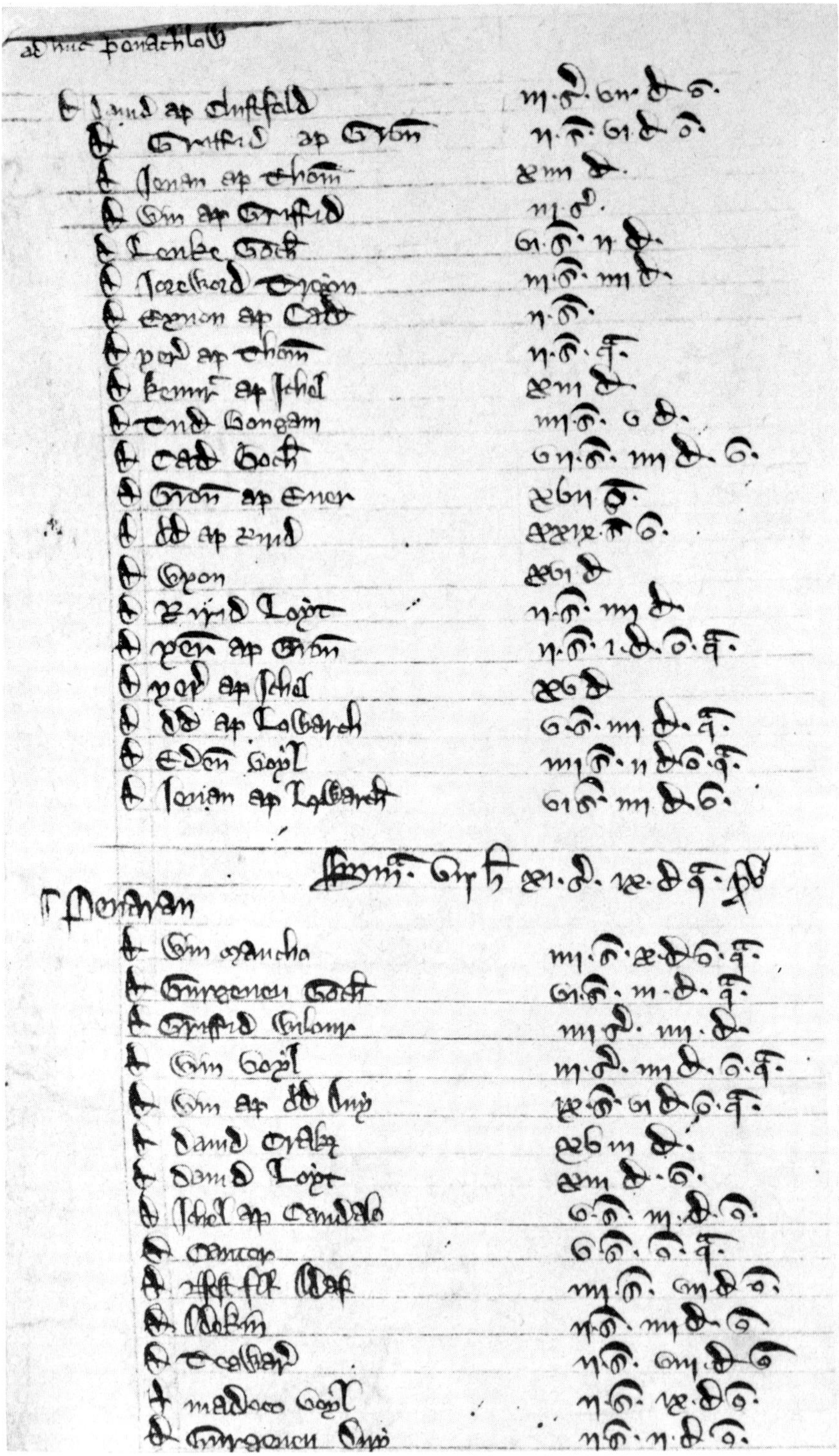

The Merioneth Lay Subsidy Roll, 1292-3
(P.R.O. E.179/242/53, *part of* m.2)

THE MERIONETH LAY SUBSIDY ROLL
1292–3

THE MERIONETH LAY SUBSIDY ROLL 1292-3

Edited by

KEITH WILLIAMS-JONES

Board of Celtic Studies, History and Law Series No. 29

Published on behalf of the University of Wales Board of Celtic Studies

CARDIFF
UNIVERSITY OF WALES PRESS
1976

ISBN 0 7083 0597 0

Printed by A. McLay & Co., Ltd., Cardiff

Contents

Acknowledgements vi

INTRODUCTION vii

Date of the subsidy xii
Assessment and collection: the supply of money xiii
Financial yield and the rebellion of 1294–5 xxiv
Population estimates xxxv
Comparative wealth of various areas lxviii
Merioneth society in the late thirteenth century lxxx
The economy in the late thirteenth century cxi
Editorial method cxxxv
App.: Statistical Tables A–F cxl

TEXT

The Merioneth Lay Subsidy Roll, 1292–3 1

APPENDIX

Fragment of a 'local' Lay Subsidy Roll for part of the commote of Penllyn, 1318 93

INDEX 103

LIST OF MAPS

Map A Relative wealth of commotes of North Wales in 1292–3 lxxiii
Map B Relative wealth of Merioneth, by parishes, in 1292–3 lxxviii
Map C Townships of Merioneth *c.* 1300 cxxxviii

ACKNOWLEDGEMENTS

The material brought together in this volume mushroomed into a book thanks largely to the encouragement of two friends, Professor J. Gwynn Williams and Mr. J. Beverley Smith. Both read the first draft of the Introduction, made valuable suggestions on how it could be improved and expanded, and kept an interested eye on the book's progress thereafter. Professor Williams kindly read the whole book in page proof. Yet another friend, Mr. Peter Crew, found time to discuss with me various points arising from the Introduction and readily agreed to draw the three maps which appear in the volume. To all these good friends I owe a great debt of gratitude. It is with gratitude, too, that I recall the assistance given by the late Professor Melville Richards in identifying some of the place names mentioned in the text. In the long arduous business of reading proofs and compiling indexes, my wife has, as always, more than halved my labours. I am much indebted, also, to Dr. R. Brinley Jones, the Director of the University of Wales Press, for his assistance in seeing the book through the press, and to the printers themselves for their forbearance and expertise.

The facsimile and transcripts of Crown-copyright records in the Public Record Office appear by permission of the Controller of H.M. Stationery Office.

Introduction

THE growing financial needs of the crown led to the development of a new form of taxation in England in the late twelfth and thirteenth centuries. This was a tax which was normally levied on the movable goods of laymen in the early years – churchmen were, at first, exempt unless they had temporal property – and in consequence it became known as a lay subsidy. The exigencies of war, especially in Edward I's reign, promoted its growth, extending its range and richly improving its yield overall. By the late thirteenth century it was no longer an exceptional tax, levied to meet a particular emergency as in the past; rather, it had become the normal way of increasing the royal revenue. Despite the many difficulties connected with its assessment and collection, it had by then emerged as the 'most efficient and profitable method of direct taxation available to the crown'.[(1)] Inevitably, resort was had to it time and time again to meet Edward I's increasing commitments at home and abroad. Lay subsidies were levied no fewer than six times between 1290 and 1301, and on a further ten occasions between 1306 and 1332. The system of assessing the tax was drastically changed in 1334 in order to expedite its collection, but the tax itself remained an instrument of financial exaction, albeit of increasingly less importance, until the seventeenth century. The original idea behind the tax was simple: a person's movable goods of large and small beasts, of grain and crops, and of other possessions were valued by local assessors and a part of the assessed aggregate value of such movables was paid as a tax (or subsidy), the proportion being expressed as a tenth or a fifteenth or whatever fraction was agreed upon by king and parliament.[(2)] In 1334 and thereafter assessments were made not so much on the basis of an individual person's property as on agreed fixed quotas payable by vills and towns as a whole.

Wales was not normally subject to parliamentary taxation in the middle ages,[(3)] but in times of need or of extensive royal influence

---

1 Michael Prestwich, *War, Politics and Finance under Edward I* (1972), p. 184.

2 The whole subject is exhaustively treated in J. F. Willard, *Parliamentary Taxes on Personal Property 1290 to 1334* (1934). For the development of the tax before 1290 see S. K. Mitchell, *Taxation in Medieval England* (1951).

3 Anthony Steel, *The Receipt of the Exchequer 1377–1485* (1954), p. 273. For a review of the position up till the end of the reign of Edward II see Joseph R. Strayer and George Rudisill, Jr., 'Taxation and Community in Wales and Ireland, 1272–1327', *Speculum*, XXIX (1954), 410–16.

it was expected none the less to make contributions by way of subsidies. For the first time, on 20 January 1291, a 'request' was made to the lords, knights, free men, and 'whole commonalty' of Wales to grant a fifteenth to Edward I as the rest of the realm had done in the previous year.(1) The reason for imposing this unprecedented burden on the Welsh was said to be the need to pay off outstanding debts incurred in ransoming the king of Sicily during Edward's long sojourn abroad in Gascony between 1286 and 1289. The mere imposition of the new tax shows how remorselessly Edward I's authority had grown in Wales by 1291, in the marches as well as the principality, though the assent of the marcher lords was, as might be expected, sedulously cultivated.(2) Despite assurances that the 'request' was not to be regarded as a precedent, another lay subsidy was levied as early as 1300 from Powys (then in the hands of the crown) and the royal lordships of Builth and Montgomery as well as North and West Wales and Flintshire.(3) Notwithstanding further pledges made on this occasion also that the grant of a subsidy was 'not to be drawn into a precedent', the principality was subjected to similar subventions in 1318, 1384, 1394–5 and at other times in the fourteenth century.(4) The financial pressure exerted by means of subsidies in the 1390s, on the eve of the Glyn Dŵr revolt, can hardly have won Richard II many friends in the southern principality, no more than can the subsidy demanded of the northern principality in the early summer of 1401, when the

---

1 *Cal(endar of) Pat(ent) Rolls 1281–92*, p. 419.

2 For individual arrangements with marcher lords for levying the tax on their lands, see ibid., pp. 500, 502, 503, 510, 511; and *Cal. Pat. Rolls 1292–1301*, pp. 52, 56. Richard de Massy and the royal clerk Adam de Bodington had prepared the ground: the latter was allowed £5 for conducting negotiations in Wales in 1291 (P(ublic) R(ecord) O(ffice) E.403/67 m.1). Mrs. Natalie Fryde is engaged on a study of subsidies granted by Wales to the crown after the conquest, largely from the point of view of 'representation' and 'consent'.

3 *Cal. Pat. Rolls 1292–1301*, pp. 503, 517–18, 526, 534; *Cal(endar of) Close Rolls 1296–1302*, p. 354. (The lordship of Ellesmere was also asked to contribute on this occasion.) Griffith de la Pole of Powys was still a minor in 1300 (*Calendar of Inquisitions Post Mortem*, III, 62).

4 P.R.O. E.179/220/131 and 132; and /242/61; *Cal. Close Rolls 1318–23*, pp. 19, 82; *Calendar of Fine Rolls 1307–19*, p. 379; *West Wales Historical Records*, XII (1927), 115; Ralph A. Griffiths, *The Principality of Wales in the Later Middle Ages: The Structure and Personnel of Government, I, South Wales, 1277–1536* (1972), 114, 178, 274, 304, 438, 463, 518, 537; William Rees, *South Wales and the March* (1924), pp. 66–7. The subsidy imposed in 1394 appears to have been an exceptionally heavy one: Merioneth itself contributed 1,000 marks (£666. 13*s*. 4*d*.) towards it (*Cal. Fine Rolls 1391–99*, p. 124).

At the instance of Hugh le Despenser, the younger, the men of the towns of Dryslwyn and Newton and the commonalty of Cantref Mawr were relieved of paying the fifteenth demanded in 1318 (*Cal. Pat. Rolls 1317–21*, p. 266). Cf. also *Cal. Close Rolls 1318–23*, p. 19.

revolt was in a fairly critical stage, have improved Henry IV's image there.(1) Nor does it appear that areas outside the two principalities were completely immune after 1300: in 1376–7, for example, the burgesses of Haverfordwest were accounting for a £40 subsidy payable to Richard II in equal sums over four years.(2) The crown's needs drove it to make further exactions in the fifteenth century – in 1417, 1430, 1451, if not at other times(3) – and Welsh landlords in particular were made liable to an experimental 'income' tax in 1450.(4) But generally, after Edward II's reign, the crown seems to have favoured what may be called extra-parliamentary devices – originally fashioned, perhaps, by marcher lords and later adapted and exploited by the importunate Black Prince – for raising extra-ordinary revenue in Wales and the term 'subsidy' was invariably extended to them: amongst these were the 'sessions and tallage, otherwise called subsidy' in the shires of West Wales; the 'subsidy' called 'hornyeld' and the 'mise, recognisance, or subsidy' in the principality of North Wales; and the 'mise' or 'subsidy' of 1,000 marks which was levied regularly in the former county of Flint every seven years, from 1346 at the latest, throughout the greater part of the later middle ages – even during the troubled years in 1402 and 1409 – and which was extended, on one occasion at least, in 1437, to Anglesey and to Chirk and Hopedale and other areas in the northern march.(5)

These numerous financial demands, sanctioned by parliament or custom or made at the 'request' of the crown, inevitably created their own records, but none of the extra-parliamentary returns for Wales seems to have survived. As for the quasi-parliamentary lay subsidy returns, 19 medieval rolls are extant, 13 of them the returns of the fifteenth requested in 1291.(6) They cover the two former counties of

1 P.R.O. E.179/242/61; Griffiths, op. cit., 304, 463, 518; J. E. Lloyd, *Owen Glendower* (1931), p. 39, n. 1; and P.R.O. S.C.6/1216/1.

2 Henry Owen (ed.), *A Calendar of the Public Records relating to Pembrokeshire*, I (1911), 131. See also Robert Somerville, *History of the Duchy of Lancaster, I, 1265–1603* (1953), 93 n. 2.

3 ibid., 184; Griffiths, op. cit., 54 n. 42, 251, 297, 372, 421, 432, 524; T. B. Pugh (ed.), *The Marcher Lordships of South Wales 1415–1536* (1963), pp. 42, 148; Francis Jones, *The Princes and Principality of Wales* (1969), p. 92. See also *Cal. Pat. Rolls 1452–61*, p. 124 for a reference, dated 12 August 1453, to a subsidy from the North Wales counties.

4 Steele, op. cit., p. 234.

5 J. Goronwy Edwards (ed.), *Calendar of Ancient Correspondence concerning Wales* (1935), pp. 223, 224; *Reg(ister of Edward the) B(lack) P(rince)*, I, 34, 67–8, 86, 87; and III, 137, 140, 162, 204, Deputy Keeper's *Reports*, XXXVI, App. ii, 434; and XXXVII, App. ii, 6, 25–7, 35, 111–16, 201, 282, 310, 347, 693–4.

6 One of the 19 rolls (P.R.O. E.179/242/48) is a schedule of the jurors and assessors appointed for South Wales and the marches regarding the fifteenth requested in

Merioneth and Flint; one vill (Aberffraw) in Anglesey; the three commotes of Cymydmaen, Cafflogion, and Creuddyn, and the vill of Nefyn in the old county of Caernarvon; the three commotes of Cynllaith, Mochnant, and Nanheudwy in what used to be eastern Denbighshire; the cantref of Arwystli, the two commotes of Cyfeiliog and Caereinion, the borough of Welshpool, and the vill of Carreghofa, all in the former county of Montgomery; the sub-lordship of Bronllys in what used to be Brecknockshire; the sub-lordships of Bleddfa, Radnor, Glasbury, Norton, and Presteign in the old county of Radnor; the sub-lordship of Cilgerran in the northern half of what was once known as Pembrokeshire; the commote of Is Cennen in the former county of Carmarthen; and the lordships of Abergavenny, Grosmont, Whitecastle, Skenfrith, and Monmouth, all part of the old county of Monmouth. Although this leaves vast areas of Wales unrepresented, these returns of the subsidy requested in 1291 are much more complete – and hence of more importance to the historian – than the five other lay subsidy rolls[1] relating to Wales which are extant for the middle ages. Their value is, of course, not entirely uniform. Only two former counties – Merioneth and Flintshire – have compact lists of taxpayers covering more or less their entire area. The north is altogether better served than the south. The returns pertaining to the former six northern shires – or parts thereof – are conveniently arranged by townships whereas those for the south are not. Again, only four rolls actually list the movables of persons assessed and they are confined to parts of Anglesey and the old county of Caernarvon.[2] Every return, however, gives a fairly comprehensive list of the main taxpayers in their respective areas and the sum at which each person was assessed. Of the 13 rolls in which the returns are kept, only four have been published, namely, those for Aberffraw, Cafflogion, and Nefyn and those for the lordship

---

1291. It is, therefore, strictly speaking, not a subsidy roll: it has been edited by Major Francis Jones in the *B(ulletin of the) B(oard of) C(eltic) S(tudies)*, XIII (1948–50), 215–25.

1 These are P.R.O. E.101/506/15 mm. 1, 2 which is a fragment of a subsidy roll relating to Merioneth for 1318 (see Appendix *infra*, pp. 96–102); P.R.O. E.179/220/131 and 132 which are incomplete assessments relating to the commotes of Cafflogion, Cymydmaen, Nanconwy, and Isaf in the former county of Caernarvon and dating possibly from Edward III's or Richard II's reign; P.R.O. E.179/242/61 which is an account of the sub-chamberlain of West Wales for the subsidy of 1394; and P.R.O. E.179/224/601 which is a roll containing portions of largely unidentified assessments dating from Edward III's reign to Charles II's: amongst them is a fragment of an assessment of the second half of the fourteenth century relating to 'Eynoon' (= ? Eifionydd).

2 i.e., Aberffraw, Nefyn, Cafflogion, and Creuddyn.

of Abergavenny and the sub-lordship of Cilgerran.[1] Amongst those hitherto unpublished are the fine subsidy roll for Flintshire and the slightly less well-preserved roll for Merioneth printed below.

No other complete subsidy roll for Merioneth has survived for the medieval period[2] so that unique importance attaches to this particular roll. However, unlike the four surviving contemporary rolls for the vills of Aberffraw and Nefyn and the commotes of Cafflogion and Creuddyn, it is not a 'local' roll, that is to say, it is not a commotal roll giving detailed particulars of the taxable movables (the number and value of cows, sheep, horses, corn, and other possessions) of individuals; rather, it is a 'county' roll, which merely lists the names of individuals under various townships and the sums at which they were assessed. Though unique, its value is therefore somewhat circumscribed. No thorough-going analysis of Merioneth's agriculture and society is feasible from its study; no indication is given of the nature of a person's movable wealth on which the tax was based. As a 'county' roll, or a roll of particulars as it would be known in the Exchequer, it is a summary – and no more – of all the detailed local commotal rolls for Merioneth which were drawn up for the purposes of the subsidy and which have since been lost. The fact that it must have been compiled from local rolls may account for certain errors of calculation in the totals of some townships, the greatest discrepancy occurring in the case of the township of Penaran where a true total of £14. 1*s.* 11$\frac{3}{4}$*d.* appears as £6. 7*s.* 6$\frac{3}{4}$*d.*[3] Errors in transcription and compilation from local rolls may account too for the omission of the names of some townships – and of the names of an unrecorded number of taxpayers in at least two instances – which cannot now be recovered.[4]

---

1 See *B.B.C.S.*, V (1929–31), 54–71 (commote of Cafflogion: roll/242/50a) and 143–8 (vill of Nefyn: roll/242/50b); *B.B.C.S.*, XIII (1948–50), 225–30 (lordship of Abergavenny and the hundred of Cilgerran: roll/242/56); and F. Seebohm, *The Tribal System in Wales* (1895), App. A.f. (vill of Aberffraw: roll/242/49). See also Henry Owen (ed.), *A Calendar of the Public Records relating to Pembrokeshire*, II (1914), 10–14, for the subsidy relating to Cilgerran. It is hoped that the rolls for Creuddyn and Cymydmaen (Caernarvonshire) will shortly be published in the *Transactions of the Caernarvonshire Historical Society*.

2 The only other extant subsidy roll for Merioneth is a fragment dating almost certainly from 1318 (P.R.O. E.101/506/15 mm. 1, 2: for a discussion concerning its date and an edited transcript of it, see Appendix, *infra*, pp. 95–102). In it details are given of the movables of persons in the townships of Penaran, Castell, Cyffty, Bedwarian, Streflyn, and possibly Llandderfel, all of them vills in the commote of Penllyn. Neither Castell nor Bedwarian figures in the 1292–3 roll.

3 *infra*, p. 11 and n. 6.

4 See *infra*, p. 21, n. 8 and p. 22, n. 3.

DATE OF THE SUBSIDY

The Merioneth subsidy roll is undated but there does not seem to be any doubt that it was compiled in response to the 'request' made for a fifteenth to the 'whole commonalty of Wales' on 20 January 1291. Subsidies are usually dated to the year when they were granted, for the actual assessment and collection were normally spread over two years. But when can the 'request' for a subsidy from Wales be said to have been granted? The political divisions of Wales and the autonomous position of the marcher lords necessitated lengthy consultations and the preparation of more complicated arrangements than existed for England. Richard de Massy and Adam de Bodington[1] clearly spent a long time in Wales trying to convince the marcher lords – and presumably the communities in the principality – of the wisdom of complying with Edward I's wishes and of co-operating in the task of assessment and collection. It was not until 10 July 1292 that they registered their first success in the marches when John de Warenne graciously consented to the 'request' in return for future immunity.[2] Similar concessions were wrung from a number of marcher lords at intervals throughout the rest of the year 1292.[3] But the patent rolls record two concessions that were not made until 27 November and 10 December 1293.[4] We know too that in the marches and principality of South Wales the assessments were carried out at various times between 20 November 1292 and early April 1293,[5] so that it might be safer to date the subsidy as a whole 1292–3, despite the fact that the assessments were to be based on goods held apparently on Michaelmas Day 1292.[6] Only one subsidy can with certainty be dated 1292 – that for Monmouth, Grosmont, Skenfrith, and White Castle. There the grant of a subsidy was conceded by the king's brother Edmund on 8 November 1292, the jurors evaluating the goods of their fellows met the same month, and the subsidy roll itself is dated 20 Edward I.[7] The subsidy roll for Flintshire is also dated 20 Edward I (20 November 1291 – 19 November 1292)[8] but one cannot be certain

1 *Cal. Pat. Rolls 1281–92*, p. 419.

2 ibid., p. 500.

3 ibid., pp. 502, 503, 510, and 511.

4 *Cal. Pat. Rolls 1292–1301*, pp. 52, 56.

5 *B.B.C.S.*, XIII (1948–50), 215–24.

6 Henry Owen (ed.), *A Calendar of the Public Records relating to Pembrokeshire*, II (1914), 10, notes that the assessment at Cilgerran took place on the morrow of Michaelmas, 1292.

7 *B.B.C.S.*, XIII (1948–50), 215; P.R.O. E.179/242/59.

8 P.R.O. E.179/242/52.

when the 'request' was agreed to by the community there. As for Merioneth and the rest of the principality of North Wales there is nothing more to go on than the reference made in 1318 to the fifteenth granted to 'king Edward, father of the present king, in the twenty-first year of his reign', that is, 1292–3.[1] Even if a date were discovered for the receipt of the subsidy roll at the Exchequer it would not materially help to solve the problem. It is recorded on the subsidy roll for Bronllys, Clifford and Middlewood, and Glasbury that it was handed in to the Exchequer on 29 April 1293; and similarly the roll for parts of the former county of Radnor was in the hands of Exchequer officials on 1 June 1293.[2] But the receipt roll for Easter 1293 records that moneys were already coming in from these very areas.[3] One suspects that the Merioneth subsidy roll was drawn up some time in 1292, but it cannot be dated any closer than 1292–3.

ASSESSMENT AND COLLECTION: THE SUPPLY OF MONEY

The procedure whereby the subsidy was levied in the principality in 1292–3 differed only slightly from that observed elsewhere. In England, it was a fairly straightforward matter of appointing chief taxors and collectors from among the more substantial persons in each county, having them sworn and instructed at the Exchequer, and charged with the task of supervising the assessment and collection of the subsidy in their respective counties. The chief taxors, in their turn, appointed assessors from each hundred and it was they who drew up the inventory of each individual's movables and collected the tax, all under the surveillance of the chief taxors, who were themselves answerable to the Exchequer.[4] This procedure seems to have been transplanted more or less intact to the marches of Wales, though Reginald de Grey as justiciar of Chester assumed an active role in the task of collection from some areas.[5] In the principality of North Wales, however, the chief taxors were not local men but bureaucrats, normally the chamberlain of North Wales acting singly or in conjunction with the controller, and assisted by the sheriffs or sub-sheriffs of the three counties.[6] Commotal assessors (*taxatores*) were usually six in number[7] and, like

1 P.R.O. E.159/95 m. 62.

2 P.R.O. E.179/242/57 and 60.

3 P.R.O. E.401/126.

4 All this is described in detail in Willard, *Parliamentary Taxes*, Chapt. II.

5 *B.B.C.S.*, XIII (1948–50), 215–25; P.R.O. E.159/67 m. 53.

6 See e.g. P.R.O. E.159/95 m. 62.

7 *infra*, pp. 7 and 91; cf. *Reg. B.P.*, I, 67–8, which required four commotal assessors in 1347.

their counterparts elsewhere, were made responsible for visiting townships and acting in concert with village jurors to make the necessary individual assessments. The assessment itself was based on stock and goods held at Michaelmas 1292 though the movables might in some cases be actually assessed months afterwards. The assessors were later expected to return to collect the sums assessed. The six local assessors in each commote were selected by the chamberlain of North Wales, who was himself accountable to the Exchequer in London.[1] All were allowed expenses for their pains.[2]

According to the instructions which were drawn up and issued to officials in Gwynedd in 1292–3 and which served as a precedent for their successors in 1318, the assessment of movable goods was to be confined to the more important domestic animals and to the main crops; to the following animals: an ox, nominally valued at 5*s*. 0*d*., a cow at 3*s*. 4*d*., a three-year old affer at 2*s*. 6*d*., a two-year old affer at 2*s*. 0*d*., a horse at 5*s*. 0*d*., a mare at 5*s*. 0*d*., a ewe at 6*d*., and a sheep at 8*d*.; and to the following crops: a crannock of corn, nominally valued at 2*s*. 6*d*., of oats at 6*d*., of ground oats at 2*s*. 0*d*., of rye at 16*d*., of barley and ground barley at 16*d*., of beans at 2*s*. 6*d*., and of peas at 16*d*.[3] It is known, however, that utensils, of an unspecified kind, were also included amongst the movables assessed in Aberffraw, skiffs and fishing nets in Cafflogion, and boats, fishing nets and merchandise in Nefyn,[4] most of them indicative of the extra-agricultural pursuits of their respective areas and, in consequence, a manifest source of taxable wealth which could not easily escape the attention of the authorities. Likewise in the lordship of Glamorgan, allowance was made for the assessment of wool in 1292,[5] which may point to the great value placed on the rearing of sheep there at the end of the thirteenth century – and that despite the epidemic of scab which decimated the sheep population of Glamorgan in 1281.[6] Whether the inhabitants of Merioneth were imposed upon in this way in 1292–3 is not known, but one can well believe that the merchant at Cynwyd was assessed on his merchandise, the artisan in Harlech on his utensils, even the fisherman at Kethugalc on his boat or fishing tackle. (In Dolgledr in 1326 Eynon ap Gronou

---

1 P.R.O. E.159/95 m. 62 and E.401/131.

2 P.R.O. S.C.8/90/4451.

3 P.R.O. E.159/95 m. 62. The crannock was to be of the standard London measure of four bushels.

4 Seebohm, *Tribal System*, App. A. f., pp. 41–4; *B.B.C.S.*, V (1929–31), 68, 70, 71, 143–7. Cf. Willard, *Parliamentary Taxes*, p. 76 and n. 2.

5 J. G. Edwards (ed.), *Littere Wallie* (1940), p. 181.

6 Rees, *South Wales and the March*, p. 196.

Voel and Gronou Loit were indeed robbed of 'sex retia'.[1]) The sheep's wool, too, in certain parts of Merioneth may (though it is very unlikely) have been of such quality as to promote its production and thereby attract the notice of the tax-gatherer. But of none of this is there any certainty. What can be said is that in none of the extant local subsidy rolls relating to Gwynedd are pigs or goats mentioned, so that one can assume that they were rarer (or smaller in number) than is generally imagined – a reading of the extent of Anglesey drawn up in 1294 does not confound that supposition[2] – or for some reason were exempted altogether from the tax, a piece of good fortune which many parts of England were unlucky enough not to share. What can be said, too, is that no unmistakable evidence has been found of farming equipment and implements as such being made subject to the subsidy; it is possible, however, that they are included amongst the unspecified *utensilia* mentioned in the Aberffraw roll.

The 'expenses' granted to assessors for their work may well have invited a great number of malpractices. Entertaining assessors on a lavish scale or offering them gifts or bribes produced startling reductions in individual assessments in some areas in England.[3] It is impossible to determine how closely officials in the principality complied with the directions given them. Variable and often perplexing instructions about taxable goods gave ample scope for local assessors to display their talents for bending the rules whenever compelled or moved to do so. Even in the best-ordered areas, peasants must have wrangled interminably about what should or should not have been included of their goods and possessions in the assessment. Angry protestations must have choked the air as the assessors went about their business. Some bribery and corruption there must inevitably have been, but in 1292–3 local communities in Wales had less experience to draw on than (say) Cheddington or Cuxham as how best to ease the burden of extra-ordinary taxation. It took time to learn the tricks of tax-evasion.[4] Though not subject to proof, under-assessment was probably universal from the beginning – even if they had wanted to adhere strictly to the rules, local assessors had no choice but to make allowances if they were to live peaceably ever after with their neighbours. As for tax-avoidance, it was almost certainly much more common than it is today. Even

1 *B.B.C.S.*, VI (1931–3), 355.

2 Printed in Seebohm, *Tribal System*, App. A. a., pp. 3–25; Cf. Paul Vinogradoff and Frank Morgan, *Survey of the Honour of Denbigh 1334* (1914), p. xl.

3 P. D. A. Harvey, *A Medieval Oxfordshire Village: Cuxham 1240 to 1400* (1965), p. 106; Willard, *Parliamentary Taxes*, pp. 187, 206, 211.

4 See ibid., pp. 345–6.

so, the preparation of the subsidy roll was no mere formality, nor lightly undertaken. The spirit, if not the letter, of the law was obeyed in procedure. The preliminary assessment was designed to corral all persons with movables valued as low as 15*d*.[1] That must have been a long and tedious process. The detailed local lists of movables which were drawn up by commotal assessors were then scrutinised by the chamberlain of North Wales and the names of those with movable property to the value of 15*s*. or more – and the sums at which they were assessed – were lifted and transferred on to the 'county' roll. It was this roll which was used for collecting the tax. Every half-year, beginning in Easter 1293 until Michaelmas 1294 the tax was paid, or ought to have been paid, in to the Exchequer in four equal portions.[2] Nothing is known of the detailed arrangements of the collection in Gwynedd – nor indeed how the subsidy was actually paid by the individuals concerned. It may have been by two or more instalments – the evidence of the receipt rolls seems to suggest some such arrangement – or (less likely) in a lump-sum payment. It is not known for certain either whether it was paid in cash or in kind by individuals for the evidence is very conflicting when it is not non-existent. As we can gather from various allegations against officials suspected of making off with money destined for the royal coffers,[3] cash must have been available in the countryside in considerable quantity to pay the royal dues in the first place. On the other hand, it is perhaps too readily assumed that with the growth of commutation and the establishment of trading centres in the thirteenth century there was a plentiful supply of money in North Wales.[4] The proceedings of various courts show that whereas the stealing of goods and chattels was a common occurrence around the turn of the century, theft of money was comparatively rare – and even then the actual sums involved were usually fairly small, whatever extravagant claims were made to the contrary.[5] Commutation had gone far in Gwynedd, as indeed it had in all parts of Wales

---

1 P.R.O. E.159/95 m. 62.

2 ibid.; cf. E.159/73 m. 76 and E.179/242/51 (where the total has been divided into four). The subsidy of 1290 in England was also to be paid in four instalments. It was the only time apparently such a scheme was adopted (Willard, *Parliamentary Taxes*, p. 185).

3 See, e.g., U(niversity) C(ollege of) N(orth) W(ales), Bodrhyddan 2335 (Flintshire Plea Roll for 1317, m. 4d.); *Cal(endar of) Inq(uisitions) Misc(ellaneous) 1219–1307*, p. 432.

4 T. Jones Pierce, *Medieval Welsh Society: Selected Essays* (ed. J. Beverley Smith, 1972), pp. 103–25.

5 See, e.g., J. Goronwy Edwards (ed.), *Flint Pleas 1283–1285* (1922), p. 24; R. Arthur Roberts (ed.), *Ruthin Court Rolls* (1893), p. 18. Cf. C. T. Martin (ed.), *Registrum epistolarum fratris Johannis Peckham archiepiscopi Cantuarensis*, II (1884), 457.

except possibly West Wales, by 1282, but there were large isolated pockets where advance had apparently been very slow: in Merioneth, for example, payments specified to be made 'in denariis' in the extent of *c.* 1284 applied only to the commotes of Tal-y-bont and Ystumanner.[1] The process of commutation was anything but complete by the time of the final conquest.

Nevertheless, it is undeniable that the thirteenth century had witnessed a dramatic leap in the use of money in Wales. Certainly the payment of tribute by Welsh princes to English kings which had usually taken the form of so many head of cattle in the past had given way to hard cash by the time of Llywelyn I (d. 1240) and Llywelyn II (d. 1282), and that in considerable amounts.[2] Even Senena was prepared to pay 600 marks to Henry III for the release of her husband Gruffydd ap Llywelyn (I) and her son Owain in 1241.[3] Whether the princes of Gwynedd minted their own coins or not, they must have realised the desirability of doing so. Llewelyn II, in particular, would have been attracted by the idea. One of the more conspicuous aspects of his policy in the late 1250s and 60s was his readiness to use money as a diplomatic weapon. He was very free with his cash as he tried to buy his way out of trouble and into princely society. In 1257 he offered 'a great sum of money' to the crown in return for recognition of his position in Gwynedd; alternatively, he intimated that he was prepared to pay 1,500 marks to secure a seven-year truce.[4] A year later a year's truce between himself and Henry III was bought for 100 marks.[5] This was a mere prelude to more ambitious schemes which were to overwhelm him completely in the course of time. Already, in 1258, the chronicler Matthew Paris notes that he had been prepared to hand over as much as 4,500 marks for a firm peace (rather than a mere truce) which recognised his past conquests; by 1259, if we are to believe another chronicler, that figure had leapt to £16,000,[6] a sum not far short of the total indemnity the crown finally agreed upon in 1267. No information seems to be available about the moneys

1 *Arch(aeologia) Camb(rensis)* (1867), pp. 185, 187.

2 J. E. Lloyd, *A History of Wales* (3rd ed., 1939), pp. 465, 546, 660, 668, 736, 741. Coins were, however, in circulation in tenth-century Wales (ibid., 337 n., 346); and in the early twelfth century, too, cash was discussed, if not actually handed over, in diplomatic arrangements of the time (Thomas Jones (ed.), *Brut y Tywysogyon* (*Red Book of Hergest Version*) (1955), pp. 62, 64, 76).

3 Edwards (ed.), *Littere Wallie*, p. 52.

4 Edwards (ed.), *Cal. Anc. Corr.*, pp. 50–1.

5 Edwards (ed.), *Littere Wallie*, pp. 13–14.

6 H. R. Luard (ed.), *Matthaei Parisiensis Chronica Majora*, V (1880), 727; H. R. Luard (ed.), *Flores Historiarum*, II (1890), 435.

bargained for in the negotiations leading to the two-year truce of 1260; nor are the extant documents any more forthcoming concerning the truce arranged in 1263, but clearly Llywelyn was prepared no less than to put Wales in pawn in return for recognition of his title and position as prince of Wales. His understanding with, first, the Earl Simon at Pipton in 1265 and, later, Henry III at Montgomery in 1267 involved the huge sum of 30,000 marks payable over a term of ten years – for although he undertook to pay 5,000 marks less than that amount in 1267, the difference was bargained for in 1270 to buy the homage of the one powerful Welsh prince (Maredudd ap Rhys of Dryslwyn) who still defied him.(1) The mere existence of the principality was to cost its inhabitants ten annual instalments of 3,000 marks.

Llywelyn II seems to have grossly over-estimated his financial resources. In the context of the Welsh economy 30,000 marks was a greater burden than the 150,000 marks (a sum that was never fully paid) England had to find to ransom Richard I in 1193. Not only that, but the machinery at Llywelyn's disposal for raising revenue cannot possibly have been as sophisticated and as well-lubricated as the crown's. It is impossible to calculate his income per annum, but even at the height of his power it would have been surprising if it had exceeded £4,500 – £5,000, which was more or less the annual income of Gilbert de Clare,(2) the powerful earl of Gloucester and lord of Glamorgan, one of the greatest men in the realm and builder of Wales's biggest castle at Caerffili. Edward of Caernarvon's total income after his investiture as prince of Wales in 1301 is estimated to have been nearly £8,800,(3) but his appanage included the earldom of Chester, Ponthieu, and the southern principality as well as most of the lands which had once been held by Llywelyn II; the principality of North Wales on its own is said to have brought in little over £3,000, but apparently much less than that in normal years, fluctuating between £2,400 and £2,800 per annum(4) – and this was twenty years after galloping commutation and after Edward's

1 Lloyd, *History of Wales*, pp. 736–7; Edwards (ed.), *Littere Wallie*, pp. 1–4.

2 G. A. Holmes, *The Estates of the Higher Nobility in Fourteenth-Century England* (1957), p. 36, estimated the value of the Clare estates at £6,000 in 1314. T. B. Pugh, 'The Marcher Lords of Glamorgan and Morgannwg, 1317–1485', in T. B. Pugh (ed.), *Glamorgan County History*, III (1971), 167, notes, however, that the possessions of the last Clare were valued at over £7,000 a year, of which the revenues of the lordship of Glamorgan amounted to £1,267. 6*s*. 9¼*d*. Between 1290 and 1295, the gross annual income of the Clare estates was about £4,500–£5,000 (Michael Altschul, *A Baronial Family in Medieval England: the Clares, 1217–1314* (Baltimore, 1965), p. 205).

3 Hilda Johnstone, *Edward of Carnarvon 1284–1307* (1946), p. 68.

4 ibid.; W. H. Waters, *The Edwardian Settlement of North Wales* (1935), p. 58 and n. 5.

ruthless ministers had picked the financial bone pretty clean. The total estimated revenue of the king himself was no more than £26,828. 3*s*. 9¼*d*. in 1284.(1)

These figures put the debt incurred at Montgomery into its proper perspective: they illustrate how deeply and improvidently Llywelyn II, with his slender means, had committed himself in 1267 by agreeing to pay 30,000 marks to the crown. His credit might not have been considered good enough to reassure prospective lenders by 1272. Such was his dilemma when Edward I ascended the throne. There seems to be little doubt that Gwynedd succumbed in 1277 partly because of Llywelyn's overweening ambition and ill-conceived policies. Intention outran capacity. Political disaster followed closely on the heels of financial troubles. The chronology of events in the early 1270s is vital to our understanding of Llywelyn's predicament. Between 1270 and 1272 he was falling more and more into arrears with his annual payments of 3,000 marks to the crown – 1,000 marks in arrears with the instalment at Christmas 1270, 2,000 marks in arrears with the next instalment a year later – before payments ceased altogether late in 1272 on Edward I's accession.(2) The withholding of fealty to Edward I early in 1273 may well have been prompted as much initially by financial difficulties as by any sudden rush of blood to the head. Nothing is more revealing of Llywelyn's financial plight at this time than his dealings with his brother Rhodri who had contracted to quitclaim all his hereditary rights to him for 1,000 marks in 1272: only 50 marks of this sum was paid in six years, the payment of the remaining 950 marks being put in hand as late as 1278.(3) Reports of desperate attempts to impose added taxation on the principality in 1273 and 1275 have the distinct ring of truth.(4) Indicative too of how crippling the annual debt of 3,000 marks must have been was that after the humiliating defeat of 1277, no more than 500 marks per annum – one-sixth the previous rate – were to be paid to discharge the outstanding sums owing to the crown.(5) Even in his reduced circumstances after 1277 instalments of 500 marks a year were more realistic than the annual payments of

1 Mabel H. Mills, 'Exchequer Agenda and Estimate of Revenue, Easter Term 1284', *Eng(lish) Hist(orical) Rev(iew)*, XL (1925), 234.

2 The payments are laid out in Edwards (ed.), *Littere Wallie*, p. li n. 1.

3 ibid., pp. 42, 85, 117.

4 *Cal. Close Rolls 1272–9*, p. 57; Edwards (ed.), *Cal. Anc. Corr.*, p. 105.

5 Edwards (ed.), *Littere Wallie*, pp. 117–18. At the same time Edward I remitted the war indemnity of £50,000 and the annual render of 1,000 marks for Anglesey (Lloyd, *History of Wales*, p. 760 n. 229). Financial pressure on Llywelyn continued to be applied, however, after 1277 (*Cal. of Chanc. Rolls* (*Various*) *1277–1326*, p. 159; Martin (ed.), *Registrum . . . Peckham*, II, 442–3).

3,000 marks required in the heyday of his power: more realistic because, no longer a mighty prince, he had fewer commitments to meet, though the added financial pressures exerted upon him by Edward I after 1277 were designed to shackle him further.

Llywelyn's ambition had overreached itself. The principality he had brought into being in 1267 was proving economically unviable in the early 70s. His outgoings must have been considerable. We know next to nothing about the people around him but he must presumably have had a sizeable body of retainers, men who had to be kept sweet by grants of various kinds. (It may have been undischarged commitments to 'his own men' which partly inspired the plot against the prince in the belfry of the church at Bangor in 1282.) Maintaining the trappings of power, in keeping with his new status as prince of Wales, must have proved a costly business. Castles had had to be built – £174. 6*s*. 8*d*. at least was expended on Dolforwyn castle in 1273–4[1] – or reinforced to secure the prince's extended dominion; boroughs or quasi-boroughs had had to be founded to galvanise its economic development. But costly as ventures of this kind – and others – were they would most probably have been fairly easily met from customary sources of revenue had it not been for the added burden imposed by the financial provisions of the treaty of Montgomery in 1267. These vast additional demands upon the principality's meagre resources cannot have eased Llywelyn's path at home. Of the 30,000 marks owing to the crown under the terms of the treaty, a total of at least 18,750 marks was paid by instalments between 1267 and 1272,[2] so that the 'tribute' alleged to have been demanded by Llywelyn in 1273,[3] when his fortunes were on the turn, may not have been the first, a fact which again, if true, would go far to explain much of the inner tensions of his principate.

How would these extraordinary demands – if such they were – have been met by the prince's subjects? By cash? English practice in the field of finance, as in every other, must have exercised a strong fascination over the prince of Wales. In late 1275 it was rumoured that he 'had imposed on the people a heavy tribute of threepence on each head of cattle', a device which, however distorted, bears a striking resemblance to the English tax on movables.[4] And ready cash was clearly the object of the tribute of 1275. It would be wrong to underestimate the amount of money in circulation at this time

1 Edwards (ed.), *Littere Wallie*, pp. 23–4.

2 ibid., p. li n. 1 for details.

3 *Cal. Close Rolls 1272–9*, p. 57.

4 Cf. Edwards (ed.), *Cal. Anc. Corr.*, pp. 105 and 179.

or to underrate its impact on the contemporary Welsh mind: the sole entry *sub anno* 1279 in the *Brut y Tywysogyon* concerns the 'new money' Edward I had struck that year. In that first recoinage of the reign in 1279, English mints produced £500,000 in coins, and it has been estimated by Dr. Prestwich that there was about £800,000 current coin – a sum more or less equivalent, apparently, to the total amount of direct taxation raised by Edward I – in circulation at any given time during the reign.(1) Inevitably, a fair proportion of this money must have found its way to Wales, if only in the wages of all those masons and carpenters and other workers who laboured so magnificently to build Edward's fortresses. The plantation of boroughs by Edward I was deliberately designed to promote the use of money: it rounded off and hastened a process already set in motion by marcher lords and Welsh princes alike. The conquest of Wales made its inhabitants more familiar than ever before with the business of dealing in hard cash. Commutation progressed apace. It need occasion little surprise that counterfeiting money was already an established practice and that turning a dishonest penny was not beyond the wiles of some.(2) The quickening circulation of coins sharpened the need for money. Welshmen, as well as immigrant English burgesses, were able to take advantage of the new opportunities that opened up before them. A fourteenth-century Flintshire man, one Cynwrig Sais, left at his death, amongst his other possessions, as much as £120 in money.(3) Clearly some men had goodly fortunes which enabled them to speculate and invest in land when opportunity allowed, but those with capital on any appreciable scale were probably few in number. Even so important a personage as a bishop who wished 88 marks (£58. 13*s*. 4*d*.) to be distributed at his death had to make it conditional on 'sufficient money' being left 'in the Bishop's treasury'.(4) Consideration money noted in legal transactions of the late thirteenth and early fourteenth centuries might, on rare occasions, reach £100,(5) but usually much smaller sums were involved.(6) Even in the seventeenth century, over four hundred years later, Wales suffered from a 'chronic shortage of cash' which was only alleviated periodically, it was said, when the

---

1 Prestwich, *War, Politics and Finance*, pp. 194–5.

2 See, e.g., Edwards (ed.), *Flint Pleas*, p. 45; *B.B.C.S.*, I (1921–3), 267; Martin (ed.), *Registrum . . . Peckham*, II, 451.

3 C. R. Williams (ed.), *The History of Flintshire*, I (1961), 99.

4 *Arch. Camb.* (1919), p. 186.

5 e.g., U.C.N.W., Mostyn 1627, 2940, 2941.

6 ibid., 2167, 2168, 2441–4, 2633, etc.; Nat(ional) Lib(rary of) Wales, Plas Iolyn 284, 285; and Powis Castle 16261, 16263, 16264, 16266.

' "Spanish fleet" reached port'.[1] In 1300 the drovers had long to wait before winning renown as the unofficial bankers of the age. The whole balance of economic life for the average peasant was so delicately poised that a bad harvest or murrain or a similar disaster placed him at the mercy of the money-lender. Those who held office and who were entrusted with collecting dues were in a better position than most to lend money, but the professional money-lender as such, so ominous a figure in village life in India and parts of Europe, has never been all that prominent in Welsh life. Though lending was fairly widespread the actual sums of money borrowed were apparently not very large:[2] that is to say, they do not seem to have been sufficiently great to create new ties of dependence strong enough to sever ancient ties of kinship. Potentially very damaging and disruptive though it was, the incurring of debt was probably not a significant factor in the break-up of the old social order in Wales. The limitations of the Welsh economy were such, in any case, that they were not normally likely to attract Jewish or professional financiers. Though there were Jewish merchants and artisans in South Wales in the thirteenth century[3] and even as late as 1386–7 in the commote of Maenordeilo (in the former county of Carmarthen),[4] not many ventured west of Hereford at any time. Certainly no evidence has been found of their presence in North Wales: though charters to the royal boroughs carried a clause prohibiting them from residing there, that was merely common form. It seems more likely that when in need of ready cash, the Welsh peasant turned to wealthy relatives or friends or neighbours; alternatively, he sought out the towns, a prospect which long filled him with dismay: men from Merioneth, bound for the continental war as foot-soldiers in 1345, stubbornly refused to enter the town of Conwy even to draw their wages before departure.[5] For many a long day the English borough and the Welsh hinterland collided rather than met. Their activities were as far from being complementary as their interests were divergent. The persistence of a natural economy spelt stagnation, if not disaster, for the town, whereas in the countryside money remained a scarce commodity which was not in constant demand and use.

1 See A. H. Dodd, *Studies in Stuart Wales* (1952), p. 23.

2 e.g., Roberts (ed.), *Ruthin Court Rolls*, pp. 27, 33, 36.

3 E. A. Lewis, 'The Development of Industry and Commerce in Wales during the Middle Ages', *Trans*(*actions of the*) *Roy*(*al*) *Hist*(*orical*) *Soc*(*iety*), XVII (1903), 129 n. 5.

4 Rees, *South Wales and the March*, p. 222 n. 4.

5 Edwards (ed.), *Cal. Anc. Corr.*, p. 247.

Of course, it is one of the oldest tricks in the book to plead poverty with tax-collectors hammering on the door. But when agriculture was not as yet fully geared to a money economy, when the economy as a whole was still largely one of subsistence, the plea had real substance. The measures which had to be taken to acquire money were almost as painful as the act of parting with it. In answer to a petition from West Wales, Edward II agreed in 1315–16 that *gwestfa* there could be paid to the bailiff in the form of 'the cow which the tenants offer or five shillings' (provided the cow was worth five shillings!).[1] When, later, the crown demanded a subsidy from the principality in 1318, the community of West Wales expressed the hope that since they were 'never accustomed to have money in the Welshry' the king would 'receive the fifteenth from them both in beasts and in corn' for they had 'no other chattels'.[2] The prayer, which seems to have gone unanswered, was probably inspired by memories of the difficulties experienced in having to pay cash at the time of a previous subsidy. It might have reached a sympathetic ear. The crown was not averse to receiving payments in kind – 120 oxen were driven from North Wales to Windsor as a 'present' to the king in 1326–7[3] – and the usual method of distraint for non-payment invariably involved the forfeiture of goods.[4] Purveyance, indeed, an evil which increased dramatically during Edward I's reign, was to prove even more burdensome to the poor than lay subsidies. But there was a limit to what the king's court could consume and what the royal farms could take as stock. Despite safeguards, the posibility of being inundated with a horde of sad and worthless animals was too real to be ignored; at the same time, individual payments in kind were not flexible enough to deal with minor differentials in assessments. The need for cash was in any case pressing, if only to meet the multifarious demands of war; and subsidies were levied specifically to raise money. In the event, livestock or grain or some other goods had, in the majority of cases, to be sold at the few appointed local markets available to meet the financial demands of the crown. This was an additional source of irritation which made the subsidy of 1292–3 even more unpopular in Wales.

It envenomed relations between crown and people further because it short-circuited the usual procedures. The normal unit of assessment and collection was the *gwely* or the vill, but the subsidy of 1292–3 was aimed directly at the individual's personal property.

1 Ivor Bowen, *The Statutes of Wales* (1908), p. 28.

2 Edwards (ed.), *Cal. Anc. Corr.*, p. 179.

3 *Cal(endar of) Mem(oranda) Rolls 1326–7*, p. 304, no. 2148.

4 Harvey, *A Medieval Oxfordshire Village*, p. 105.

Whether intentional or not, it helped to subvert the established social order in Wales, and as such it was yet one more factor which caused resentment.

FINANCIAL YIELD AND THE REBELLION OF 1294–5

The subsidy of 1292–3 has received little attention from historians. No estimate of Edward I's total revenue has ever taken account of the money raised by it. The reason for this neglect is not far to seek. J. F. Willard was able, many years ago, from information conveniently assembled in the pipe roll for 1295, to draw up a useful table showing the total amount charged against individual English counties in 1290 on the basis of the assessment rolls.[1] Welsh historians never have it quite so easily. No amount of painstaking research would yield so precise and comprehensive a picture for the old Welsh counties. Only two county totals – Merioneth's and Flintshire's – can be recovered without resorting to conjectures. The contribution from Wales and the marches as a whole cannot be accurately assessed. The sum of £1,939. 9*s.* 11¾*d.*, computed from adding up the totals from the available evidence of the existing subsidy rolls themselves, represents but an unknown fraction of the whole. Since the area covered by the existing rolls is no more than about one-fifth of the land surface of Wales, a crude reckoning would suggest that the subsidy of 1292–3 raised between £9,500 and £10,000 from Wales. A similar figure is arrived at when the reasonable assumption is made, on the basis of estimates for the sixteenth-century, that the population of Merioneth and Flintshire – assessed at £566 and £464 respectively in 1292–3 – was around 9 and 10 per cent of that of Wales.

An estimate of about £10,000 is by no means absurdly high. The subsidy demanded in 1300 was not as burdensome as that of 1292–3 and yet it raised quite substantial amounts for the crown: a fixed sum of 2,000 marks (£1,333. 6*s.* 8*d.*) was drawn on the northern principality; 1,100 marks (£733. 6*s.* 8*d.*), equivalent apparently to a twentieth, from the southern principality; and a notional 500 marks (£333. 6*s.* 8*d.*), as against £464 in 1292–3, from Flintshire.[2] In the latter case, that represents a drop of nearly one-third on 1292–3 figures. If the same reduction applied in the contribution of the northern principality, the latter's assessment in 1292–3 could have

---

1 J. F. Willard, 'The Taxes upon Movables of the reign of Edward I', *Eng. Hist. Rev.*, XXVIII (1913), 517–21.

2 *Cal. Close Rolls 1296–1302*, p. 354; Joseph R. Strayer and George Rudisill, Jr., 'Taxation and Community in Wales and Ireland, 1272–1327', *Speculum*, XXIX (1954), 410 and n.; information about Flintshire's contribution kindly supplied by Mrs. Natalie Fryde.

been around £1,800, which, from other evidence, would seem a likely figure. That is one reason for thinking that the contribution of the three former counties of Anglesey, Caernarvon, and Merioneth in 1292–3 was somewhere in the region of £2,000. There is another.[1] We know, from the clear evidence drawn from the subsidy of 1318, that Merioneth's assessment in relation to Anglesey and Caernarvonshire was in the ratio of 3:4·3:5;[2] and since we know further that Merioneth's assessment in 1292–3 was £566, it would follow that, if the 1318 ratio applied in 1292–3, Anglesey could have been asked to contribute £812 and Caernarvonshire £944 in 1292–3, making a total of £2,322 for the principality of North Wales as a whole. (In 1318, the total was only £929, but Merioneth's contribution then, at £227,[3] was less than a half of what it was in 1292–3, at £566.) If, therefore, it could be accepted, from these admittedly unsatisfactory but reasonable deductions, that the northern principality contributed about £2,000 to the subsidy of 1292–3; and if it could be further accepted, on the basis of valuations and papal tithes payable in accordance with the taxation of *c.* 1291,[4] that Gwynedd's contribution to the subsidy of 1292–3 represented at the most one-fifth of the total demanded of Wales, then the fifteenth granted in 1292–3 might – again – reasonably be expected to have produced, at a conservative estimate, an additional bonus of at least £10,000 to the crown from Wales. There can be little doubt that, on average, individual assessments in some areas of the march were not as heavy as those in the northern principality or in the former county of Flint, and it may be that marcher lords protected their tenants from the reach of the royal exchequer in order that they might the more easily squeeze them themselves, but it is none the less a likely assumption that Wales's contribution to the subsidy of 1292–3 was in the region of £10,000 – if not in excess of that figure.

England, on the other hand, with most probably well over twelve times the population of Wales, was assessed at less than £120,000 in 1290,[5] in comparison a surprisingly low figure in view of the

---

1 Cf. also *infra*, p. xxxi, n. 5.

2 P.R.O. E.359/14 m. 13d. The ratio of 3 : 5 which characterised payments from Merioneth and Caernarvonshire occurred at other times (see, e.g., *Welsh Hist(ory) Rev(iew)*, III (1966–7), 154).

3 P.R.O. E.359/14 m. 13d.

4 *Taxatio ecclesiastica . . . Nicholai IV, c. 1291* (1802).

5 J. F. Willard, art.cit.: the precise sum was £116,346. 12*s*. 11½*d*. According to Professor Russell (*British Medieval Population*, p. 246) the population of pre-plague England, at 3,700,000, was over 18 times that of Wales. If Wales's population was 300,000, as will be tentatively advanced here, that was still less than one-twelfth that of England's. Professor Postan has, however, argued that England's pre-plague population was nearer 6,000,000 (*Camb. Econ. Hist. of Europe*, I, 561–2).

vastly superior wealth and resources of England. The taxable capacity per square mile of one of England's wealthiest counties, Lincolnshire, was reckoned at £3. 8*s.* 0*d.*, less than twice that of the area covered by the old county of Flint at £1. 18*s.* 0*d.* The tax bore more heavily on a poorer people – though the view that English settlers in Wales got off more lightly than Welshmen must be firmly rejected.[1] Of the English counties, both Cornwall and Rutland were to contribute less than Merioneth;[2] even large or important counties like Lancashire (£1,166), Middlesex (£1,148), Staffordshire (£1,342), and Worcestershire (£1,352), only a little over twice as much.[3] Devonshire's contribution per thousand acres in 1334, when it was higher than in 1290, was only 15*s.*,[4] a mere half or so of that of Merioneth's in 1292–3. A straight comparison, based on county population, is virtually impossible; nor are there any local assessment rolls for upland English counties for 1290 which would make a comparative study of individual assessments in any way realistic. But the conclusion seems inescapable: either Wales was not as sparsely populated and as impoverished in the thirteenth century as is generally imagined, or the local assessors in 1292 carried out their work too conscientiously, taking their cue perhaps from those who had prepared the new, startlingly-high assessment of Welsh dioceses for Pope Nicholas IV in *c.* 1291.[5] The latter proposition may be the more likely. Despite the vast outlay of expenditure on military fortifications in the years after 1282–3, the conquest of Wales held out more promise of immediate financial return to Edward I than has been generally recognised. The conquest was certainly not a benevolent act of state. Edward I and his armies, like the Normans before them, 'conquered for their own profit'.[6] All potential assets were to be exploited to the full – even German miners were specially

---

1 D. L. Evans (ed.), *Flintshire Ministers' Accounts, 1328–1353* (1929), p. xl and n. 7, noted apropos the tax of 1347 that the heaviest burden 'fell on the Welsh of Englefield, the boroughs being predominantly English', but the subsidy of 1292–3 did not discriminate in favour of English settlements in north-east Wales: the vill of Caerwys, for example, with an almost entirely Welsh population of 43 taxpayers, contributed £7. 1*s.* 8¾*d.*, whereas the vill of Hope, with its 35 English taxpayers, was assessed at £7. 18*s.* 7¼*d.* Of course, if this reflects the relative poverty of Welsh areas, it shows also that English communities did not escape the taxman's attention.

2 It should be noted, however, that the tin-mining population of Cornwall was exempted from paying royal taxes, and consequently many 'affluent persons managed to evade payment by claiming to have mining interests' (John Hatcher, *Rural Economy and Society in the Duchy of Cornwall, 1300–1500*, (1970), p. 9).

3 *Eng. Hist. Rev.*, XXVIII (1913), p. 519.

4 Audrey M. Erskine (ed.), *The Devonshire Lay Subsidy of 1332* (1969), p. xi.

5 Glanmor Williams, *The Welsh Church from Conquest to Reformation* (1962), p. 59.

6 The observation is that of J. E. Morris, *The Welsh Wars of Edward I* (1901), p. 2.

recruited to explore the possibilities of working the copper mines at Diserth.[1] It is true that the issues of the archbishoprics of York and Dublin and those of the king's land in Ireland had to be diverted to help finance the construction of the castles, but that applied for the most part to extra-ordinary expenditure.[2] It is also true that the principality's accounts were heavily in arrears in the early years after 1282–3. But the aim of making the principality self-supporting was soon achieved: by 1300 it 'had ceased to be a financial burden to the king' and more than half the proceeds of the principality's revenue found its way to the royal coffers.[3] Further, it was only to be expected that a strong, calculating monarch would, sooner or later, seize the opportunity his vast new power in Wales gave him of exacting some kind of payment from the marcher lords in return for removing the threat which Llywelyn II had once posed for them. The subsidy of 1292–3 was one way of discharging the debt and proved fairly lucrative from the point of view of the crown – far more so, in sum and proportionately, than the 'new' subsidy demanded in 1543 immediately after the 'Union'. If we are correct in assuming that Wales's contribution to the subsidy of 1292–3 amounted to about £10,000, it follows that as much as one-twelfth of the total raised by the corresponding subsidy in England came from Wales. The amount Wales was expected to furnish in 1543, however, was only £4,291 out of a total of £74,070[4] – or about one-eighteenth of the whole. In one particular field, at least, Edward got a better bargain out of his conquest than Henry VIII did in forging the 'Tudor Union'.

This is not to say that even after the conquest revenue from some sources did not dwindle as time went on – as in the case of subsidies. The contribution expected of Merioneth, if not the principality as a whole, from the fifteenth granted in 1318 was much lower than that of 1292–3: instead of £566, Merioneth was assessed at only £227 in 1318[5] (and Caernarvonshire at £377 and Anglesey at £325, making £929 in all, a drop even by the values of 1300, let alone 1292–3 – though the subsidy imposed in 1300 was for a fixed sum of £1,333 and not for a regular fifteenth, so that the figure for 1300 is in no way comparable with that of 1292–3 or of 1318). Mrs. Natalie Fryde has suggested that the fall in Wales's contribution by 1318 can be

---

1 Arthur Jones (ed.), *Flintshire Ministers' Accounts 1301–1328* (1913), pp. 95–6.

2 *Cal. Pat. Rolls 1281–92*, pp. 149, 193; *B.B.C.S.*, XIV (1950–2), 237, 240–1, 307.

3 *B.B.C.S.*, IX (1937–9), 51; ibid., XVI (1954–6), 110.

4 Pugh (ed.), *Glam. County Hist.*, III, 574.

5 P.R.O. E.359/14 m. 13d.

attributed to the disturbances associated with the revolt of Llywelyn Bren in 1316 and to the general disenchantment in Wales with Edward II and his policies.[1] That may be so, but it is a difficult viewpoint to defend. The revolt of Llywelyn Bren was largely a local affair. Though it caused general alarm amongst the authorities in Wales, it scarcely affected any area outside Glamorgan, a region to which the subsidy of 1318 did not in any case extend. It is doubtful too – to stand the argument on its head – if it was exactly Edward I's popularity amongst the Welsh which was responsible for the large sums accounted for in 1292–3. The decline in amounts received from subsidies was fairly general throughout the country after 1290–3. Of more relevance perhaps in 1318 was the complaint expressed at the time which noted the 'great dearth of victuals that then was in those parts',[2] a reference to the effects of the terrible famine that swept most of northern Europe in 1315–17. It can hardly be doubted that the 'agrarian crisis' of the second decade of the fourteenth century extended to the principality of North Wales, though it is impossible in any way to measure exactly how far the area was affected by it. Mortality amongst man as well as beast could have been high. The number of taxpayers in Penaran fell from 74 to 27 between 1292–3 and 1318, and in Cyffty from 19 to 13. There is this, too, that by 1318 local assessors had grown that much wiser with the years. Where comparison is possible with the surviving fragment of the Merioneth assessment for 1318,[3] it can be seen that the 1292–3 figure is usually the higher. The total the vill of Penaran was assessed at went down from over £14 to £4, that of the vill of Cyffty from 65*s*. to 31*s*.; of individual assessments, two show small increases of a few pennies, two are assessed at the same sum (in itself a possible indication of laxity on the part of local assessors), and five have been substantially reduced. The overwhelming impression remains that local assessors in 1292–3 had done their work too well – at least for the liking of the assessed.

Willard, in his important study of parliamentary taxation on personal property, expressed the view that 'there was little serious opposition to the collection of taxes',[4] and it is easy, as Dr. Titow has pointed out, to exaggerate the hardship endured by lord and

---

1 Natalie Fryde (ed.), *List of Welsh Entries in the Memoranda Rolls 1282–1343* (1974), p. xviii.

2 *Cal. Mem. Rolls 1326–7*, p. 46, no. 284. Cf. Ian Kershaw, 'The Great Famine and Agrarian Crisis in England 1315–1322', *Past and Present*, 59 (May 1973), 14, 20, 29.

3 See *infra*, Appendix, pp. 93–102.

4 Willard, *Parliamentary Taxes*, p. 197; cf. Prestwich, *War, Politics and Finance*, p. 193.

peasant alike.[1] Tithes were a bigger burden and purveyance a greater evil. It is almost certain that the under-assessment of movables was common. Everywhere, assessors were as open to bribery as they were in Cuxham or Cheddington.[2] Nevertheless, an Act concerning assaults on the collectors of tenths in Salop was passed in 1414 and communities in both England and Wales are known to have resisted or refused the payment of taxes.[3] How best to provide for the defence of the principality 'without stirring the Welsh' was a problem which faced more than one king. Fear of unrest expressed itself whenever new forms of taxation were introduced: the Black Prince's demand for a subsidy in 1347 was accompanied by powers delegated to assessors in the principality to 'arrest and take all who are contrariant or rebellious in the matter'.[4] The nervousness of those in authority was by no means unjustified. The imposition of a heavy tax by itself might not always 'precipitate a rising' but it was an essential ingredient in many rebellions, as witness those in Flanders (1323–8) and France (1358 and 1363).[5] In England the collection of the poll tax was the immediate occasion for the rising of 1381.[6] And if England had been subject to parliamentary taxation before the 1290s, Wales had not. Reasons which might have impressed prospective English taxpayers – the deceit of the French, the treachery of the Welsh, the disloyalty of the Scots – were hardly likely to arouse much enthusiasm in others. The request for a subsidy in 1291 confirmed the worst fears of the Welsh. The last remnant of independent Wales had only been finally subjugated a decade earlier. To ask the Welsh to bear, at that particular time, a taxation load proportionately heavier than England was bound to provoke a fierce and widespread reaction. For what is remarkable about the great revolt of 1294–5 is not so much that it came so soon after the final conquest of 1282–3 but that it affected almost every part of Wales, even those areas which had long since fallen to the crown and marcher lords, and which had thereafter remained firmly in their grasp. Wounded national pride, the 'strain of a new discipline upon the Welsh', the mustering of troops for a foreign war, the blighted hopes of the old Pétainist Welsh 'aristocracy', confiscations and expropriations, contemptuous attitudes and gratuitous acts of

---

1 J. Z. Titow, *English Rural Society 1200–1350* (1969), p. 63.

2 Willard, *Parliamentary Taxes*, p. 206; Harvey, *A Medieval Oxfordshire Village*, pp. 105–08.

3 *Rotuli Parliamentorum*, IV, 31; Pugh (ed.), *Marcher Lordships*, p. 42 n 5.

4 *Reg. B.P.*, I, 67–8.

5 Rodney Hilton, *Bond Men Made Free* (1973), pp. 115–17.

6 ibid., pp. 162–4.

oppression by arrogant officials[1] – all were explosive issues in post-conquest Wales, though Welshmen had, it must be remembered, served in English armies (even abroad)[2] before disagreement with France broke out into open war in 1294, and towering castles and alien ways had long been familiar to many of them. Disturbances and acts of lawlessness were endemic in the principality as in the marches.[3] The famine of 1294, too, may have contributed to Madog's war, but nothing, perhaps, in the two years immediately preceding it, stoked up the fires of resentment throughout the length and breadth of the land quite so effectively as the collection of the fifteenth of 1292–3. The men of West Wales, no less than those of North Wales, were said to be 'much troubled and irritated' by the action of royal officials before Madog's war in 1294–5.[4] Their 'grievances and hardships' were most probably of long standing, but Rhys ap Maredudd, who rose from their midst in rebellion, remained an isolated figure in 1287. It was taxation which turned local restiveness into national revolt in 1294. The mustering of Welsh troops for the French war in September that year merely provided the pretext and the occasion for concerted action. It could well be significant that an area like the lordship of Chirk escaped the full fury of the revolt: there, despite the strained relations between lord and tenants,[5] the inhabitants generally were more lightly assessed than they were elsewhere, the average tax paid there being as low as 1*s.* 9*d.* as against 3*s.* 7*d.* in Flintshire and 4*s.* 3*d.* in Merioneth.[6]

---

1 F. M. Powicke, *The Thirteenth Century* (1953), pp. 437–43; Morris, *Welsh Wars of Edward I*, pp. 240–3; Michael Prestwich, 'A new account of the Welsh campaign of 1294–95', *Welsh Hist. Rev.*, VI (1972–3), 89, 93; Glyn Roberts, *Aspects of Welsh History* (ed. by A. H. Dodd and J. Gwynn Williams, 1969), p. 306; Historical Manuscripts Commission, *Report on MSS. in various collections*, I (1901), 246–50; *Cal. Pat. Rolls 1292–1301*, p. 165; Martin (ed.), *Registrum . . . Peckham*, II, 439.
No fewer than 102 persons from Merioneth – 74 of them from the commote of Penllyn, many of them men of some consequence – were fined for not attending county and hundred courts during the short period from Easter to Michaelmas 1288. (P.R.O. E.101/614/3).

2 See, e.g., P.R.O. E.159/65 m. 21d. Welshmen had been recruited for expeditions to France in 1226, 1242, and 1253 (*Patent Rolls 1225–32*, p. 35; *Close Rolls 1237–42*, pp. 458, 497–8, 514; ibid., *1242–7*, p. 76; ibid., *1251–3*, p. 483; and *Cal. of Liberate Rolls 1240–45*, p. 178). Cf. Charles Oman, *A History of the Art of War in the Middle Ages*, I (2nd ed., 1924), 404–05.

3 e.g., P.R.O. E.159/67 m. 9d. where it is alleged that John Giffard acted against the king's peace in West Wales and that Welshmen were involved in murder, theft, etc.

4 Edwards (ed.), *Cal. Anc. Corr.*, pp. 140–1.

5 Llinos Beverley Smith, 'The Arundel Charters to the lordship of Chirk in the fourteenth century', *B.B.C.S.*, XXIII (1968–70), 154.

6 Averages above Merioneth's were Monmouth (5*s.* 6*d.*) and Bronllys (4*s.* 7*d.*). Ranged between 3*s.* 0*d.* and 4*s.* 0*d.* were the following: Welshpool, Grosmont, Skenfrith, Whitecastle, and Abergavenny; and between 2*s.* 0*d.* and 3*s.* 0*d.*: Mathrafal, Radnor,

Heavy assessments inevitably made for uneasy collection. The principality of North Wales, the most sensitive area of all, had already been subjected to heavy financial pressure during the abnormal years both immediately before and after the conquest. In the early 1290s the three sheriffs of Anglesey, Caernarvonshire, and Merioneth in turn reported heavy arrears and rents in decay 'propter paupertatem tenencium'.[1] Imposing an additional burden on the area in 1292–3, proportionately heavier than that on the marches, simply ensured that it became the storm-centre of the revolt in 1294–5.

Difficulty experienced in collecting the tax had been apparent in 1293. A sharp reminder of royal displeasure at the tardiness with which the money came in from parts of Wales and Cheshire was issued in late December of that year and John de Godelegh was sent to investigate the delay[2] – and not without reason. The collectors of the subsidy, who were expected to stagger the payments over four half-yearly terms, had been active in Wales before Easter 1293, when the receipt roll records a total of £344. 18*s.* 5½*d.* received from the first instalment of the fifteenth from Wales.[3] But this was followed by a second contribution of only £250. 7*s.* 10*d.* in October 1293,[4] a desperately small sum which must have prompted the despatch of Godelegh later in the year to remind the Welsh sharply of their obligations. Godelegh seems to have been fairly successful in his mission. The next term – April 1294 – saw a distinct improvement in the situation from the crown's point of view, £2,026. 14*s.* 2*d.* being paid in, of which £1,070 was accounted for by Robert de Belvero and Adam de Whetenhall, chamberlain and controller respectively of the principality of North Wales.[5] This substantial sum, paid in at the third instalment of the subsidy in April 1294, may not have been at all to the liking of the Welsh. Thereafter only the small sum

---

Cyfeiliog, Arwystli, Cafflogion, Cilgerran, and Glasbury. Only one area with a 'county' roll had a lower average than the lordship of Chirk and that was Is Cennen at 1*s.* 8*d.* For detailed average assessments in Stapleton, Bleddfa, Radnor, Winforton, Knighton, Norton and Presteigne, see M. A. Faraday, 'The Assessment for the fifteenth of 1293 on Radnor and other marcher lordships', *Transactions of the Radnorshire Society*, XLIII (1973), 79.

1 *B.B.C.S.*, IX (1937–9), 53, 58, 60.

2 *Cal. Pat. Rolls 1292–1301*, p. 109; *Calendar of Chancery Rolls* (*Various*) *1277–1326*, p. 353.

3 P.R.O. E.401/126.

4 P.R.O. E.401/128.

5 P.R.O. E.401/131. If £1,070 represents half the sum owing from the northern principality, that is another reason for thinking that the area was assessed at around £2,000, as has been contended above (*supra*, p. xxv). However, Easter 1294 was the time the third, rather than the second, instalment was due.

of £29. 15*s.* 6*d.* was handed in at the Receipt from Wales and the marches in October 1294.[1] By then, the Welsh were in revolt.

A total of £2,651. 15*s.* 11½*d.* in all is recorded on the receipt roll as having been received from Wales and the marches. Some payments were, however, entered directly in the pipe roll: £346. 0*s.* 6¾*d.* inclusive of expenses and allowances from Flintshire, £139. 2*s.* 11*d.* from Bromfield, and small sums of £20 and £14 from Merioneth and Caernarvonshire respectively.[2] Added to this must be the £25. 19*s.* 10½*d.* paid in by the widow of one of the collectors in West Wales in 1304–05,[3] so that we can account for at least £3,169. 19*s.* 2¾*d.* in amounts handed in at the Exchequer. This latter sum is but a fraction of what was received by the crown from the fifteenth in Wales and the marches. Vast areas of Wales are unrepresented in the receipt rolls: the greater part of the north-east; the whole of Glamorgan except Gower; and most of the old county of Monmouth. Furthermore, whereas the central march and the former county of Pembroke are fairly fully represented, only a single instalment is recorded as having been paid from the principality of North Wales, from the area once referred to as Cardiganshire and parts of the former county of Carmarthen. The total sum received can probably never be finally known – the activities of the Wardrobe in these years made nonsense of established Exchequer practice – but to judge from the mere handful of entries one has been able to follow, it can be said that no more than about one-half to three-quarters of the money due had been paid in by the time the storm broke in the autumn of 1294.[4] Arrears from various parts of Wales probably remained unpaid after the revolt, though seemingly only the collectors in Flintshire (for some undiscovered reason) were hounded for their remissness by the Exchequer. With £118 out of £464 still remaining in arrears, the Flintshire collectors complained in vain in 1300 that they had not been able to levy anything since the revolt because several of those assessed had been 'killed . . . and their lands, tenements, goods, and chattels entirely destroyed', while others had little to support themselves.[5] The complaint went unheeded: as late as 1338 the unfortunate heirs of the collectors in

1 P.R.O. E.401/133.

2 P.R.O. E.372/140 mm. 24 and 25; /146 m. 24; and see E. B. Fryde (ed.), *Book of Prests of the King's Wardrobe for 1294–5* (1962), p. 215.

3 Myvanwy Rhys (ed.), *Ministers' Accounts for West Wales 1277–1306* (1936), pp. 384–5.

4 See *infra*, pp. lxix–lxx, for the amounts paid. Willard notes that some moneys from the 1290 subsidy for England were receipted at the Wardrobe (*Parliamentary Taxes*, p. 231).

5 P.R.O. E.159/72 m. 66; /73 m. 76.

Flintshire were still held answerable to the Exchequer for the arrears of the fifteenth of 1292–3.[1]

There is, of course, no way of deciding whether or not the collectors of Flintshire – or elsewhere – would have met their obligations in October 1294 by paying in the fourth and final instalment of the subsidy if the revolt had not intervened. Certainly only small sums were received in the Exchequer from this particular source in Michaelmas 1294. No evidence has been found of collectors being assaulted or in any way molested or prevented from carrying out their duties; but neither is there any record that the local communities in the principality gave their assent in the first place to the 'request' made for a fifteenth in 1291. Those who had 'unduly burdened the Welshery' were not easily forgiven. There is no doubt that the beginning of the revolt coincided with the mustering of Welsh troops at Shrewsbury on 30 September 1294, that is to say, on the very eve of the collection of the fourth and last instalment of the subsidy in the autumn of 1294. That, surely, is more than a coincidence. One chronicler linked the revolt with the imposition of the new and odious tax.[2] It is certain that many of those taxed were killed. The subsidy may well have strained the loyalty of men in the middle stream of Welsh society who were yet influential locally, men like Llywelyn ap Cadwgan, assessed at the fairly substantial sum of 16*s.* 7*d.* in Gwrych in Ystumanner, Gronw ap Heilyn, assessed at 10*s.* 4*d.* in Llanddwywe in Ardudwy, and Peredur [ap Llywelyn], assessed at 8*s.* 2*d.* in Llwyngwril in Tal-y-bont, all of them wealthy enough to command, if not to hold, commotal offices but who died fighting against Edward in Madog's war.[3] Similarly, in north-east Wales, in the former county of Flint, Madog Goch and his brother Nynnyaw, who burnt the royal manor of Overton in 1294, were assessed fairly heavily in the townships of Bangor, Penley, Overton Foreign, and possibly elsewhere in the same county.[4] The two brothers were pardoned early in 1295 but amongst the inhabitants of the former county of Flint who did not survive was one David ab Iorwerth of Kelston, who had held land, extended at 42*s.* 11*d.* annually, in twelve townships.[5] Even the loyalty of a more notable figure like Madog ab Iorwerth, assessed at 30*s.* in Pennant-lliw and

1 *Cal. Pat. Rolls 1338–40*, p. 31; see Willard, *Parliamentary Taxes*, p. 27, for entry in memoranda roll for 1331. It is not known when the debt ceased to be entered in the pipe roll, but it was there in 1338.

2 H. R. Luard (ed.), *Flores Historiarum*, III (1890), 91.

3 See *infra*, pp. 30, n. 1, 41, n. 2, 56, n. 1.

4 P.R.O. E.179/242/52; *Cal. Inq. Misc., 1307–49*, p. 16, no. 56; *Cal. Pat. Rolls, 1292–1301*, p. 128.

5 ibid., p. 138.

one of the most powerful men in Penllyn, in the very heart of Merioneth, may have been in doubt during these years.[1] The crown remained very wary of such men: a grant of an office to the king's yeoman Gruffydd ap Dafydd, lord of Hendwr and one of the barons of Edeirnion, in July 1295 was made 'at the king's will', that is, it had to be explained, 'so long as he is useful and faithful to the king'.[2] As the tributes allegedly exacted by Llywelyn II in 1273 and 1275[3] may have exacerbated feelings against him, so too the imposition of the fifteenth by the crown in the early 1290s may have been the last straw for many of the leading Welsh *uchelwyr*. The post-conquest period was clearly a time of crisis for them. It is significant that few of the ancestors of families who became prominent in Merioneth in Tudor and Stuart times seem to be listed in the assessment rolls; equally significant is it that most of the affluent families (in terms of movables) in 1292–3 have left little subsequent trace of their existence or activities – though it is not suggested, of course, that they all came to grief during Madog's revolt. As in Glyn Dŵr's day there were clearly sharp grievances in Welsh society in the 1290s which the disillusioned Welsh 'aristocracy' was able to exploit. Even Edward I acknowledged as much when he set up an enquiry after the revolt to look into 'serious' complaints by the men of the community of North Wales against the 'injuries, extortions, oppressions, and very serious damage' inflicted upon them by royal officials since the conquest.[4] Likewise in West Wales a commission was appointed to look into reports of oppressions there.[5] Seething discontent was clearly rampant in the middle and upper reaches of Welsh society in the 1290s.

And if leading *uchelwyr* had much to complain about, how much more the lower orders of society and the less well-off. A man like Cynwrig Foel who held just 12 acres of Welsh land in the vill of Madryn in Llŷn was hanged in Madog's war.[6] There were many such who met a similar fate. Well-to-do villeins in the old counties of Merioneth and Caernarvon are known for certain to have suffered for the part they played in the events of 1294–5.[7] For the unfree, even more than the free, the post-conquest period in these areas brought further insecurity and added burdens. All, no matter what their legal

---

1 See *infra*, p. 7, n. 6
2 *Calendar of Chancery Warrants 1244–1326*, pp. 63–4.
3 *Cal. Close Rolls 1272–9*, p. 57; Edwards (ed.), *Cal. Anc. Corr.*, p. 105.
4 *Cal. Pat. Rolls 1292–1301*, p. 165.
5 ibid., p. 246.
6 *B.B.C.S.*, VI (1931–3), 258.
7 P.R.O. S.C.6/1170/5.

status, were made liable to the fifteenth of 1291, though it would be too much to hope that 'none of the richer sort' was 'spared from contributing according to his means'.[1] One can only imagine what ill-usage accompanied its collection: significantly, it was the man with overall responsibility for the collection of the subsidy in Anglesey – Roger de Pulesdon, the sheriff of the island – who was singled out to be lynched as the rebels swept into Caernarvon town and stormed the castle there in 1294;[2] at the same time they did not forget to burn records and memoranda and every kind of incriminating evidence they could find of outstanding debts.[3] And the wider the net, the more likelihood was there of a violent reaction, as social groups hitherto unburdened by extra-ordinary taxation came within the frosty reach of the royal exchequer. Taxation promoted national unity in Wales as effectively as it heightened Welsh national feeling. Whatever else may be said of Madog's war it was more than a mere 'revolt of the disinherited'. The element of surprise, which characterised its opening, depended on widespread support throughout Wales – and that at every level. Despite English fears, reflected in their panic defensive measures throughout Wales, the rising of Rhys ap Maredudd in 1287 remained an isolated affair; but the great rebellion of 1294–5 involved every section of Welsh society.

POPULATION ESTIMATES

Historians have, perhaps not altogether without good reason, usually fought shy of making use of medieval subsidy rolls for demographic purposes. Even Professor Josiah C. Russell, well-known for his 'adventurousness' in this field, refrained from doing so. He accepted Willard's caveat about them and dismissed the idea of utilising them for measuring population.[4] Numerous others, far more cautious than Professor Russell, have expressed even stronger disapproval of subsidy rolls. One recent writer has condemned them outright as being 'useless'.[5] Many of the objections raised against placing excessive reliance on subsidy rolls are justified, but it is difficult to see why a source of this kind should be so comprehensively rejected out of hand in this way. Medieval subsidy lists are, on the face of it, no more imperfect a source for measuring population

1 The government was clearly aware of what was going on locally whenever taxes had to be paid (see, e.g., *Cal. Pat. Rolls 1281–92*, p. 178).

2 *Flor. Historiarum*, III, 91.

3 P.R.O. E.159/70 m. 60d; *Cal. Close Rolls 1302–07*, p. 398.

4 J. C. Russell, *British Medieval Population* (Albuquerque, 1948), pp. 33, 364; J. F. Willard, op. cit., pp. 174–82.

5 W. B. Stephens (ed.), *Sources for the History of Population and their Uses* (1971), p. 8.

than other taxation lists upon which population figures are based – figures which, despite lordly scepticism in some quarters, are still accepted by and large as working hypotheses by most historians. Nothing more is claimed for them than that. Uncertainty attends all deductions based on assessment returns, but some forms of taxation records are more useful and reliable than others. Equally, greater credence can be placed on figures based on certain taxation lists for particular years than for others. Hearth tax assessments for 1670 are, it is known, more reliable than those for the 1660s and, with caution, can be, and are, used for demographic purposes.[1] Though the contrary may well be true of medieval lay subsidies, that the amounts raised by each levy declined as subsidies became more frequent and that there was a general tendency towards a reduction in the number of people paying the tax between 1290 and 1334,[2] it follows that some of the early subsidy rolls, or at least those relating to certain areas, may be more trustworthy than later ones. They have not degenerated into being mere formal documents. The returns of the 1290 subsidy for England are very meagre and fragmentary and are, generally, an unprofitable source of information to the English historian. The parallel returns for Wales, on the other hand, the first of their kind, though equally meagre, are much more useful since they are for the most part not fragmentary. What has survived is more or less complete and consequently of great potential value to the historian. No accurate estimate of the total population of the whole of Wales at the end of the thirteenth century is remotely possible from the returns – they cover less than a quarter of the country – but they do provide, despite numerous problems attaching to them, the best basis for estimating roughly the population of various parts of Wales soon after the Edwardian conquest.

The main difficulty about the Merioneth subsidy roll of 1292–3 is that one cannot compare it with any other for the area as a whole for the medieval period. It is different in kind from the extents of *c.* 1284 and the early fifteenth century[3] which are, in any case, either incomplete or not uniformly compiled. In the one instance where a direct comparison between the extent of *c.* 1284 and the subsidy of 1292–3 can be made, there is agreement on numbers in the bond township of Crogen: the extent specifies that there were

1 Lydia M. Marshall, 'The Levying of the Hearth Tax, 1662–1688', *Eng. Hist. Rev.*, LI (1936), 629–30; Leonard Owen, 'The Population of Wales in the Sixteenth and Seventeenth Centuries', *Trans*(*actions of the*) *Hon*(*ourable*) *Soc*(*iety of*) *Cymm*(*rodorion*) (1959), pp. 99–113.

2 J. F. Willard, op. cit., pp. 179, 343–4.

3 See *Arch. Camb.* (1867), pp. 184–92, and H. Ellis, *The Record of Caernarvon* (1838), pp. 261–92.

5 villeins there and the subsidy that there were 5 taxpayers, but one of these, Ithel Dapifer, was hardly likely to have been a villein.[1] What can be claimed for the subsidy of 1292–3 is that, although it is imperfect, it is fairly comprehensive, for only one parish – Llanelltud – in the whole county as it was then constituted is unrepresented.[2] Undeniably, too, the degree of supervision exercised by officials of the central exchequer at Caernarvon over the assessment was impressively high; it is apparent at every turn in the corrections and emendations of the totals at which townships were assessed. Furthermore, it seems that local officials, on the whole, carried out the preliminary work of assessment conscientiously, if slowly, in the early 1290s, being particularly careful about not grossly under-assessing their own contributions. Barely ten years after the conquest, they were probably trying to impress their new taskmasters with their competence and probity. Indeed if, as we have already tried to argue,[3] the collection of the subsidy sparked off the great revolt of 1294–5, then it could be that they had been over-assiduous in carrying out their initial duties, for royal complaints in December 1293 that 'certain taxors and collectors' had been negligent and remiss were concerned essentially with the prickly task of collection, not assessment.[4]

Nevertheless, the greatest care must be exercised when using the roll for estimating the population of Merioneth in the late thirteenth century. There are any number of sound reasons why that should be so. To begin with, one cannot be absolutely certain of the total number of those assessed in 1292–3. It must be accepted that a few persons had movables, and were therefore liable to be taxed, in more than one township, but it has proved impossible to discover exactly how many. Identification becomes extremely hazardous when, for example, as happens on more than one occasion in this roll, two brothers might be called by the same name, or when two

1 *infra*, p. 16, and *Arch. Camb.* (1867), p. 189.

2 Dr. Colin Thomas's view, as expressed in *Journ(al of the) Mer(ioneth) Hist(orical and) Rec(ord) Soc(iety)*, VI (1969–72), 122, that 'for Ardudwy . . . evidence for only six full townships survives' seems to be based on what is immediately legible of the roll. A number of townships which are known to have existed at this time do not, however, figure in this subsidy roll: they include Rhagad, Bonwm, Castell, Bedwarian, Rhyddallt, Brynbanon, 'Alltuelin', Trefeirion, and 'Keventeylloyn'. Some, like Gwernhefin, granted by Llywelyn II to Basingwerk abbey in 1247, were in the hands of ecclesiastics (*Calendar of Charter Rolls*, II, 291); others, like Bala, were in the hands of the crown (*Cal. of Chanc. Rolls (Various) 1277–1326*, p. 328). Prysor is mentioned in a coroner's account for 1325–6 (P.R.O. S.C.6/1170/16 m. 4); significantly, Edward I's itinerary in 1283 seems to have taken in 'Castell' Prysor (*Cal. of Chanc. Warrants 1244–1326*, p. 13).

3 *supra*, p. xxx. Cf. Waters, *Edwardian Settlement*, pp. 28–9.

4 *Cal. of Chanc. Rolls (Various) 1277–1326*, p. 353, and *Cal. Pat. Rolls 1292–1301*, p. 109.

men with the rather unusual name of Adaf ab Purrewyn were not only assessed in the same township but also listed next to each other in the roll.[1] It is not clear either how many were, strictly speaking, non-Merioneth people: in Alan de Ruthin and Lawrence de Montgomery we may have two interesting early examples of enterprising burgesses with interests in Merioneth who were probably resident outside the county; in Gwyn Mautho an intruder from the lordship of Mawddwy, which did not become a part of the shire of Merioneth until 1536; and in the 26 taxpayers of Abertanat men who were residents of an area which ceased to be part of the county in the same year.[2] But too much can be made of difficulties of this kind. They are no reason for throwing our hands up in despair. An effort must be made to arrive at as accurate a figure as possible; otherwise our appreciation of the scale of human need is severely limited. Not that we should forget, on the other hand, that we are dealing in terms of possibilities, not certainties. All the 'difficult' cases referred to above are fairly marginal and comparatively few in number. 2,669 names are recorded on the roll, incomplete as it is; even allowing for duplication and non-residence, the total number of Merioneth taxpayers in 1292–3 cannot have been much less than 2,600.

But that merely disposes provisionally of one problem. There is an added complication: the number of taxpayers does not correspond to the number of households. Despite the difficulties attending identification which have already been noted, one gains the distinct impression from reading certain parts of the Merioneth roll that wives and mature children were sometimes assessed alongside the head of the family as if this were in the nature of a poll-tax return. This is particularly noticeable in such areas as Bodgadfan, Rhydcryw, Peniarth, Corwen, Bodorlas, and Pencraig.[3] In Ceiswyn, on the other hand, an unidentifiable number of sons or daughters seem to have held movable property in common and were made liable collectively to the tax.[4] The inclusion of sons alongside their fathers in the lists does not seriously affect one's estimate of the total number of taxable households in Merioneth at the end of the thirteenth century since most of them, it is reasonable to assume, were householders themselves. But, clearly, women are in a different category and it is crucially important to distinguish between those who were most probably wives and those who were not. Around 10 per cent of those assessed were women. About half of these were

---

1 *infra*, pp. 34, 75, and 92..
2 *infra*, pp. 6, 9, 29, 91–2.
3 *infra*, pp. 36–40, 75, 76, and 90.
4 *infra*, pp. 33–4.

seemingly unattached widows or spinsters (though none of them is actually described as such) while the other half were apparently wives and daughters who were assessed alongside their menfolk. Roughly 100 or so must, therefore, be subtracted from the estimated total of 2,600 taxpayers and we may conclude tentatively that there were about 2,500 households liable to the subsidy of 1292–3 in Merioneth.

What proportion of the total population of the county did these constitute? Here we are almost completely in the dark. Not only were outright paupers naturally omitted from the roll but so too were those whose assessed tax came to less than 1*s.* – or possibly more, since 1*s.* 4*d.* seems to have been taken as the 'conventional minimum' in some areas, 1*s.* 6*d.* in others.(1) No one in the whole commote of Ystumanner was assessed at less than 1*s.* 3*d.*, nor does a single cleric appear (at least not a single cleric has been identified for us) in the lists for the commote – it surely cannot be that there were no clerics with temporal property worth 15*s.* or more in Ystumanner? Some assessors were clearly more accommodating than others. If one or two hearth tax returns of the seventeenth century were any guide in these matters, the number of the untaxed could be as numerous as those liable to the tax.(2) There is no warrant for making such an assumption in this case, though there are parallels. It seems likely that if more 'local' commotal rolls had survived, the submerged mass of the untaxed might be more accurately gauged, because we know that in Gwynedd, at least, local assessors were required to draw up a list of all those who had movable property valued at as little as 15*d.* or more on Michaelmas day 1292.(3) Local assessors in Nefyn, Creuddyn, and Cafflogion, areas lying in the old county of Caernarvon, carried out this part of their instructions to the letter. Their returns reveal that more than half (48 out of 93) of those named in Nefyn, a third (about 40 out of 128) of those originally assessed in the commote of Creuddyn, and at least 35 of the 201 persons for the commote of Cafflogion had movables worth in all between 15*d.* and 15*s.* in value and were therefore exempt from paying the subsidy.(4) Their names would simply not have been

1 e.g., seven persons were assessed at 1*s.* 4*d.* in Llanfrothen (*infra*, pp. 64–5), and no one at less than that sum. On the 'conventional minimum' see J. F. Willard, op. cit., p. 90.

2 See the 1670 returns for Pembrokeshire in *West Wales Historical Records*, IX (1920–23), 218–40; X (1924), 177–216; XI (1926), 113–37. J. C. Russell, op. cit., p. 146, allowed only five per cent. for the 'indigent and untaxed' for estimating the population of England in 1377, but this has not found general acceptance.

3 P.R.O. E.159/95 m. 62, and cf. App., *infra*, pp. 96–102.

4 P.R.O. E.179/242/51; *B.B.C.S.*, V (1929–31), 54–71, 143–8. The only other 'local' roll for Gwynedd dating from 1292–3 which has survived – that for Aberffraw in Anglesey – does not list those with movable property of less than 15*s.*, so that the population of the vill may have been bigger than that of Nefyn's (cf. ibid., 142 n. 4).

entered on the (now lost) county roll for Caernarvonshire.[1] Of course, in Nefyn as well as in Creuddyn and Cafflogion some persons may have been completely destitute, without movable property to the value of 15*d.*, in which case they would not have made even the 'local' roll, so that the number of those exempted from paying the tax could well have been higher. It almost certainly was, for none of these calculations takes into account hired servants or certain clergymen who possessed no temporal property; but the existing evidence only allows us to say that the untaxed population could, at the very least, be between about one-sixth and one-half of those assessed. An average based on these figures would give us one-third.

This is a very crude measuring-rod. The number of those unassessed cannot be known entirely, though one surmises that they formed a considerable percentage of the population of Merioneth in the late thirteenth century. But even if the number of the untaxed as well as the taxed were known, there would still be difficulties. Controversy still rages about the size of the medieval household in England. It may have been the 3.5 consistently favoured by Professor Russell for the whole of England and Wales throughout the middle ages – which seems unlikely – or 4.3 or 5.9 or higher estimates preferred by others for particular areas at different times.[2] The debate is rather unreal for allowance must be made for regional and periodic variations. More than that, what exactly constitutes a household is still open to question. Should dependants or servants or farm-hands or apprentices be included in the calculation? On all these matters there is, unfortunately, very little evidence on which to base a judgement as far as Merioneth – or even Wales – is concerned.

The roll is, therefore, hardly an ideal instrument for measuring the population of late thirteenth-century Merioneth. It says nothing of those who did not pay the subsidy; it gives no indication of the size of a Merioneth household; it does not include the names of taxpayers from one parish in Ardudwy or from a scatter of townships in the commotes of Edeirnion, Penllyn, and Tal-y-bont. Even the number of those assessed cannot be exactly computed. Nevertheless it is, taking the area as a whole, far and away the best available indicator for the period, for it is fairly comprehensive in its coverage and shows every sign of having been drawn up with

1 Cf. *B.B.C.S.*, XIII (1948–50), 230, where it is noted that five jurors in the hundred of Cilgerran in the former county of Pembroke had 'not 15*s.* value' and therefore 'paid nothing'.

2 For a convenient summary of part of this growing literature, see J. C. Russell, 'The Pre-plague Population of England', *The Journal of British Studies*, V, No. 2 (1966), 17–20. In ibid., p. 14, Professor Russell gives a revised estimate of the 1377 population of England which he gave in his *British Medieval Population*.

care. As it happens, there is an additional piece of evidence which not only largely corroborates the information given in this roll but also provides an accurate index of the size of a family in a small Merioneth borough at this time. In Harlech in April 1295 there were, apart from the reinforced garrison and their dependants, resident there 11 men (as compared with the 12 recorded as taxpayers in 1292–3, though the names of nearly half of them differ), 12 women, and 21 children, making 44 in all which gives an average of 4 to a family.[1] If this figure were applied generally and uniformly to the whole of Merioneth as then constituted, it would give us a population of around 10,000. Almost certainly that would be an underestimate, for the simple reason that it does not take into account the number of those unassessed and their families who must have been fairly numerous in the wholly rural areas of Merioneth at the end of the thirteenth century. Household goods and certain items of clothing, for example, were classified as movables in towns but not in the country, so that tax-exemption and tax-evasion proved far more difficult there than in rural areas.[2] A newly-established borough like Harlech, with its easily identifiable though fluctuating population was, in any case, in a special category of its own as far as Merioneth was concerned. If we could assume that the unassessed in country areas formed a mere 10 per cent of the population it would leave us with a global figure for the county of about 11,000. That is most probably a low estimate. If the unassessed generally totalled on the average one-third of those assessed, as the meagre evidence drawn from other areas of North Wales suggests,[3] the population would be in the region of 13,333. Even if the normal

1 J. Griffiths, 'Documents relating to the rebellion of Madoc, 1294–5', *B.B.C.S.*, VIII (1935–7), 149–50. Professor Russell, in estimating the population of Harlech at this time, ignored those in the castle in April 1295, but included in his calculations not only the 44 persons described clearly and simply as being 'de villa de Hardelach' but also the seven men who 'came with John de Havering' in December 1294 as well as the 14 women and children 'de castro'. He concluded accordingly that there were 18 heads of families and a total population of 65 in Harlech in 1294–5 which conveniently gave him an average of 3.6 to a family and thus fitted in perfectly with his theory of about 3.5 per household for England and Wales in the Middle Ages (*British Medieval Population*, pp. 338–40). But this will not do: either the men in the castle should have been included or the women and children described as being 'de castro' should have been omitted from his calculations. It is very doubtful, too, if the seven men who 'came with John de Havering', the deputy-justiciar of North Wales, should be numbered amongst the ordinary inhabitants of Harlech. During times of trouble the population of castellated boroughs was bound to fluctuate: reinforcements were sent, for example, to Harlech during Rhys ap Maredudd's revolt (*B.B.C.S.*, XIV (1950–2), 307) and similarly to Cricieth during Madog's revolt (E. A. Lewis, *The Mediaeval Boroughs of Snowdonia* (1912), p. 195, and *B.B.C.S.*, III (1926–7), 151, 152).

2 J. F. Willard, op. cit., pp. 75–8.

3 *supra*, p. xl.

multiplier of 5 were adopted, the figure would be 12,500. But we are now really groping in the shadows.

* * *

A population probably well in excess of 10,000 at the time of the conquest of Wales comes as something of a surprise. Perhaps more people may have inhabited Merioneth than might be suspected from reading Gerald of Wales's account of his brisk tour through the area a century earlier. As early as 1123 the sons of Gruffydd ap Cynan of Gwynedd, in their struggle against Powys, are said to have carried off to Llŷn the whole population of the cantref of Meirionnydd and their property[1] – a singularly futile exercise unless the numbers justified it. But the marked increase in population probably came, as T. Jones Pierce said, later in the twelfth century and, to judge from Europe as a whole, is likely to have continued in the thirteenth century: it makes Llewelyn II's ambitious policy in the 1260s and the 1270s all the more credible. What does seem inescapable is that the population of Merioneth by the end of the thirteenth century was more than the considered estimate of 9,760 conjectured by Leonard Owen for the same area by the mid-sixteenth century.[2] Most individual townships and parishes in Merioneth seem to have been more densely populated in the late thirteenth century.

How trustworthy are the conjectured totals for the mid-sixteenth century and are they in any way comparable with those of 1292–3? One may disagree with Leonard Owen's methods and findings in detail, but his estimates are rightly based on figures derived from the two principal sources available, namely the returns of the new (to Wales) subsidies voted in 1543 and the 'Bishops' Census' of 1563.[3] The latter, but not the former, is generally acknowledged to be fairly accurate.[4] Independent corroboration of its accuracy – if such it is – is confined to a single instance as far as Merioneth is concerned: according to the Bishops' Census, the number of families in the parish of Llanaber was 60, a figure which, when multiplied by 5,

1 Thomas Jones (ed.), *Brut y Tywysogyon: Peniarth MS. 20* (1941), p. 82. The cantref of Meirionnydd consisted of the two commotes of Tal-y-bont and Ystumanner.

2 Leonard Owen, art. cit., p. 111. The total of 10,520, calculated by Leonard Owen using a multiplier of five, includes 760 for Mawddwy, an area which did not become part of Merioneth until 1536.

3 There are useful general observations on the 1543 subsidy in W. R. B. Robinson, 'The First Subsidy Assessment of the Hundreds of Swansea and Llangyfelach, 1543', *Welsh Hist. Rev.*, II (1964–5), 125–45; for the 1563 household returns for Merioneth see *Roy*(*al*) *Comm*(*ission on*) *Anc*(*ient*) *Mon*(*uments*): *Inv*(*entory for*) *Merioneth* (1921), p. xxii.

4 See, e.g., W. G. Hoskins, *Provincial England* (1964), p. 186, and *Victoria County History: Leicestershire*, III (1955), 138.

gives us 300, the precise number of 'parsones' mentioned in a petition to the court of requests by the 'tenauntes and freholders' of Llanaber in Henry VIII's reign.(1) But it seems that the 1563 figures are themselves in some cases estimates only: in no fewer than 13 out of the 21 Merioneth parishes covered the totals are expressed in round multiples of ten – which makes them rather suspect. Unfortunately, too, the Census figures of 1563 are available for only three Merioneth hundreds, namely, Ardudwy, Tal-y-bont and Ystumanner, but where comparison is possible with the earlier returns of the subsidy of 1543 there is a fairly close correspondence between them.(2) Commotal totals for Ystumanner and Tal-y-bont are 323 and about 350 respectively from the returns of 1543,(3) and 338 and 336 from the returns of 1563. When the totals tally as closely as this, it is difficult to see why the subsidy lists of 1543 should be under such a thick cloud of suspicion. On the other hand, English historians have reported substantial increases in the population of various parts of England in the forty years or so between 1524 and 1563, so that one would naturally expect the 1543 figures for Wales to be lower than those for 1563, as they certainly are in the case of Pwllheli.(4) Doubts, therefore, inevitably remain about these mid-sixteenth century totals for Welsh areas, but they have at least been derived from two independent sources and they can, consequently, with the usual reservations, be accepted as generally accurate.

If the taxpayers of 1292–3 were herded into 'households' and parishes, a valid comparison could be made with the ecclesiastical returns of 1563. The results are revealing in that they show that in 16 out of 21 parishes in the three western commotes of Merioneth the 1563 figures are lower than those of 1292–3. The number might be even higher than 16, for full details are not available for the two parishes of Pennal and Llanelltud. In the three remaining parishes no substantial increases can be discerned by 1563 except in the case of the parish of Ffestiniog, but in the thirteenth century that parish had been very sparsely populated indeed. The Table below giving details of the 1292–3 and the sixteenth-century lists clarifies these points. Included also in the Table for good measure and largely for the sake of interest are the number of tenements returned in a crown survey of 1592 in the commotes of Penllyn,

---

1 *Roy. Comm. Anc. Mon.: Inv. Merioneth*, pp. xxii and 40.

2 Cf. W. R. B. Robinson, art. cit., p. 139 n. 29.

3 The 1543 returns for these two commotes (P.R.O. E.179/222/309 and 311) were not used by Leonard Owen in his calculations; they are, for the most part, illegible.

4 Jones Pierce, *Medieval Welsh Society*, p. 183.

Tal-y-bont, and Ystumanner;[1] the number of names entered in the hearth tax lists for the whole of Merioneth (apart from Mawddwy) in 1670;[2] the number of families listed in the visitation returns of the Bishop of Bangor for parishes located mainly in Ardudwy in the mid-eighteenth century;[3] and the population of parishes as given in the first census of 1801. It should be understood that the figures in this statistical table merely provide, for the most part, a rough index of the position at various dates and are not necessarily to be taken as indicating trends. Where blanks occur information is not available.

The value of the 1292–3 assessment, and many of the reservations about it, are equally applicable in the case of the returns of the new subsidy of 1543. Every person having lands or goods worth £1 or more was liable to the assessment of 1543 (in 1292–3 it had been movable goods to the value of 15*s*. and above) so that, in theory, every householder except an outright pauper was a potential taxpayer.[4] The untaxed proportion of the population is as difficult as ever to measure, but on the face of it, if we allow for the fall in the value of money, the number of those taxed should have equalled, if not exceeded, that of 1292–3. As the Table below shows, the returns of 1543 are not dissimilar to those of 1563 and gain respectability by virtue of that fact. In one respect at least they are of more value for comparative purposes than the ecclesiastical returns of 1563 because they are arranged under townships rather than parishes. Detailed comparison is, however, confined to the commote of Edeirnion and part of the commote of Tal-y-bont. The results are of interest in that they bear out what has already become clear, from a comparative study of the subsidy lists of 1292–3 and the ecclesiastical returns of 1563, about the relatively higher population density prevailing at the end of the thirteenth century. The figures relating to the commote of Edeirnion do not point quite so conclusively in that direction but nevertheless even there indications of a drop in numbers overall by the mid-sixteenth century are unmistakable. Only 6 out of 21 identifiable townships in Edeirnion had more taxpayers in 1543 than in 1292–3 and none of those showed appreciable increases. On the other hand, it has to be said that the 1292–3 totals for the remaining 15 townships are not substantially higher than those of 1543 and the assumption must be that the mid-sixteenth century total for Edeirnion as a whole cannot have been

1 P.R.O. L.R.2/236.

2 P.R.O. E.179/222/400a.

3 A. I. Pryce, *The Diocese of Bangor during three centuries* (1929), pp. 165–6.

4 W. R. B. Robinson, art. cit., pp. 129–30.

Parishes	Taxed 1292–3	Taxed 1543	Households 1563	Tenements 1592	Taxed 1670	Families 1749	Pop. 1801
Llanaber	101	45	60		141	145	1,463
Llanenddwyn	50	73	60		69		567
Llanddwywe	25		30		66		308
Llandanwg	48	32	27		53		461
Llanbedr	31	25	23		63		319
Llandecwyn	35	31	32		39		387
Llanfihangel-y-Traethau	85		30		56	52	669
Llanfair	55	35	32		37	50	369
Ffestiniog	21		50		79	106	732
Maentwrog	55		40		62	88	593
Trawsfynydd	105		70		151	?400	1,232
Llanfrothen	92		40		43	25	646
Llanelltud			38		59	40	398
Tywyn	209		200	188	305		2,092
Pennal	38+		56	59	111	72	554
Tal-y-llyn	78		50	76	92	108	633
Llanfihangel-y-Pennant	67		32	39	48	61	366
Llangelynnin	100	69	60	129	123	141	754
Dolgellau	154	158	140	130	307		2,949
Llanfachreth	112		76	79	166	80	1,069
Llanegryn	108	78	60	92	110		623
Llanfor	179			144	222		1,705
Llangywer	27			22	69		430
Llanuwchllyn	104			41+	147		1,191
Llanycil	93			104	230		2,445
Llandderfel	84			46	111		815
Betws Gwerful Goch	17	26			52		241
Corwen	164	64+			211		1,369
Gwyddelwern	67	62			112		1,143
Llandrillo	127	75			140		800
Llangar	79				65		203
Llansanffraid	12	7					88

considerably lower than that of the late thirteenth century.[1] Whether that in its turn argues for a remarkable degree of stability – or for a measure of recovery after disasters in the interval – is highly problematical.

The 1543 subsidy returns for the commote of Tal-y-bont,[2] though fragmentary, are more interesting. Here, two parishes are represented: Llanegryn, which shows a clear drop from 108 to 78, reflecting accurately most probably the comparative decline in the area's economic importance by the sixteenth century; and the old parish of Dolgellau, which shows a small increase from 154 to 158, mainly due to the growth of the 'town' of Dolgellau. The number of households in Dolgellau was not 140 as Leonard Owen and others after him have maintained on the basis of the 1563 returns[3] – that number refers to households, not in the town, but in the old parish of Dolgellau which consisted of eight townships – but nearer 23, the number of taxpayers in the town in 1543, as against only 3+[4] in 1292–3; and it is possible that this increase from 3+ to 23 by the mid-sixteenth century was due to an influx of people from the neighbouring easterly and southerly (and in one instance former bond) townships of the old parish of Dolgellau, as the Table below shows.

Dolgellau Parish	Taxpayers	Taxpayers
Townships	*1292–3*	*1543*
Dolgellau	3+	23
Dyffrydan	20	21
Dolgledr	21	29
Cefnyrowen	10	12
Garthmaelan	22	10
Garthgynfor	34	28
Brithdir	41	25
Gwanas	3	10
TOTAL	154	158

1 Leonard Owen assumed wrongly that the 1543 subsidy for Edeirnion was complete (art. cit., p. 105).

2 P.R.O. E.179/222/309.

3 Leonard Owen, art. cit., p. 111. Cf. the map in Joan Thirsk (ed.), *The Agrarian History of England and Wales, 1500–1640*, IV (1967), p. 146, where Dolgellau is shown to be almost as big as Caernarvon and Denbigh and bigger than Beaumaris, Conwy, and Welshpool: that certainly was not the case.

4 See *infra*, p. 50, n. 1 for the reason why 3+ is used here.

The growth of Dolgellau may have been very modest indeed by the time of the 'Union', but Leland accurately described it in the 1530s as the 'best village in this commote' of Tal-y-bont.(1) And village or no, it had larger ambitions. It is of some interest to note that the 'town' of Dolgellau by the mid-sixteenth century was bigger than one of its main rivals, namely Bala, under which 13 taxpayers are recorded in 1543, but had yet possibly to overtake the 'county' town of Harlech, with its 25 men ready at the muster in 1539. Already, however, Dolgellau was in a strong position to challenge the claims of other towns to be the administrative centre of Merioneth. As early as 1546 it was playing host to quarter sessions; in 1553 even the court of great sessions was summoned to meet there.(2)

Two main conclusions emerge from a comparative study of the thirteenth and sixteenth century statistics available for Merioneth as a whole. Firstly, the overall population of the county was almost certainly bigger in the late thirteenth century than in the mid-sixteenth century. Secondly, the population of individual townships, especially rural townships, was, in the main, higher in the late thirteenth century, but decline was not uniform throughout the area: at least one growth point – Dolgellau – is discernible by the mid-sixteenth century. In truth, areas with urban characteristics – trading and administrative centres – seem generally to have been more flourishing and populous by the time of the 'Union' of England and Wales. The confidence of the authorities in the urban potential of Harlech may have been misplaced but in 1539 they were prepared to invest in it and ordered that the castle and town walls be 'substantyally reapared and amended'.(3) Harlech, indeed, by then may have nearly doubled in size since its foundation, though it was still in fact little more than a small village and ill-equipped to meet the future. As for migration in the later middle ages, if it occurred at all, it seems to have taken place for the most part intra-commotally. There had, apparently, been no great shift in the population, for each commote maintained the same percentage of the total population of the county to two or three degrees at the two dates – Ardudwy, Tal-y-bont, and possibly Penllyn also, with the same consistent percentages of about 27 per cent, 20 per cent, and 18 per cent respectively, and Ystumanner (up from about 15 per cent to 18 per cent of the whole by 1543) edging into fourth place ahead of Edeirnion.

* * *

Have these conclusions any general validity? Commotal figures – where available and as they stand – seem to indicate that Maelor

1 Lucy Toulmin Smith (ed.), *The Itinerary in Wales of John Leland* (1906), p. 77.

2 P.R.O. E.179/222/307, 310; *Letters and Papers of Henry VIII*, XIV, pt. i, 321–2; Nat. Lib. Wales, Merioneth Plea Rolls, Wales 23/1 m. 5d. and Wales 23/2 m. 9.

3 *Arch. Camb.* (1846), pp. 248–9. Harlech, however, had no town walls.

in the former county of Flint, Cynllaith, Mochnant, and Nanheudwy in what used to be eastern Denbighshire, Arwystli (if not Cyfeiliog) and Caereinion in the old county of Montgomery, and Radnor in the late county of Radnor had a higher taxable population in 1292–3 than in 1543 or possibly a greater number of households than in 1563, whereas figures for Cafflogion, Creuddyn, and Cymydmaen in the old county of Caernarvon, Cilgerran in the northern part of what used to be Pembrokeshire, and Abergavenny and Skenfrith in the former county of Monmouth show an increase by the sixteenth century. But a crude comparison of this kind reveals many inconsistencies. The evidence for the most part is too fragmentary or inconclusive to allow for accurate global comparisons to be made. More than half the townships of the commote of Creuddyn, for example, no longer figure in the defective roll of 1292–3.(1) Even a fairly close analysis, parish by parish, let alone commote by commote, allows too much scope for error and distortion. Indeed one cannot be certain that a comparative analysis township by township is always entirely reliable unless all hamlets and settlements are accounted for.(2) That, however, is the best that could possibly be expected, and the inclusion of hamlets or sub-townships must in the vast majority of cases be assumed. Unfortunately, apart from the former counties of Merioneth and Flint, a really valid detailed comparison, township by identifiable township, is limited to a mere handful of instances, many of them areas remote from each other. Nevertheless, an examination of the relevant figures is not without interest. The rural townships of Aberffraw (Anglesey) and Carreghofa (formerly in Montgomeryshire) follow the pattern noted in Merioneth and show a reduction in numbers.(3) With urban centres, the picture is slightly more complicated. An overall pattern is difficult to discern. Towns like Denbigh and Llanidloes show an increase; Pwllheli and Machynlleth have the same number or fall just below the late-thirteenth century figure; Nefyn shows a considerable drop by about a half, but there the wide difference is due to the inclusion of a great number of persons who were not liable to the tax on the 'local' subsidy roll of 1292–3.(4) It would be unwise to draw firm conclusions from these few isolated examples but the abiding impression remains that the towns generally were as popu-

---

1 P.R.O. E.179/242/51.

2 In the township of Penaran in the commote of Penllyn there were, for example, six gavells of free land and four gavells of bond land.

3 From 69 to 54 in the case of Aberffraw (Seebohm, op. cit., and B(ritish) M(useum), Harl. MS 594); from 27 to 21 in that of Carreghofa (P.R.O. E.179/242/55 and U.C.N.W., Bangor MS. 13492).

4 These conclusions are based on P.R.O. E.179/242/50a, 50b, and 54; B.M. Harl. 594;

lous – if not more so – in 1543 as they had been in the early 1290s, whereas rural townships were not. Unless agricultural productivity had increased significantly by the sixteenth century, this seems to disprove the notion that a thriving urban economy was dependent upon a prosperous countryside.[1]

There can be little doubt that living in towns became more attractive in the sixteenth century whatever impression to the contrary may have been given by reading John Leland's *Itinerary*. Journeying with Leland through Wales in the 1530s is altogether a depressing experience as he wanders from one necropolis to another, morbidly reciting how this 'toun is wonderfully decaied' while the other 'is totally yn ruine'. But even he could not resist observing that Carmarthen had 'incresid', or that Abergavenny was 'meately welle inhabited', or that Holt seemed 'a praty riche Walshe toune'; nor could he disguise the fact that a town like Denbigh, though 'clere defacid with fier by hostilite' in 1468, was still very much a going concern.[2] Inevitably some boroughs, like Newport (Dyfed),[3] fared badly in the Tudor age. Many, unsupported by the castle, failed to stand on their own two economic feet. The late sixteenth century in particular seems to have been a crucial period for them. It was their failure to develop then, in an expansive age, which hastened their final demise as boroughs. But at the time of the 'Union' the fate of many towns of medieval origin remained as yet uncertain. Leland must be read with some caution. The outlook for some of the towns was by no means as gloomy as he would allow. If he omits to mention that a town was 'in decay' one can take it almost for granted that it was not. Wrexham is a case in point, as is Brecon, Haverfordwest, Carmarthen, and Caernarvon.[4]

Even so, if one were able to take a census of the urban population in the first decade or so of the fourteenth century and then make a comparison with mid-sixteenth century data, the result would probably favour the earlier period, for there appears to have been, despite the rebellion of 1294–5 and the havoc caused by it, an urban

---

B.B.C.S., III (1926–7), 151–2; John Williams, *The records of Denbigh and its lordship* (1860), p. 99. Cf., however, Jones Pierce, *Medieval Welsh Society*, p. 183, where it is noted that Pwllheli's population increased from 21 to 36 between 1543 and 1565.

1 Cf. A. R. Bridbury, *Economic Growth: England in the Late Middle Ages* (1962), p. 74.

2 Toulmin Smith (ed.), *Itinerary*, pp. 45, 59, 69, 97.

3 B. G. Charles, 'The Records of the Borough of Newport in Pembrokeshire', *National Library of Wales Journal*, VII (1951–2), 36, 120.

4 Leonard Owen, art. cit., pp. 107–10. Some of the urban figures cited by Leonard Owen need to be treated with caution, however, because many of them relate to parochial, rather than strictly urban, estimates. The whole question needs to be re-examined.

explosion in many parts of Wales at the turn of the thirteenth century, a late spasm of the 'borough-fever' that had gripped the preceding age.[1] Perhaps the most spectacular growth occurred in the mid-Wales town of Welshpool which had 106 taxpayers in 1292–3 and no fewer than 173 burgesses by 1309;[2] by the mid-sixteenth century, however, the number of households there had dropped back to the pre-1300 level. Urbanisation at its medieval peak possibly stood higher than at the 'Union' though developments did not follow a uniform course, since they were subject to the vagaries of local conditions.

Lack of adequate evidence unfortunately precludes a detailed examination of the population of the vast proportion of townships in Wales at the end of the thirteenth century and the mid-sixteenth century. The schedules of assize rents dated 1302–03 for the old counties of Cardigan and Carmarthen[3] which Professor Russell used for estimating the population of Wales[4] and which at first sight seem so promising are not in fact likely to yield very satisfactory results. Measuring the population of West Wales in *c.* 1300 from them is difficult for two reasons: in the first place, added to the names of a good number of the tenants listed as paying rents of assize are the words 'cum coheredibus suis' with no indication whatever of exactly how many; in the second place, the number of those owing suit of court at the county court of Cardigan for the commote of Iscoed Is Hirwern is almost double the number of tenants for the same commote who owed assize rents.[5] If we were to take the latter as the basis of our calculations the population of the former county of Cardigan at the time of the Edwardian conquest could have been about 10,000, but if we were to take the number owing suit of court as roughly equivalent to the number of households in the county, the population would be nearer 20,000 – or 3,000 more than Leonard Owen's estimated total for the county in 1545/63[6] which would tend to confirm our findings about other areas. But even if this were so – and the evidence is by no means as conclusive as one would wish – any detailed comparison of the figures for the early fourteenth century and the mid-sixteenth century for West Wales is impossible for there is very little correspondence between how they were drawn up at the two different periods.

---

1 Cf. Ralph A. Griffiths, 'The Medieval Boroughs of Glamorgan', *Glam. County Hist.*, III (1971), 339–40, and 343; *National Library of Wales Journal*, XVI (1969–70), 8–9.

2 P.R.O. E.179/242/54; *Montgomeryshire Collections*, I (1868), 153.

3 P.R.O. S.C.11/770 and 773.

4 Russell, *British Medieval Population*, pp. 331–7.

5 P.R.O. S.C.11/770 m. 1 and m. 1d.

6 Leonard Owen, art. cit., p. 108.

Thus, apart from Merioneth, the only other area where a comparative study, township by township, on any significant scale is possible is the former county of Flint. But here the evidence, though fairly full and comprehensive, is complicated by the fact that it is based mainly not on the subsidy and ecclesiastical returns of the 1540s and 1560s but on the muster roll of 1539 for the county.(1) Muster rolls as sources of population, especially for the mid-Elizabethan period, have found a champion in Dr. E. E. Rich.(2) Welsh historians have, rightly on the whole, been reluctant to make use of the muster rolls of the late 1530s for the Welsh counties. The returns are very uneven, but there is an urgent need to look afresh at them in detail. They provide, if nothing else, corroborative evidence at certain times: 160 persons appear on the muster roll of Tenby in 1539 and 164 on the subsidy returns of 1543 for the town; likewise, in the lordship of Cilgerran, the two returns show a close correlation.(3) The value of muster rolls as far as the former shire of Flint is concerned can be well demonstrated by the Table below, which allows a detailed comparison to be made not only between thirteenth and sixteenth-century returns for Maelor but also between the muster roll of 1539 and the subsidy return of 1543 for the hundred, the only one extant for the county.(4) (N.I. stands for 'no information'.)

MAELOR *townships*	1292–3	1539	1543
Worthenbury	89	63	63
Bangor	73	68	45
Overton Foreign	16	53(5)	31
Overton Villa	56	26	23
Knolton	23	22	20
Penley	49(6)	25	19
Erbistock	14	16	9
Tybroughton	23	21	19
Is-coed	39	40	35
Bronington	N.I.	34	29
Bettisfield	29	26	23
Hanmer	19	55	46
Willington	40	34	32
Halghton	57	41	46
TOTAL	527+	524	439

1 P.R.O. S.P.1/146, pp. 179–219.
2 E. E. Rich, 'The Population of Elizabethan England', *Econ(omic) Hist(ory) Rev(iew)*, II (1950), 247–65.
3 Owen (ed.), *Calendar of Public Records . . . Pembrokeshire*, II, 52–67; III, 73, 239–41.
4 P.R.O. E.179/242/52; /221/207; and P.R.O. S.P.1/146, pp. 179–219.
5 The hamlet of Asney is included in the total.
6 The township of Bodidris [y Traean?] is included in the total.

Despite the disparate totals, the figures for 1539 and 1543 are, with two exceptions, fairly consistent with each other. Further, though the subsidy return includes the names of women, there is some correlation between the names entered on both returns. The Flintshire muster roll may, therefore, with the usual reservations, be used for comparative purposes: if, from our point of view, it errs at all, it is on the high side, since every male above the age of 16, whether he held property or not, was required to be listed. The totals noted for the three other divisions of medieval and Tudor Flintshire in the Table below are of *identifiable* townships only. (N.I. stands for 'no information'.)

Division	Townships	1292–3	1539	1543
Coleshill	23	701	650	N.I.
Prestatyn	16	271	277	N.I.
Rhuddlan	10	386	357	N.I.
Maelor	14	527+	524	439

These figures for the former county of Flint, like those for Merioneth, point inexorably to the same conclusion: that the overall population of the county was bigger and individual townships were generally more densely populated in the late-thirteenth century than in the mid-sixteenth century. The decline, similarly, was by no means uniform. The northern commote of Prestatyn had advanced relatively more than the others, but again there does not appear to have been a great shift in population within the county. As for the towns, the well-established boroughs of Flint and Overton had shrunk to less than half their size – which seems indisputable: Leland corroborates the evidence of the muster rolls about Overton by saying that 'now there is not 20 houses' there.(1) Rhuddlan, however, had lost little ground and the vills of Caerwys and Holywell had grown appreciably by Tudor times.(2) Thus while the old English boroughs had suffered mixed fortunes, if not certain decline, native Welsh centres were showing positive signs of life and the overall urban population of the late county of Flint, despite appearances to the contrary, may not have been dramatically lower in the mid-sixteenth century than it was at the end of the thirteenth. Indeed it may have been higher than it was in the second quarter of the fourteenth century. The rot seems to have set in early at Flint and Overton, so that the mid-sixteenth century figures may reflect a slight

1 Toulmin Smith (ed.), *Itinerary*, p. 67.

2 The figures for Flint are 76–35; for Overton 56–26; for Rhuddlan 75–67; for Caerwys 43–63; for Holywell 26–37.

upturn in their fortunes. During Madog's war in 1294–5, the English themselves set fire to the town of Flint to save the castle[(1)] – a not uncommon practice in the middle ages[(2)] – and the Overton area too was badly ravaged in the same rebellion.[(3)] Life may have proved difficult thereafter for the two boroughs, especially for Overton. When the Black Prince sought an aid in 1347 Flint, the most prosperous town in the county in 1292–3, was assessed at merely half the sum demanded of Rhuddlan and only a little more than Caerwys, while Overton was not included for assessment amongst the boroughs at all[(4)] – the castle there may have been 'throuen doune by the violence of Dee Ryver chaunging his botom' in the early fourteenth century.[(5)] And this was before the Black Death and the great Glyn Dŵr rebellion. Rhuddlan, on the other hand, which 'lost its primacy to the parvenu borough of Flint' in the 1280s and 1290s,[(6)] obviously fared better. It suffered at the hands of Welshmen and plague at various times, but already by 1428 there were probably upwards of 90 persons holding burgages there.[(7)] Like other towns, it succeeded in breaking out of its medieval shell: as early as 1486, reference is made to 'le olde towne' of Rhuddlan.[(8)] Its resilience is still apparent at the time of the 'Union'.

Of the more rural townships in the former county of Flint only two, Hanmer and Ysgeifiog, showed substantial increases by the mid-sixteenth century.[(9)] Hanmer in particular drew the fair comment of Leland's that it had 'a greate deale more riches then all the residew of Englisch Maylor'[(10)] and that is amply reflected by the strength of its showing in the muster rolls. In most of the other 60-odd rural

---

1 Arthur Jones, 'Petitions to King Edward I by the burgesses of Flint, 1295–1300', *Flints(hire) Hist(orical) Soc(iety) Journ(al)*, 9 (1922), 43.

2 Cf. John Williams ab Ithel (ed.), *Annales Cambriae* (1860), p. 71, *sub anno* 1214 when the burgesses of Carmarthen set fire to their own town; and H. R. Luard (ed.), *Annales Monastici*, I (1864), 39, *sub anno* 1232 when the town within the gates of Kenfig was set on fire by the burgesses.

3 *Cal. Inq. Misc., 1307–49*, p. 16, no. 56.

4 Evans (ed.), *Flintshire Min. Accounts*, pp. 21–2. Flint had been assessed at £23. 10*s*. 6½*d*. in 1292–3, Rhuddlan at £22. 15*s*. 4¾*d*., Overton at £12. 12*s*. 9¾*d*., and Caerwys at £7. 1*s*. 8¾*d*.

5 Toulmin Smith (ed.), *Itinerary*, p. 67.

6 A. J. Taylor, 'Rhuddlan Cathedral: A 'Might-have-been' of Flintshire History', *Flints. Hist. Soc. Journ.*, 15 (1954–5), 51.

7 Edwards (ed.), *Cal. Anc. Corr.*, pp. 231–2; Evans (ed.), *Flintshire Min. Accounts*, pp. 41–2; Arthur Jones, 'A Fifteenth Century Document of Rhuddlan', *Flints. Hist. Soc. Journ.*, 5 (1914–15), 45–90.

8 Nat. Lib. Wales, Gwysaney 375.

9 From 19 to 55 and 36 to 62 respectively.

10 Toulmin Smith (ed.), *Itinerary*, p. 68.

townships, the population had fallen, though nowhere so catastrophically as in Calcot: whereas the assessors of 1292 found 38 taxpayers, muster masters could rely on only two men from there in 1539. Despite this, it seems likely that the former county of Flint had not been as badly affected as Merioneth by the disasters of the fourteenth and fifteenth centuries or had recovered more quickly from them. Certainly its population was relatively bigger than Merioneth's by the early sixteenth century, but neither there nor in most other areas where valid comparisons by townships can be made was it as high as in the late thirteenth century. Unquestionably rural areas had suffered decline in the aggregate. It does not necessarily follow, of course, that the population of Wales as a whole was smaller at the 'Union' than at the Edwardian conquest, but it does sustain the presumption that that was so.

A proposition of this kind would surprise few English historians. Not all would agree with Professor Postan that the thirteenth-century peak in rural areas may not have been reached 'until the very eve of the industrial revolution of the eighteenth century',[1] but evidence 'in favour of a low level of population until well into the sixteenth century is too strong to be disregarded' by some historians.[2] Wales probably lagged behind England before its population too surged dramatically in the latter half of the sixteenth and seventeenth centuries. If the mid-sixteenth century figures reflect an upward swing – as is likely – population must have fallen equally dramatically in some areas in the fourteenth and fifteenth centuries: it was by no means as universally static between 1300 and 1550 as a superficial acquaintance with the relevant figures might lead one to suppose. Two major disasters overtook Wales during this period: the Black Death and the Glyn Dŵr revolt. Measuring the impact of either on Wales's population with any degree of accuracy is virtually impossible. The Black Death in particular presents enormous problems for the demographer. A very confused picture emerges from the evidence as it stands.[3] In north-west Wales the boroughs apparently escaped but, to judge from the ministers' accounts, the countryside (especially Anglesey and parts of Llŷn) did not; in the north-east corner of Wales, on the other hand, it was not so much the countryside but the towns (Rhuthun, Rhuddlan,

---

1 M. M. Postan, 'Medieval Agrarian Society in its prime: England' *The Cambridge Economic History of Europe*, I (2nd ed., 1966), p. 570.

2 Julian Cornwall, 'English Population in the early Sixteenth Century', *Econ. Hist. Rev.*, XXIII (1970), 44. Cf. *Vict. County Hist.: Leicestershire*, III, 138.

3 The best account is still William Rees, 'The Black Death in Wales', *Trans. Roy. Hist. Soc.*, III (1920), 115–35.

Holt, and others excepting possibly Wrexham,[1] Caerwys and a few more) which seem to have suffered most – though various parts of the countryside were hit too; in the south-east, whereas one lordship might, at different times, be badly affected, its neighbour might not; and whilst much of mid-Wales was spared the worst, after the first outbreak West Wales seems to have been completely free of the scourge. It cannot be doubted that many towns suffered grievously, but the granting of charters (to, amongst others, Hope, Pwllheli, and Nefyn) and even the founding of new boroughs or quasi-boroughs (like Dinas Mawddwy in 1394 with no fewer than 35 burgesses)[2] in the post-Black Death era is not entirely compatible with declining numbers. One's whole view of the plague is vitiated by a natural tendency to generalise from the particular. Estimated mortalities of one-half, or up to two-thirds, of the total may not be gross exaggeration for some areas, but it is doubtful if such figures should be applied to Wales as a whole. Even the commonly-accepted average of one-third overall may be a bit high. Where plague struck, it struck very hard indeed,[3] but it must be recognised that over large parts of Wales its incidence appears to have been slight.

It must be admitted too that firm statistics about the Black Death are few and far between and that when they do occur we tend to over-dramatise them, to shape them in the image of our own pre-conceptions. A reference to a great number of lands and tenements being 'vacant and unoccupied' in the lordship of Llanstephan on account of 'the great pestilence lately prevalent in the country there'[4] would doubtless be seized upon – and made much of – if the records in which it is found were dated 1349–50 rather than 1500–01. Whatever the impression gained from reading ministers' accounts for 1349–50 or 1350–51, that lead-mining in Holywell (Clwyd) came to an end because of the Black Death, the irrefutable fact is that miners 'for the most part [had] died and the survivors [were refusing] to work there' in 1347–8 *before* the first visitation of the plague.[5] Again, whatever conclusions we might leap to on reading – to take

1 Wrexham seems to have prospered greatly in the second half of the fourteenth century, usurping the position held by the borough of Holt (Brian Evans, 'Grant of Privileges to Wrexham (1380)', *B.B.C.S.*, XIX (1960–2), 42–7).

2 B. G. Charles, 'Court Rolls and other Records of the borough of Dinas Mawddwy and the manor of Mawddwy', *Journ. Mer. Hist. Rec. Soc.*, I (1949–52), 44–5.

3 As at Rhuthun where 77 died in two short weeks in June 1349 (William Rees, art. cit., p. 120). On clerical mortality, see especially Williams, *Welsh Church*, pp. 146–8.

4 *West Wales Historical Records*, XIII (1928), 85.

5 Evans (ed.), *Flintshire Min. Accounts*, p. 19. Mining must have been regarded as an extremely hazardous occupation. Cf. the situation in West Wales in 1304–05 when there were only four men working the lead mine at Llanbadarn: more men could not be found to work it (Rhys (ed.), *Min. Accounts for West Wales*, pp. 390–1).

the most celebrated statistic of all – that 97 out of 104 *gabularii* in the commote of Mefenydd (Dyfed) did not survive the plague must be qualified by the thought that the story was regarded with some scepticism even at the time by the chamberlain of West Wales.[1] It was much more sensible – less incriminating and more advantageous – for local officials to explain away their failure to collect the prescribed dues by recording the death of tenants rather than their flight. Such was the new situation created by the plague that the unfree found that they could successfully exercise the threat to leave their townships if their financial burdens were not eased by the lord – or so the evidence from the lordship of Denbigh would suggest.[2] Temporary, if not indeed in many cases permanent, flight may well have been as prevalent as death in these years. An examination of the Rhuthun court rolls covering the period of the Black Death by no means entirely dispels that impression. Loss of revenue does not necessarily indicate loss of lives. One has no wish to minimise the horror, but it is all too easy to exaggerate the overall mortality rate for the plague years.

On the other hand, there can be little doubt about the combined calamitous effects of plague and rebellion on population. Some North Wales boroughs which could boast of a fairly stable population in the fourteenth century did not escape the ravages of war in the fifteenth.[3] Evidence of depopulation during the second half of the fourteenth and fifteenth centuries is in fact clear and increasingly voluminous. Plague ravaged various communities[4] and rebellion turned a number of towns into empty shells or otherwise stunted their growth. Recovery from these disasters was doubtless swift in many instances, but it certainly did not follow a set uniform pattern. The tempo differed from place to place: if Pwllheli or Cardiff still felt the residual effects of rebellion at the end of the fifteenth century,[5] Monmouth had, with 201 burgesses in 1441, largely recovered, being not far short of the number (266) mentioned there in

---

1 William Rees, art. cit., p. 22, and cf. D. L. Evans, 'Some Notes on the history of the principality of Wales in the time of the Black Prince (1343–1376), *Trans. Hon. Soc. Cymm.* (1925–6), p. 80.

2 Holmes, *Estates of Higher Nobility*, pp. 98–9.

3 See, e.g., Jones Pierce, *Medieval Welsh Society*, pp. 155–8; *Trans. Caerns. Hist. Soc.*, 18 (1957), 44–6; *West Wales Historical Records*, II (1911–12), 106.

4 As at Rhuthun (see *supra*, p. lv, n. 3). In 1315 there had been 159 burgesses in Holt; by 1391 there were but 78 burgage holders there (D. Pratt, 'The Medieval Borough of Holt', *Denbighshire Hist(orical) Soc(iety) Trans(actions)*, 14 (1965), 15, 49–50. Early in Elizabeth's reign, tenants and copyholders there may only have numbered about 70 (P.R.O. S.C.12/17/93).

5 Jones Pierce, op. cit., pp. 157–8; *Glam. County Hist.*, III, 349; cf. B. G. Charles (ed.), *Calendar of the Records of the Borough of Haverfordwest 1539–1660* (1967), p. 1.

1610;[1] Rhuthun, too, was by 1465 probably as flourishing as it was a hundred years later when it was on the verge of a period of spectacular growth.[2] But the cumulative effect of the disasters on some rural communities was permanently debilitating. The lordship of Chirk, for one, was 'a region of insidious and progressive depopulation, a process never sufficiently reversed in following centuries.'[3] Bond vills in particular were deeply affected. In Henry V's reign, the bond vills of the commotes of Tal-y-bont and Ystumanner which supported upwards of 150 families in 1292–3 were said to be 'completely depopulated'.[4] For the commotes of Ardudwy and Penllyn, too, there is ample evidence of deserted holdings in Henry V's reign.[5] Generations of officials wrestled with the problem of loss of revenue from un-tenanted townships without any great success, and in the former counties of Merioneth and Caernarvon, as well as elsewhere, the deserted bond vills became a battleground for rival gentry families hungry for land.[6] Of course, the depopulation or decay of bond vills is not, in itself, an indication of a fall in overall population because of the possible migration or temporary flight of individuals and communities to other areas,[7] but what evidence there is for Wales as a whole seems to bear out Professor Duby's conclusions about rural depopulation in the medieval west, that the 'disaster' had indeed been 'astonishingly far-reaching'. And not only far-reaching, but also possibly of long duration. Professor Duby claims that as late as 1470 'in most European villages households were still only half as numerous as at the beginning of the fourteenth century',[8] a claim fully borne out by the studies of Édouard Baratier, at least as far as Provence is concerned.[9] Can it be true also of

---

1 K. E. Kissack, *Mediaeval Monmouth* (1974), p. 60. At about the same date, Brecon had just over 70 burgesses (Theophilus Jones, *A History of the County of Brecknock* (1898 ed.), p. 86).

2 Melville Richards, 'Records of Denbighshire Lordships: I. The Lordship of Dyffryn Clwyd', *Denbighshire Hist. Soc. Trans.* XV (1966), 18–26; P.R.O. S.C.12/24/2A. There were 90 burgesses there in 1496 (R. Ian Jack, 'The Seigneurial Charters of the Borough of Ruthin', *National Library of Wales Journal*, XVI (1969–70), 85.

3 Llinos Olwen Wyn Smith, 'The Lordships of Chirk and Oswestry, 1282–1415' (unpub. Ph.D., University of London, 1970), p. 359.

4 J. Beverley Smith, 'Crown and Community in the Principality of North Wales in the reign of Henry Tudor', *Welsh Hist. Rev.*, III (1966–7), 152–3.

5 See, e.g., *Rec. of Caernarvon*, pp. 262, 278, 282.

6 Jones Pierce, *Medieval Welsh Society*, pp. 43–8, 62–85.

7 Cf. R. R. Davies, 'The Social Structure of Medieval Glamorgan', *Glam. County Hist.*, III, 308–09.

8 Georges Duby, *Rural Economy and Country Life in the Medieval West* (trans. by Cynthia Postan, 1968), p. 300.

9 Édouard Baratier, *La Démographie Provençale du XIIIe au XVIe Siècle* (1961), pp. 75–94, 109–18, and App. II in particular, pp. 131–87.

Wales? It can well be believed of bond townships, for leading freemen had, by then, no more than marginally exploited them; but as for the free vills themselves, which were far more numerous than bond vills by 1470, the evidence is by no means clear. It is, of course, possible to find deserted free holdings[1] – and that is only to be expected, for the very fact that the unfree were leaving their areas and migrating elsewhere suggests in its turn that free townships were underpopulated at various times. In parts of north-east Wales in 1474, if not elsewhere about the same period, tenants were enticed to take up tenements for terms of four years 'without paying anything for the same' and thereafter on favourable terms for life; and rewards were given for rebuilding tenements 'lying waste and fallen to the ground'.[2] However, towards the end of the fifteenth century, if not, to a lesser extent, for some considerable time before, the average size of escheated holdings in lowland areas was much smaller than in the fourteenth century. Jones Pierce, whose belief in a generally stable population remained unshakeable, attributed this partly to the 'growing physical limitation on expansion'[3] but equally plausible would be to view it as the result of pressure of population building up over a period. In the uplands the position may have differed little from the low-lying areas, except that appropriations from the waste were still possible there to accommodate growing numbers of people. Only the chronology is uncertain.

The individual and cumulative effects of recession and plague and rebellion on population are largely unquantifiable and cannot be adequately assessed as far as Wales is concerned. There are no fourteenth-century poll-tax returns for Wales as for England; while the extant fifteenth-century rentals for various lordships, omitting as they normally do details about sub-tenants, are more or less entirely unsatisfactory for demographic purposes. In consequence of all this, little of any general statistical significance for the fourteenth and fifteenth centuries can be contributed towards the important debate on precisely when population began to fall or when it began to rise again – and in what areas and to what extent. The sudden reduction in population following the pestilence of 1349–50 may have stimulated the birth-rate for a while before further outbreaks of plague and the widespread devastation associated with the Glyn Dŵr revolt crippled it further. Regional or particu-

1 e.g., *Rec. of Caernarvon*, pp. 263, 264.

2 W. Bell Jones, 'Hawarden Deeds', *Flints. Hist. Soc. Journ.*, 7 (1919–20), 32–3. Cf. *B.B.C.S.*, XIX (1960–2), 46–7; Owen, *Calendar of Public Records . . . Pembrokeshire*, I, 135–40.

3 T. Jones Pierce, 'Landlords in Wales, the Nobility and Gentry', *Agrarian History of England and Wales*, IV, 361–2.

lar instances notwithstanding, it could well be that the years of the great rebellion and its immediate aftermath at the beginning of the fifteenth century marked as low a point generally in Wales's population between the Edwardian conquest and the 'Union' as the years of the plague. Many Welsh towns seem to have suffered even more at the hands of Glyn Dŵr than they did in the wake of the great pestilence and it was not until after the revolt that the old social order in the Welsh countryside was demolished beyond repair. Inheritance customs seem to have withstood the effects of the Black Death much better than the great rebellion. It may be an impression gained from the accident of record survival, but it appears as if there was a more fluid land market in the post-Glyn Dŵr period than after the plague and the better-placed families were not the only ones to benefit from it. Competition from undue numbers had been reduced by then: plague and rebellion were appalling disasters for the peasantry as a whole, but for those who survived the opportunities had never been greater.

By making some fairly large assumptions, not least amongst them the supposition that the demographic trends in the former counties of Merioneth and Flint and elsewhere in North Wales between the thirteenth and the sixteenth centuries were representative of Wales as a whole, it could be maintained that Wales was possibly more densely populated at the conquest than at the 'Union' – on the basis of the very slender evidence available, about one-tenth more densely populated than at the 'Union'. If that is so, it follows that previous low estimates of Wales's population at the end of the thirteenth century must be revised. The population of Wales at the 'Union' has variously been given as 125,000; 225,000; 275,000; 325,000; and 350,000.[1] Recent research has tended to favour a figure of about 275,000; the population at the conquest could therefore have been in the region of 300,000.[2] But this latter figure, it must again be emphasised, is a very crude estimate indeed, no more reliable than a supposition founded upon a supposition.

* * *

The evidence is so exiguous for parts of the former shires of Anglesey,

---

1 David Williams, 'A Note on the Population of Wales, 1536–1801', *B.B.C.S.*, VIII (1935–7), 359–63; Leonard Owen, art. cit.

2 For the 1536 estimate, see Frank Emery, 'The Farming Regions of Wales', *Agrarian History of England and Wales*, IV, 142–3. Professor Russell estimated the pre-plague population of Wales to be 200,000, and the post-plague population in 1377 to be 125,000, which was to double by 1545 and thus tally more or less with Rickman's estimate (Russell, *British Medieval Population*, pp. 360–1). This calculation takes no account of the Glyn Dŵr rebellion and rejects implicitly the notion that Wales was more densely populated at the time of the conquest in 1282–3 than it was in 1536–43.

Caernarvon, Montgomery, and Denbigh that very little of value can be said about the distribution of population in North Wales at the end of the thirteenth century. The general pattern probably remained much what it was until the great upheaval of the industrial revolution, though the figures indicate a shift in population in certain areas by the sixteenth century: at least the population of the late county of Flint seems to have been greater than Merioneth's by then, but whether that had come about by migration or some other factor cannot be ascertained. There were more people per acre in the Flintshire of the 1290s than in Merioneth, but fewer lived there at that time (2,553 taxpayers as against 2,669 in Merioneth). Merioneth, with almost half its area over 1,000 feet – hardly any permanent settlements were to be found above that height anywhere in Wales – and with by far the lowest proportion of arable land in the whole of England and Wales,[(1)] was physically a more fragmented and isolated – and thus a somewhat less easily governable – community than the former county of Flint but, 'racially', the latter was much more divided than Merioneth, mainly because of the presence of solid contingents of immigrant Englishmen in the 'merchant towns' of Flint, Rhuddlan, and Hope. Of the other two merchant towns in the county, Overton was three-quarters English, Caerwys almost entirely Welsh. In the Merioneth boroughs of Bere and Harlech, one-third of the taxpayers had Welsh names, a fact which disproves the often-held view that Welshmen were excluded from dwelling or holding burgages in Edwardian castellated boroughs. So, too, with the borough of Aberystwyth where nearly half the burgesses were Welsh.[(2)] Even some of the mighty strongholds of English influence in North Wales – Conwy and Beaumaris – were patently not opposed to having Welshmen as burgesses in their midst,[(3)] no more than were some of the newly-founded boroughs in the northern march: Rhuthun, the very first town which Glyn Dŵr attacked in the autumn of 1400, ostensibly partly on 'racial' grounds, could claim that about one-third of its inhabitants were Welsh as early as 1324.[(4)] Of course, those who were accepted into the burghal fold in this way were

1 L. Dudley Stamp, *The Land of Britain: Report of the Land Utilization Survey*, Part 33: *Merioneth* by L. A. Holliday (1940), pp. 178, 182.

2 *B.B.C.S.*, XV (1952–4), 283.

3 There were possibly two Welshmen at Conwy (P.R.O. S.C.12/17/87) and three or four at Beaumaris (P.R.O. S.C.11/767). No person bearing a Welsh name is listed amongst the burgesses of Caernarvon in 1298 (P.R.O. S.C.12/17/86). It is clear that Welshmen resided in the immediate environs of the boroughs though they might not be admitted as burgesses. Of the three chaplains to be elected to serve the parish church of Conwy in 1284, one was to be an 'honest Welsh chaplain by reason of the difference of the language' (*Cal. of Chanc. Rolls* (*Various*) *1277–1326*, p. 287).

4 R. Ian Jack, 'Records of Denbighshire Lordships: II. The Lordship of Dyffryn Clwyd in 1324', *Denbighshire Hist. Soc. Trans.*, 17 (1968), 13–18.

Welshmen by birth and name only. One can hardly believe that a person like Dafydd ab Einion, the most prominent burgess in Beaumaris after its foundation, who held lands also in Conwy and who readily assisted, as a supplier of goods, in the building of Harlech castle in the 1280s and in the victualling of English garrisons in the late 90s,[1] was warmly committed to the Welsh cause (though it is tempting to identify him with a man of the same name who had served Llywelyn II loyally before the conquest).[2] Nationality mattered less than political and economic circumstances to such men: the exigencies of the hour overrode all other considerations.

Nor should the preposterous idea that Welshmen *qua* Welshmen were averse to living in towns be allowed to gain added currency any longer. Llan-faes was a success story before the conquest of Gwynedd and had to be uprooted to make way for Beaumaris after Madog's war. Other small Welsh settlements were acquiring urban characteristics at about the same time.[3] In the embryonic town of Wrexham in 1315 Welshmen outnumbered Englishmen by over 4 to 1 (36 Welshmen as against 8 Englishmen); and already by the end of the thirteenth century Welshmen had gained a foothold in some of the English border towns, being foreign members of Shrewsbury town guild by then if not burgesses of the town itself.[4]

Edward I prevaricated – with good reason – before accepting Pecham's advice about making burgesses of Welshmen in order to 'civilise' them and win them over to English ways. Such was the ease and rapidity with which some Welshmen took to town life that their progress threatened not only the livelihood of immigrant Englishmen but the very stability of the new order itself. The Edwardian borough was, after all, an integral part of the English defensive system and consequently was expected to be manned by 'true' Englishmen, loyal to the crown. Vital as that might be, it nevertheless required nerves of steel on the part of immigrants to withstand a hostile as well as an alien environment over a great length of time. Englishmen were far from home and longed for smoother pastures. Significantly, orders had to be issued fairly early on to confiscate the burgages of those who were non-resident.[5]

1 P.R.O. S.C.11/767; S.C.12/17/88; R. Allen Brown, H. M. Colvin, and A. J. Taylor, *The History of the King's Works*, II (1963), 1034 (as David ab Eynon of Lanuays); *B.B.C.S.*, XV (1952–4), p. 148. His son Ieuan was acting as one of the bailiffs of Beaumaris in 1317 (Nat. Lib. Wales, Pitchford Hall, 216).

2 Edwards (ed.), *Littere Wallie*, pp. 4, 46, 82, 102.

3 Jones Pierce, *Medieval Welsh Society*, pp. 121–2.

4 A. H. Dodd (ed.), *A History of Wrexham* (1957), p. 24; *Trans. Roy. Hist. Soc.* (1903), p. 130. A William Vahghan is mentioned as a burgess of Shrewsbury in 1282 (*Cal. of Chanc. Rolls* (*Various*), *1277–1326*, p. 227).

5 P.R.O. S.C.11/767.

But as the roll of desertions grew longer, new recruits were difficult to find. Compromises were inevitable. Willing Welshmen were at hand to fulfil the economic, if not the military, hopes of the conqueror and were successful in intruding themselves more and more into the very bastions of English power in North Wales. Nowhere in the first half of the fourteenth century did the Welsh advance appear more menacing to the English authorities than at Beaumaris, in that south-east corner of Anglesey where urban impulses had been at their strongest before the Edwardian conquest. Other Welshmen apart from the descendants of Dafydd ab Einion were prominent in the life of the community there in the 1320s;(1) and clearly some of the immigrants themselves were 'going native' there by then, adopting the Welsh form 'ap' for 'son of', giving their children Welsh names,(2) and, most alarming of all, flouting authority by freely leasing and alienating lands and tenements to Welshmen and granting them the liberties of the town. By the early 1330s there were more Welsh than English burgesses there, a fact which moved the justiciar of North Wales to order in *c.* 1334 that all lands and tenements which had been alienated or leased to Welshmen be taken into the hands of the crown. Notwithstanding this particular injunction, the burgesses of Beaumaris, like their counterparts in other, less prestigious, North Wales towns, continued to violate ordinance and convention by allowing Welshmen to live in their midst, granting them the liberties of the town as well as the right to hold lands and tenements there. In *c.* 1345 their waywardness finally led to the town's liberties being temporarily suspended by the prince's officials.(3) These efforts in the 1330s and 1340s to stem the Welsh advance may have been prompted partly by the misfortunes which struck Newborough (in south-west Anglesey) in 1331 – after a third of the borough's lands was destroyed by moving sands in that year,(4) a number of the inhabitants there may have drifted back to the Beaumaris area from whence their fathers had been driven after 1295 – or they may be seen as a reaction to the seething unrest which led to the Shaldeford murder in 1345. Be that as it may, the drastic measures affecting Beaumaris in the 1330s and 1340s make nonsense of the supposition that Welshmen did not take to living in towns – as does the evidence from elsewhere: in Cricieth, for example, three burgages were taken into the king's hands in 1337 because they were held by Welshmen.(5)

1 Nat. Lib. Wales, Pitchford Hall, 216, 452, 516, 590.

2 ibid., 461, 1365.

3 P.R.O. E.315/166f. 8.

4 Lewis, *Mediaeval Boroughs*, p. 53.

5 ibid., p. 186.

Nevertheless, the urban population of Wales was predominantly English in the thirteenth century. In contrast, the countryside was overwhelmingly Welsh. The tide of English immigration had flowed quite strongly at the Edwardian conquest but it was by no means a flood. It was, in any case, more often than not streamed into well-defined parts of the country, usually areas of good agricultural land. Apart from the eastern confines of the lordship of Denbigh,[1] the Flintshire area was probably unique in North Wales – certainly the lordships of Chirk and Bromfield and Yale (excluding the town of Holt) as well as the greater part of the lordship of Rhuthun were as solidly Welsh as the rest of North Wales[2] – in having at this time a fairly high number of persons with English-sounding names in areas outside the main towns: 68 in the commote of Coleshill, 64 in Maelor Saesneg, 36 in Prestatyn, but only 5 in the commote of Rhuddlan. As many as three-quarters of the taxpayers of the township of Prestatyn had English names, a half of those of Eston and Ewloe, a third of those of Wulfinton and Bettisfield, a quarter of those of Sychdyn and Agyston. The 'nova villa' of Mostyn had not a single Welshman among its complement of taxpayers. Overall, however, less than 1 in 15 in rural areas of the late county of Flint could be considered English and that in percentage terms represented only 8 per cent of the population of Coleshill and Prestatyn commotes and a mere 1 per cent of that of the commote of Rhuddlan.[3] This compares favourably with about 1 in 6 in northern and eastern Gwent and a less than 1 in 10 concentration in parts of the old counties of Radnor and Brecon – though the variations even within these areas could be wide: whereas the sub-lordship of Bleddfa was more or less 100 per cent Welsh, that of Radnor was only 47 per cent.[4] Cilgerran and Is Cennen in West Wales were largely uncontaminated,[5] as indeed was the greater part of Dyfed away from the southern half of the former county of Pembroke and the old established boroughs.[6] What the various proportions might have

1 David Huw Owen, 'The Lordship of Denbigh, 1282–1415' (unpub. Ph.D., Univ. of Wales, 1967) pp. 147, 157–8.

2 P.R.O. E.179/242/55; T. P. Ellis (ed.), *The First Extent of Bromfield and Yale, A.D. 1315* (1924), pp. 4, 6; D. Pratt, art. cit., p. 15; R. Ian Jack, art. cit., pp. 18–53.

3 All this is based on P.R.O. E.179/242/52.

4 P.R.O. E.179/242/56, 57, 59, and 60. See also M. A. Faraday, 'The Assessment for the fifteenth of 1293 on Radnor and other marcher lordships', *Transactions of the Radnorshire Society*, XLIII (1973), 79.

5 P.R.O. E.179/242/56 and 60.

6 See particularly P.R.O. S.C.11/770 and 773, and S.C.12/20/32. The small borough of Lampeter was entirely Welsh except for one or two Englishmen (P.R.O. S.C.11/771 m .4).

been by the sixteenth century it would be unwise to speculate, for it would be wrong to assume that an English name automatically indicated an English person by then.

The greatest difference between Merioneth and other counties of North Wales in the late thirteenth century lay in the number and size of towns, those prime agents of social change in the middle ages. Less than 2 per cent of Merioneth's population lived in towns as against 11 per cent or so in the former county of Flint, a percentage which was in fact higher than the proportion for England as a whole, estimated at between 8 and 9 per cent, and not falling far short of Spain's with just over 15 per cent.(1) One of the few places in Merioneth which resembled a 'town' in the 1290s was Cynwyd, with a merchant, a doctor, and two cobblers amongst its 45 taxpayers. It failed to develop into a borough, but at the end of the thirteenth century it clearly had as much potential as either the vills of Tywyn and Dolgellau with a mere 12 taxpayers between them or the chartered boroughs of Harlech and Bere with only 12 and 16 taxpayers respectively.(2) In contrast, 106 taxpayers, almost all of them with smooth Anglo-Norman names, inhabited the important mid-Wales borough of Welshpool alone and there were 61 liable to the subsidy in neighbouring and less well-favoured Machynlleth.(3) Even the unprepossessing settlements at Lampeter (Dyfed) and Llanfyllin (Powys) boasted 22 and 30 burgesses respectively by 1303 and 1309; while the borough of Carmarthen, the queen of them all, already had 181 burgesses some years before the Edwardian conquest.(4) Those assessed in the 'merchant towns' of the old county of Flint in 1292 numbered 285 in all – 76 in Flint, 75 in Rhuddlan, 56 in Overton, 43 in Caerwys, and 35 in Hope.(5) In 1298, soon after the terrible ravages of Madog's war, the names of no fewer than 62 burgesses are entered on a rental of Caernarvon; about the same time, 110 persons held burgages in Conwy and there were between 62 and 83 burgesses in Beaumaris.(6) In the early fourteenth century, Aberystwyth had 112 burgesses, Cardigan 102; Holt, on the eastern edge of the former county of Denbigh, could boast 159 burgesses

1 Denys Hay, *Europe in the Fourteenth and Fifteenth Centuries* (1966), pp. 76–7.

2 *infra*, pp. 30, 49–52, 65–6, 86–7.

3 P.R.O. E.179/242/54.

4 P.R.O. S.C.11/771 m. 4; *Montgomeryshire Collections*, I (1868), 159; Lloyd, *History of Wales*, p. 751.

5 P R.O. E.179/242/52.

6 P.R.O. S.C.11/767; S.C.12/17/86 and 87. S.C.11/767, the extent of the curtilage lands held by the burgesses of Beaumaris, is more of a 'working-copy' than the other two documents and contains a number of alterations. The total number of those listed is 83, but there were only 62 curtilage holders in residence.

by 1315.[1] It is possible, of course, that the turn of the thirteenth century saw as spectacular an expansion in the urban population of Merioneth as happened elsewhere – for example, Denbigh increased threefold from 39 burgesses to 120 between 1290 and 1311, Llanidloes five-fold from 13 in 1292–3 to 66 in 1309[2] – but apart from the founding of Bala in *c.* 1310 there is little to prove that that was so; indeed, the very reverse, for Bere almost certainly ceased to exist as a borough during this period: it lost its *raison d'être* as the castle's strategic position was seen to be no longer of any consequence. In any case, the inhabitants of medieval Bala, like other towns in Merioneth, appear to have remained few in number. The impulse to grow was seemingly as weak there as it was in Cricieth.[3] Stagnation took root early on in Harlech too. Perhaps, in consequence of all this, social change was slower in Merioneth and areas like Eifionydd than it was in the environs of the major North Wales boroughs.

Not that any town in North Wales is likely to have sheltered much over 1,000 souls in 1300 – which is not surprising, since the urban population of England too at this period was small. Apart from London, Bristol, and York, the population of an English town, in contrast to many towns in Italy or Flanders, rarely exceeded 4,000. In the vast majority of cases, that is to say, the small market towns, the population was probably much less than 2,000.[4] They were normally not much bigger than the main North Wales boroughs, though clearly considerably more important than the Merioneth boroughs. The latter were insignificant even in the context of the economy of North Wales.

But if the Merioneth towns were small in comparison with others, the taxable population of vills and hamlets varied almost as much in the rest of North Wales as it did in Merioneth, though nowhere except in Merioneth did it fall below 2 or rise above 90. In Merioneth more than one 'single-taxpayer' township is to be found and only there did the taxable population of two or three townships exceed 100[5] – which can be explained by the fact of pressure on scarce resources on the one hand and the vast extent of some territorial units, like Trawsfynydd and Nannau, on the other. The average

1 *B.B.C.S.*, XV (1952–4), 282–93; Ellis (ed.), *Bromfield and Yale*, p. 6.

2 D. H. Owen, 'The Lordship of Denbigh' (Ph.D., Wales, 1967), p. 239; P.R.O. E.179/242/54 and *Montgomeryshire Collections*, I (1868), 161.

3 Lewis, *Mediaeval Boroughs*, pp. 199–200; Colin A. Gresham, 'Tre Ferthyr and the Development of Cricieth', *Trans. Caern. Hist. Soc.*, 27 (1966), 17–19; *B.B.C.S.*, III (1925–7), 64.

4 R. H. Hilton, *A Medieval Society* (1966), pp. 167–8.

5 See the Tables forming the Appendix to this Introduction.

number of taxpayers per vill in parts of North Wales varied from 13 in the lordship of Chirk (Clwyd) to 16 in Llŷn (Gwynedd), 22 in Merioneth, 29 in the late county of Flint, and 36 in western areas of the former county of Montgomery. But these figures conceal the wide differences that existed between one commote and another: in the old county of Flint, for example, the average number of taxpayers per vill in the commote of Coleshill was 42, in the commote of Prestatyn only 14; in Merioneth it was as low as 11 in Ystumanner and as high as 46 in Ardudwy. The disparity within individual commotes was considerably greater even than this: in Ystumanner, the number of taxpayers per vill ranged from 1 to 41, in Edeirnion from 1 to 45, in Penllyn from 2 to 74, in Ardudwy from 6 to 105, and in Tal-y-bont from 3 to 112. How do we explain these variations in vill population? Not so much by reference to whether the vills were in lowland or upland – or even coastal – regions, though lowland vills tended generally to be more densely populated than those in mountainous areas; neither does it seem to have been on the basis of whether vills were bond or not, for the bond vill of Pennal was one of the most heavily populated townships in the commote of Ystumanner as the free township of Nannau was in the commote of Tal-y-bont. (Pennal, however, appears to be something of an exception in this respect.) Bond vills, situated for the most part in lowland areas or along the coast, tended on the whole to be smaller and agriculturally richer than free townships, but they were not necessarily less populous. Even remoteness seems to have had little to do with it: Pennant, closeted amongst one of the most outlandish and mountainous areas in Merioneth, had yet more taxpayers than eight other kindlier-placed townships in the parish of Llandrillo. Population depended rather on a number of other factors, namely, size, resources, security, the land-holding pattern, and probably stage of development. It may well be that a number of (un-named) subsidiary townships or hamlets lie concealed in the Merioneth subsidy roll of 1292–3 and that their inhabitants were included amongst the taxpayers of bigger 'parent' townships – the township of Penaran in the parish of Llanuwchllyn with the highest number of taxpayers (74) in the commote of Penllyn in 1292–3 and only 27 in 1318, and with six gavells of free land and four gavells of bond land in the early fifteenth century,[1] suggests as much – but to argue *e silentio* in this way is dangerous: to maintain that every vill or hamlet mentioned in succeeding centuries was already in being in 1292–3 would be to strain credulity and crush all belief in any kind of development. Agricultural potential, arguably one of the basic considerations

---

1 P.R.O. E.101/506/15; *Rec. of Caernarvon*, pp. 261–2.

governing the original size of townships, was not revealed *in toto* to our distant forefathers. It can readily be conceded that the vast majority of settlements were in being by the time of the Edwardian conquest, if not long before – but by no means all. The task of wood clearance was certainly not complete by the end of the thirteenth century,[1] while some temporary settlements (*hafodau*) flowered 'into permanent farms or even into hamlets in the late Middle Ages'.[2] The modern period appears to have witnessed the creation, as well as the dissolution, of a number of administrative townships or sub-townships in parts of Merioneth.[3] Nevertheless, why some townships were considerably larger than others may never be adequately explained. What is incontrovertible is that on the evidence before us 65 per cent of the vills in Merioneth had taxable populations of 20 or less in 1292–3; only about 10 per cent (as against 25 per cent in the late county of Flint and 42 per cent in parts of the former shire of Montgomery) had taxable populations of over 40 and all but a few of these were concentrated in the two commotes of Ardudwy and Tal-y-bont. In short, vills with a population of over 500 – if we were to accept a multiplier of about 4 or 5 overall – were very much the exception in thirteenth-century Merioneth. As likely as not, a vill would consist of about 100 inhabitants or less – and the same would be true of Llŷn and the lordship of Chirk; in the former county of Flint it could possibly be anything up to 150, in western areas of the old county of Montgomery up to 200. These numbers appear pretty well insignificant but they must be read in their proper context: in the West Midlands at around the same date, nearly half the villages had populations of only about 150 to 300 people;[4] while an estimate based on the total number of parishes and total population of England as a whole puts the average population of a rural parish at this time at about 300 and of a non-rural parish at only 200.[5]

---

1 References to orders to fell trees, 'thick coverts', etc., at the time of the Edwardian conquest are legion and apply to many parts of Wales. See, e.g., *Cal. of Chanc. Rolls* (*Various*), *1277–1326*, pp. 168, 171, 182–8, 232, 251, 253–4, 274, 277, 281, 293, 313–14, 318–19. For the sixteenth century cf. Toulmin Smith (ed.), *Itinerary*, pp. 78, 118.

2 Maurice Beresford and John G. Hurst (edd.), *Deserted Medieval Villages* (1971), p. 254; cf. Jones Pierce, *Medieval Welsh Society*, p. 222 and n. 68.

3 e.g., the township of Maesmawr in the parish of Llangelynnin in the commote of Tal-y-bont was in being by the eighteenth century (K. Williams-Jones (ed.), *A Calendar of the Merioneth Quarter Sessions Rolls 1733–65* (1965), 171). Tithe Apportionment Awards for various parts of the county reveal the existence of a number of new sub-townships by the late 1830s and the 1840s.

4 R. H. Hilton, op. cit., p. 91.

5 J. R. H. Moorman, *Church Life in England in the Thirteenth Century* (1946), p. 5.

COMPARATIVE WEALTH OF VARIOUS AREAS

Conclusions about population must necessarily be very tentative. If there were more to go on, one would be on safer ground in using subsidy rolls for mapping the distribution of taxable wealth within England and Wales and within individual counties and commotes.[1] But such is the paucity of evidence that the subsidy rolls have disappointingly little to tell us of the relative wealth of various regions of Wales in 1292–3. Nothing much can be gleaned either from other sources about the assessment of areas not covered by the extant subsidy rolls. The receipt rolls do, however, reveal payments made from some parts of Wales for which no subsidy rolls have survived (as well as areas for which they have survived) and though there are difficulties about determining exactly what percentage of the various assessments was paid in at the Exchequer, the information contained in the receipt rolls does extend our knowledge and broaden the picture. Where three more or less equal payments have been recorded on the receipt rolls[2] – or when the second payment is twice the first – we may safely take it for granted that the instalments represent three-quarters of the total at which the areas concerned were assessed. This is clear from data relating to the commote of Is Cennen and the sub-lordship of Radnor. We may, consequently, draw up the Table below in which the totals in square brackets are derived from entries in the receipt rolls and the others from the extant subsidy rolls. Where only one or two unrelated payments have been entered on the receipt rolls it is impossible to make any accurate estimate of what the total assessment might have been: these have, therefore, all been ignored, except the one payment of interest, that of the round sum of £200 received from the former county of Cardigan and 'the land which belonged to Rhys ap Maredudd', made in Easter 1294.[3] Added for comparison, in the right-hand column, are county assessments and, where relevant and possible, commotal assessments for the new-style subsidy voted for in 1543.[4] (N.I. in the centre column stands for 'no information'.)

---

1 See, e.g., R. E. Glasscock, 'The Distribution of Wealth in East Anglia in the early fourteenth century', *Trans(actions of the) Inst(itute of) Br(itish) Geog(raphers)*, XXXII (1963), 113–23.

2 The relevant returns are recorded on P.R.O. E.401/126, 128, 131, and 133.

3 P.R.O. E.401/131.

4 From P.R.O. E.359/42. The roll is fairly comprehensive and brings together information about the assessments of 1543 in a most useful way, but there are omissions – e.g., the third payment made from western Glamorgan (Swansea, Llangyfelach, Neath, etc.) has not been entered; likewise, it is not clear whether or not the second and third payments recorded for the former counties of Merioneth and Caernarvon refer to the counties as a whole or to a group of hundreds in those counties. The hundred of

Former County and Division	*1292–3*	*1543*
Anglesey	N.I.	£532. 4*s*. 7*d*.
Malltraeth	£53. 5*s*. 1¼*d*.	
Brecknockshire	N.I.	£555. 14*s*. 9*d*.
Talgarth	[£52. 0*s*. 0*d*.]	
Bronllys	£28. 16*s*. 5¾*d*.	
Caernarvonshire	N.I.	£514. 4*s*. 10*d*.
Cafflogion	£24. 2*s*. 11½*d*.	
Creuddyn	£16. 12*s*. 1½*d*.	
Cymydmaen	£111. 18*s*. 8½*d*.	
Nefyn	£6. 16*s*. 0½*d*.	
Cardiganshire	[£200. 0*s*. 0*d*. +]	£338. 9*s*. 10*d*.
Carmarthenshire	N.I.	£681. 3*s*. 1*d*.
Is Cennen	£10. 17*s*. 5*d*.	
Denbighshire	N.I.	£982. 14*s*. 2½*d*.
Cynllaith	£15. 15*s*. 5*d*.	
Mochnant	£20. 8*s*. 1*d*.	£36. 4*s*. 7*d*. +
Nanheudwy	£28. 18*s*. 0*d*.	
Flintshire	£464 18*s*. 11*d*.	£396. 9*s*. 7*d*.
Maelor and Hope	£122. 6*s*. 3*d*.	£103. 12*s*. 2*d*.
Coleshill	£148 10*s*. 1*d*.	
Prestatyn	£64. 4*s*. 10*d*.	£292. 17*s*. 5*d*.
Rhuddlan	£96. 1*s*. 4½*d*.	
Mold	N.I.	
Glamorgan	N.I.	£910. 4*s*. 10*d*.
Merioneth	£566. 11*s*. 10½*d*.	£181. 17*s*. 0*d*.
Ardudwy	£148. 15*s*. 2*d*.	
Edeirnion	£114. 4*s*. 6*d*.	
Mawddwy	£12. 0*s*. 7*d*.	
Penllyn	£98. 8*s*. 6*d*.	
Tal-y-bont	£122. 2*s*. 2*d*.	
Ystumanner	£83. 1*s*. 6*d*.	
Monmouthshire	N.I.	£1,231. 3*s*. 7*d*.
Abergavenny	£88. 18*s*. 6*d*.	
Monmouth	£96. 5*s*. 1*d*.	
Grosmont	£26. 11*s*. 9*d*.	
Skenfrith	£15. 19*s*. 11*d*.	
Whitecastle	£21. 18*s*. 9*d*.	

Mawddwy which was not part of Merioneth in 1292–3 was, however, included in some returns for the county in 1543. Mawddwy contributed £12. 0*s*. 7*d*. to the subsidy of 1292–3 (P.R.O. E.179/242/54) and that sum should, for comparative purposes, be added to the Merioneth total of £566. 11*s*. 10½*d*. for that year.

Former County and Division	*1292–3*	*1543*
Montgomeryshire	[£415. 14*s*. 2½*d*.+]	£286. 2*s*. 11½*d*.
Arwystli	£75. 7*s*. 10*d*.	£107. 14*s*. 10*d*.
Cyfeiliog	£44. 2*s*. 6*d*.	
Caereinion	£48. 13*s*. 4½*d*.	£34. 18*s*. 10*d*.
Deuddwr and Ystrad Marchell	[£71. 7*s*. 4*d*.]	
Mechain + Mochnant	[£65. 8*s*. 2*d*.]	£42. 6*s*. 1*d*.
Montgomery	[£60. 0*s*. 0*d*.]	
Welshpool town	£20. 15*s*. 0*d*.	£23. 16*s*. 7*d*.
Pembrokeshire	N.I.	£911. 9*s*. 1*d*.
Cilgerran	£18. 2*s*. 11¾*d*.	
Pembroke	[£120. 0*s*. 0*d*.]	
Haverfordwest	N.I.	£149. 18*s*. 8*d*.
Radnorshire	N.I.	£338. 9*s*. 1*d*.
Radnor	£68. 0*s*. 9*d*.	£151. 2*s*. 4*d*.

It will be seen at once from the above particulars how fragmentary is our information about county assessments in 1292–3. Nevertheless, the relative importance of the two southernmost counties of northern Wales at the end of the thirteenth century is clearly shown: Merioneth certainly, and possibly the former shire of Montgomery too, counties with large tracts of inhospitable and unproductive countryside, were more highly assessed than ancient Flintshire, though not of course in terms of taxable capacity per acre. But by the mid-sixteenth century, if the figures are to be believed – and some of them are questionable[1] – there had been a spectacular change. It would, despite some clever advocacy recently on the part of Dr. Schofield,[2] probably be unsafe for us to draw a straight comparison between assessments for 1292–3 and 1543 which would illustrate the rise or fall in real values between those two dates, but a lateral comparison of county assessments as a whole in 1292–3 with those in 1543 reveals that the late county of Flint by the Tudor period was much wealthier than the former shires of Merioneth and Montgomery even in absolute terms, and clearly infinitely wealthier in real terms. Merioneth, with its minute burghal population, was by far the poorest county in Wales by the time of the 'Union': little wonder that, alone of the Welsh counties, it was relieved of having to return a member of parliament to represent its boroughs in 1536. The later middle ages probably saw as dramatic a shift in the balance of local wealth

1 See previous footnote.

2 R. S. Schofield, 'The Geographical Distribution of Wealth in England 1334–1649', *Econ. Hist. Rev.*, XVIII (1965), pp. 483–510.

as seems to have occurred in England,[1] but whereas the movement in England was largely southwards, in Wales the drift seems to have been away from the centre towards the periphery. The problem of mid-Wales is a long-standing one – though the paralysis had not, seemingly, for some reason, crept as far south as the former county of Radnor by Henry VIII's reign. Only the rise of the woollen industry in the sixteenth and seventeenth centuries redressed the balance somewhat in favour of the mid-Wales counties before that too sank without trace.

A thorough analysis of the relative wealth of various areas in Wales in the mid-sixteenth century must await further study. As for the late-thirteenth century, the information about the communities in South Wales is so disconnected that analysing the data relating to them for comparative purposes would be a pointless exercise. Even for the North Wales counties the evidence is by no means as comprehensive as one would wish: most of the subsidy rolls for the former counties of Anglesey, Caernarvon, and Denbigh are missing. The criticism that has been levelled against using subsidies for measuring the relative wealth of various areas is, in any case, valid in many ways: they are a tax on movables, not on total wealth; some areas seem to have been more heavily assessed than others; bribery and under-valuation distorted total assessments; most of the church's wealth was excluded from the tax; assessments were made according to the 'location of the ownership of wealth' and not according to the 'location of wealth'.[2] More serious still, the revenue derived from them varied enormously from time to time. The fifteenths imposed on England in 1275, 1290, and 1301 realised total sums as divergent as £81,054, £116,346, and £49,755 respectively. Confronted with fluctuations of this magnitude, English historians have turned to the 1334 subsidies (rather than others) for measuring comparative wealth, since they are based not so much on the value of an individual's movables as on fixed quotas payable by different communities. It is possible, however, that the 1290 assessments for England would repay closer study because from that year the Exchequer took greater cognisance of the assessment and collection of subsidies. In any case, the Welsh historian has no choice in the matter. The subsidy of 1334 is not available to him; and he must assume, as indeed he has good reason to do, that the subsidy of 1292–3 (the equivalent of the English subsidy of 1290) reflects roughly the probable taxable situation of Wales at that time.

---

1 ibid., p. 483.

2 ibid., p. 485; R. E. Glasscock, art. cit., pp. 115–16; Harvey, *A Medieval Oxfordshire Village*, pp. 108–09; Prestwich, *War, Politics and Finance*, pp. 180–1, 193.

It is undeniable that subsidies are, at best, little more than frail guides to the relative wealth of various areas. They are none the less guides – the best available to us – and on the accompanying map of North Wales (Map A on the opp. page) an attempt has been made to illustrate, to the nearest shilling, the relative wealth of various commotes of North Wales according to their taxable capacity per 1,000 acres. The commotes comprising the old county of Flint and, inexplicably, the westernmost commote of Llŷn – Cymydmaen – occupy a league to themselves: they would easily stand comparison with some of the more wealthy regions of England. The impressive showing of north-east Wales may owe a great deal to the presence of rich mineral deposits in the area, an asset which certainly did not remain unexploited in the late thirteenth century.[1] More surprising is the fairly high placing of some of the upland areas of mid-Wales, and in particular the south-western and eastern commotes of Merioneth and the comparatively well-provided-for commotes forming the eastern portion of the old county of Montgomery. The nearness of the thriving borough of Welshpool doubtless accounts for the latter, but whatever the reason, the relative economic buoyancy of some of the areas lying along or in the vicinity of the eastern middle march at the end of the thirteenth century could not be more clearly demonstrated.

* * *

Within Merioneth itself, the most populous commote by far at the end of the thirteenth century was Ardudwy – which is not surprising since it was also the biggest commote in the county, being over twice as large as any other except Penllyn. It was Ardudwy, too, which contributed most to the subsidy of 1292–3 and it was there, at Harlech, that Edward I planted his only borough in Merioneth that proved remotely viable. But as the Tables appended to this Introduction show,[2] Edeirnion, followed by Tal-y-bont and Ystumanner, was, in relation to its size, far more densely populated than Ardudwy. In terms of taxable capacity per acre which, it can be argued, bears some relation to movable wealth, the commote of Edeirnion was well ahead of the field, being more than twice as valuable as Penllyn or Ardudwy. An English invading force in 1282–3 (or possibly during the earlier campaign of 1277) found that the Welsh had a 'great lair' there, with a 'great abundance of corn

---

1 Edwards (ed.), *Flint Pleas*, pp. xviii–xix; Jones (ed.), *Flintshire Min. Accounts*, p. xliii, rather overstates the case however.

2 Most of this section is based on the information laid out in the Tables forming the Appendix to this Introduction.

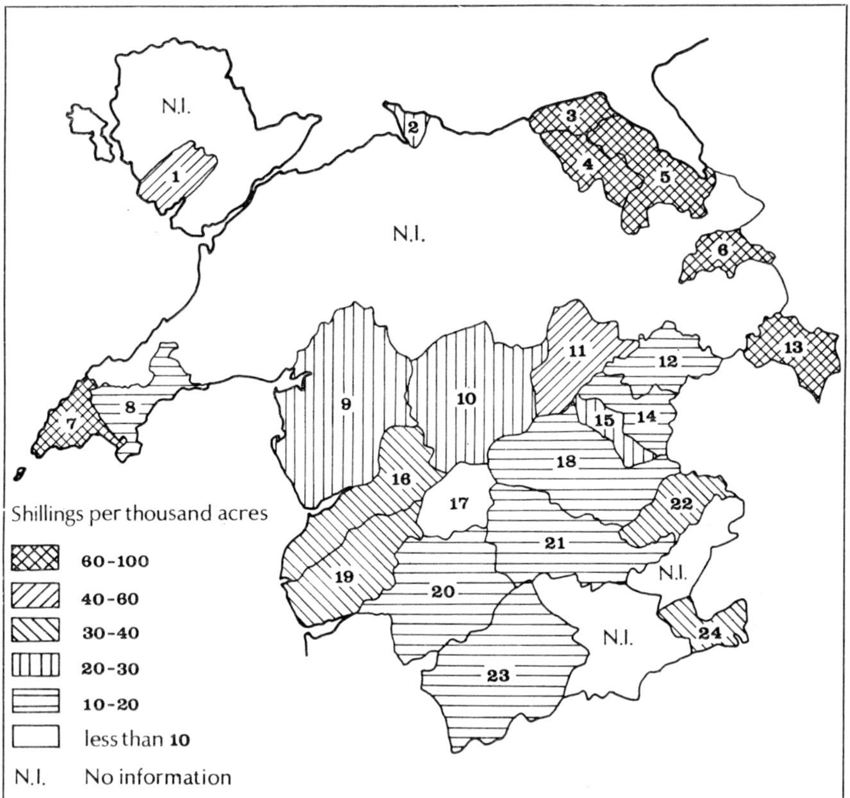

MAP A Relative wealth of commotes of N. Wales in 1292-93

1. Malltraeth
2. Creuddyn
3. Prestatyn
4. Rhuddlan
5. Coleshill
6. Hope
7. Cymydmaen
8. Cafflogion
9. Ardudwy
10. Penllyn
11. Edeirnion
12. Nanheudwy
13. Maelor
14. Cynllaith
15. Mochnant Is Rhaeadr
16. Tal-y-bont
17. Mawddwy
18. Mochnant and Mechain
19. Ystumanner
20. Cyfeiliog
21. Caereinion
22. Deuddwr and Ystrad Marchell
23. Arwystli
24. Montgomery

collected into heaps and in well covered granges' and 'great plenty of beasts'; without doubt, it was reported, 'much assistance in supplies' was at hand for the king's enemies there.[1] The evidence of the papal assessment of *c.* 1291 confirms the fact that Edeirnion was pre-eminent amongst the commotes of Merioneth.[2] It is not surprising that Henry of Monmouth was able to say of it, even in the middle of the Glyn Dŵr revolt, that it was 'une beau paiis et bien enhabite'.[3] But as for individual wealth, the average assessment was higher in the commote of Tal-y-bont than elsewhere. A greater proportion of those with movable wealth of £5 and over inhabited this commote than any other – about 1 in 5 of the total as compared with nearly 1 in 10 in Penllyn and 1 in 8 in Ystumanner. Indeed, if land over 1,000 feet were discounted, the taxable capacity of Tal-y-bont would exceed that of Edeirnion. The importance of Tal-y-bont is reflected in the extent of *c.* 1284, where its value to the crown is given as £77. 18*s.* 5*d.*, over £5 more than the much bigger commote of Ardudwy and nearly £20 more than either Penllyn or Ystumanner.[4] Tal-y-bont's comparative affluence possibly sprang from the fact that its long coastal strip and extensive area of adjacent upland pasture gave it a more balanced agricultural economy than any other commote (excepting Edeirnion), though it needed the stimulus of the woollen industry in the sixteenth and seventeenth centuries to give it any kind of pre-eminence. Bere, the one borough within its confines, was bigger than Harlech in 1292–3. The evidence of this subsidy roll makes nonsense of the idea that it was a 'borough in name only', but it seems to have withered overnight, probably in the wake of Madog's revolt when the castle lost its strategic importance. Its dissolution left the way clear for the emergence of Dolgellau which, despite its poor showing in this subsidy roll, contrived to prosper in a small way as the administrative and economic centre of Tal-y-bont.[5]

In almost every respect, the poorest commote in Merioneth at the end of the thirteenth century was Penllyn, but the devastation wrought there in the years of conquest had been very great, as the evidence on every side testifies.[6] The church, in any case, possibly claimed a greater proportion of its landed surface than it did in any

1 Edwards (ed.), *Cal. Anc. Corr.*, p. 172. Sir Goronwy's assumption that the 'Diriyon' of the document is Edeirnion is most probably correct.

2 *Taxatio ecclesiastica . . . Nicholai IV, c. 1291*, p. 291.

3 Henry Ellis (ed.), *Original Letters illustrative of English history*, 2nd series, I (1827), 12.

4 *Arch. Camb.* (1867), pp. 184–92. Cf. however, *B.B.C.S.*, IX (1937–9), 59.

5 Waters, *Edwardian Settlement*, pp. 99, 108.

6 e.g., *Arch. Camb.* (1867), p. 188; *Cal. of Chanc. Rolls (Various) 1277–1326*, p. 328; Martin (ed.), *Registrum . . . Peckham*, II, 455–8.

other commote, the two Cistercian houses of Basingwerk and Strata Marcella in particular holding large tracts of upland territory there. Much of the commote was barren and unproductive but it was not a total wilderness. The abbot of Basingwerk, it is true, probably had part of Penllyn as much as any other area in mind when he complained to the prince in 1346–7 of the 'incredibly sterile' possessions which his house had in Wales and Cheshire,[1] but since he was faced then with a tax bill his words carry that much less weight. At the time of the conquest in 1283 Roger Lestrange, one of the triumphant English commanders, had included Penllyn as well as Edeirnion in his calculations as he mused over the possible obtainment of a marcher lordship for himself in North Wales.[2] Penllyn was not without its attractions, not without potential, as Lestrange must have discovered. But notwithstanding its vaccaries and vast sheepwalks it yet lagged behind the other areas until apparently the late sixteenth and seventeenth centuries despite the confident plantation of a projected borough there in 1310.[3] Its relative wealth *vis-à-vis* the other commotes of Merioneth in the mid-Tudor period cannot, however, be adequately assessed because of the unyielding nature of the evidence.

There was great diversity within each commote. Tal-y-bont contained, within its bounds, not only the most populous and the most highly assessed township, namely Nannau, in the whole county but also one of the least populated and one of the lowest assessed, the vill of Dolgellau. Nannau and Dolgellau were near neighbours, but the one cannot usefully be compared with the other because Nannau was the largest township in the commote and Dolgellau one of the smallest. It is a matter of the utmost regret that the boundaries of many medieval townships cannot now be recovered. Some have disappeared altogether without trace. Even the great surveys of the late sixteenth and seventeenth centuries, valuable and compendious though they are, do not, at all times, faithfully reflect the medieval picture since the extensive concealments and encroachments by the gentry in the Tudor and Stuart periods intentionally obscured or distorted it.[4] A full-blown comparative study, based on the taxable capacity per acre of townships is, therefore, out of the question. By grouping townships together

1 Edwards (ed.), *Cal. Anc. Corr.*, p. 185.

2 ibid., p. 124. His wishes came to nothing.

3 Lewis, *Mediaeval Boroughs*, p. 55.

4 A comparison of the Ystumanner portion of the survey of 1592 (P.R.O. L.R.2/236) with the rental of 1633 (E. D. Jones, 'A Rental of Crown Lands in the commote of Estimanner, 1633', *Journ. Mer. Hist. Rec. Soc.*, II (1953–6), 312–24) brings this out clearly.

under their respective parishes, however, a study of the relative economic importance of various areas within the commotes is at least possible, though it should be understood that it would be wholly misleading to think in terms of even density of settlement or uniform development within each parish – and totally erroneous to imagine that the boundaries of the parishes drawn on Map B necessarily correspond to some of the parochial boundaries as they may have existed in 1292–3.

Which were the most populous and the wealthiest areas? Expressed in bald figures, the eleven leading parishes (out of a total of thirty-three) in the county were Tywyn (with 209 taxpayers), Llanfor (179), Corwen (164), Brithdir and Dolgellau (154), Llandrillo (127), Llanfachreth (112), Llanegryn (108), Trawsfynydd (105), Llanuwchllyn (104), Llanaber (101), and Llangelynnin (100). All the other twenty-two parishes of the county had fewer than 100 taxpayers each, as is revealed in Tables B–F, which are appended to this Introduction. Total assessments more or less followed the same pattern, with Tywyn again ahead of the other parishes with £40 and Llanegryn in eleventh place with £21. (The remaining parishes were assessed at totals less than £20.) What is significant here is that four out of five parishes in the commote of Tal-y-bont – Dolgellau, Llanfachreth, Llanegryn, and Llangelynnin – are included amongst the top eleven, showing that its comparative prosperity was fairly evenly spread. But as the accompanying Map (Map B on pages lxxviii–lxxix) shows, a somewhat different pattern emerges when one considers the taxable capacity (per 1,000 acres) of the parishes. The foremost parish turns out to be Penrhyndeudraeth in the north-west corner of the commote of Ardudwy. What explains that is not immediately apparent. It had no high moorland, a distinction – and advantage – it shared with only one other parish in the county, namely, Betws Gwerful Goch, and, like the comparatively prosperous Llanaber area, it was a source of supply of lime, drawn upon for extensions or repairs at Harlech castle in the early fourteenth century.[1] The presence of the fort of Aber Ia[2] or Castell Deudraeth within its bounds may provide a clue to its early economic as well as strategic importance at the mouth of two estuaries. With a taxable capacity of over £7 per 1,000 acres, it was more than twice as important as its nearest rival Llanegryn in the commote of Tal-y-bont. The economic importance of the Llanegryn area during the thirteenth century is, however, again demonstrated. Some way behind these two parishes came Betws Gwerful Goch, Llangelynnin, Llansan-

1 Stamp, *The Land of Britain*, Part 33, p. 197; *Arch. Camb.* (1846), pp. 247–8.
2 *Arch. Camb.* (1963), pp. 78, 87, 104.

ffraid Glyn Dyfrdwy, Llanfair, Corwen, Llandanwg, Llangar, and Gwyddelwern. All the other parishes had a taxable capacity of less than £2 per £1,000 acres. The main wealth of the county lay in the western areas bordering upon the sea on the one hand and in the eastern-most parishes facing the English border on the other. The broad acres of the mainly upland parishes in between fared less well, though there were clearly, as the next section shows, pockets of comparative affluence there too. Three other matters of interest emerge from this analysis: firstly, not a single parish in the commote of Penllyn or in the commote of Ystumanner had a taxable capacity of £2 or over per 1,000 acres; secondly, all the parishes except one in the prosperous commote of Edeirnion had taxable capacities of over £2; and lastly, the greatest disparity occurred in the large commote of Ardudwy, for the parish of Ffestiniog had the miserably low taxable capacity of 6*s*. per 1,000 acres as against over £7 per 1,000 acres in nearby Penrhyndeudraeth. Ffestiniog, indeed, seems to have been the most backward area in the whole county – the least inhabited and the poorest – at the end of the thirteenth century. What advance had been made there in relation to other areas by the sixteenth century – or what degree of economic change had occurred in other parishes in the meanwhile – is not quantifiable.

* * *

It may be objected that finer instruments than subsidy rolls are at our disposal for measuring the comparative wealth of various areas. That claim can hardly extend to the 'new' papal assessment drawn up for Pope Nicholas IV in the early 90s.[1] The *taxatio* of *c*. 1291 has been described as 'the most precious survey of ecclesiastical property in the middle ages'[2] but churches valued at less than £4 were not subject to the new valuation and in consequence only a handful of Merioneth parishes are represented in the returns.[3] The 'new' papal assessment of *c*. 1291 is of value only insofar as it identifies for us the wealthiest livings. Nor can it be claimed that the earlier valuation 'of Norwich' of 1254 or the undated 'Annuals due from the churches of the diocese' preserved in Llyfr Coch Asaph[4] provide a more comprehensive and detailed view of comparative

---

1 *Taxatio ecclesiastica . . . Nicholai IV c. 1291.*

2 Powicke, *Thirteenth Century*, p. 498, n. 1.

3 See *Taxatio ecclesiastica* . . . , pp. 286, 287, 291.

4 W. E. Lunt, *The Valuation of Norwich* (1926), pp. 196, 472; O. E. Jones, 'Llyfr Coch Asaph' (unpub. M.A., Univ. of Wales, 1968), p. 4. (The 'Annuals' are undated, but they are presumed to be within the years 1293–1346 by Mr. O. E. Jones. Their relative values differ little from the Valuation of Norwich, though the actual sums are smaller.)

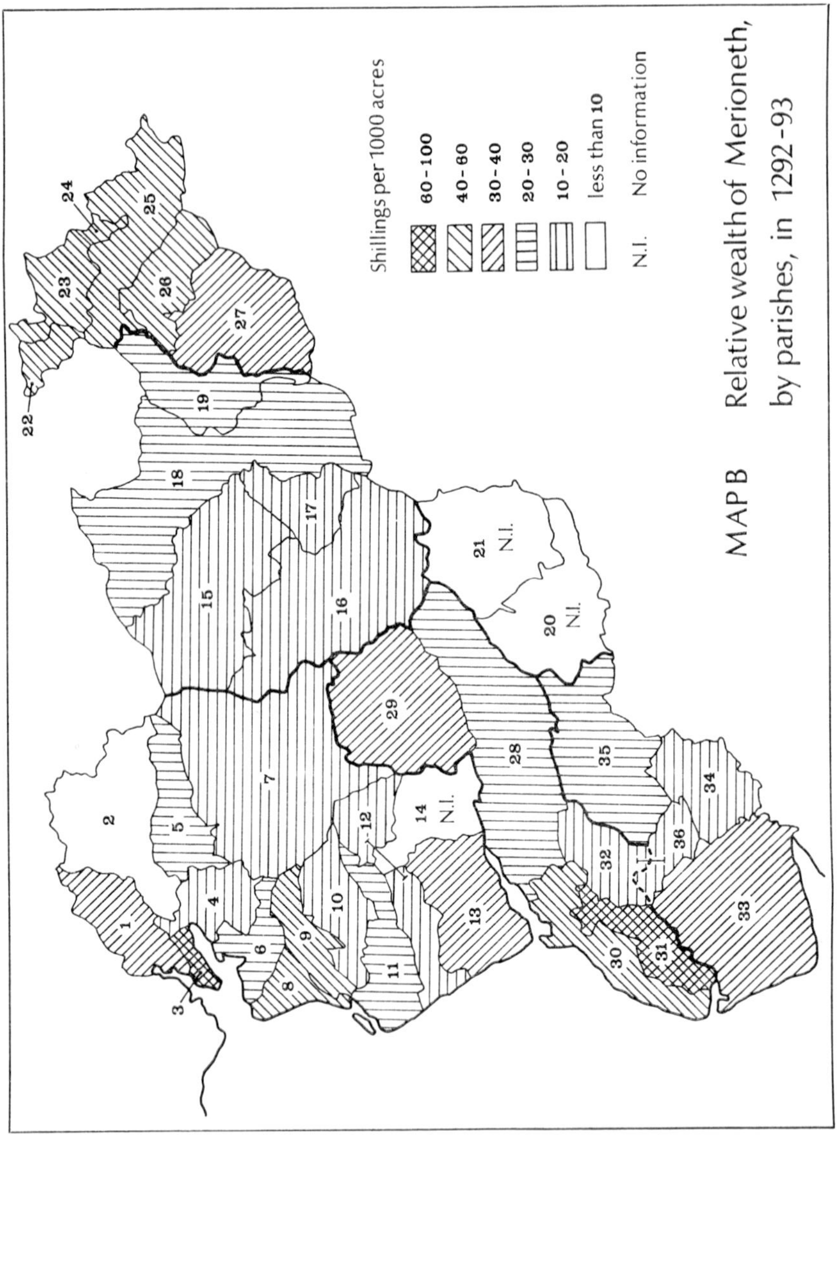

MAP B Relative wealth of Merioneth, by parishes, in 1292-93

ARDUDWY
1. Llanfrothen
2. Ffestiniog
3. Penrhyndeudraeth
4. Llandecwyn
5. Maentwrog
6. Llanfihangel-y-traethau
7. Trawsfynydd
8. Llandanwg
9. Llanfair
10. Llanbedr
11. Llanenddwyn
12. Llanddwywe
13. Llanaber
14. Llanelltud

PENLLYN
15. Llanycil
16. Llanuwchllyn
17. Llangywer
18. Llanfor
19. Llandderfel

MAWDDWY
20. Mallwyd
21. Llanymawddwy

EDEIRNION
22. Betws Gwerful Goch
23. Gwyddelwern
24. Llansanffraid Glyndyfrdwy
25. Corwen
26. Llangar
27. Llandrillo

TAL-Y-BONT
28. Brithdir and Dolgellau
29. Llanfachreth
30. Llangelynnin
31. Llanegryn
32. Llanfihangel-y-Pennant (part)

YSTUMANNER
33. Tywyn
34. Pennal
35. Tal-y-llyn
36. Llanfihangel-y-Pennant (part)

wealth than subsidy rolls. Professor Glanville Jones has argued, fairly persuasively, that there is a close relation between settlement patterns and the relative economic prosperity of various areas of Anglesey as revealed by a study of the valuation of Norwich of 1254,[1] but even in the valuation of Norwich, the most useful of all the ecclesiastical returns, the picture is indeterminate and distorted as far as Merioneth is concerned: no fewer than 6 of the 17 Merioneth parishes covered by it are assessed at the same sum, while others are given what seem to be conventional assessments of so many shillings or marks.[2] A comparison between the ecclesiastical valuation of 1254 and the lay subsidy returns of 1292–3 for Merioneth confirms W. E. Lunt's findings from other areas[3] that there is in fact little correspondence between them, except in the general sense that the high – and low – valuations of 1254 tended, on the whole, to be vaguely reflected in the total parochial assessments of 1292–3. If this does little to enhance the value of using subsidy rolls for assessing comparative wealth, it raises even greater doubts about the wisdom of relying on the ecclesiastical returns of 1254 or *c.* 1291.

Of course, the particular taxes to which the clergy were subjected were based on incomes rather than on movables so that differences between the two assessments were bound to occur. It is a moot point which of the two – incomes or movables – more accurately reflects the wealth of various areas. In the context of the times movables possibly provided a more sensitive indicator of wealth than tithable income. But there is no certainty about that. For breadth and depth of detail there is nothing to touch the subsidy rolls; their accuracy, however, is not subject to real proof.

MERIONETH SOCIETY IN THE LATE THIRTEENTH CENTURY

Though the most populous and the wealthiest vills in the county tended on the whole to be free, there is little to distinguish generally between free and bond townships. Nor can one detect all that much difference, as far as economic resources are concerned, between upland and lowland vills: the township of Pennant, lodged in the shadows of the Berwyn mountains, appears to have been blessed with more assets than many a vill lying on the valley floor. Apart

1 G. R. J. Jones, 'The Distribution of Medieval Settlement in Anglesey', *Transactions of the Anglesey Antiquarian Society and Field Club* (1955), pp. 51–3.

2 The highest assessed parish was Llanfor (at 66*s.* 8*d.*), followed by Corwen (53*s.*4*d.*), Tywyn, Llandrillo, and Gwyddelwern (each at 40*s.*), Llangelynnin, Llanegryn, Dolgellau, Llanfachreth, Pennal, and Llanfair (each at 20*s.*), Llanfihangel-y-Pennant, Llanfihangel, and Llandderfel (each at 6*s.* 8*d.*), Llangar and Betws Gwerful Goch (both at 5*s.*), and Llansanffraid Glyn Dyfrdwy (2*s.*). Lunt, op. cit.

3 ibid., pp. 613–14.

from the quasi-parochial townships like Nannau and the territorial units of the commote of Ardudwy, the most populous and prosperous township of all in the county was the large mixed vill of Penaran, the area of largely fertile land around and to the south of the village of Llanuwchllyn, at the south-western end of Bala lake. Two persons who had movables in this township were chosen to do homage and fealty to the English prince of Wales in 1301.[1] In the vicinity stand the old Roman auxiliary fort at Caergai and the native stronghold of Castell Carndochan, the home, so it is said, of Madog ab Iorwerth, one of the most powerful men in the commote of Penllyn in Edward I's day. Next in importance to Penaran was the township of Peniarth, lying in the shadow of three ancient hill forts, in the lower reaches of the Dysynni, in the parish of Llanegryn, in south-west Merioneth. It, too, occupied comparatively good land and lay near to important cross-country routeways. More compact than Penaran and Peniarth and potentially more dynamic than either of them was the vill of Cynwyd in Edeirnion which had all the makings of a goodly market town, frequented by doctors, cobblers, and merchants. Other vills well-grown and well-lined above the average were Gwyddelwern, Rhyd-cryw, Cefnrhos, Brithdir, and Gwernefail, all of them townships with broad acres of good pasture-land and lying on the edge of fair-sized villages. The average sum of 11*s*. 7*d*. for Hendwr in the commote of Edeirnion was the highest by far of any vill in the county with more than one taxpayer.[2] A high average assessment usually indicated that a vill was in the hands of a few persons of comparatively great wealth. Conversely, where there was a large number of taxpayers assessed at small modest sums, as in Llanfrothen or Maentwrog,[3] it is possible that it was an area of predominantly very small holdings of land, a supposition that the extent of Merioneth of *c*. 1420 tends to confirm.

The smaller the number of taxpayers and the greater the differential in assessments between them, the more likelihood was there of a vill being dominated by one person or family. The tendency in any case was in this direction, especially in free townships. If society in Merioneth as a whole, as shadowily revealed in this subsidy roll, were to be represented in the form of a diagram, it would resemble, not so much a pyramid, as a decanter bottle with a phenomenally long thin neck, for over 85 per cent were assessed at less than 6*s*. 8*d*. (i.e. had movable property worth less than £5) and the remainder at various sums ranging up to 44s. More people – 91 in all – were

1 *infra*, pp. 9–10.
2 See the Tables appended to this Introduction for an analysis of the township returns.
3 *infra*, pp. 63–5, and 73–4.

assessed at the lowly sum of 1*s*. 4*d*. than any other amount. The same pattern more or less is discernible in the Flintshire subsidy roll though the highest individual assessment there is 75*s*.[1] The gulf between the richest and the next-to-poorest in the former counties of Flint and Merioneth was not as wide as it was, for example, in the lordship of Abergavenny where the lord John Hastings was assessed at £8 and no fewer than 555 of the remaining 574 at less than 7*s*. 4*d*., 143 of them at 1*s*.;[2] nevertheless, one cannot in any sense regard Merioneth – or Flintshire – society as being egalitarian in the late thirteenth century: on the contrary, it was both complex and stratified.

At ground level, however, county society in Merioneth assumed a different shape, since the highest assessment in one township might not be much more than the median in another. Fairly sharp differentials existed at the local level but they were not as stark and pronounced as they would have been if set against the whole gamut of county assessments. Viewed at ground level, county society was made up not of one vertical, but many: it resembled an assortment of upturned funnels of varying sizes, as each township had its thick basic quota of close and evenly-spaced assessments at the bottom with, more often than not, one or two much higher assessments standing well apart and above the rest. The same phenomenon is displayed elsewhere even in some bond townships: in the vill of Aberffraw in Anglesey, for example, 67 were assessed at various sums ranging from 1*s*. to 8*s*. and two persons, clearly much wealthier than the others, at 22*s*. and 24*s*.[3] Where more than one member of a family was assessed in the same vill, the disparity could be very great. Perhaps the best example is the free vill of Bodgadfan in the commote of Tal-y-bont where a certain Madin ap Adaf Hen was assessed at 24*s*., the highest in the township. Entered in the lists immediately before him were, almost certainly, his two sons Adaf ap Madin and Wir ap Madin, assessed respectively at 13*s*. 3*d*. and 7*s*. 10*d*., so that the total assessment of this family as a group came to no less than 45*s*. 1*d*. The next highest assessment in the township was 10*s*. 4*d*. and there were 17 others assessed at less than that sum.[4] The influence that could have been exerted in the area by the

1 P.R.O. E.179/242/52. The highest assessed person was, significantly, a burgess of Flint.

2 P.R.O. E.179/242/56. It has been said, however, that the lords 'were able to pass much, perhaps even the whole, of their liabilities on to tenants of every kind including their villeins, and that it was the common folk who became the main payers of the new taxes'. (M. M. Postan, *The Medieval Economy and Society* (1972), p. 173).

3 Seebohm, *Tribal System*, App. A.f.

4 *infra*, p. 36–7.

Adda Hen clan must, in consequence, have been considerable. Unfortunately, nothing is known of Madin ap Adaf Hen's progenitors or of the fortunes of his family, but the pattern described here seems to lend substance to the notion of a powerful patriarchal ancestor and his dependants being given exclusive rights and privileges in a certain locality.

Attempts at relating any of these findings to the *gwely* structure as such have, however, proved fruitless. Nor have endeavours to relate taxable wealth to landed possessions been very successful: for what it is worth, two persons who were assessed at about 10*s*. were said to have held 6 bovates of land each,[1] that is to say, probably 24 customary acres each, which works out at 2.4 acres per shilling assessed. In very different circumstances, the son and heir of a certain Richard de Welles (a Hertfordshire gentleman who was killed fighting the Welsh as a member of Edward I's armies in Anglesey in 1283) inherited an estate of 68 acres from his father and was assessed at 33*s*. 8*d*. in 1290:[2] although these figures are in no way to be taken as conclusive, they do again point to a ratio of about 2 acres to every 1*s*. 0*d*. of assessment. If all this has any general relevance, a person assessed at the lowest possible sum of 1*s*. 0*d*. would have been in possession of about 2–2½ acres of land; likewise, the median assessment of 3*s*. 1*d*. would have meant the equivalent of about 7½ acres of landed property which may not be all that wide of the mark in actual fact in certain parts of Gwynedd;[3] again, those with over 4 bovates of land (or 16 customary acres) who owed suit of court at the county court[4] would have been amongst the élite with chattels worth £5 in their possession for which they would have been assessed at 6*s*. 8*d*. in 1292–3. According to this analysis, less than 15 per cent of Merioneth's population could lay claim to 16 acres of land or more.

A great deal of this is inferential and open to question. But what of the élite? It is of some interest, in view of one of the original meanings of *tref*, that a number of farms or small estates, like Ucheldref, Cynlas, Cyffty, Cefnyrowen, Rhiwerfa, Bron-prys, and others adopted or inherited the names of small townships in which one person or family had a preponderant interest in the 1290s. Of equal interest is it that the larger estates of later times, such as Nannau, Peniarth, Rhywedog, Rhiwlas, Corsygedol, many of which

1 See *infra*, p. 51, n. 1, and p. 56, n. 1.

2 P.R.O. C.133/11/488; and E.179/120/2.

3 Cf. Jones Pierce, *Medieval Welsh Society*, p. 216; also *infra*, p. cxix.

4 Waters, *Edwardian Settlement*, p. 101, but cf. Edwards (ed.), *Cal. Anc. Corr.*, pp. 179–80.

also assumed the names of the vills in which they were situated, had their main seat in areas which in the 1290s seem to have contained more than the usual number of assessments in the middle range. Competition was clearly fiercer there amongst diverse lusty equals: it both steeled and spurred them on to greater things. If it is true that, as T. Jones Pierce said, in Gwynedd at this time 'rarely did a man's chattels exceed five pounds in value, if we exclude the prince and possibly a handful of leading *uchelwyr*',[1] throughout Merioneth as a whole nearly 400 families (15 per cent) stood poised to advance themselves in the 1290s. This was substantially higher than in many other areas: in the former county of Flint 261 (or 10 per cent, of whom, significantly, as many as 1 in 5 were resident in the county's boroughs) had movables worth more than £5; in the lordship of Bronllys, formerly in Brecknockshire, 7 out of 123 (5.7 per cent); in the lordship of Chirk only 17 out of 662 (2.6 per cent). Even in parts of Merioneth's neighbour, in the old county of Montgomery, as few as 66 (of whom 20 – or 1 in 3 – were burgesses from Welshpool) out of 1,429 paid a subsidy of 6*s*. 8*d*. or over – a percentage of only 4.6. In the commote of Is Cennen in West Wales not a single person was assessed at more than 6*s*. 8*d*., that is to say, had movables worth £5 in value. These figures point surprisingly to a higher degree of affluence in Merioneth in the late thirteenth century – or can it be that an area only recently made obedient to the king's will was a more vulnerable target for the taxator?

The key to the success of Norman and later English rule in Wales lay partly in the practice of allowing Welshmen a share, at a subordinate level, in the governance of the land. Indeed, the co-operation of Welshmen in the running of local affairs was at all times a prime necessity and recognised as such by wise governors. The king's viceroy in West Wales was bluntly reminded in 1244 of the simple truth that it was 'not easy to control the Welsh except through one of their own race'. Prudence decreed, not so much excluding Welshmen from office, as following the example of the earl of Pembroke who had shrewdly given two baronies 'to a certain Welshman . . . in order to hold down the Welsh through him'.[2] Without a working relationship of that kind, effective local government in Wales would have broken down sooner or later; at the same time, to deny Welshmen the opportunity to participate, at however humble a level, in the administration of their localities was liable to provoke rebellion, for office-holding was an important avenue of advancement economically as well as socially – so important, indeed, that Welshmen were

1 Jones Pierce, *Medieval Welsh Society*, p. 133.

2 Edwards (ed.), *Cal. Anc. Corr.*, p. 48.

prepared to go to extraordinary lengths to secure offices, buying their way in and paying heavy entry fines like the men of Rhos or Mefenydd,[1] or even betraying their native princes and handing them over captive to the English authorities, as Dafydd Fychan of West Wales and Ynyr Fychan of Nannau (in Merioneth) are said to have done.[2]

Clearly, in all this, the vast reservoir of patronage at the disposal of the prince excited the keenest attention; equally clearly, for the more lowly, that patronage could scarcely be tapped except through the good offices of intermediaries, whether top local administrators or influential courtiers. Burleigh's advice to his son to 'Be sure to keep some great man thy friend' might well have been given to any aspiring office-holder in medieval Wales. However, only those who were amenable and already of some consequence locally had much hope of attracting the support of the powerful. These twin qualifications become critically important in post-conquest Gwynedd.

The competition for offices was fierce, made all the more so by the rapacity of English immigrant families anxious to advance themselves.[3] Almost every office of any importance which Welshmen sought had its price. It followed, of course, that claimants for office had invariably to possess a modicum of wealth and political discretion in the first place. How much personal wealth? That in some measure depended upon what offices were available at different times. In the immediate post-conquest period no Welshman could ever hope to storm the commanding heights of the principality's administration – though assuming the important role of deputy was clearly not beyond the determination of one Rhys ap Hywel early in Edward II's reign, for he served as the justiciar's lieutenant in West Wales in 1312–13.[4] Nor would it in any way have been politic to entrust the custody of a great royal castle to a Welshman in the years following 1282–4. Gruffydd ap Tudur, it is true, managed to hold on to the small fortress at Dolwyddelan and drew 40 marks per annum for it,[5] but no such expectations were entertained about the Edwardian castles: a much less exalted office than that of con-

1 Martin (ed.), *Registrum . . . Peckham*, II, 449, 462; Griffiths, *The Principality of Wales in the Later Middle Ages*, I, 66n. Cf. *B.B.C.S.*, VII (1933–5), 147.

2 Rhys (ed.), *Min. Accounts for West Wales*, p. 359; *Rec. of Caernarvon*, p. 220.

3 See, e.g., ibid., pp. 224–5. Cf. A. L. Poole, *From Domesday Book to Magna Carta* (1951), p. 9 n. 1, for sums offered by those seeking offices under the crown in Henry I's day.

4 Griffiths, *The Principality of Wales in the Later Middle Ages*, I, 97. He was in fact made justiciar in 1326–7 (ibid., 98).

5 *Cal. of Chanc. Rolls* (*Various*), *1277–1326*, p. 288. He was appointed 22 August 1284. Cf. ibid., pp. 162, and 178 for appointment of Hywel ap Meuric as custodian of Builth castle.

stable, the janitorship of Harlech castle, worth 2*d.* a day and a robe as well as various fees, was held by an Englishman in the 1290s.[1] The ambitions of Welshmen were focused for the most part on the opportunities available in the second and third tier of local government, the shire and the commote. As it was, only a privileged few could rise to the shrievalty, which was worth, excluding perquisites, £40 in the early years (until 1286) because of the 'newness of the office', and £20 thereafter.[2] To be sheriff, the highest position a Welshman could normally aspire to, a person's movable wealth, to judge from the case of Gruffydd ap Dafydd, lord of Hendwr and sheriff of Merioneth in 1301, had to be in the region of £20 at least, that is to say, he had to be liable in the sum of 25*s.* or over.[3] Not all in that category automatically qualified for the office of sheriff, for other considerations were taken into account as well, but relative wealth too was a *sine qua non.* The more affluent could lay claim to offices seemingly well below their dignity, but those on the verge of penury, on the other hand, had little hope of holding high office. The haves, as usual, were better placed than the have-nots to further their own ends. Those in the upper bracket of Merioneth society in the 1290s were, however, as we shall see, comparatively few in number. Hence, perhaps, the reason why the local assessors of the Merioneth subsidy of 1292–3 were drawn from a fairly wide spectrum of Merioneth society: only two out of 29 were in Gruffydd ap Dafydd's class and eight were assessed at less than 6*s.* 8*d.*

It was the local offices under county level which Welshmen had their eyes on mainly. Here again the rewards were real enough. The biggest commotal prize was that of rhaglaw, a quasi-shrieval office which had mushroomed in the age of the princes and which lay securely in the custody of their more affluent subjects: Rhirid ap Madog, for example, Llywelyn II's rhaglaw (*constabularius*) in Penllyn in 1282, was assessed at 11*s.* 11*d.* in 1292–3.[4] As the prince's lieutenant, the rhaglaw had important administrative, judicial, and fiscal functions to perform in the commote. The perquisites of the office after the Edwardian conquest seem to have become more important than the executive powers once exercised by the holders of the office. The precise range of those perquisites are, however, difficult to discover. They were not, apparently, universally uniform. According to the mid-fourteenth century proceedings arising from writs of *quo*

1 *infra*, p. 65.

2 *Cal. of Chanc. Rolls* (*Various*), *1277–1326*, pp. 283, 305. Cf. *B.B.C.S.*, I (1921–3), 268.

3 See *infra* p. 82 n. 3.

4 He is probably the same man as is mentioned in Martin (ed.), *Registrum . . . Peckham*, II, 455.

warranto issued in 1348, the rhaglaw of Ardudwy, who rendered £4 a year for the office, received a share of all fines and amercements imposed on the inhabitants of the commote, a percentage of the proceeds from all mead and beer exposed for sale in the commote, a tenth share of reliefs paid to the prince, and 20*s*. for every meeting of the turn.[1] Elsewhere, in Bromfield and Yale, Eifionydd, Twrcelyn, West Wales and other areas, a great number of additional bonuses accrued to the rhaglaw, amongst them provender for his horse and perquisites from the sale of all victuals and forfeited goods.[2]

The perquisites of office were, of course, additional to the normal dues and amercements exacted; and sweet as were the fees and perquisites of office, even sweeter was the power – and especially the fruits of power – that went with it. The scope it gave the holder for lining his own pocket was immense, particularly when he held it at farm. The administration could be manipulated in favour of kinsmen and followers; the law itself could be made to serve as a convenient cloak for illegal practices. Charges preferred against a person allegedly acting 'sub colore officii sui' are numerous.[3] One of the most accomplished practitioners of the art of extortion was Cynwrig Sais, rhaglaw of the cantref of Englefield for four years from 1335. In 1340 he was accused and found guilty of numerous crimes – of pressing many false indictments, of exacting exorbitant fees and wrongful reliefs, of levying enormous corn dues – and was compelled to submit to a huge fine of £200. His 'instincts and bearing', it has been said, 'were those of a lord of a commote, not of its bailiff'[4] and it is small wonder that he was still paying for his crimes when he died in 1348. It is not surprising either that the rhaglawry of Englefield was held at farm at various sums of upwards of £85 a year[5] and that the person who held the office in 1292–3, one Gruffydd ap Tudur, was assessed at £3. 12*s*. 11*d*., far and away the highest recorded for any office-holder in North Wales.[6] The rhaglawry of Englefield was unique in many respects. It was an office comparable in importance and status to that of sheriff, for it embraced the three commotes of Rhuddlan, Prestatyn, and Coleshill, but the potential value of the office to the holder was equally apparent elsewhere and this is reflected in the movable wealth of those in Merioneth who claimed the office:

1 *Rec. of Caernarvon*, pp. 156–7.

2 ibid., pp. xi, 154, 170; Rees, *South Wales and the March*, p. 97.

3 See, e.g., U.C.N.W., Bodrhyddan 2335, mm. 3 and 4; P.R.O. E.163/5/21.

4 Evans (ed.), *Flintshire Min. Accounts*, p. xxviii.

5 ibid., pp. 19, 46, 69; Jones (ed.), *Flintshire Min. Accounts*, p. 87.

6 P.R.O. E.179/242/52 *sub* commote of Prestatyn.

Gwrgenau Fychan, for example, who was appointed rhaglaw of Penllyn in 1306 was assessed at over 11*s.* in 1292–3.[1] Though Ynyr Fychan of Nannau, the rhaglaw of Tal-y-bont from 1303 to *c.* 1330, was assessed at only 8*s.* 6½*d.* in 1292–3, those seeking or holding the office of rhaglaw normally possessed movables valued at £7. 10*s.* 0*d.* at the very least (or were assessed at well over 10*s.*).

So too, to a lesser degree, with the office of rhingyll or bailiff which was nominally subordinate to that of rhaglaw, but executively of greater importance after 1282 in most parts of Wales except Englefield. The fees and perquisites attaching to the two offices covered much the same ground[2] – though less accrued to the rhingyll – and attracted much the same class of taxpayer in Merioneth: only those assessed at well over 6*s.* 8*d.* (that is, 'leading *uchelwyr*', if we are to accept Jones Pierce's norm) are known to have claimed the office. Sometimes the same person held both offices or combined them with other offices, such as keeper of vaccaries or forests[3] – which in itself is indicative of the great value placed by important men on local offices. Equally the bailiffs of Harlech were substantial taxpayers and one at least – the wealthiest inhabitant there in 1292–3 – is known to have held the office of rhingyll of Ardudwy in the early fourteenth century.[4] Because of lack of information, little can be said about the relationship of movable wealth to the holding of lesser local offices. The watchman, a 'boneddig gwlad' according to Dr. William Rees,[5] was clearly a person of some substance in Merioneth, being usually assessed at sums above the average for the county as a whole, but certainly not on a par with those holding the chief commotal offices.

The Edwardian conquest ushered in the days of 'superabundance of bailiffs'. One office in particular which attracted the attention of office-hunters was that of woodward, which seems to have been much more important in Merioneth than various other parts of Wales, including well-wooded Nanconwy.[6] The woodward received apparently little more than 4*d.* for every proven vert offence and some other undisclosed perquisites, but offers of £9 and £10 were made in the fourteenth century for the woodwardship of Ardudwy, more than twice what was offered for the rhaglawry of the same com-

1 *infra*, p. 3.

2 *Rec. of Caernarvon*, pp. 154, 170.

3 ibid., pp. 152, 156, 171.

4 P.R.O. S.C.6/1170/5.

5 Rees, *South Wales and the March*, p. 10.

6 *Cal. of Inq. Misc., II, 1307–49*, p. 430. The woodwardship of Nanconwy was worth £7 in 1341.

mote[1] and nearly twenty times what the office of woodward fetched in parts of the former county of Flint.[2] Quite wealthy men, those with movables well over £5 in value, were eager to lay their hands on the office, a fact which points to its profitability on the one hand and to the supreme importance at the time of timber and woodland on the other.

But not all offices imported at the conquest proved all that lucrative. The office of coroner, for example, carried no emoluments.[3] Coroners, however, were not drawn from the ranks of the destitute: a person assessed at 3*s*. 3*d*. (that is, worth £2. 10*s*. 0*d*. in movables) in 1292–3 was acting as coroner of Penllyn in 1304–05.[4] This probably gives a fair indication of the degree of social importance which Welshmen attached to the office, for the coroner was elected in the county court by Welsh freeholders.

All this provides merely a very rough and ready indicator of the relative status of a number of local offices, for the assessments themselves are not totally reliable guides to personal wealth and give no indication of the 'family circumstances' of those taxed. It is fairly clear none the less that the choice in the upper reaches of Merioneth society was severely limited. If only persons in the first category referred to above, namely, those with movable wealth of about £20 and upwards, are to be classified as leading *uchelwyr* then there were less than a dozen such families in late-thirteenth century Merioneth – three in Penllyn, three in Tal-y-bont, two in Edeirnion, and one each in Ardudwy and Ystumanner. This may account for the fact that persons in the very top rank of county society were able – or possibly had – to serve more than one rhaglawry in the county, for some aptitude for office-holding was probably considered necessary even in the 1290s. As compared with those similarly assessed in Hertfordshire in 1290[5] they scarcely qualified as 'middling gentry' but in the context of Merioneth society they were immensely wealthy and consequently a power in the land.

Even so, it seems that leading *uchelwyr* in Merioneth, in the estimation of the inhabitants if not of outsiders, numbered far more than a dozen or so. Welsh society at this time was radically different from English society in many respects. It was rooted in a different soil, was governed by different precepts, and responded to different needs. English yardsticks cannot be fairly applied to Wales, but it

1 *Rec. of Caernarvon*, p. 215.

2 Jones (ed.), *Flintshire Min. Accounts*, pp. 27, 58.

3 Waters, *Edwardian Settlement*, p. 141.

4 See *infra*, p. 5 n. 1.

5 P.R.O. E.179/120/2.

is doubtful if even in Merioneth a person could be regarded as a leading *uchelwr* in the county if he had not at his disposal movables valued at around £10 or more. Ynyr Fychan of Nannau, one of nature's opportunists, with movables valued at about £6. 10*s.* 0*d.*, cannot, at least by this token, be considered among the élite of the county in the early 1290s, though fortune seems to have soon favoured him and his house. About 75 to 80 persons – nearly three per cent of the total taxable population who were assessed at 13*s.* 4*d.* or over, that is, had movables valued at £10 or more – may be regarded as substantial *uchelwyr* in the county, a figure which works out at just over one to every two townships or administrative units. (It is significant that about 90 *uchelwyr* from Merioneth made homage and fealty to the prince of Wales in 1301.)[1] They were fairly evenly distributed throughout the five commotes but not within each commote: in half of the parishes of Ardudwy, for example, there were no *uchelwyr* of this kind, though in the parish of Llanaber there were four – a fact which may not be unconnected with another, namely, that Llanaber was a mixed vill with apparently a fairly big bond population.[2] The area, in fact, is fairly rich in prehistoric monuments and hill forts. At all events, it is not to be wondered that there is a very fine early thirteenth-century church at Llanaber.[3] In the county as a whole, the greatest concentration of substantial *uchelwyr* was in the parish of Tywyn, which had seven, followed by Llanuwchllyn and (the much smaller parish of) Llandrillo with six each.[4] In the early years after the Edwardian conquest the more responsible commotal offices were probably discharged by them, and though a wide gulf by no means separated them from the 80 or so in the £7. 10*s.* 0*d.* – £10 group immediately below or indeed the throng of *uchelwyr* in the £5 – £7. 10*s.* 0*d.* range, the difference between the highest and the lowest assessed – and especially the non-assessed – *uchelwr* was considerable, much more so than a reading of the Welsh laws might lead one to suppose. Economic and social condition was in reality as divisive a factor in Welsh life as legal status. An *uchelwr* of very slender means would, quite naturally, take pride in his legal status and be grateful for it, since it relieved him of many of the burdens endured by the unfree,

---

1 See Edward Owen, *A List of those who did homage and fealty to the First English Prince of Wales in A.D. 1301* (1901), pp. 12, 13, 17, 20, 24–6; *Cal. Pat. Rolls 1343–45*, pp. 232–3.

2 *Rec. of Caernarvon*, p. 277.

3 *Roy. Comm. Anc. Mon.: Inv. Merioneth*, p. 47.

4 For further details of those assessed at 13*s.* 4*d.* and over, see Tables B–F which are appended to this Introduction.

but to enjoy a life-style appreciably different from his fellows,[1] to taste the delights of a 'teg blas' ('fair hall') rather than experience the miseries of a 'tŷ taeog blwng' ('wretched serf's house'),[2] and to exercise power and authority he had to be a man of some substance in the first place. Whatever else, a well-lined purse provided the means to enlarge one's stake in the land and thereby enhanced the prospect of securing for one's family in the course of time an honoured place in society. The importance which contemporaries attached to being well-born cannot be gainsaid, but much as the poets might insist that only 'bonedd . . . a fag y bendefigaeth', ('it is lineage which fosters the aristocracy')[3] the supposition that social pre-eminence in the late thirteenth century had nothing to do with material wealth is as naïve as the egalitarian view of Welsh society still so fondly adhered to in some quarters. The term '*uchelwr*', it is true, retained its primary meaning of 'free man' until at least the first quarter of the sixteenth century,[4] but the word had always carried with it also connotations of a more 'aristocratic' flavour, consonant with the worldly possessions and wide authority of some.[5] A yawning gap, in fact, existed between what constituted a legal class and a social class. Hence the perennial ambiguity surrounding *uchelwyr* as a group and the consequent blurring of class differences in Welsh life. The ranks of the *uchelwyr* were in fact riven with economic differences. Wealth mattered. It is simply inconceivable that a man who could not make the taxpayer's roll in 1292–3, unless exempted for some special reason, would have been considered for any local office of consequence. Wealth may not have been the sole or the main criterion, but it was the promise of service under a lord which a degree of wealth, however acquired, made possible that conferred eminence on a man and helped to distinguish him from the mass of the peasantry both free and unfree. Clearly, being able to lay claim to and hold an important local office marked a person out

---

1 Though they date from the latter half of the fourteenth century and are concerned with 'princely homes', Iolo Goch's famous *cywyddau* to Sycharth and the court of the bishop of St. Asaph are of relevance here, as revealing of trends if nothing else. (See Henry Lewis, Thomas Roberts, and Ifor Williams (edd.), *Cywyddau Iolo Goch ac Eraill* (1937), pp. 36–8, 82–4.)

2 Thomas Parry (ed.), *Gwaith Dafydd ap Gwilym* (1963), No. 39, l.8.

3 Thomas Parry (ed.), *The Oxford Book of Welsh Verse* (1964), p. 146.

4 Clwyd Record Office (Flintshire), D/PT/1090. In parts of north-east Wales 'frankeleyn' was also an alternative (P.R.O. S.C.2/221/2 mm. 13 and 23; /226/25 m. 2; Nat. Lib. Wales, Pen. 404D, p. 39).

5 Cf. Thomas Jones (ed.), *Brut y Tywysogyon: Red Book of Hergest Version*, pp. 16–17, 28–9. Thomas Jones translated *uchelwyr* as 'chief men', *sub annis* 984 and 1075. In the Low Countries, the free were apparently equated with men of noble status (Hilton, *Bond Men Made Free*, p. 54.)

from his fellows and fostered the notion that he was a member of the 'gentry' class.[1]

Social and political influence did not, of course, depend, no more than it does at any other time, on personal wealth alone. Though the activities of many highly-assessed persons in 1292–3 are shrouded in mystery through lack of adequate evidence to pursue them, we may be fairly certain none the less that some of them were not as influential or as prominent in comital affairs as their place in the assessment table would have us believe. Important as wealth was, there were other considerations as well. Native shrewdness and natural aptitude may have counted for something; dynastic connexions counted for far more. Office-holding tended to run in families, as did trades like smiths and carpenters. Gruffydd ap Dafydd, lord of Hendwr, who became sheriff of Merioneth in 1301, owed as much to his 'aristocratic' descent as to his wealth – though of course the one went with the other more often than not: when Llywelyn Bren and his followers in Glamorgan surrendered after their brief rebellion in 1316 more than half the livestock that fell into the hands of the crown as a result of their action belonged to the leader himself.[2] Certainly, birth and pedigree continued to dominate social attitudes. In 1345, a principality official suggested that if Welshmen enlisting for the French wars were to be led by Welshmen, such leaders should be of baronial status and not 'men of lesser estate'.[3] Glyn Dŵr's appeal to his fellow Welshmen indeed was mainly based not so much on his 'baronial' as his princely descent and connexions. But those of 'aristocratic' or princely descent were a dying breed after 1282. Their place was being taken by prominent *uchelwr* families – and, increasingly as time went on, by 'new' men, flush with newly-acquired riches, endeavouring to make their way in the world. Accumulated wealth, more than ever before, laid the foundation of public advancement, as the reaction to it proves only too well. The whole savage thrust of Gruffydd Llwyd's famous *cywydd* to Glyn Dŵr in the latter half of the fourteenth century is directed in the first instance against social upstarts:

Aml iawn gan y mileiniaid
Ariant ac aur, ni roent ged,
A golud, byd gogaled; . . .

1 Siôn Tudur (d. 1602) was contemptuous of such an idea in the late sixteenth century. As he remarks with heavy sarcasm: 'O chaiff swydd . . . Ef â'n hawdd yn fonheddig' ('If he gets an office he quickly joins the ranks of the gentry') (Parry (ed.), *Oxford Book of Welsh Verse*, p. 224), but the argument has more force than he would care to admit.

2 Ralph Griffiths, 'The Revolt of Llywelyn Bren, 1316', *Glamorgan Historian*, II (1965), 194.

3 Edwards (ed.), *Cal. Anc. Corr.*, p. 248.

A fu isaf ei foesau
Uchaf yw, mawr yw'r och fau:
A'r uchaf cyn awr echwydd
Isaf ac ufuddaf fydd,

. . .

Hyn a wna, hen a newydd,
Y drygfyd. Pa ryw fyd fydd?[1]

An honoured place in Welsh society was not won overnight! To be in the running at all was an achievement in itself. So many factors (quite apart from the fulsome prejudice of long-established families) militated against the success of aspiring social climbers: failure of male heirs, disease, incapacity, profligacy, political indiscretions, natural catastrophes, the very misfortunes in fact which gave the fortunate few who escaped or survived these disasters the opportunity they required to carve greater things for themselves and their families. In the early 1290s their hour had not yet arrived. Not all that many taxpayers in the Merioneth subsidy roll appear to have been recognisable ancestors of those who were to emerge as the 'natural' leaders of society in the Tudor and Stuart age. That particular social revolution had hardly begun in the late thirteenth century. The majority of those who eventually won through were clearly drawn from the ranks of newly-founded, rather than old-established, families.

The unfree, like the free, were subject to the subsidy of 1292–3, but the roll does not distinguish between them. The number of free townships in Merioneth greatly exceeded that of bond by the end of the thirteenth century, but the bond population was by no means negligible despite appearances to the contrary. The extent of *c.* 1284 referred to the 40 villeins of 'the whole commote' of Penllyn of whom there 'are 10 surviving',[2] but the picture drawn in the extent is incomplete. Areas under the control of the church, for example, lay outside the purview of royal surveyors. Measuring the bond population presents difficulties for other reasons too: some persons might be assessed on goods in townships in which they did not reside; there were mixed vills like Penaran, Rhyd-cryw, and Llanfihangel[3] where it is difficult to assess the proportion of free to

---

1 Lewis *et al.* (edd.), *Cywyddau Iolo Goch ac Eraill*, p. 125, 11. 6–8, 13–16, 21–2. 'The villeins very often have silver and gold – they bear no gifts – and riches, a niggardly world; . . . he whose manner of living was lowest is now the highest, loudly do I bewail it, and the highest before mid-day will be the lowest and the most obedient. . . . This is what makes, old and new, an evil world. What is this world coming to?'

2 *Arch. Camb.* (1867), p. 188.

3 *Rec. of Caernarvon*, pp. 261–2, 272–3, 281–2.

unfree; a number of bond settlements – in the commote of Ardudwy especially[1] – were swallowed up in bigger units in the undiscriminating subsidy roll. More perplexing still, some bondmen, like Heylin ap Roger of Tal-y-bont, lived in free townships;[2] on the other hand, some freemen apparently lived (or at least had movables) in bond townships: the two chaplains listed under Llanfendigaid ought clearly not to be subsumed in the bond total, nor the steward at Crogen, nor the smith (traditionally a freeman) at Llanycil.[3] In view of all these anomalies the evidence as it stands and as far as it can reasonably be stretched allows us to say no more than the ratio of bond to free in 1292–3 was, at a crude estimate, between 1 to 3 and 1 to 4[4] – and nearer 1 to 4 than 1 to 3 – in the commotes of Ardudwy, Penllyn, Tal-y-bont, and Ystumanner. No comparable estimate is possible for the commote of Edeirnion.

The average bondman was not necessarily more destitute than the average freeman. In some ways indeed the free peasant was worse off than his unfree counterpart, since his holding would be subject to division by inheritance, whilst that of the bondman's was, in theory at least, preserved as a unit in the lord's interest. Though that much more difficult, it was still possible for a bondman to make his way in the world. Capacity and wealth could remove barriers as effectively as birth. Heylin ap Roger, the villein from Tal-y-bont who was allowed to live at Tywyn, was assessed at 4*s.* 11*d.*, the highest in the township. Some bondmen, it is known, had their own sub-tenants and servants.[5] (All social classes in the middle ages were encumbered with hierarchies.) The upper layers of society were naturally crowded with the free rather than the unfree, but the latter did not wear poverty as a badge. The economic condition of many bondmen differed little from that of the ordinary *uchelwr*. Assessments in the bond vills of Llanddwywe and Llanfendigaid ran to over 10*s.*, which was far higher indeed than those in a number of free townships.[6] Of course, the unfree, because of their lowly status, were more

---

1 See, e.g., ibid., pp. 283–5; G. R. J. Jones, 'The Distribution of Bond Settlements in North-west Wales', *Welsh Hist. Rev.*, II (1964–5), 22.

2 *Arch. Camb.* (1867), p. 184.

3 *infra*, pp. 16, 20, and 36.

4 Cf. G. R. J. Jones, 'The Tribal System in Wales: a Re-assessment in the light of Settlement Studies', *Welsh Hist. Rev.*, I (1961–2), 125.

5 Vinogradoff, *Honour of Denbigh*, p. lxxi; G. R. J. Jones 'The Distribution of Bond Settlements in North-west Wales', *Welsh Hist. Rev.*, II (1964–5), 23. The law sometimes caught up with villeins who had under-tenants: the jury at the hundred court of Clun in 1344 found that a person was 'not so free that he can have under-tenants'. (G. E. A. Raspin, 'Clun Court Rolls, 1328–1561' (unpub. thesis, Diploma in Archive Administration, Univ. of London, 1963), 552/1/10 p. 3).

6 *infra*, pp. 35–6, and 55–6.

vulnerable than the free and their assessments may, in consequence, be artificially high. That would have been in keeping with their economic disabilities as a group. The more substantial *uchelwyr* were, after all, particularly well-placed not only to press their own views upon the authorities[1] but also to defend the interests of the free as a whole. In 1315–16, for example, basing their case on what they claimed was the custom in the age of the princes, they were able to persuade Edward II to pass an ordinance relieving freemen of the burden of taxation where the goods of villeins and advowry tenants were sufficient to meet the charge.[2] The unfree, in contrast, had no voice of any kind in the councils of the realm. Fiscal pressure was more easily applied in their case. Furthermore, the conquest of Wales was a greater disaster for them as a group than for the free, for commutation, which had progressed much less amongst bondmen, was thereafter imposed upon them universally almost at a stroke.[3] The labour services they had to perform, though not so far removed from those of the free as they were in England, were also increased somewhat after the conquest, as were their communal obligations. Their position was exploited in so many ways: whereas freemen owed suit of court at the new courts set up after 1284, the unfree had to provide for the maintenance of the turn in addition to making presentments there.[4] But apart from heavier labour services and tenurial differences – the unfree were 'bound to the soil' – what really differentiated them as a group from the free was the fact that the charge upon a bond vill (at least this was invariably the case in a *trefgyfrif*) remained fixed irrespective of the number living there, a crippling burden in times of famine and plague when death claimed so many. Only in the course of time, and possibly then only in certain areas, did the unfree secure the right to be charged per head and not on a communal basis.[5]

The difficulties arising from their normally weak bargaining position were compounded by the fact that their economic progress was impeded in so many different ways. A career in the church, that most promising of all avenues of advancement, was as a rule closed to them. Nor were they legally entitled to earn a living as smiths or to practise the craft of poetry. Scratching any kind of living required just that little bit more effort and ingenuity on their part. The free

---

1 e.g., *Rec. of Caernarvon*, p. 132, and *Cal. Pat. Rolls 1292–1301*, p. 223.

2 Bowen, *Statutes of Wales*, pp. 27–8. Cf. Postan, *The Medieval Economy and Society*, p. 173.

3 Jones Pierce, *Medieval Welsh Society*, pp. 39–40.

4 Waters, *Edwardian Settlement*, pp. 119–20.

5 See, e.g., Holmes, *Estates of Higher Nobility*, pp. 98–9, for the easing of the financial burdens of the unfree in the lordship of Denbigh in the 1370s and 1390s.

even seem to have claimed for themselves what must have been the best lands for grazing in some areas: in 1325, for example, one Cynwrig ap Gwion of Nanconwy, presumably a bondman, was fined 18*d.* for pasturing his animals on the lands of freemen.[1]

And at the root of their personal degradation was the stigma attaching to their status. The personal constraints endured by the unfree were not always as dire as the letter of the law implied: if a bondman was recognised as a poet, he could possibly, like the thirteenth century bard Prydydd y Moch, succeed in enfranchising his progeny; the lord's permission to marry was probably hardly ever withheld, nor was it impossible for a villein like Argaun of Crogen to pay for a 'licence to dwell elsewhere in the commote at his will'; free land found its way into bond hands.[2] But deliverance from personal servitudes depended much upon the whim of personalities or the dictates of circumstances. More than that, the very state of bondage was beneath contempt – Glyn Dŵr, whose revolt at the beginning of the fifteenth century enabled many to escape from their thraldom, was himself unlikely to have felt well-disposed to villeins[3] – and mortifying to those subject to it: the image that sprang to the poet's mind was *limbo patrum.*[4] The use sometimes by the poets of the word 'caeth' for 'bondman', with its overtones of slavery, may not be without some significance. A Frenchman who had been taken captive during the French wars in Edward III's time by Gruffydd Fantach and who had been brought over by him to his house (*mansio*) in Llanfair in the commote of Uchaf (in former Caernarvonshire) was regarded as his captor's own man and villein (*ut de homino suo captivo et villano*) and by virtue of that fact Gruffydd Fantach's heir, Dafydd, was able to claim that he could take possession of all his goods.[5] It was accepted as a matter of course that a lord could appropriate the chattels of his villeins: the latter's only defence often enough, as in the case of Ieuan ap Madog Fychan, a *villanus* of Dafydd ap Gruffydd Fantach's manor of Dwygyfylchi, was simply to protest that he was descended of an adventitious English family and thus, by implication, was a free man.[6] Bondmen were another 'race' (as Sir John Wynn of Gwedir put it) and though not without rights were yet in a way entirely at the mercy of their

1 P.R.O. S.C.2/215/51.

2 G. R. J. Jones, 'The Tribal System in Wales: a Re-assessment in the light of Settlement Studies', *Welsh Hist. Rev.*, I (1961–2), 126–7; Dafydd Jenkins, *Cyfraith Hywel* (1970), p. 36; *Cal. of Inq. Misc., II, 1307–49*, p. 43.

3 cf. Lewis *et al.* (edd.), *Cywyddau Iolo Goch ac Eraill*, p. 33, l. 12.

4 ibid., p. 267, l. 26.

5 P.R.O. Wales 20/1 m. 12.

6 ibid., m. 12d.

lords. The plight of the unfree was sometimes cruelly exposed. In 1416, well over a hundred years after this roll was compiled, a *nativus* called Hwlcyn Bach, 'with all his household and progeny, goods and chattels, reliefs, amobrau, and other services and bondages (*bundagiis*) whatsoever', was sold to the master of Penrhyn 'for a certain sum of money'.[1] Even in mid-century, in 1449 and again in 1456, bondmen and their posterity, as well as all their goods and services were still being traded like so many cattle.[2] Indeed, bondmen, with their names carefully recorded in some instances like so many items in an inventory to a will, were conveyed along with lands and tenements from one landowner to another as late as 1503.[3] Despite the celebrated charters granted to his subjects in North Wales by Henry VII between 1504 and 1508, villeinage continued in some areas until Edward VI's reign, if not even later;[4] and an unfree ancestry remained a source of grave embarrassment to the famous and not-so-famous for years later: Sir John Wynn of Gwedir's caustic gibe about the unfree origins of bishop William Morgan (the translator of the Bible into Welsh in 1588) was meant to discredit as well as wound.[5]

* * *

The roll is hardly more forthcoming about the number of clergy than it is about the numbers of the free and the unfree. Twenty-eight clergymen, nearly half of them from Ardudwy, are listed, a proportion of one clergyman to about 350 laymen which stands in stark contrast with an estimated 1 to only 55 laymen in 1377 and 1 to 180 at the Reformation.[6] But there were certainly more than 28 clergymen in Merioneth in 1292–3. Those without any temporal property were not assessed at all; those in the commote of Ystumanner appear to have been fortunate enough to have been overlooked altogether; and of the religious only three are named in the lists. Furthermore, it is fair to assume that a large number of persons inhabited the 'semi-clerical underworld' of Merioneth at the end of the thirteenth century – the sobriquet 'esgobyn' or 'clerkin', for example, or even the epithets 'athro' or 'ysgolhaig' in some instances, may hint at

1 U.C.N.W., Penrhyn 219, 220.

2 ibid., 394; Howell T. Evans, *Wales and the Wars of the Roses* (1915), p. 27.

3 U.C.N.W., Baron Hill 1276, 1278; and cf. U.C.N.W., Penrhyn 11, 217–18, 386, 393, 394, 397, and 407. Bondmen could of course be disposed of by will (ibid., 5).

4 E. A. Lewis and J. Conway Davies (edd.), *Records of the Court of Augmentations relating to Wales and Monmouthshire* (1954), pp. 185, 310. Cf. *Cal. Pat. Rolls 1560–3*, pp. 536–7, and *Cal. Pat. Rolls 1566–9*, pp. 343–4.

5 J. Ballinger (ed.), *The History of the Gwydir Family* (1927), p. 65.

6 Russell, *British Medieval Population*, p. 328; Williams, *The Welsh Church*, p. 326.

posturing of a kind; while Madog the palmer could have been an itinerant monk as well as, or rather than, a simple pilgrim.[1] Whatever the proportion of clergy to laity may have been, it was more than 1 to 350. There is no sure way of knowing whether it was nearer 1 to 55 than 1 to 180 in 1292–3. If we could assume that the decrees of the Council of Oxford of 1222 were fully implemented, that is to say, that every large parish (in Wales as elsewhere) would thereby have been burdened with at least two or three fully-fledged priests as well as deacons and subdeacons; and if we could assume further, on the basis of the Norwich valuation of 1254 and the *Taxatio* of *c.* 1291, that twenty-one parishes had been carved out in Merioneth by 1300, the ratio of clergy to lay could have been at least 1 to 127. That is little more than mere surmise. The number was, however, probably excessive for a county with such limited resources as Merioneth. Of the estimated 26 churches and chapels in existence in Merioneth at the end of the thirteenth century, no fewer than nine were too poor to be considered at the Norwich valuation of 1254 or the new valuation of *c.* 1291.

The church was taxed directly for the first time by the crown in 1294 – and that at rates much higher than it had been taxed before by the pope and the Welsh princes.[2] What effect this had on its attitude towards the new ruler of Wales is open to question, but the medieval clergy were as likely to incite rebellion as to support the establishment when their interests were threatened. They were present at times of unrest in 1345 and 1400,[3] and though they did not play as prominent a part in Welsh life as their counterparts in England – Welsh law, for example, was the preserve of laymen for the most part, whereas royal judges were invariably clerics until Edward I's reign – at parish level, if no higher, they closely identified themselves with their flocks and probably exerted considerable influence over them. Inevitably, conflicts must have arisen over the payment of tithes, especially during periods of famine or other disaster, but the parish clergy must, too, have shared their parishioners' anxiety about their common economic lot. To judge from the assessments in the subsidy roll, only two or three at the most amongst the parish clergy could have enjoyed anything resembling a life of ease and luxury. Poverty or punishing taxation may have driven some to the side of the rebels in 1294–5, for most were doubtless very lowly paid. The value of many English livings was small but it has been observed,

1 *infra*, pp. 35, 42, 61, 84, 92; *B.B.C.S.*, VI (1931–3), 356, for 'Iorwerth athro' at Dolgledr in 1326.

2 Williams, *The Welsh Church*, p. 59; Prestwich, *War, Politics and Finance*, pp. 186–7.

3 Williams, *The Welsh Church*, pp. 124, 216–19.

on no less an authority than archbishop Pecham's, that 'a figure to be regarded as a satisfactory minimum income for English livings must be halved for those in Wales'.[1] It is impossible to generalise, but the stipend of chaplains in charge of outlying chapels in England could be as low as five marks a year in the thirteenth century,[2] and they must be accounted amongst the most important of those acting as assistants to incumbents. The income of 'annual' chaplains was lower, no more than about 40*s*. a year in many cases, the equivalent of what an unskilled labourer might earn.[3] Deacons and others might earn even less than that. The plight of these and other brethren in Wales must have been worse. Even at the Reformation nearly a quarter of Welsh benefices were worth less than £5 a year.[4]

Details about the possessions of men in minor orders in the Welsh church at the time of the Edwardian conquest are extremely rare. The only cleric as such who is mentioned in extant 'local' subsidy rolls is Madog *clericus* of Nefyn in the old county of Caernarvon. He was probably typical in many ways of fellow priests elsewhere who served their communities, being indistinguishable for the most part from some of his parishioners, with four oxen, one horse, two crannocks of grain, fishing nets and 'merchandise' amongst his movables and assessed at around the median sum of 2*s*. 9*d*.[5] Madog clearly held land, but the tithe on hay which he and others presumably claimed was important for feeding their animals; it must, however, have been a constant source of friction between them and their parishioners. As for the horse, it was an expensive possession for many an incumbent, but in mainland Wales especially, where some parishes covered vast acres of land, it was none the less essential, for it enabled him to visit outlying parts of his parish.

Madog's total movable taxable wealth came to only 41*s*. A bishop possessed what would be regarded, in contrast, as enormous riches. The will of Anian, the bishop of St. Asaph who died in 1293, has been preserved for us. His bequests included not only silver vessels and plate, and books and money, but also a stud of horses, over 300 head of cattle, and a number of sheep and pigs.[6]

Of all the professions and occupations, that of the cleric was, of course, potentially the most rewarding materially. Only the temporal goods of churchmen were liable to the subsidy of 1292–3, but the

1 ibid., p. 283.

2 Moorman, *Church Life in England*, pp. 13–14.

3 ibid., p. 55.

4 Williams, *The Welsh Church*, p. 283.

5 *B.B.C.S.*, V (1929–31), 143.

6 *Arch. Camb.* (1919), pp. 186–7.

tax effectively segregated most of them and reflected their official positions in the church. A humble *offeiriad* or parochial chaplain might be assessed at around 1*s*. 4*d*. to 2*s*. 2*d*. or, in one instance, at Llanfendigaid, as high as 8*s*. 5*d*. The latter and the two parish priests assessed at 8*s*. 9*d*. (at Taltreuddyn) and 10*s*. 8*d*. (at Llanfor)(1) could have rubbed shoulders with middle-ranking *uchelwyr*, but they were very much the exception. Those assessed over 10*s*. 0*d*. were usually rural deans who, we may rest assured, were from 'good' families, though they remain shadowy figures, unclaimed by Le Neve. Most of those who started at the foot of the ladder remained there, their morals an affront to archbishop Pecham and his co-reformers, as such entries as 'Adaf ab Referyot' (Adam son of the priest) and 'Phelip ab menach' (Philip son of the monk) and 'uxore persone' affirm.(2) Rather surprisingly, two clerics with the title of *magister*, that is with university degrees, are mentioned, the one (Gregory) under Llanbedr and the other (Cadwgan) under Ffestiniog in northern Ardudwy.(3) They may – the latter in particular – have been in the service of the native prince of Wales before 1282 and they may thereafter have been engaged by the king or the bishop of Bangor in some fairly important administrative capacity, but nothing seems to be known of them. They were assessed at relatively modest sums.

The exact significance of the term 'escop' as applied in the roll is not known. It may be no more than a playful nickname, or it may refer to an illegitimate offspring of a bishop, or again it may be a survival from an earlier monastic dispensation. But whatever else he may have been, 'Yerword Escop', assessed at 2*s*. 8*d*. in Llanenddwyn,(4) was not a bishop – though bishops were, of course, not necessarily exempt from the subsidy, and it is of some interest that the bishop of St. Asaph was answerable for £1. 2*s*. 10*d*. for the movables he kept in the distant commote of Tal-y-bont.(5) The importance of their Merioneth lands to a number of religious houses is also well brought out in this roll. The chattels of the Cistercian monks of Basingwerk (in the old county of Flint) were valued at about four times that of Valle Crucis (in the former county of Denbigh) and Strata Marcella (in the late county of Montgomery) and at just under half that of the Merioneth house of Cymer itself: the four abbots were assessed at £3. 3*s*. 0*d*., 16*s*. 2*d*., 13*s*. 1*d*., and £6. 7*s*. 3*d*. respectively.

1 *infra*, pp. 5 and 58.

2 *infra*, pp. 83, 87, and 89.

3 *infra*, pp. 67 and 72.

4 *infra*, p. 57.

5 *infra*, p. 43.

Occupations are only occasionally mentioned in the subsidy roll and even then it is not always clear whether the appellation refers to a person's surname or his calling. This can be very misleading, especially when, in any case, most rural occupations were probably part-time in nature. Is it likely that David Saer, who was assessed at 16*s*. 3*d*. in Gwernefail and possibly also at 6*s*. 3*d*. in Dwygraig in the same commote of Penllyn,[(1)] was a working carpenter or builder? Should one decide on 'David Carpentarius' or 'David carpentarius' when the taxable sum against his name in the vill of Garthiaen in Edeirnion reads 11*s*. 2*d*.?[(2)] Such tools as were necessary to a man's trade were not included in the assessment,[(3)] but could these men have been carrying a large amount of stock when the assessment was taken? That too seems unlikely. Carpenters and *seiri* were the builders of the age and their skills were probably in some demand. Wales was famous for its timber. These high assessments, however, must give pause. The daily wage of a carpenter at the end of the thirteenth century was no more than 3*d*.[(4)] Though relatively prosperous by peasant standards a craftsman was far from being well-off. Men such as David Saer or David Carpentarius must have been engaged in activities other than building and supplying the needs of agricultural communities, but they acquired their surnames from what may have been their distinctive occupation or the traditional calling of their families. In consequence of all this, no thorough analysis of occupations and their relative status is possible. Nevertheless, the Table below gives some indication of the range of occupations in late-thirteenth century Merioneth and their distribution. They have been arranged in order of the highest assessment, though for reasons already given the sum assessed may not be an accurate reflection of the relative status of individual crafts in Welsh society at the turn of the thirteenth century. It needs to be emphasised, too, that it is likely that not all occupations have been identified: words like *corthur*, *mendour*, *welour*, *sipac*, suggest some occupation or other but their exact meaning is not clear; and if one can accept that weavers were particularly numerous in rural Merioneth at this time it is not at all certain that a glazier (?*gwydraus*) or a tailor or just possibly tiler (*tylour*) should be included in the list of occupations.

1 *infra*, pp. 12 and 19.

2 *infra*, p. 81.

3 Willard, *Parliamentary Taxes*, p. 80. But cf. *supra*, p. xv.

4 Hilton, *Medieval Society*, p. 5.

	Occupation or Office	*Assessment* Highest	Average	*Commotes* Ardudwy	Edeirnion	Penllyn	Tal-y-bont	Ystumanner
1.	saer/carpenter	16*s.* 3*d*	6*s.* 10*d.*	5	1	4	3	1
2.	secular clergy (excl. bishops)	13*s.* 6*d.*	4*s.* 5*d.*	13	7	4	4	
3.	telynor/harpist	11*s.* 10*d.*	8*s.* 0*d.*			1		1
4.	*carbonarius*/charcoal burner	11*s.* 6*d.*	11*s.* 6*d.*	1				
5.	*medicus*/doctor	10*s.* 3*d.*	3*s.* 11*d.*	1	5	1	1	
6.	tournour/?turner	10*s.* 0*d.*	6*s.* 2*d.*	1		1		
7.	*sutor*/cobbler	9*s.* 8*d.*	3*s.* 0*d.*	9	4	6	6	1
8.	ysbydwr/hosteler	8*s.* 6*d.*	7*s.* 10*d.*	1		1		
9.	gwehydd/weaver	8*s.* 2¾*d.*	3*s.* 11*d.*	12	6	4	5	2
10.	mendour/= ?	7*s.* 8*d.*	7*s.* 8*d.*		1			
11.	*forestarius*	7*s.* 7½*d.*	7*s.* 7½*d.*			1		
12.	*faber*/smith	7*s.* 3½*d.*	3*s.* 3*d.*	2	4	4	5	2
13.	*aurifaber*/goldsmith	7*s.* 0*d.*	2*s.* 9*d.*	3	3		1	1
14.	(g)welour/= ?watchman	6*s.* 11*d.*	4*s.* 5*d.*	1	1	1		
15.	*janitor*/porter	6*s.* 3½*d.*	6*s.* 3½*d.*	1				
16.	hebogydd/falconer	5*s.* 11*d.*	3*s.* 11*d.*		1	1		
17.	*pelliparius*/skinner	5*s.* 6*d.*	4*s.* 9*d.*	2				
18.	porthour/porter	5*s.* 3*d.*	5*s.* 3*d.*					1
19.	*dapifer*/steward	5*s.* 0½*d.*	5*s.* 0½*d.*			1		
20.	bardd/poet	4*s.* 8*d.*	3*s.* 3*d.*	1	1		1	1
21.	melinydd/miller	4*s.* 6*d.*	3*s.* 3*d.*			1		1
22.	crythor/crowder	4*s.* 5*d.*	2*s.* 9*d.*		2	2	1	1
23.	*sacrista*/sexton	3*s.* 11½*d.*	2*s.* 11*d.*			2		
24.	tylour/= ?tailor	3*s.* 5*d.*	3*s.* 5*d.*				1	
25.	*suttanor*/	2*s.* 6½*d.*	2*s.* 6½*d.*		1			
26.	*garcio*/groom or servant	2*s.* 5*d.*	2*s.* 5*d.*	1				
27.	gwydraus/= ?glazier	2*s.* 3*d.*	2*s.* 3*d.*				1	
28.	alafwr/herdsman	2*s.* 3*d.*	2*s.* 3*d.*		1			
29.	*pictor*/painter	2*s.* 2½*d.*	2*s.* 2½*d.*		1			
30.	*piscator*/fisherman	2*s.* 2*d.*	2*s.* 2*d.*	1				
31.	*scriptor*/scribe	2*s.* 1*d.*	2*s.* 1*d.*	1				
32.	corthur/= ?	2*s.* 0*d.*	2*s.* 0*d.*	1				
33.	telyniadur/= ?harpmaker	2*s.* 0*d.*	2*s.* 0*d.*					1
34.	*carnifex*/butcher	1*s.* 10½*d.*	1*s.* 10½*d.*	1				
35.	pendafad/= ?shepherd	1*s.* 6*d.*	1*s.* 6*d.*	1				
36.	pannwr/fuller	1*s.* 5*d.*	1*s.* 4½*d.*	1	1			
37.	*mercator*/merchant	1*s.* 2½*d.*	1*s.* 2½*d.*		1			

As the above Table shows quite clearly, there can be no question of the continued importance of the carpenter and the smith in Welsh society, a reminder of the classic days of the Welsh laws when there had been no other craftsmen (excepting always the poets) to compete against them.[1] The diverse needs of husbandry and warlike pursuits ensured their supremacy amongst artisans, and all, whether practising or not, were invariably quite highly assessed. But many other specialised skills had sprung up by 1300, prominent among them being the cobbler's. Weavers apart, there were more cobblers than other craftsmen and two of them – if indeed they followed their craft – were assessed at the high sums of 7*s.* 8*d.* and 9*s.* 8*d.*[2] Their skills were clearly in great demand: the slightly pointed, heel-less, ankle-high shoe of the period[3] was worn by more Welshmen than might be imagined after reading Gerald of Wales.

The roll does not provide a comprehensive inventory of all trades and occupations – or of numbers engaged in them – in late thirteenth-century Merioneth. It is strange, for example, that no mention is made anywhere of a *porthmon* (dealer or drover), a familiar enough figure in contemporary Nefyn (in former Caernarvonshire) or Lampeter (in former Cardiganshire).[4] Missing, too, are the expected references to some of those who must have met the daily needs of society, such as the brewers or bakers – or the tailors who, whether itinerant or not ('chwipio'r gath' would have been the curious Welsh expression used centuries later) were employed by some in shaping the linen cloth of the day for their short robes and jackets or sleeveless tunics and mantles.[5] But the fact that some trades or occupations are not mentioned does not necessarily mean that Merioneth society was bereft of their services. The prime concern of the compiler of the subsidy roll was, after all, with identification and assessment. There could have been no mistaking who 'Gwen Vaur Goch' was in Maentwrog whatever her occupation! It would be wrong to assume on the bare evidence of the roll that there was only one merchant in Merioneth (at Cynwyd) at the end of the thirteenth century, since a certain 'mercator de Ardudwy', for example, is mentioned in arch-

1 E. A. Lewis, 'The Development of industry and commerce in Wales in the middle ages', *Trans. Roy. Hist Soc.*, (1903), p. 140.

2 *infra*, pp. 44 and 49.

3 See Edwards (ed.), *Littere Wallie*, frontispiece, and facsimiles opp. pp. 139 and 158. Gerald of Wales, however, noted a century earlier that Welshmen went about for the most part barefooted (James F. Dimock (ed.), *Giraldi Cambrensis Opera*, VI (1868), 181).

4 *B.B.C.S.*, V (1929–31), 146; P.R.O. S.C.11/771 m. 4.

5 See, e.g., U.C.N.W., Bodrhyddan 2335 and *B.B.C.S.*, VI (1931–3), 355–6, for theft of these garments and other articles.

bishop Pecham's correspondence.[1] Indeed it is known, from the same source and elsewhere, that quite a brisk trade was carried on between the eastern commotes of Merioneth on the one hand and Oswestry, Shrewsbury, and Chester on the other, not always to the advantage of Welshmen seemingly.[2] It is quite possible too that the two interlopers mentioned in the Merioneth roll – Alan de Ruthin and Lawrence de Montgomery – may have been engaged in trading activities as merchants of one kind or another. That they are not described as such need not disturb us unduly. The contemporary subsidy roll for such a comparatively important commercial centre as Nefyn in the former county of Caernarvon does not include a single reference to a merchant, though 'merchandise' there was certainly assessed.[3] Local markets must have attracted *mercatores* from further afield, though the range of their activities is difficult to determine: it may, as yet, with such small individual flocks of sheep (always excepting of course those belonging to the main Cistercian houses) have been confined mainly to dealing in hides. The fact that the one merchant mentioned in the subsidy roll was the lowest-assessed of all those designated as working at an occupation may be revealing of the fairly primitive state of trading in Merioneth at the end of the thirteenth century. On the other hand, it must be remembered that much merchant property was in the form of cash and thus not subject to assessment in the first place.

Evidence of urban activity *per se* is almost non-existent, for the smiths, the numerous cobblers, the carpenters, the skinners, and other artisans were just as likely to have been country dwellers pure and simple. Joinery on a large scale, for example, is said to have been carried on at this time in the rich timber countryside around Ewloe and Buckley in the former county of Flint.[4] Much as the towns of North Wales resembled the countryside, perhaps in none of them except the embryonic borough of Bangor, where Sir Gruffydd Llwyd had a stake,[5] did local men of substance have an interest at the end of the thirteenth century. As beleagured outposts of English influence and power, many of the towns were isolated and largely thrown in upon their own resources. Those in Merioneth were not very well served in that respect. Not only were they, as we have seen,[6]

1 Martin (ed.), *Registrum . . . Peckham*, II, 457.

2 ibid., 443, 457; Edwards (ed.), *Cal. Anc. Corr.*, pp. 85, 90; *Trans. Roy. Hist. Soc.*, (1903), p. 130.

3 *B.B.C.S.*, V (1929–31), 143, 144.

4 Jones (ed.), *Flintshire Min. Accounts*, p. xliii.

5 *Rec. of Caernarvon*, p. 92.

6 *supra*, p. lxiv.

much less populous than the major boroughs of North Wales, but they seem also to have been less colourful and exciting places to live in. There were shops at Caernarvon and Rhuthun, fulling mills at Rhuddlan, a crier and mercers at Conwy, bakers and brewers at Beaumaris, tailors at (even) Bangor and Cricieth.[1] Evidence of similar manifestations of urban life in Merioneth is non-existent – which is not to say that such in fact was the case. Some time later, in 1327, a person called William le Taylour held a burgage of land in Harlech,[2] – and the town, without doubt, had a butcher already by 1292–3. If, as seems likely, a pastoral demesne was created and developed by the burgesses in the environs of the town, at Lasynys or elsewhere,[3] his duties may well have extended, as did those of his counterpart in Cuxham (Oxfordshire), to certifiying 'the natural death of animals on the demesne'.[4] At all events, one can well imagine that he was as alive as any of the other burgesses, whose wealth lay chiefly in the number of their several herds and flocks, to the profits that could be made from stock-breeding. Animals bought for a song in the autumn could be sold for a handsome profit come the following spring provided the means of acquiring winter fodder was available.[5]

In the early years of Harlech's existence, however, the needs of the town and its inhabitants were subordinated to that of the castle. It was the castle, of course, which provided the borough with its *raison d'être*. Many of Harlech's taxpayers assessed in this roll had been engaged in the hectic business of building the castle in the 1280s, and in particular in the carting of lime, sand, stone, iron, and wood from Chester or Caernarvon or from the 'free' quarries in Anglesey or nearby Egryn.[6] They had, too, busied themselves in supplying various commodities, such as lime for making a chimney in one of the chambers in the castle, charcoal for the king's forge at Harlech, or sticks and straw for 'roofing the houses in the castle'.[7] As charcoal burners or smiths or whatever they had doubtless assisted materially also in the actual building of the castle. They were a motley crew: Savoyards and Frenchmen were as thick on the ground as Englishmen and, together with the Welsh and Scots, perhaps

1 P.R.O. S.C.2/215/714; S.C.11/767; S.C.12/17/87; *Rec. of Caernarvon*, p. 92; Jones (ed.), *Flintshire Min. Accounts*, p. xliii; *B.B.C.S.*, II (1923–5), 153; *B.B.C.S.*, IX (1937–9), 241.

2 Nat. Lib. Wales, Brogyntyn, 4548.

3 Lewis, *Mediaeval Boroughs*, pp. 54–5.

4 Harvey, *A Medieval Oxfordshire Village*, p. 145.

5 Duby, *Rural Economy and Country Life*, pp. 148–50.

6 Brown *et al.*, *History of the King's Works*, II, 1030–33.

7 ibid., 1033–5.

outnumbered them. There must have been a cosmopolitan flavour about Harlech in its early pioneering days which it seems to have lost fairly quickly in the course of the fourteenth century. One Savoyard, however, Adam Baynard, settled down at Harlech, became a burgess, and served as bailiff of the town in 1291–2, 1296–7, and 1300–01.[1] Gilbert Boynard, probably his descendant, was active on behalf of the borough in the mid-fourteenth century.[2]

Adam Baynard disappears from our view in 1301. Not so the immigrant Englishman John Carbonarius (or John le Colier as he was otherwise known) who, by his industry and enterprise, seems to have firmly laid the foundations of the fortunes of the Colier family, whose services to the borough of Harlech were not matched by any other throughout the middle ages. Already by the time this subsidy roll was being compiled in 1292–3 he was the wealthiest burgess in Harlech in terms of movables. His beginnings may have been rather more humble. John Carbonarius's surname most probably accurately describes his occupation on his arrival at Harlech. As a charcoal burner he must have been engaged in the years after the conquest in preparing wood fuel for 'the king's forge' near the castle and possibly also, later on, in producing nails or other iron objects for the benefit of his fellow burgesses and the agricultural community in the surrounding countryside.[3] For certain, it was he who built, at his own expense, the mill under the castle at Harlech and who petitioned the prince in 1305 that he might hold the same without rendering farm for it.[4] It was he, too, for certain, who was engaged, along with others of the inhabitants of Harlech, in the carting business in the 1280s, hiring horses to bring heavy materials to the site for the building of the castle.[5] That particular experience was not wasted upon him. In 1307, for example, we find him submitting an account for the carriage of wine and materials – lime bought at 'Le deutrayth' and gravel and timber – for the castle.[6] Like William de Doncaster and other immigrant Englishmen who had answered the call to colonise the new towns in Wales he was determined to make the most of his privileged position. He kept well in with the authorities, declared his readiness in 1316 to furnish the castle 'with all his goods', and thereby secured the right to supply 'the said castle, when need

---

1 ibid., 1038–9; and see *infra*, p. 66.

2 *Rec. of Caernarvon*, p. 194.

3 Brown *et al.*, *History of the King's Works*, II, 1033. Cf. Jean Birrell, 'Peasant Craftsmen in the Medieval Forest', *Agric(ultural) Hist(ory) Rev(iew)*, 17 (1969), 106.

4 *Rec. of Caernarvon*, p. 225. For the mill see *B.B.C.S.*, XVI (1954–6), 114. Cf. Rhys (ed.), *Min. Accounts for West Wales*, pp. 40–1.

5 Brown *et al.*, *History of the King's Works*, II, 1030, 1032.

6 *Arch. Camb.* (1846), pp. 247–8.

be, with 2,000 of his own cheeses'.[1] A veritable Jack-of-all-trades, he had the happy knack of turning his hands to any kind of business and making a success of it. By 1316 he had obviously branched out successfully as a dairy farmer and the fortunes of his house were subsequently bound up with the rearing of stock and the marketing of dairy produce. During Glyn Dŵr's revolt members of the Colier family are said to have suffered considerable losses – more than 200 cattle as well as a number of horses, sheep, and goats.[2] Nevertheless they survived and remained prominent burgesses of Harlech until Tudor times. Throughout the middle ages they followed the lead of their founder and served both borough and (at times) commotal offices.

John le Colier's career clearly shows how difficult it is to classify people according to occupations at the end of the thirteenth century. The charcoal burner could be a carter one minute, a farmer or a builder the next. Whilst those attached to the households of the great might exercise their trade or art to the exclusion of any other, most had to be prepared to tackle tasks not directly related to their main occupation. At the best of times only one trade per person is revealed in the roll. Evidence of 'industrial' activity in late thirteenth-century Merioneth is very thin indeed as might be expected. In view of the large number of livestock, it is surprising that so few skinners or workers in leather or hide make an appearance: more likely than not, they have not been identified for us by the scribe. Of great possible interest are the references to two fullers – a Heylin Pannor in Kethugalc, which unfortunately has not been identified, and a son of Pannour in Corwen.[3] If it could be assumed that the presence of a fuller at this time was a clear indication of the existence of a fulling mill, then here we would have indirect evidence of the earliest known fulling mills in North Wales;[4] but fulling was an old craft and was carried on 'by hand' or 'by foot' long before – and long after – the invention of the fulling mill.[5] As for the corn mill, it was well and truly established by the end of the thirteenth century, there being more than ten corn mills scattered fairly evenly throughout the five commotes.[6] Strangely, however (or perhaps understandably), not a single miller, a person traditionally associated with low cunning

1 *Cal. of Fine Rolls 1307–19*, p. 271.

2 P.R.O. E.163/6/38.

3 *infra*, pp. 67 and 75.

4 J. Geraint Jenkins, *The Welsh Woollen Industry* (1969), pp. 101–02; R. Ian Jack, 'The Cloth Industry in Medieval Ruthin', *Trans. Denbighshire Hist. Soc.*, XII (1963), 10–25. It should be noted, however, that Aberconwy Abbey had a fulling mill at Rhedynog Felen in the early 1290s. (Rhŷs W. Hays, *A History of the Abbey of Aberconway 1186–1537* (1963), p. 113.)

5 E. M. Carus-Wilson, *Medieval Merchant Venturers* (2nd ed., 1967), pp. 184–98.

6 *Arch. Camb.* (1867), pp. 185–91.

in financial matters, is mentioned in the lists for the commotes of Ardudwy, Edeirnion, or Tal-y-bont. Perhaps, again, the compiler of the roll failed to identify them for us. Purely rural occupations and pursuits are not at all well represented, but we can at least be certain that there was a falconer (*hebogydd*), a herdsman (*alafwr*), and a huntsman (*cynydd*) in late thirteenth-century Merioneth. These take us back to the old Wales of Hywel Dda and beyond. More surprising than this is it to find a hostel-keeper (*ysbydwr*) gaining such prominence at Maestran, now an obscure vill on the Llanuwchllyn/Llanycil border in the commote of Penllyn, but then a possible stopping-place between Bala and Murycastell on the formerly important mountain road, much traversed by royal armies, leading to Caernarvon and the western coast of Merioneth. Maentwrog, where another hosteler (Wilim *Spedor*) appeared amongst those assessed, had already one foot in the tourist trade. Hostelries were not unknown in Wales at this time, but elsewhere – or at least in Nefyn in the former county of Caernarvon – the person who kept them was known as 'y guestur'.(1) And if hostelries were already a part of the Merioneth scene, the more lowly tavern had probably long been in existence, though our earliest reference is to one kept without licence in Rhyd-cryw in 1326.(2) The existence of both hostelries and taverns suggests that active trading was very much a normal part of economic life in Merioneth in the late thirteenth century.

The highest-assessed artist in the roll was the harpist Madog Chitharista, the sole taxpayer in the unidentified township of Arnarou (or possibly Arvaron) in Ystumanner. His playing must, many times, have charmed away the cares of princes for he was clearly a person of considerable means, being taxed in 1292–3 at the heavy sum of 11*s*. 10*d*., in itself a remarkable testimony to the standing of harpists in Welsh society, amply confirming Gerald's impression that they were held in higher esteem than men of learning by the *uchelwyr*.(3) Harpists were indeed the third highest assessed of all whose occupations are recorded on the roll, though even amongst them there were, naturally, varying degrees of excellence and reward: a 'country' minstrel at this time could earn as little as 1*d*. for his playing, whereas the services of a 'courtly' musician, proficient enough to be maintained by a person of 'sufficient consequence', might not be bought for under 2*s*.(4) Be that as it may, to anyone familiar with the Welsh

1 *infra*, pp. 13 and 73; *B.B.C.S.*, V (1929–31), 145, and XXV (1972–4), 423–4.

2 *B.B.C.S.*, VI (1931–3), 356.

3 Dimock (ed.), *Opera*, VI, 183. For the little that is known about Madog Chitharista, see *infra*, p. 26, n. 4.

4 John Webb (ed.), *A Roll of the Household Expenses of Richard de Swinfield, Bishop of Hereford, during part of the years 1289 and 1290* (1854), pp. 148, 152, 154.

world, it was only to be expected that harpists, if not a harp-maker (? = *talennyatur*), players of the *crwth* (one of them a *crouthores*), and poets would be amongst those assessed. And though there is only one unmistakable reference to a painter – in the vill of Llandrillo in Edeirnion[1] – it yet serves to remind us once again of the importance of the visual arts in medieval Wales. More than at any other time, painting performed a didactic as well as an aesthetic function in the middle ages. The ceilings and walls of parish churches, both large and small, formed splendid ready-made canvasses for the painter to exercise his art and bring home to churchgoers in a vivid way allegorical themes and stories from the Gospels.[2] The painter of Llandrillo was probably not an isolated figure as surviving examples of painting from the Clwyd area testifies. The English border towns were certainly rich enough to attract and support painters,[3] and a school of sculptors flourished in north-east Wales in the fourteenth century.[4] (An Englishman, as one would expect, was responsible for securing an 'image' for the 'chapel of Harlech'.)[5]

Illuminating manuscripts, too, was an art, but it is doubtful if a professional scribe (*scriptor*), whose son was assessed in the respectable sum of 2*s.* 1*d.*, was engaged on such work in Llandecwyn in northern Ardudwy in the 1290s.[6] Indeed it is by no means clear what particular needs called for his rather special skills at Llandecwyn at this time, unless it be that, as a product of apparent attempts to 'modernise' Welsh administration in the thirteenth century, his work increased enormously in the post-Settlement period and carried him to all parts of the commote of Ardudwy, if not the whole of Gwynedd. Might not he be one of the persons who compiled the present roll? Scribes do not seem to have been particularly well paid: the thirteen clerks engaged in transcribing the accounts of the three sheriffs of Gwynedd in 1304–05 received only 10*s.* between them.[7]

The presence of a number of goldsmiths, artists of another kind, in late thirteenth-century Merioneth – three in Ardudwy, three in Edeirnion and one in both Tal-y-bont and Ystumanner – may also appear at first sight surprising, but their art was well-nigh indispensable to a church and society which needed sacred vessels and ornaments of all kinds, objects which could none the less be melted

1 *infra*, p. 83.
2 Williams, *The Welsh Church*, pp. 446–8.
3 See, e.g., Nat. Lib. Wales, Wynnstay MS. 86.
4 Colin A. Gresham, *Medieval Stone Carving in North Wales* (1968), pp. 4–10.
5 Brown *et al.*, *History of the King's Works*, II, 1035.
6 *infra*, p. 60.
7 *B.B.C.S*, I (1921–3), 271.

down and sent to the nearest mint whenever – and the paying of this subsidy was one of those occasions – the need for money arose.[1] Not that this was in any way incompatible with the increasing use made of coins for exchange purposes. So closely associated in the popular mind was the goldsmith with the outward symbols of wealth that a person found in possession of counterfeit money in 1284 was suspected of having been a goldsmith.[2] But of the exploitation of Merioneth's precious mineral there is still no indication; the gold apparently came from outside the county.

What particular consolation country doctors at this time were able to offer is somewhat problematical. Some canny, if vague, appreciation of the properties and effects of herbs, a certain expertise with the knife, and an acquaintance with the mysteries of the black arts were probably the limit of an ordinary physician's qualifications and medical knowledge.[3] To attempt to distinguish between a doctor and a quack at this period would be completely unreal, but the 'doctor' as such had had an honoured place in the court of the old Welsh kings and there is little reason to doubt that the services of those with some medical skill, however crude, were valued in the community, especially those areas, perhaps, which were more advanced than others. Doctors (*meddygon*) were fairly numerous in Edeirnion – one of the five appearing under the commote was assessed as highly as 10*s.* 3*d.*[4] – and are mentioned once in the lists for every other commote except Ystumanner. Nowhere in the roll is there any suggestion that medical practitioners with greater pretensions or knowledge than simple *meddygon* were practising their skills in Merioneth at the end of the thirteenth century, but some were to be found in other parts of North Wales at this time, such as the barber surgeon at Conwy and the physician (*physygwr*) at Bangor.[5] (The latter, significantly, was described as *magister* – which tends to support the view that clerics dabbled in medicine.) Edward III's surgeon did, however, hold the woodwardship of the commote of Penllyn in the mid-fourteenth century, though whether the inhabitants would have gained more from his presence in the commote than from his absence is a moot point.[6]

---

1 Marc Bloch, *Land and Work in Mediaeval Europe* (trans. by J. E. Anderson, 1967), pp. 197–8.

2 Edwards (ed.), *Flint Pleas*, p. 45.

3 G. Penrhyn Jones, 'Some Aspects of the Medical History of Caernarvonshire', *Trans. Caern. Hist. Soc.*, 23 (1962), 71–2.

4 *infra*, p. 84.

5 P.R.O. S.C.12/17/87; *Rec. of Caernarvon*, p. 92.

6 ibid., pp. 190–1. He had had an interest in Penllyn since at least 1328 (*Cal. Pat. Rolls 1327–30*, p. 244).

Society as revealed in this subsidy roll was thus more complex than that delineated in the Welsh laws or as it appeared to Gerald of Wales a century earlier. Some facets of it are clearly much older than written record, but equally arresting are the new and sometimes unexpected features of the social scene – the goldsmith, the merchant, the fuller, the innkeeper. This was, however, by no means a sophisticated society: urbanisation had yet to gain a recognisable foothold, let alone tread the path of innovation.

THE ECONOMY IN THE LATE THIRTEENTH CENTURY

Hardly anything of the economy supporting the society described above is revealed in the subsidy roll. It can safely be assumed, thanks to the researches of Professor Glanville Jones, that settlement naturally gravitated by and large to the areas of good but scarce cultivable land, though Gerald of Wales made the Welsh peasant out to be a herdsman rather than a cultivator. Writing at the end of the twelfth century, Gerald said that the Welsh lived on meat and oats, milk, cheese and butter. He added that they ate a great deal of meat and only a little bread, but he noted too that they baked thin large 'oat-cakes' every day.[1] Their partiality for milk and butter is confirmed by a Flemish chronicler at the end of the thirteenth century,[2] but again both Welsh law and documentary evidence testify to more normal needs. Though not the exclusive concern of the unfree, tilling the soil was certainly not neglected by them, as the extents drawn up after the Edwardian conquest make abundantly clear. The activities of many manors in south – and especially south-east – Wales were of course almost entirely geared to the raising of corn, but in other areas, too, arable cultivation assumed considerable importance. Anglesey's reputation as the 'granary of Wales' is not wholly unfounded and even parts of Llŷn could afford to supply corn for the castles in some years after the conquest,[3] a fact which seems all the more credible when one recalls Leland's remark in the sixteenth century that there was 'very good plenty of corne and grasse' between Nefyn and Aberdaron.[4] Nor did the supreme importance which was attached to pasture elsewhere preclude the growing of corn there. Corn renders, in accordance with the requirements of Welsh law, were general among the free as well as the unfree, even in the upland interior.[5] Punitive raids along the craggy

1 Dimock (ed.), *Opera*, VI, 179–80, 183.

2 D. L. Evans, 'Some Notes on the History of the Principality of Wales in the time of the Black Prince (1343–1376)', *Trans. Hon. Soc. Cymm.* (1925–26), p. 46 n. 1.

3 *B.B.C.S.*, XV (1952–4), 142.

4 Toulmin Smith (ed.), *Itinerary*, p. 87.

5 See, e.g., *Cal. of Inq. Misc., II, 1307–49*, p. 43.

frontier area between Gwynedd and Powys in the early twelfth century had led to corn being burnt as well as stock being killed.[1] In addition to 'great plenty of beasts', a 'great abundance of corn' was reported to be held in 'well-covered granges' in the commote of Edeirnion at the time of the final conquest.[2] The early extent of Merioneth in *c.* 1284 confirms that other, less well-favoured, commotes in the county were by no means devoid of corn-growing areas.[3] Any number of mills for grinding flour dotted the countryside. There were at least two millers in business in Merioneth in 1292–3, as the subsidy roll makes clear. Ploughing could be the subject of contract – in 1326 in the hundred court of Ardudwy a man was prosecuted for failing to fulfil his part of a contract to plough five acres of land in return for a sum of money and flour (*farina*).[4]

Nor should the demands of a society attuned to the needs of warfare be overlooked. The 'war-horses' of leading *uchelwyr*, if not the sumpter-horses supplied by the unfree, depended on their quota of oats if they were to function properly. The importance of corn to the pastoral economy must not in any case be underestimated. The economy revolved around animals. Humans were largely dependent on them for sustenance and traction-power. But the animals themselves had to be fed – throughout the year: they lived off the varied produce of the land, which in its turn needed manure to restore its fertility. There was a remorseless logic about this cycle, about the close relationship between one activity and another. However insufficient the deposit of manure – and where stall-feeding was restricted because of lack of fodder during the winter months, manure was bound to be haphazardly and inefficiently applied – it was still the best fertilizer known to medieval man. Arable and pasture were interdependent and interrelated: the one could not thrive without the other. Even where the economy was preponderantly pastoral was this true. Having a certain amount of land under cultivation was essential to the successful ordering of a stable and largely self-contained pastoral economy. The problem, therefore, that concerns us is not whether corn was grown or not, but whether it was grown in sufficient quantities to meet the day-to-day needs of pastoral areas on the one hand and the extraordinary demands sometimes made upon the economy by war or natural calamity on the other.

---

1 Jones (ed.), *Brut y Tywysogyon*, p. 68.

2 Edwards (ed.), *Cal. Anc. Corr.*, p. 172.

3 *Arch. Camb.* (1867), pp. 185–91.

4 *B.B.C.S.*, IV (1927–8), 157.

What, then, of the overall requirements – and resources – of pastoral areas? For the vast majority, economic life was governed by basic needs. The peasant economy in 1300 still aimed to do two things essentially. In the first place, it sought to provide sufficient wealth to pay rents and tithes and taxes: whereas in England wheat was mainly grown for this purpose,[1] in Wales cattle and oats were the main medium of exchange. Secondly, it strove to provide, at the very minimum, sufficient sustenance to maintain the peasant and his family. What kind of subsistence economy was it? Our answer to this important question must necessarily rest for the most part on the fairly slender evidence provided by the extant 'local' subsidy rolls.

Only five 'local' rolls giving detailed information about taxable movables have survived for Wales. Four of them date from 1292–3: those for Aberffraw in Anglesey, and Creuddyn, Cafflogion, and Nefyn in the former county of Caernarvon.[2] The fifth 'local' roll is a fragment of the commotal roll for Penllyn in Merioneth dating almost certainly from 1318 and it covers the townships of Penaran, Castell, Cyffty, Bedwarian, and Streflyn in the western half of the commote, and a part of another unidentified township.[3] There is no way of knowing how accurate these detailed local returns of movables are. No wills or inventories or comparable lists from this period have survived to test their veracity. The presumption must be that they were not very exact, for though the assessment was traditionally based on goods and stock held at Michaelmas, that is, around harvest time when the granaries were full, the movables were actually assessed sometimes months afterwards. The good faith of assessors cannot, in any case, always be taken on trust: some inevitably were softhearted and others susceptible to bribes.[4] But if seed in the ground could have been concealed, livestock and grain could not (all that easily) and if we allow for the fact that human error and frailty and the capacity for subterfuge are not peculiar to one area, a general comparison of the five lists may not be out of place here. The Table below sets out the crude totals of the tax-payers, animals, and main crops in the five localities. (It must be

1 Hilton, *Medieval Society*, p. 111; Titow, *English Rural Society*, p. 81; Harvey, *A Medieval Oxfordshire Village*, p. 166.

2 See Seebohm, *Tribal System*, App. A.f., pp. 37–45; *B.B.C.S.*, V (1929–31), 55–71, 143–8; P.R.O. E.179/242/51. The subsidies relating to Aberffraw, Nefyn, and Cafflogion have been fully analysed in Colin Thomas, 'Thirteenth-century Farm Economies in North Wales', *Agric. Hist. Rev.*, 16 (1968), 1–14.

3 P.R.O. E.101/506/15 mm. 1 and 2. For an edited transcript, see *infra*, pp. 96–102.

4 Cf. Harvey, *A Medieval Oxfordshire Village*, pp. 105–09; Willard, *Parliamentary Taxes*, pp. 138–41; Prestwich, *War, Politics and Finance*, pp. 180–1, 193.

emphasised, however, that the figures for western Penllyn are not those for 1292–3 but those for nearly thirty years later when for some reason or another assessments were generally lower and probably less accurate than in the early 1290s.)

Area	*Nos. listed*	*Oxen*	*Cows*	*Horses*	*Mares*	*Affers*		*Sheep*	*Crannocks of*		
						2-year	*3-year*		*Wheat*	*Oats*	*Barley*
Aberffraw	69	136	265	72	36	87	41	757	117	296	51
Cafflogion	201	278	767	179	—	35	149	711	98	564	15
Creuddyn	128	127	293	22	37	39	—	548	195½	429	46½
Nefyn	93	87	175	48	—	26	16	205	33	81	24½
Penllyn (part)	76	125	463	—	54	149	92	409	—	865	—

These figures are revealing in a number of ways. In the first place, cattle, the main source of wealth, were more important in western Penllyn than elsewhere, but individual large herds of cattle were nowhere common, the largest herd – of 36 – belonging to Iorwerth Foel of Aberffraw, Anglesey. A family group in Bodfel in the commote of Cafflogion in the old county of Caernarvon was recorded, however, as being in common possession of 90 head of oxen and cows, but that was very much the exception. The largest herd in the parts of Penllyn covered by the fragment of 1318 numbered only 33. The average for all areas was about five, but a substantial *uchelwr* must have kept at least 40–50 head of cattle; and, in comparison, a minor prince of the church like bishop Anian of St. Asaph (d. 1293) or a Welsh rebel lord like Rhys ap Maredudd (d. 1291) or Llywelyn Bren (d. 1316) counted his herds in the hundreds.(1) Cattle clearly were the mainstay of the national as well as the individual family's economy. They had formed a vital ingredient in the prince of Wales's military thinking before the conquest. In the overall defence of his principality, great reliance was laid on a series of strategically-placed vaccaries for ensuring food supplies.(2) That partly explains why many vaccaries are to be found in areas far from the environs of the Edwardian castles built later: there were no fewer than four in the *ffridd* near Aber,(3) an important residence of the prince of Gwynedd's, half-way along the coast between Caernarvon and Conwy. But vaccaries were not confined to royal lands; for example, Aberconwy abbey had its vaccary at Llyn Cymer in *c.* 1291, Pwllheli its *magister vaccariarum* in 1350–1.(4)

Secondly, sheep were not as numerous as cattle in Penllyn, Cafflogion, or Nefyn, whereas in Aberffraw and Creuddyn there

1 *Arch. Camb.* (1919), pp. 186–7; Rhys (ed.), *Min. Accounts for West Wales*, p. 38; Pugh (ed.), *Glam. County Hist.*, III, 85.

2 G. R. J. Jones, 'The Defences of Gwynedd in the Thirteenth Century', *Trans. Caern Hist. Soc.*, 30 (1969), 38–9.

3 *B.B.C.S.*, VII (1933–5), 151.

4 Hays, *Aberconway Abbey*, p. 106; *B.B.C.S.*, VI (1931–3), 265.

were considerably more sheep than cattle. In Aberffraw, men had flocks of 50, 46, 44, 40, 30, 25, and 24, figures which could not be matched in any other area; in the four other localities the biggest flock of sheep numbered merely 20. Sheep were not in favour amongst the mighty either. The beneficiaries named in the will of bishop Anian of St. Asaph (d. 1293) could count on the distribution of only 24 sheep amongst them.[1] Neither the lordship of Denbigh nor the Mortimer lordships included many sheep among their stock.[2] (In the south, however, the tenants of the lord of Glamorgan appear to have invested quite heavily in them, for the lord conceded that a fifteenth on wool be included in the subsidy of 1292–3.)[3] The comparatively small number of sheep generally in North and other parts of Wales at this time is surprising at first sight, for the sheep was a most useful animal, of value as a source not only of wool and meat but also of milk (for cheese) and dung (for tillage). More perhaps than any other domesticated animal, sheep require comparatively little attention. And they are so easy to please. They can graze at heights of 700 feet in winter and up to 2,000 feet in summer.[4] They seem as ideally suited to the broad acres of central Wales as to the Cumberland hills and Yorkshire dales. Their great value does not seem to have been fully realised even by the Cistercian houses of mid-Wales by the end of the thirteenth century. The evidence of the *Taxatio* of *c.* 1291 need not be taken completely at face value, but the wide difference between numbers of sheep belonging to border or south-eastern monasteries and those of mid-Wales cannot be ignored. Whereas Margam, Neath, and Tintern were said to have had 5,245, 4,204, and 3,264 sheep respectively, Strata Marcella had only 110 sheep, Cwmhir 300, and Cymer a mere handful of 25. None is mentioned under Valle Crucis. The only mid-Wales Cistercian abbey with a fairly substantial number of recorded sheep in *c.* 1291 was Strata Florida, with 1,327[5] – which tallies well with the fact that a thirteenth century charter to the house was witnessed by, amongst others, 'magistris ovium et

---

1 *Arch. Camb.* (1919), pp. 186–7.

2 P.R.O. S.C.6/1182/6 m. 6; Vinogradoff, *Honour of Denbigh*, p. xl; Rees, *South Wales and the March*, pp. 196, 218; B. P. Evans, 'The Family of Mortimer' (unpub. Ph.D., Univ. of Wales, 1934), pp. 453–4.

3 Edwards (ed.), *Littere Wallie*, p. 181.

4 Stamp, *Land of Britain*, Part 33, p. 192.

5 *Taxatio ecclesiastica . . . Nicholai IV, c. 1291*, pp. 277, 282, 284, 289, and 293. The point discussed here has already been made by G. R. J. Jones, 'The Distribution of Bond Settlements in North-west Wales', *Welsh Hist. Rev.*, II (1964–5), 29. Cf. R. A. Donkin, 'Cattle on the Estates of Medieval Cistercian Monasteries in England and Wales', *Econ. Hist. Rev.*, XV (1962–3), 43.

vaccarum'.[1] Whether strictly accurate or not, these figures from the *Taxatio* of *c.* 1291 suggest that the mid-Wales area was still too wild and unsafe for sheep-rearing on a large scale. Sheep needed more protection than cattle against dogs and natural predators. Hence one reason for the delay in the development of the wool trade, and later the woollen industry, in the mid-Wales area. (In Cornwall, by contrast, where sheep were particularly numerous, a thriving textile industry sprang up in the fifteenth century.)[2] There were other reasons for the small numbers of sheep, not least amongst them sheep-disease, which was fairly prevalent and devastating in its effects, and the deeply-entrenched conservatism of the Welsh peasant. Equally important, perhaps, was the fact that, although some of the best wool in the kingdom came from the south-east corner of Wales, much Welsh wool at this period was of indifferent quality,[3] not much sought after, cheaper, and consequently not worth investing in: bigger flocks could come with better quality, for pastoral activities on any level above the most rudimentary were at the mercy of the market. Marketing itself in the upland interior must have presented enormous problems for merchants at this time. Even determined attempts in the 1370s to encourage sheep-farming on a large scale on the Bohun estates came to nothing.[4] Whatever the reasons for these failures, all the evidence points to a comparatively small number of sheep in 1300 – and that is a fact of major importance when considering the viability of the Welsh economy at the turn of the thirteenth century.

In the third place, western Penllyn was the only district which apparently grew one crop, and one crop only, namely oats,[5] and that on a much greater scale than in the other four areas. It seems as if there had been no advance there since Gerald of Wales's day.[6] Elsewhere, there was more variety: a small amount of beans was grown possibly in Ardudwy, certainly in Creuddyn – even as late as the second half of the seventeenth century Creuddyn was still the only part of the old county of Caernarvon where beans were found[7] – and according to the extent of 1294 in the commote of

1 Stephen W. Williams, *The Cistercian Abbey of Strata Florida* (1889), App., p. xvii.

2 Hatcher, *Rural Economy and Society*, pp. 169–70.

3 *Cal. Pat. Rolls 1340–43*, p. 272, where the wools of Wales are described as being 'coarse and of little value'.

4 Rees, *South Wales and the March*, pp. 256–7.

5 Cf. *Arch. Camb.* (1867), p. 188.

6 Dimock (ed.), *Opera*, VI, 179.

7 Gareth Haulfryn Williams, 'A Study of Caernarfonshire Probate Records 1630–1690' (unpub. M.A., Univ. of Wales, 1972), p. 228.

Twrcelyn in Anglesey too;[1] rye in small quantities was accounted for in both Creuddyn and Nefyn; and peas were not far less plentiful than rye in the parts of Anglesey and Caernarvonshire covered by these lists. In general, oats was four to five times more important than any other crop grown in the five localities, but in Aberffraw and Creuddyn, where wheat was widely grown, the ratio was not much more than about 2 to 1 – and that compares favourably with parts of Oxfordshire.[2] In all areas where it was grown, barley was less important than wheat.

Fourthly, western Penllyn, with its much poorer soil, had to support as many draught animals (oxen usually for drawing the plough, horses or affers for carting and harrowing)[3] as Aberffraw. It must have depressed the standard of living in Penllyn quite appreciably, for a sizeable force of draught animals was expensive to maintain, but the large herds pastured there made that necessary. An economy based principally on cattle rather than on sheep – and the distinction is by no means of little account – was at once more complex and vulnerable, if more lucrative. The harvest, for one thing, assumed much greater importance, because cattle were less self-supporting than sheep in winter. But apart from that, preparing the land and bringing in the harvest required the services of draught animals, amongst them horses, which in their turn needed additional or special nourishment at certain times of the year.

It follows, therefore, fifthly, that although, of the five areas, western Penllyn was the most pastoral, mixed farming of a more restricted kind than elsewhere was practised there, too, for the raising of oat crop, to judge from the figures, was clearly of major importance in the commote and directly related to the raising of stock there. It was grown not only to provide food for humans but also to provide fodder, being fed to the cattle during the lean winter months as well as to the horses and affers then and at other times of the year.[4] It was certainly inadvisable to let good horses 'remain in the open' even in the early spring if the weather was not 'fit';[5] nor could they have functioned properly at any time if they had had to rely solely on the fruits of pasturing. Even sheep needed extra sustenance when unable to provide for themselves in the depth of severe winters. Exclusively animal husbandry must have been exceptionally rare, if

1 Seebohm, *Tribal System*, App. A. a., p. 24; cf. also R. Arthur Roberts (ed.), *The court rolls of the lordship of Ruthin* (1893), p. 8.

2 Harvey, *A Medieval Oxfordshire Village*, pp. 46–8.

3 F. G. Payne, *Yr Aradr Gymreig* (1954), p. 181; and cf. Harvey, op. cit., pp. 59–60.

4 ibid., pp. 47–8.

5 Edwards (ed.), *Cal. Anc. Corr.*, p. 71.

indeed it was practised at all, in North Wales at this time. Crops might be grown at heights of at least 1,000 feet above sea level,[1] especially in the favourable climatic conditions prevailing in the thirteenth century.[2] Significantly, the poet Iolo Goch in the fourteenth century singled out the ploughman, and not the herdsman, as the chief sustainer of life in his *Cywydd y Llafurwr:*

Nid bywyd nid byd heb ef.[3]

Such sentiments had a fairly long ancestry in European thought,[4] but there is no reason to doubt the Welsh poet's sincerity in expressing them. The team of oxen which drew the plough was proverbially much-prized and well looked after.[5] Crop-growing was so essential that the most unpromising terrain had to be exploited, for grain was not readily obtainable by purchase and trading was a major operation beyond the resources of some communities. Diversification and some degree of specialisation took place only where it was possible; even then, as a component of general husbandry, livestock was an indispensable factor in the process of soil renewal. And that remained true also of primarily corn-producing areas.

* * *

Western Penllyn was probably not representative of every part of Merioneth. The economy there resembled that of Cafflogion's more than any other area, but in the coastal districts of the county the economy may have been shaped more like Aberffraw's and Nefyn's, and that of the eastern commote of Edeirnion more like the lusher parts of Creuddyn. (Breath-taking generalisations about Wales and Welsh life, drawn from Gerald of Wales or elsewhere, no longer serve much purpose; even the division of Wales into 'mixed farming lowlands' and 'pastoral stock-rearing uplands' disguises the infinite variety of local conditions.) Nothing could be gained from comparing the valuation of the fragmentary Penllyn subsidy of 1318 with that of other areas because they are dated at different times, but a rough estimate of the movables in the possession of an 'average' householder in the five areas may not come amiss at this point.

---

1 This was the case south of Pumlumon as Lhuyd discovered at the end of the seventeenth century (*Agrarian Hist. of Eng. and Wales*, IV, 116). Cf. M. M. Postan, 'Village Livestock in the Thirteenth Century', *Econ. Hist. Rev.*, XV (1962–3), 228.

2 J. R. Bray, 'Vegetational Distribution, Tree Growth and Crop Success in relation to recent climatic change', *Advances in Ecological Research*, 7 (1971), 182–3, 210–12.

3 'No life no world without him'. (Lewis *et al.* (edd.), *Cywyddau Iolo Goch*, p. 79.)

4 Hilton, *Bond Men Made Free*, pp. 53–4.

5 Payne, *Aradr Gymreig*, p. 182.

This is expressed in median figures in the Table below. (The figures in parentheses represent the number of those who were recorded as having none of the items listed.)

Area	*Nos. listed*	*Oxen*	*Cows*	*Horses*	*Affers*	*Sheep*	*Crannocks of grain*
Aberffraw	69	2(18)	4(2)	2(8)	2(20)	13(22)	2(3)
Cafflogion	201	2(87)	3(21)	1(68)	2(103)	6(99)	2(47)
Creuddyn	128	2(41)	2(12)	1(52)	1(74)	6(27)	2(15)
Nefyn	93	2(61)	2(19)	1(54)	1(69)	6(67)	1(32)
Penllyn (part)	76	2(34)	4(2)	1(25)	2(22)	6(20)	8(12)

If these five areas are representative of the north-west of Wales as a whole, then a notionally typical middle-of-the-road tax-paying Gwynedd farmer around 1300 might be said to have had two oxen, three cows, one horse, two affers, six sheep, and two crannocks of grain to support himself and his family. (The median number of cattle in North Wales would have risen to anywhere between eight and fourteen by the seventeenth century and the number of sheep to between twenty-five and forty,[1] which points to a considerable expansion in sheep-rearing in the intervening period and consequently to relatively greater basic security.) According to the common estimation of a number of farmers in the area anything from eight to twenty acres of normal farming land in north-west Wales, depending upon its quality and yield, would have been required to support a unit of that kind. If the level of agricultural productivity was, as has been suggested, at least three times lower in the middle ages than today,[2] farms would have had to be considerably bigger than the eight to twenty-acre unit specified, but for a largely pastoral economy these calculations may not be applicable at all.

Most homesteaders had at least a cow, but those with the bigger herds had, significantly, also more grain than others. The possession of sheep made up for the want of cattle among some, especially in Creuddyn where some degree of specialisation may have begun to take place, but again it is noticeable generally that the richer cattle-owners tended also to have the biggest flocks of sheep.[3] When one considers the great utility of the sheep, it is surprising that so many had no sheep at all: nearly one half of those in Cafflogion and as

1 Brian Morgan Evans, 'Settlement and Agriculture in North Wales 1536–1670' (unpub. Ph.D., Univ. of Cambridge, 1966), pp. 228–31. Dr. Evans's figures are, however, based on an admittedly small sample. In his study of Caernarvonshire's probate records from 1630 to 1690, Mr. G. Haulfryn Williams, using a much bigger sample, found that the median number of cattle for the county in the seventeenth century was nearer 16 and the median number of sheep about 22 (unpub. M.A., Univ. of Wales, 1972, p. 253). These calculations, it needs to be said, are based on surviving probate material.

2 Titow, *English Rural Society*, p. 76.

3 Cf. M. M. Postan, art. cit., p. 244.

many as two-thirds in Nefyn. Even in Aberffraw where the biggest flocks were to be found, almost a full third of those assessed had no sheep at all. Only the wealthy could normally afford to be sheep-farmers – and that on a very modest scale indeed. Some (27 out of the total of 567 listed from all areas) had neither a cow nor a sheep: their existence must have been precarious in the extreme. And the median figure for grain, if the assessments are to be believed, is remarkably low. Most of the individual holdings of grain recorded cannot have been sufficient to support a family and it may be that only measures surplus to the needs of peasants were taxed. Not many could provide a full team of oxen to draw even the light plough, so that one can safely assume that co-operative tillage was practised, as indeed it still was as late as the seventeenth century.[1] If we allow, as we must, that poultry, pork, fish, and game (occasionally) supplemented the diet and that cheese, eggs, and milk, cabbages and leeks (in some areas) and possibly honey were fairly plentiful, it is still more than likely that our 'average' tax-paying farmer from Gwynedd and his family must have been living at bare subsistence level. Ensuring adequate sustenance must have necessitated a great deal of supplementary activity like labouring or carting or domestic work of one kind or another. (A boarded-out *garcio* appears in the list for Harlech.)[2] Otherwise a family would have had difficulty in making ends meet in a fairly good year; a bad harvest or an additional burden might have spelt real disaster. The imposition of the subsidy of 1292–3 could have dealt a punishing blow to a family in the median range, for a payment of 3*s.* 1*d.*, though staggered over a period of two years, was more or less equivalent to the loss of a cow or four or five sheep in terms of taxable values. (The actual market value of animals naturally varied from year to year.) Very many others – possibly anything up to two-thirds of the total population – were, it must be remembered, worse off than they were. At a rough estimate, based on the evidence of 'local' subsidy rolls, about a third of the population was not subject to the subsidy at all, their total movable goods being valued at less than 15*s.* This was the official poverty line but the actual threshold could have been higher. Those whose goods were valued at 15*s.* and who were thus assessed at the lowest possible sum, had to pay 1*s.*, the wages for a full week's work for most peasants. It is not surprising that the three sheriffs of Gwynedd were in arrears with their accounts in the early 1290s, partly on account 'of the poverty of the tenants'.[3] And the normal

---

1 Payne, *Aradr Gymreig*, p. 108.

2 *infra*, p. 66.

3 *B.B.C.S.*, IX (1937–9), 53, 58, 60.

diet in an area like western Penllyn, where no other crop but oats seems to have been grown, must have been monotonous in the extreme even for the fairly affluent. Of course, trade was done with the market towns in the marches and the richer English border county towns (how good *cwrw Caer* or *cwrw 'mwythig* must have tasted after the ale brewed from oat malt in western Penllyn!) and the efforts of Llywelyn II and Edward I to create urban centres in Gwynedd certainly fostered the growth of trade in North Wales. Salt had from time immemorial been imported from the wiches of Cheshire.(1) Other necessaries of life were more and more by 1300 being met by trade. But little of this is reflected in the subsidy rolls.

* * *

Such are some of the main conclusions that can be drawn from a study of the 'local' subsidy rolls. If the data they contain reflect the situation in general before the conquest – as they conceivably do – they nevertheless have little to tell us how far the economy was geared to the military needs of the Welsh princes. There is nothing to confirm the fact that vaccaries were formed in various places. During periods of crisis we may take it that flocks and herds could be easily moved from one place to another, for the Welsh were long familiar with the practice of transhumance. Pasturing became a matter of the gravest critical concern only when defensive positions had to be held for more than a season or two. It is surely of some significance that when open war broke out between England and Wales the crown tried to starve the Welsh into submission by imposing a blockade on the country. Corn, wine, salt, iron, armour, and 'other things' were all made subject to the embargo on goods entering Wales.(2) It is impossible to assess the effectiveness of these particular sanctions, but they were pursued with some vigour and hope of success, which in itself is revealing of how slender Welsh resources must have appeared to English eyes. The princes of Gwynedd themselves were clearly fully aware of their dependence on some imported goods and of the weakness in their defensive position. As Professor Glanville Jones has shown, elaborate plans seem to have been made by them to establish vaccaries at various strategic places within their domains as one solution to their victualling

---

1 E. A. Lewis, 'The Development of industry and commerce in Wales in the middle ages', *Trans. Roy. Hist. Soc.* (1903), pp. 124, 130, 166; H. J. Hewitt, *Medieval Cheshire* (1929), pp. 112–13. What has been described as an 'extensive salt marsh' in the Dyfi basin does not seem to have been exploited until the sixteenth century (*Nat. Lib. of Wales Journ.*, VIII (1953–4), 420).

2 *Cal. of Chanc. Rolls* (*Various*), *1277–1326*, pp. 240–7, 254, 273.

problems.[1] But the princes of Gwynedd assumed a strictly defensive posture for only short periods of time in the thirteenth century. Their whole instinct was for following a vigorous aggressive expansionist policy. Llywelyn II was as deeply committed to extending his dominion over Wales as Edward I was. Even after his greatest triumph at Montgomery in 1267, which saw him elevated for the first time as prince of Wales in the eyes of the outside world, he was preoccupied, not so much with consolidating hard-won gains (as J. E. Lloyd would have had him do) as with advancing his cause still further in south-east Wales, smashing Caerffili castle and humbling the great earl of Gloucester in the process.[2] Taking the offensive in this spectacular way entailed more than the building of castles or the formation of vaccaries: it called for planning in terms of campaigns rather than of temporary shows of force; it necessitated the adoption of sophisticated military equipment and methods; it required more flexible arrangements, longer and more reliable military service – all of which had revolutionary implications in the economic and social field.

We still know too little about the armies at the disposal of the princes of Gwynedd, about their numbers, their deployment, their cohesion. Quite considerable forces could seemingly be mobilised when the princes and their satellites were bent on waging war, though what degree of integration was attained by them is entirely unknown. Nor have the changing tactics they employed been investigated in minute detail. What can be said is that two main problems confronted a Welsh expeditionary force in the field: there was on the one hand the daunting prospect of having to engage in open warfare (in addition to the traditional guerilla activity) and on the other the ever-mounting difficulties surrounding the seizure of castles. (These problems in their turn hatched a dozen others, inviting solutions which had ramifications well beyond the military sphere.) The reduction of castles was central to the whole operation; failure there would put victory beyond the invaders' grasp. But the building of castles became a fine art in the thirteenth century and subduing them became increasingly more laborious and costly in terms of money and resources as time went on.[3] Welsh rulers had, of course, long been familiar with siege warfare. Burning, tunnelling, and direct assault had been favourite tactics of theirs in the early years,[4] but they were alive to other stratagems. The use of 'engines' for breaching

1 *Trans. Caern. Hist Soc.*, 30 (1969), 38–9.

2 Lloyd, *History of Wales*, pp. 750–4.

3 Oman, *History of the Art of War*, p. 43.

4 Jones (ed.), *Brut y Tywysogyon*, pp. 34, 86, 122.

the walls of Aberystwyth castle was considered by a number of them as early as 1116,[1] though it was not until the end of the twelfth century that such devices seem to have come into general use in Wales. Catapults and 'diverse engines' and 'siege-contrivances' were certainly employed at the sieges of Ystrad Meurig in 1193, Painscastle in 1196, Dinefwr in 1213, Cardigan in 1231, Brecon in 1233, Diserth or Mold in 1245.[2] Llywelyn II, too, was not without similar or even more refined instruments[3] at his disposal during his campaigns in the 1260s when a string of castles fell to him in mid-Wales – and again in 1270 when he utterly devastated Caerffili castle. The scale of some of these latter operations must have resembled those at Dryslwyn and Newcastle Emlyn in 1287–8 when at least 60 oxen and 120 pack-horses were employed in dragging a siege-engine into position and feeding it with cartloads of boulders and lead, when a cavalry troop and a large contingent of infantrymen were given the task of protecting it, when carpenters and blacksmiths and other workmen were recruited to construct and work it.[4] The provision of ordnance and other supplies must have taxed the energies and ingenuity of a Welsh invading force. The number of horses of various kinds required for diverse military purposes must surely, in proportion to manpower, have been fairly high by Llywelyn II's day. According to Welsh law, the unfree were expected to supply, amongst other things, sumpter-horses for the prince's army. Doubtless most bond townships could normally provide the prescribed quota of pack-horses when required to do so, but when the mules of the bishop of Bangor's lay tenants had to be pressed into the prince's service, as happened in 1261,[5] it was highly indicative of the extreme pressure on the principality's resources.

Advances in the art of warfare could not be ignored by ambitious princes if they wished to keep abreast of developments and benefit fully from them – provided, of course, their economies could shoulder the burden of paying for them. In particular, it was essential to create a more 'professional' fighting force suitably horsed and equipped in the increasingly expensive gear of the time. It is highly

---

1 ibid., p. 94.

2 ibid., pp. 176, 196, 198, 230; Edwards (ed.), *Cal. Anc. Corr.*, p. 22.

3 Builth castle was being besieged with missile-firing engines (*machinis*) in 1260 by Llywelyn II (W. W. Shirley (ed.), *Royal and other Historical Letters illustrative of the reign of Henry III*, II (1866), 150; Cnwclas succumbed 'prae timore machinarum' in 1262 (John Williams Ab Ithel (ed.), *Annales Cambriae* (1860), p. 100). For thirteenth-century developments in the art of siege warfare, see Oman, *History of the Art of War*, pp. 44–6, 49–51.

4 Morris, *Welsh Wars of Edward I*, pp. 212–16.

5 *Trans. Caern. Hist. Soc.*, 30 (1969), 40.

significant that Llywelyn II was reported as having upwards of 300 barded, as well as 'uncovered', horses at his command during campaigns in mid-Wales in the early 1260s.[1] Despite the different tactics generally employed in waging war, Anglo-Norman military practice exerted a powerful influence on the thinking of Welsh rulers. The latter could claim the services of every freeman whenever and as often as they wished within their domains but for only six weeks beyond their borders. That provision was simply not sufficient to meet the advanced military needs of the second half of the thirteenth century – which explains why a new-style 'knight-service', modelled on the English system, was devised by the princes of Gwynedd to enable them to carry out extended military operations beyond their borders.[2] It seems to have been done not so much as part of a systematic overall review of their military needs as in response to urgent local problems. None the less, however indeterminate the design, the appearance of a 'special *corps d'élite*', as T. P. Ellis called it,[3] involved major adjustments to the social structure. Military service for a few became a 'due attached to land' rather than a privilege 'incidental to status'.[4] In return for more continuous military service, certain groups, notably the Tudors and their kindred, were granted lands free from the usual services and obligations.[5] Military needs led, in short, to the rise of a new privileged legal class in Wales, a military aristocracy in embryo, distinct from free and bond alike.

The implications of these new trends in Welsh military thinking go beyond changes in the social structure. Reports of the use of barded horses by Llywelyn II in the 1260s tell us little how far developments in Wales had kept pace with those in England, but clearly the Welsh had embarked on a policy which would impose severe strains on their economy. The protective armour worn by barded horse and iron-clad knight alike had become so elaborate and heavy by the late thirteenth century that no 'ordinary' horse could carry the weight, and as the defensive accoutrements of rider and mount became more elaborate the cost of equipment increased proportion-

---

1 In Edwards (ed.), *Cal. Anc. Corr.*, p. 18, a figure of 180 is given for the campaign of 1263; in *Foedera*, I, 423, Llywelyn was said to have entered the lands of Roger Mortimer in 1263 'cum trescentis equitaturis armatis'. Three years previously, in 1260, Llywelyn, while attacking Dyfed, is reported as having had in his army 240 'equos loricatos cum jumentis nudis' (Ab Ithel (ed.), *Annales Cambriae*, p. 98). Cf. also M. Paris, *Chronica Majora*, V, 597, 614.

2 For details, see *Trans. Caern. Hist. Soc.*, 30 (1969), 40–1.

3 T. P. Ellis, *Welsh Tribal Law and Custom in the Middle Ages*, I (1926), 339.

4 ibid., 336.

5 Vinogradoff, *Honour of Denbigh*, pp. 205, 228, 251, 261, 297, 303.

ately.[1] There is no way of knowing whether the barded horses in the Welsh army were true *dextrarii*, the great war-horses which were worth anything up to £80 or more by Edward I's day and which were considered almost as valuable as the barons and rich bannerets who rode them; or whether they were *equi*, priced at around £15 to £30, which were the mounts of other knights, or the rounseys of the ordinary trooper costing about £5 to £8, for they too were strong enough to carry a less heavily-armed rider.[2] Certainly the *dextrarius* was not unknown in Wales, for the Welsh equivalent – *amws* – of the Latin term takes us back at least as far as 1200.[3] In the past, indeed, Wales had had something of a reputation as a nursery of horses. During the Viking age Welsh horses were exported to Ireland and were much prized there.[4] Gerald of Wales spoke of the country's 'swift and generous steeds' on which the upper ranks went to battle,[5] a reference perhaps to the sturdy native horse which Edward of Caernarvon spoke so disparagingly about over a century later.[6] Gerald mentioned, too, horses of 'majestic proportion and astonishing fleetness' which the earl of Shrewsbury had imported to Powys from Spain[7] and which would have admirably suited the contemporary knight. These presumably were *dextrarii*, but by the time of Edward I they were apparently heavier and were still imported from the continent. And as there was then 'a great lack in the realm of great horses suitable for arms'[8] their price went up. If an English king experienced difficulty in procuring horses of sufficient weight and stamina to carry *homines ad arma* we can be sure that a Welsh prince did. Even the number of *equi* mentioned in 'local' subsidy rolls is very small indeed.

The formation and maintenance of a cavalry corps was a ruinously expensive business. Securing a suitable supply of armoured horses was merely the first step. A large auxiliary force attendant on

---

1 For a useful summary of thirteenth-century developments, see Helen M. Chew, *The English Ecclesiastical Tenants-in-Chief and Knight Service* (1932), pp. 89–90. Horse armour was introduced in the later years of Henry III's reign at the same time as 'the transition from chain to plate began with the application to such exposed parts of the body as the elbows, knees, and shins of plates of metal strapped on above the mail'.

2 Morris, *Welsh Wars of Edward I*, pp. 82–3.

3 Jones (ed.), *Brut y Tywysogyon*, p. 188; Dafydd Jenkins (ed.), *Llyfr Colan* (1963), pp. 80–1.

4 B. G. Charles, *Old Norse Relations with Wales* (1934), p. 162.

5 Dimock (ed.), *Opera*, VI, 180.

6 Johnstone, *Edward of Carnarvon*, p. 64.

7 Dimock (ed.), *Opera*, VI, 143.

8 *Cal. of Chanc. Rolls (Various), 1277–1326*, pp. 216–17, 252–3. Cf. Edwards (ed.), *Cal. Anc. Corr.*, pp. 21–2, 80.

dextrarii and their riders had to be maintained: if the English pattern was in any way followed, there were at least two troopers in attendance of one 'knight'.[1] Furthermore, since *dextrarii* were war-horses pure and simple, other horses – palfreys – had to be used to convey 'knights' to the battle;[2] and since *dextrarii*, too, had to be specially fed to enable them to function properly, elaborate precautions had to be taken to ensure supplies. The logistics problem became more acute, the need for corn (particularly) more pressing. Looting and pillaging and living off the land by no means made provisioning superfluous. It is surely significant that at the conquest the English army found at Edeirnion, on the eastern frontier of Llywelyn's principality, 'great abundance of corn collected into heaps' which was kept in 'well covered granges' there.[3] They found also as many as 50 horses there as well as 300 head of cattle. This 'great lair' at Edeirnion may not have been the only one which the princes had in reserve to enable them to launch their attacks on mid-Wales. But there was a limit to what the Welsh economy could bear. Shortage of fodder, the subject of a complaint made in 1277,[4] was not a problem confined to West Wales. If Edward I, with much greater resources at his disposal, had to send out his officials 'in all directions' – to Ireland and Scotland as well as throughout the length and breadth of England – 'to sweep in both food and material for war' for his troops,[5] Llywelyn II must have been even more hard put to it to provide adequately for the armies at his command, despite having to cope with smaller numbers. It may not be altogether too fanciful to suggest that, other considerations notwithstanding, military need itself generated the drive to south-east Wales – as it may have done to the north-east, for there the lead of Englefield, amongst other things, was essential 'to feed the engines of war'.[6] To support his pretensions, Llywelyn II required a firmer economic base for his principality. Expansion became a necessity; it fed on its own need.

At all events, it seems fairly clear from the evidence of the 'local' subsidy rolls that horses of various kinds were barely to be found in sufficient numbers to serve agricultural as well as advanced military needs. Resources were too finely stretched to cope with the demands of both over a long period. A protracted offensive was out of the

1 Morris, *Welsh Wars of Edward I*, pp. 54–5.

2 Jenkins (ed.), *Llyfr Colan*, p. 81.

3 Edwards (ed.), *Cal. Anc. Corr.*, p. 172.

4 ibid., p. 72.

5 Morris, *Welsh Wars of Edward I*, pp. 83–4.

6 Edwards (ed.), *Flint Pleas*, p. xix.

question; even a short campaign, by drawing on essential resources, could lead to economic stress and hardship. At the same time, providing for a large force of 'war-horses' called for reserves beyond the capacity of the Welsh economy. It could not be done without radically changing its character – or entirely re-drawing the boundaries of the principality. Wales could ill afford an aristocracy. It remains, indeed, a moot point how far the pressures placed upon the Welsh economy by Llywelyn II's policies were ultimately responsible for his downfall.

* * *

The crucial question about the economy of Wales is whether it was basically sound at the turn of the thirteenth century. This is hardly the occasion for a thorough examination of the problem, but such is its general importance, in view of the economic disasters of the fourteenth century, that it cannot be altogether avoided. The few observations offered here are to be taken as being exploratory in scope and the conclusions as being merely tentative in nature.

We may take it that a number of English historians now accept in broad outline the thesis first propounded and later elaborated by Professor Postan that it was the relative overpopulation of the late thirteenth century and the overexploitation of the soil consequent upon it that lay at the root of the economic disasters of the fourteenth century.[1] In the twelfth and thirteenth centuries land had had to be turned to arable to meet the needs of a rapidly expanding population, but the more arable that was made available, the less pasture there was; and the less pasture, the fewer the animals upon whose dung the land depended for renewal. A delicate balance had to be struck between the amount of land under the plough and land left for pasture. Once the 'limits of safety' were crossed, once there was insufficient pasture to support the number of animals needed to fertilise the arable, disaster beckoned, for a starved soil could not support a stagnant, let alone a growing, population. This point was reached in most parts of lowland England around the turn of the thirteenth century – and population began to decline.

This thesis – or 'working hypothesis', as Professor Postan called it – has been subjected to some critical pounding of late,[2] but whatever else may be said of it, it serves as a useful starting-point for

---

1 The thesis is rehearsed in Professor Postan's book, *The Medieval Economy and Society* (1972), pp. 33–9, 57–72. Needless to say, this brief paragraph does not begin to do justice to Professor Postan's persuasive arguments.

2 See, e.g., Barbara F. Harvey, 'The Population Trend in England between 1300 and 1348', *Trans. Roy. Hist. Soc.*, (1966), pp. 23–42; and review by R. H. Hilton in *History*, 58 (1973), 424–5.

our enquiry. It raises a number of important questions for the Welsh historian. Are there any indications that Wales was 'overpopulated' by *c.* 1300 and that her economy was unable to cope with it? Does the beginning, rather than the middle years, of the fourteenth century mark a turning-point in population increase and economic growth as far as Wales is concerned? Are the implications of Professor Postan's thesis, which relies almost entirely on evidence drawn from the heavily-manorialised districts of south-east England, also applicable to the upland regions of the country where pasture was relatively plentiful and arable scarce? Or did the mainly pastoral areas, which had probably not shared to the same extent in the prosperity of the thirteenth century, survive the economic storms of the fourteenth century better than the arable areas, simply because of the different nature of their economies?

Our answers to these questions must, at best, be tentative. There are many problems attached to them. To begin with, the evidence available is scanty, fragmentary, and, when not negative, difficult to interpret if not plainly contradictory at times. There is, for example, every reason for thinking, as has been argued above,[1] that the population of Wales was fairly large by the end of the thirteenth century, but in the early 1260s Llywelyn was compelled to recruit youngsters under the age of 14 years for his armies, such was the manpower shortage at the time.[2] The lead-mining industry in Llanbadarn in the former county of Cardigan was similarly undermanned, for only four men could be found to work there in 1304–05.[3] Likewise, there was clearly 'no pressure of population' in the lordship of Denbigh in 1334 since pasture was plentiful there and hardly any restriction was placed on cultivation.[4] But significant as this could be it is not exactly conclusive. What may be true of one area may not be true of another; nor is it entirely relevant when considering 'relative overpopulation' at the turn of the century: after all, the lordship of Denbigh suffered economic stagnation in the years following 1300 and was affected by the 'agrarian crisis' of the second and third decades of the fourteenth century.[5] In any case, it is the reason for that stagnation which is exactly the point at issue. Evidence of 'relative overpopulation' is implicit rather than overt: in the former county of Flint, for instance, sums received from

1 *supra*, p. lix.

2 *Trans. Caern. Hist. Soc.*, 30 (1969), 40.

3 Rhys (ed.), *Min. Accounts for West Wales*, pp. 390–1.

4 Vinogradoff, *Honour of Denbigh*, p. xxxvi.

5 David Huw Owen, 'The Lordship of Denbigh 1282–1425' (unpub. Ph.D., Univ. of Wales, 1967), p. 143; J. R. Maddicott, *Thomas of Lancaster 1307–1322* (1970), pp. 31–3.

reliefs were higher in 1300 than even in the famine years of 1315–16 when escheats were 50 per cent up on those of 1301;[1] while in Gwynedd in the 1290s there was a combination of heavy arrears of rent and high rents which suggests pressure on available land.[2] The dramatic drop in numbers paying the subsidy of 1318 in parts of Penllyn – from 74 (in 1292–3) to 27 in Penaran and from 19 to 13 in Cyffty[3] – may itself be indicative of the shaky foundations of the Welsh economy and of its capacity to support the existing population; but there is no certainty about that.

A complicating factor is presented by the political changes of 1282–4 which may have been as crucial in some respects as the chill economic winds blowing across Europe after 1300. Here again one has to contend with conflicting evidence. The 'greater prosperity resulting from post-conquest stability'[4] and the stimulus to the economy provided by the policy of exploitation pursued by the new conqueror must be set against the grim financial returns of the sheriffs in the 1290s and the havoc caused by the conquest itself and the great rebellion of 1294–5.[5] The devastation wrought by war in the last two decades of the thirteenth century left deep and possibly lasting scars, especially on some towns. But in one direction at least the conquest did not spell regression. The massive programme of castle-building undertaken by Edward I and the founding of new boroughs could hardly have failed to boost the Welsh economy. The immediate contribution of the borough, though obviously large, cannot easily be measured; the economic importance of the castle, though less evident, can just as easily be underestimated, especially in the early years. Both the borough and the surrounding countryside benefited economically from the presence of the castle even after building had been completed. After all, the castle had to be maintained, and its garrison – of 30 men at Conwy, Harlech, and Cricieth, 40 at Bere and Caernarvon, 50 at Aberystwyth[6] – had to be fed and clothed and provided with all kinds of appliances, domestic as well as military. The obligations of the bond population of the various castelries towards the store (*staurum*) of the castle were for the most part only indirectly related to the problem of victualling and contributed only marginally to solving it. Other means had to be found

1 Jones (ed.), *Flintshire Min. Accounts*, p. 101.

2 *B.B.C.S.*, IX (1937–9), 53, 58, 60; Jones Pierce, *Medieval Welsh Society*, p. 118.

3 *infra*, pp. 9–11 and 97–9; and 12–13 and 100–01.

4 Williams, *The Welsh Church*, p. 59, and cf. p. 79.

5 *B.B.C.S.*, IX (1937–9), 53, 58, 60; Rhys (ed.), *Min. Accounts for West Wales*, p. 116. For some effects of rebellion, see, e.g., *B.B.C.S.*, VII (1933–5), 151–3, and *B.B.C.S.*, XVI (1954–6), 115–17.

6 Lewis, *Mediaeval Boroughs*, p. 25.

to meet the need. Supplies for Dinefwr castle, with its garrison of only 25 men, in 1298–1300 included 70 oxen and cows, 20 ox carcases, 41 pigs, 592 bushels of oatmeal, 33 quarters of salt, 8 casks of wine, and 168 gallons of honey.[1] All this was clearly contracted for and purchased, some of it locally. Similar consignments were bought for the castles at Aberystwyth, Cardigan, Dryslwyn, and elsewhere,[2] and although the vaccaries serving the northern castles were reasonably well stocked at times,[3] additional supplies had to be purchased there too – again, some of it from local sources.[4] In the same way, the numerous castles in the marches, some like Neath or Llantrisant castles, housing as many as 40 to 50 people or more in the 1260s,[5] must have stimulated the economies of the areas in which they were situated and probably contributed to the growth of local droving. Like a modern military establishment, too, surplus stock – 'dead stores' – was periodically sold, *propter vetustatem*,[6] doubtless at favourably-reduced prices, to the Welsh peasant, a practice which may well have encouraged the greater use of money and swollen local trading. Sold also were the hides of animals which had died of murrain.[7] But the part played by the castle in stimulating the Welsh economy must not be exaggerated. With the comparative stability of the fourteenth century, the castles fell into disrepair and neglect. The normal garrisons of even the three great castles of Conwy, Caernarvon, and Beaumaris hardly ever exceeded 16 men throughout the greater part of the fourteenth century and fell sometimes as low as 8; in a smaller castle like Cricieth, it might be no more than 5.[8] A number of boroughs seem in consequence to have stagnated in the wake of this development. Furthermore, even in the more settled years, it must be noted that not all castle provisions were secured locally. Only very exceptionally did Llŷn or other areas in the former counties of Caernarvon and Anglesey provide corn for the castles. Corn, particularly, as well as the best beer, malt, peas, honey, were among the provisions shipped in from Bristol, Chester, and Ireland.[9] (Edward I made sure that even his fish was imported from East Anglia when he was encamped in

1 Rhys (ed.), *Min. Accounts for West Wales*, p. 132.

2 ibid., pp. 134, 146, 162, 176.

3 *B.B.C.S.*, IX (1937–9), 63.

4 *B.B.C.S.*, XV (1952–4), 145–51.

5 Altschul, *A Baronial Family*, p. 246 n. 12.

6 e.g., Rhys (ed.), *Min. Accounts for West Wales*, p. 212.

7 e.g., ibid., p. 4.

8 Lewis, *Mediaeval Boroughs*, pp. 107-08.

9 See, e.g., *Cal. Close Rolls 1296–1302*, pp. 147, 177; *Cal. of Chanc. Rolls* (*Various*), *1277–1326*, p. 355; *B.B.C.S.*, XV (1952–4), 141, 147, 149–50.

Anglesey in 1283.)[1] Only beef and pork – apart from small items of victuals – seem to have been normally procured locally.

Unsatisfactory evidence and political upheavals notwithstanding, perhaps the greatest difficulty we face in trying to assess the economic condition of Wales around 1300 is bound up with what may be called the 'English connexion'. Wales was not a homogeneous economic entity. The whole land was virtually in the hands of the crown or of marcher lords; each unit or lordship they held was part of a much bigger complex with its nerve-centre lying outside Wales. It is highly debatable whether we can usefully discuss the economic health of constituent parts of a great lord's estate without considering the condition of the estate as a whole and the degree of cohesion it had managed to attain. Certainly the Welsh lands were not neglected by the lord and his council. A substantial part of the income of the prince of Wales, as of the earls of Lincoln and Gloucester and others, came from their Welsh estates,[2] and the evidence suggests that individual Welsh lordships shared not dissimilar fortunes with other portions of a great lord's estate, as witness the Clare or Lancaster inheritances.[3] But the economic inter-relationship between the 'English' and 'Welsh' lands – and even between the Englishries and Welshries in individual marcher lordships – is not so clear. The economy of the one was in many respects complementary to the other, if only because, theoretically, the stock of upland areas could have been called upon to make up the shortage of animals in the manorial lowlands, and supplies of corn from the latter areas could have replenished the larders of the uplands. Store cattle, the main source of wealth of upland Wales, did play a part in the overall economy of the estates of great lords. If there is no certainty that the de Lacys at the end of the thirteenth century made use of cattle from the lordship of Denbigh for their vast cattle-breeding farms near Rossendale in Lancashire,[4] there is ample evidence that the prince of Wales as earl of Chester in the mid-fourteenth century brought cattle from parts of Clwyd to the important stock-rearing station he set up at Macclesfield Park in Cheshire.[5] And then there were the cattle destined for royal or baronial kitchens. If more arable had become available to support humans and livestock – or if the produce of arable, by means of imported cereals or improved

---

1 Edwards (ed.), *Littere Wallie*, p. 205.

2 e.g., the Welsh estates brought in around £2,000 annually to the last earl Gilbert de Clare out of a total income of about £6,000. (Altschul, *A Baronial Family*, p. 297).

3 ibid., pp. 296–7; Maddicott, *Thomas of Lancaster*, pp. 29–33. The subject requires, however, much further research.

4 See P. A. Lyons (ed.), *Two 'Compoti' . . . of Henry de Lacy, Earl of Lincoln* (1884).

5 Hewitt, *Medieval Cheshire*, pp. 54–6.

techniques, had become more abundant – the pastoral economy of Wales would have been capable of expansion. Already Welsh cattle had been on the move eastwards from parts of the southern marches since the middle of the thirteenth century[1] and the royal conquest of Gwynedd appears, by the early fourteenth century, to have shown the way for the drovers of North Wales too. The stimulus given to the Welsh cattle trade – and by implication to the Welsh economy as a whole – by royal and baronial and even departmental households like the Chancery's[2] was of immense importance. But murrain took its toll from time to time, especially in the years around 1320;[3] and in any case, markets for pastoral produce naturally contracted as population fell in the fourteenth century.

There is no sure way of knowing but it seems that on a superficial view at least the economy of the manorial belt in Wales was stronger generally than that of pastoral areas in 1300. Doubts have already been expressed about the soundness of various sectors of the Welsh economy in the age of the princes.[4] Policies pursued by Llywelyn II in particular were seemingly beyond the capacity of his principality to bear them. Nevertheless it is clear that the potential of the pastoral economy had not been fully exploited by him. Vast areas remained un-reclaimed, being woodland and waste which could, at least theoretically, be turned into pasture and arable.[5] Furthermore, the needs of pastoral areas were not as complex or as sophisticated as those of the manorial lowlands. The complement of individual herds was on the whole so small that winter feeding in the more well-favoured localities may not have presented a major problem for some households. In addition, oats, the main crops of these areas, was sturdier than wheat or barley or rye and less liable to fail as a result of bad weather. The likelihood is that corn-growing persisted throughout the later middle ages in the poorer oatlands, though the very suitability of oats to the soil and climate of upland areas left little incentive to improve its quality. Being able, in any case, on occasion to live 'off the hoof' was not only more expedient but also more wholesome: meat and lactic products, which formed the bulk of the Welshman's diet according to Gerald, were exceedingly rich

1 H. P. R. Finberg, 'An early reference to the Welsh cattle trade', *Agric. Hist. Rev.*, 2 (1954), 12–14.

2 Caroline Skeel, 'The cattle trade between Wales and England from the fifteenth to the nineteenth centuries', *Trans. Roy. Hist Soc.*, (1926), p. 137; *Cal. Mem. Rolls 1326–7*, p. 304, no. 2148.

3 e.g., *B.B.C.S.*, IX (1937–9), 52, 55; *B.B.C.S.*, XVI (1954–6), 112, 125; Rhys (ed.), *Min. Accounts for West Wales*, pp. 4 and 454; Maddicott, *Thomas of Lancaster*, p. 31.

4 *supra*, pp. xix–xx.

5 Cf. Vinogradoff, *Honour of Denbigh*, p. xxvi.

in protein, much more so than the carbohydrate diet the Midlands' peasant had primarily to live on.[1]

Even so, the weaknesses were equally apparent. If, in theory, colonisation and land reclamation were a possibility and in fact continued in the fourteenth century,[2] in practice more arable was difficult to come by, for the nature of the soil in many areas rendered it unsuitable for tillage. Shortage of animal feeding stuffs must have assumed critical proportions in some regions. The percentage of meadow-land remained, as ever, very small: in the lordship of Denbigh in 1334, it was invariably rated as being of higher value than arable[3] – 50 per cent higher, a valuation doubtless equalled, if not exceeded, elsewhere. Grass, that most fundamental of all crops on which the others depend, was far from plentiful in some areas. Even today, as much as two-thirds of Merioneth is heathland, moorland, and rough pasture; only a quarter of its surface has permanent grass.[4] The pressure on pastoral resources was probably much greater in the thirteenth and early fourteenth centuries. Good pasture-land was valued as highly as arable in the lordship of Denbigh in 1334.[5] Even in coastal townships – at least in Merioneth – common pastures were apparently reserved for winter use only.[6] The boundaries of pasture-lands were carefully drawn.[7] Without doubt, the *hafod* was a prime necessity of agricultural life. It would not be at all surprising if the winter feeding of animals in many districts had to be strictly rationed, with hay and forage being reserved for the more 'useful' animals, though in the coastal and low-lying areas of Gwynedd 'wintering' must have been a happier experience, especially when the weather was mild, for here was ideal country in many respects for grazing animals.

At all events, the success of the harvest was crucial to survival whether in lowland or upland areas. That was the basic, inescapable fact of economic life, subservient as it was in the pastoral regions of Wales to the needs of cattle. The importance of cattle must be re-emphasised. Here was the prime source of wealth, the main prop of the economy. Because of the lack of diversification it could not

1 Hilton, *Medieval Society*, p. 111.

2 e.g., Rees, *South Wales and the March*, p. 180 and n. 2.

3 Vinogradoff, *Honour of Denbigh*, p. xxxix.

4 Stamp, *Land of Britain*, Part 33, pp. 183–4.

5 Vinogradoff, *Honour of Denbigh*, pp. xxxviii–xxxix.

6 *B.B.C.S.*, IV (1927–8), 162.

7 ibid. David ap Guyon was found guilty in 1326 of pasturing his animals in the pasture of Llanaber *post crucem et deffensionem super pasturam illam positam*. Numerous persons were fined in the late county of Caernarvon in 1324–5 for similar offences (P.R.O. S.C.2/215/51).

be otherwise. The economy was at its most vulnerable at precisely this point. The great 'agrarian crisis' in the second decade of the fourteenth century, which struck as cruel a blow to the pastoral economy of England as it did to arable cultivation there,(1) could have severely crippled Welsh farming. It took longer to recover from loss of stock than from loss of crops. The incidence of murrain and cattle disease in Wales during these years has yet to be fully investigated;(2) already, however, it is clear that the famine years following 1315 exposed the shortcomings of Wales's pastoral economy in no uncertain manner: a 'great dearth of victuals' was then reported in north-west Wales, receipts from escheats were running twice as high as hitherto in north-east Wales, 'great dearness' was experienced in Glamorgan, men from Cantref Mawr (in the former county of Carmarthen) were pardoned the fifteenth granted in 1318 and Merioneth's contribution to the same subsidy fell from £566 in 1292–3 to only £227.(3)

But quite apart from periodic harvest failures and disease and other natural calamities, it is by no means certain that even in normal years the resources available to cope with the 'relative overpopulation' in Wales(4) – if we are right in postulating such a phenomenon – by the end of the thirteenth and the beginning of the fourteenth centuries were equal to the task. Sheep-farming on any appreciable scale had not as yet got off the ground except possibly in Glamorgan and south-east Wales so that full advantage could not be taken of the potentially vast sheepwalks in the central uplands. And although there were a number of well-known extensive vaccaries there is some doubt about the capacity of certain upland areas to support a great number of cattle: of Moel y Feidiog in Merioneth, for example, estimated to be around 2,000 acres, it was said in *c.* 1284 that it could sustain only 60 cows; and even on the vast acres of nearby Prysor in the same parish of Trawsfynydd no more than 120 cows.(5) Nor can it be claimed that the less sophisti-

---

1 Ian Kershaw, 'The Great Famine and Agrarian Crisis in England 1315–1322', *Past and Present*, No. 59 (May 1973), 20–31.

2 See ibid., pp. 14 n. 72, and 25; Maddicott, *Thomas of Lancaster*, p. 31; *Glam. County Hist.*, III, 85.

3 *Cal. Mem. Rolls 1326–7*, p. 46 (no. 284); Jones (ed.), *Flintshire Min. Accounts*, p. 101; *Glam. County Hist.*, III, 78; *Cal. Pat. Rolls 1317–21*, p. 266; P.R.O. E.359/14 m. 13d. The assessment and collection of the subsidy in North Wales too may have been delayed and postponed because of famine (*Cal. Close Rolls 1318–23*, p. 19).

4 Cf. J. Beverley Smith, 'The Lordship of Senghennydd', *Glam. County Hist.*, III, 316–17.

5 *Arch. Camb.* (1867), p. 191; G. R. J. Jones, 'The Distribution of Bond Settlements in North-west Wales', *Welsh Hist. Rev.*, II (1964–5), 29. It seems strange in contrast that the 650 acres of moorland pasture at Hafodelwy near Denbigh could support 180 animals in 1334 (Vinogradoff, *Honour of Denbigh*, p. xxxviii).

cated pastoral economy of Wales was necessarily more resilient than that of lowland England. Wholesale damage to stock, through lack of fodder or disease, could prove much more serious than damage to crops because building up herds took a long time while fields could be tilled from year to year. Moreover, on the social side, the constraints imposed by the Welsh law of inheritance acted as depressants.[1] The grimly ironical fact must be faced that had it not been for the frequent wars and rebellions and occasional famine of the late thirteenth century which skimmed off some of the 'surplus' population and ensured that there were that much fewer mouths to feed and heirs to satisfy, the old social order in *pura Wallia* would probably have begun to crumble sooner than it did.

EDITORIAL METHOD

In editing the roll, the original intention had been to identify and supply extended notes on the taxpayers. That hope proved to be almost entirely still-born, despite endless hours spent browsing in all the usual contemporary sources. Fewer than 1 in 200 taxpayers have been positively identified; the remainder stubbornly refused to come to life. The ancestors of a number of gentle families who have escaped the notice of the editor may lie buried in these lists. Some notable figures (including, it seems, Owain Glyn Dŵr's great-grandfather) seem to have been uncommonly successful in engineering their own exits from Merioneth's subsidy roll which makes its study all the more puzzling to the modern researcher. Not all the barons of Edeirnion appear in the roll; not all who assumed some importance in their own localities are listed. It is surprising how few of the ninety-or-so persons from Merioneth who made homage and fealty to the prince of Wales in 1301 presented themselves to the tax-assessors in 1292–3. The sums at which some of them – or those with similar names – were assessed in 1292–3 were so ludicrously small that one hesitates to identify them with the members of the county's élite in 1301. Of course, problems of identification are by no means confined to the Merioneth roll, as the case of David ab Iorwerth Geyrgogh of Kelston (Clwyd) for one shows: though he is said to have held lands in twelve townships in the old county of Flint before they escheated to the crown in 1295,[2] his exact contribution to the 1292 subsidy is almost impossible to ascertain. The very nature of the subsidy in taxing movable rather than landed wealth or income largely accounts for many of these anomalies.

---

1 *Glam. County Hist.*, III, 317.

2 *Cal. Pat. Rolls 1292–1301*, p. 138; Edwards (ed.), *Cal. Anc. Corr.*, p. 207.

Identification clearly is a general problem. So, too, is the less important matter of tracking down celebrities. The Merioneth roll may conceal the names of men who were prominent in their own circles: if Eynon Offeriot, assessed in Penaran, cannot be identified with the author of the earliest metrical grammar in Welsh, it is reasonable to assume that the Legeth Gour appearing under the vill of Carrog is none other than the poet from Edeirnion – Llygad Gŵr.[1] But no one else of national importance is included as far as can be discovered. Nothing seems to be known of three other poets appearing in the roll – Eynon Predith of Pennal, Heylin Predith of Maentwrog or the simply-named Barth of Garthgynfor.

The roll consists of 7 membranes (mainly of about 30 x 8 in. each) and is well preserved apart from a section of membrane 5 which, being longer than the other membranes, acted as the outer cover of the roll. Consequently, a part of membrane 5 is badly worn, which makes reading it difficult if not impossible at times even with the assistance of an ultra-violet lamp. The text was written in two columns as far as the dorse of membrane 6 when it proceeds in a single column to the end. It seems often that the townships, as entered on the roll, follow a set geographical pattern, but that is by no means always the case and it would be unwise to assume at all times that an unlocated township is to be found in the vicinity of the one which precedes or follows it in the roll. No arrangement of any kind seems to have determined which name appeared first or last in the lists but family groupings are now and then discernible. The various total sums at which townships and commotes were assessed have clearly been scrutinised carefully, corrected (according to contemporary lights) where necessary in an impatient business-like hand, and 'approved' (*probatur*).

The roll is, however, for the most part, the work of two hands[2] – clerks presumably to the local assessors – the one acting in the four commotes of Ardudwy, Penllyn, Tal-y-bont, and Ystumanner, and the other in the commote of Edeirnion, an arrangement which reflects the semi-autonomous position of the latter. The one used 'ap', the other 'ab', for 'son of', but both sometimes lapsed into the Latin 'filius', possibly as an indication of the adoption of Anglo-Norman ways by some. Every effort has been made to attain at an exact, accurate, but intelligible transcription of place and personal names, and the late Professor Melville Richards, the acknowledged authority in this field, generously gave of his advice. But difficulties remain,

1 J. E. Lloyd and R. T. Jenkins (edd.), *The Dictionary of Welsh Biography down to 1940*, p. 596; see *infra*, p. 77.

2 See frontispiece for facsimile of one of the hands.

especially over the correct reading of minims and the distinction between 'c' and 't'. With some of the well-known Welsh names, the Welsh form has at all times been adopted, although 'Ithel', for example, invariably appears as 'Ichel' in the MS. and 'Wentliana' (the modern Gwenllian) sometimes as 'Wenchana'; as for non-Welsh names, what appeared to be the most likely – or the most kindly – reading has been adopted; for example, 'Devenith' rather than 'Devenich', but 'Scot' rather than 'Stot' (literally, a young castrated ox). The meaning is by no means always as clear as one would wish it to be. At one point *Kefn* suggests itself when the MS. itself dictates 'Kesu'; at another *Glassoc* when the precise reading is certainly 'Glaffoc'. Improbable as some of these readings appear they have none the less been preserved. The distinction between 'e', 'o', and 'a' is sometimes difficult to discern but an attempt has been made to adhere strictly to the letters used in the MS.: hence we have, for example, 'Tudgech' instead of (presumably) 'Tudgoch', 'Hagor' instead of 'Hager', and 'Candalou' or 'Candolou' instead of 'Cendalo' or 'Candelou'.

The roll has been transcribed in full except that the word 'de', appearing before every personal name, has been omitted. Little purpose would have been served in retaining it and repeating it *ad nauseam*, but its presence in the original MS. accounts for the ablative form of some of the Christian names transcribed. All extensions of personal names are marked in italics, in accordance normally with the practice adopted by the individual scribes. Thus the form *Phelip* – used also by the scribe who wrote out the roll for Cymydmaen in the former county of Caernarvon – has been chosen because the scribe favoured it and wrote the name out in full once in that particular form. Each scribe had his own idiosyncratic way of spelling some names. The compiler of the Edeirnion lists usually preferred 'Groneu' and 'Iarward' to 'Gronou' and 'Iorword', the forms chosen by his colleague in the other commotes. These distinctions have been preserved. Both scribes were clearly familiar with Welsh, so that the roll is a valuable source for the study of personal and place names. Wherever possible, an attempt has been made to identify and locate all place names. The names of townships are preceded by a number in brackets which corresponds to the number appearing on Map C (showing the medieval townships of Merioneth).

The amounts at which taxpayers were assessed and all total sums have been rendered in arabic instead of the original roman. Shillings and pence have not been decimalised, mainly because of the difficulty of converting fractions of a penny into decimal values.

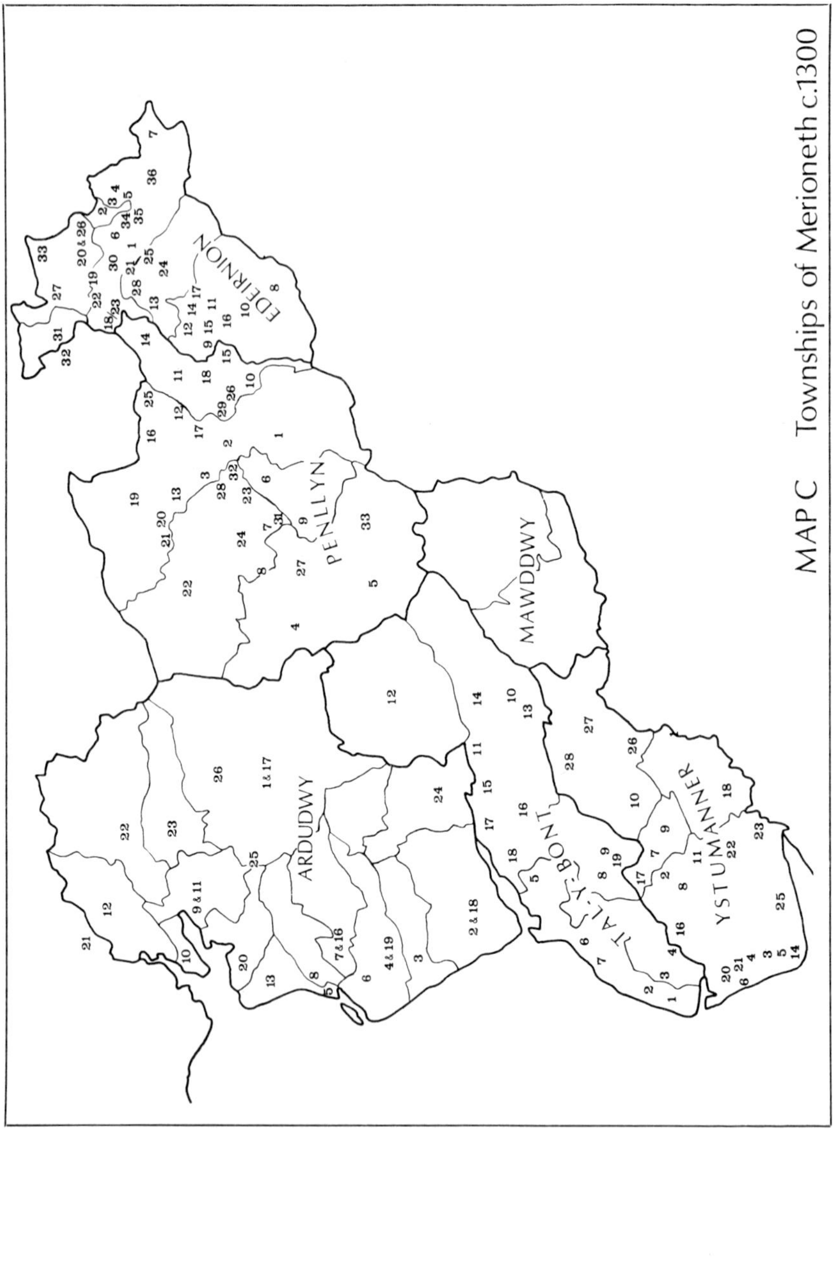

MAP C Townships of Merioneth c.1300

ARDUDWY
1. Trawsfynydd
2. Llanaber
3. Llanddwywe
4. Llanenddwyn
5. Llandanwg
6. Taltreuddyn
7. Llanbedr
8. Llanfair
9. Llandecwyn
10. Penrhyndeudraeth
11. Llandecwyn §
12. Llanfrothen
13. Harlech
14. 'Kethugalc' *
15. 'Tyinmeyron' *
16. Llanbedr §
17. Trawsfynydd §
18. Llanaber §
19. Llanenddwyn §
20. Llanfihangel-y-traethau
21. Nanmor Deudraeth
22. Ffestiniog
23. Maentwrog
24. Llanelltud ‡
25. Cefn-y-clawdd ‡
26. Prysor ‡

EDEIRNION
1. Corwen
2. Llansanffraid
3. Bodorlas
4. Tirllannerch
5. Carrog
6. Trewyn
7. Mwstwr
8. Pennant
9. Branas
10. Garthiaen
11. Moelysgediw
12. Tyfos
13. Gwnnodl
14. Hendwr
15. Cilan
16. Llandrillo
17. Faerdref Uchaf
18. Dôl
19. Llygadog
20. Gwyddelwern
21. Aberalwen
22. Ucheldref

EDEIRNION—*continued*
23. Dôl §
24. Faerdref Isaf
25. Cynwyd
26. Gwyddelwern §
27. Bodgynfel
28. Llangar and Cymer
29. 'Brythyr' *
30. Rug
31. Pencraig
32. Llanfihangel
33. Llanaelhaearn
34. Rhagad ‡
35. Bonwm ‡
36. Rhyddallt ‡

PENLLYN
1. Rhywedog
2. Llanfor
3. Penmaen
4. Pennant-lliw
5. Penaran
6. Dwygraig
7. Cyffty
8. Maestran
9. Llangywer
10. Selwrn
11. Nanffreuer
12. Nantlleidiog
13. Llaethgwm
14. Hengaer
15. Crogen
16. Caergeiliog
17. Cynlas
18. Doldrewyn
19. Ucheldref
20. Garn
21. Ciltalgarth
22. Gwernefail
23. Llanycil
24. Streflyn
25. Cymysgadwy
26. Llandderfel
27. Castell ‡
28. Bedwarian ‡
29. Brynbanon ‡
30. 'Alltuelin' ‡*
31. Gwernhefin ‡
32. Bala ‡
33. Cynllwyd ‡

TAL-Y-BONT
1. Llanfendigaid
2. Bodgadfan

TAL-Y-BONT—*continued*
3. Rhyd-cryw
4. Peniarth
5. Cregennan
6. Morfa Maenog
7. Llwyngwril
8. Nantcaw
9. Llanfihangel
10. Gwanas
11. Garthmaelan
12. Nannau
13. Garthgynfor
14. Brithdir
15. Dolgellau
16 Dyffrydan
17. Dolgledr
18. Cefnyrowen
19. Bere
20. 'Keventeylloyn' ‡*

YSTUMANNER
1. 'Winas' *
2. Pencoed
3. Caethle
4. Botalog
5. Cefnrhos
6. Penllyn
7. Rhiwerfa
8. Llannerchgoediog
9. Maestrefnant
10. Llangedris
11. Trefrion
12. 'Arnarou' *
13. Bylan †
14. Trefeddian
15. Maesmor †
16. Gwyddelfynydd
17. Llanllwydau
18. Pennal
19. Gwrych †
20. Tywyn
21. Bron-prys
22. Cynfal
23. Penmaen
24. 'Treffeden' *
25. Trefrydd
26. Corris
27. Ceiswyn
28. Ystradgwyn

MAWDDWY
No information

* Unidentified
† Unlocated
‡ Contemporary vills not included in 1292–3 roll
§ Additional list for part of township.

Numbers correspond to those in the text as well as on the map.

TABLE A	Acreage	No. of taxpayers	Poss. pop. dens. per 1,000 acres	Nos. assessed at –6*s.* 8*d.*	Nos. assessed at 6*s.* 8*d.* +	%age assessed 6*s.* 8*d.* +	Average	Assessed up to 25%	Assessed up to 50%	Assessed up to 75%	Total	Tax. capacity per 1,000 acres
MERIONETH	392,661	2,669*	33.9	2,280	389	14.9	4*s.* 3*d.*	1*s.* 11*d.*	3*s.* 1*d.*	5*s.* 0*d.*	£566. 11*s.* 10*d.**	£1. 8*s.* 10*d.*
Commotes												
ARDUDWY	129,992	737	28.3	639	98	11.9	4*s.* 0*d.*	2*s.* 0d.	3*s.* 1*d.*	4*s.* 10*d.*	£148. 15*s.* 2*d.*	£1. 2*s.* 11*d.*
EDEIRNION	47,460	519*	54.7	433	86	16.5	4*s.* 5*d.*	1*s.* 10*d.*	3*s.* 4*d.*	5*s.* 7*d.*	£114. 4*s.* 6*d.**	£2. 8*s.* 2*d.*
PENLLYN	98,721	493	24.9	439	54	10.9	3*s.* 11*d.*	1*s.* 7*d.*	2*s.* 7*d.*	4*s.* 4*d.*	£98. 8*s.* 6*d.*	19*s.* 11*d.*
TAL-Y-BONT	63,654	523	40.9	423	100	19.1	4*s.* 8*d.*	1*s.* 11*d.*	3*s.* 4*d.*	5*s.* 9*d.*	£122. 2*s.* 2*d.*	£1. 18*s.* 4*d.*
YSTUMANNER	52,834	397	37.5	346	51	12.8	4*s.* 5*d.*	2*s.* 1*d.*	2*s.* 11*d.*	4*s.* 11*d.*	£83. 1*s.* 6*d.*	£1. 11*s.* 5*d.*

TABLE A County of Merioneth. Commotal analysis of subsidy roll of 1292-3.
*Abertanat, now in co. Salop, is included in the total.

TABLE B	No. of taxpayers	Nos. paying more than 3*s.* 4*d.*	Nos. paying more than 6*s.* 8*d.*	Nos. paying more than 10*s.* 0*d.*	Nos. paying more than 13*s.* 4*d.*	Min.	Max.	Average	Total	Tax. capacity per 1,000 acres
Commote of ARDUDWY	737	347	98	33	13	1*s.* 0*d.*	44*s.* 0*d.*	4*s.* 0*d.*	£148. 15*s.* 2*d.*	£1. 2*s.* 11*d.*
Beddgelert Parish (part):										
Nanmor Deudraeth	9	7	3	1	1	1*s.* 11*d.*	13*s.* 4*d.*	6*s.* 1*d.*	£2. 14*s.* 10*d.*	
Ffestiniog	21	15	5	—	—	1*s.* 8*d.*	9*s.* 8*d.*	4*s.* 9*d.*	£5. 0*s.* 1*d.*	6*s.* 1*d.*
Llanaber	101	42	15	7	4	1*s.* 0*d.*	44*s.* 0*d.*	4*s.* 4*d.*	£21. 19*s.* 3*d.*	£1. 16*s.* 8*d.*
Llanbedr	31	13	4	2	2	1*s.* 3*d.*	13*s.* 8*d.*	4*s.* 2*d.*	£6. 8*s.* 4*d.*	16*s.* 1*d.*
Llandanwg Parish:	48	22	8	2	—	1*s.* 2*d.*	11*s.* 6*d.*	3*s.* 9*d.*	£9. 0*s.* 5*d.*	£2. 5*s.* 0*d.*
Harlech	12	5	3	2	—	1*s.* 2*d.*	11*s.* 6*d.*	4*s.* 4*d.*	£2. 12*s.* 7*d.*	
Llandanwg	36	17	5	—	—	1*s.* 4*d.*	8*s.* 10*d.*	3*s.* 6*d.*	£6. 7*s.* 10*d.*	
Llanddwywe	25	16	7	2	—	1*s.* 5*d.*	10*s.* 4*d.*	4*s.* 10*d.*	£6. 2*s.* 9*d.*	12*s.* 10*d.*
Llandecwyn	35	15	3	2	1	1*s.* 2*d.*	16*s.* 4*d.*	3*s.* 6*d.*	£6. 4*s.* 3*d.*	19*s.* 0*d.*
Llanenddwyn Parish:	50	21	6	2	—	1*s.* 0*d.*	12*s.* 4*d.*	3*s.* 7*d.*	£9. 0*s.* 2*d.*	£1. 1*s.* 7*d.*
Llanenddwyn	37	14	4	2	—	1*s.* 2*d.*	12*s.* 4*d.*	3*s.* 5*d.*	£6. 8*s.* 7*d.*	
Taltreuddyn	13	7	2	—	—	1*s.* 0*d.*	9*s.* 8*d.*	4*s.* 0*d.*	£2. 11*s.* 7*d.*	
Llanfair	55	32	9	3	1	1*s.* 2*d.*	14*s.* 4*d.*	4*s.* 4*d.*	£12. 0*s.* 2*d.*	£2. 8*s.* 0*d.*
Llanfihangel-y-traethau	28	10	—	—	—	1*s.* 2*d.*	5*s.* 8*d.*	3*s.* 1*d.*	£4. 7*s.* 2*d.*	£1. 0*s.* 6*d.*
Llanfrothen	92	34	6	1	1	1*s.* 4*d.*	13*s.* 4*d.*	3*s.* 3*d.*	£14. 16*s.* 11*d.*	£1. 15*s.* 6*d.*
Maentwrog	55	24	3	—	—	1*s.* 4*d.*	9*s.* 9*d.*	3*s.* 4*d.*	£9. 3*s.* 10*d.*	£1. 3*s.* 8*d.*
Penrhyndeudraeth	57	22	3	1	—	1*s.* 1*d.*	12*s.* 11*d.*	3*s.* 4*d.*	£9. 11*s.* 11*d.*	£7. 2*s.* 6*d.*
Trawsfynydd	105	65	23	8	3	1*s.* 5*d.*	19*s.* 2*d.*	4*s.* 10*d.*	£25. 5*s.* 8*d.*	15*s.* 10*d.*
Unidentified:										
Kethugalc	14	3	1	—	—	1*s.* 4*d.*	9*s.* 4*d.*	2*s.* 11*d.*	£2. 1*s.* 6*d.*	
Tyinmeyron	6	2	—	—	—	1*s.* 4*d.*	5*s.* 8*d.*	2*s.* 9*d.*	16*s.* 6*d.*	
Assessors	5	4	2	2	—	3*s.* 3*d.*	10*s.* 2*d.*	6*s.* 10*d.*	£1. 14*s.* 2*d.*	

TABLE B Commote of Ardudwy. Local analysis of subsidy roll of 1292–3.

TABLE C	No. of taxpayers	Nos. paying more than 3s. 4d.	6s. 8d.	10s. 0d.	13s. 4d.	Min.	Max.	Average	Total	Tax capacity per 1,000 acres
Commote of EDEIRNION	519	263	86	37	17	1*s.* 0*d.*	23*s.* 11*d.*	4*s.* 5*d.*	£114. 4*s.* 6*d.*	£2. 8*s.* 2*d.*
Betws Gwerful Goch Parish:	17	14	10	2	2	1*s.* 8*d.*	15*s.* 0*d.*	7*s.* 0*d.*	£5. 19*s.* 4*d.*	£2. 13*s.* 0*d.*
Pencraig	17	14	10	2	2	1*s.* 8*d.*	15*s.* 0*d.*	7*s.* 0*d.*	£5. 19*s.* 4*d.*	
Corwen Parish:	164	98	23	8	—	1*s.* 1*d.*	12*s.* 5*d.*	4*s.* 4*d.*	£35. 10*s.* 4*d.*	£2. 7*s.* 4*d.*
Aberalwen	8	5	4	1	—	1*s.* 5*d.*	10*s.* 8*d.*	5*s.* 9*d.*	£2. 6*s.* 1*d.*	
Bodorlas	11	7	1	1	—	1*s.* 6*d.*	12*s.* 1*d.*	4*s.* 3*d.*	£2. 7*s.* 6*d.*	
Carrog	15	6	—	—	—	1*s.* 9*d.*	6*s.* 4*d.*	3*s.* 5*d.*	£2. 11*s.* 5*d.*	
Corwen	24	12	3	1	—	1*s.* 2*d.*	10*s.* 2*d.*	4*s.* 0*d.*	£4. 9*s.* 8*d.*	
Dôl	20	15	2	1	—	1*s.* 5*d.*	12*s.* 5*d.*	5*s.* 0*d.*	£4. 19*s.* 10*d.*	
Llygadog	6	5	2	1	—	1*s.* 11*d.*	10*s.* 9*d.*	6*s.* 5*d.*	£1. 18*s.* 8*d.*	
Mwstwr	20	11	3	1	—	1*s.* 8*d.*	11*s.* 6*d.*	4*s.* 2*d.*	£4. 3*s.* 9*d.*	
Rug	4	4	1	—	—	3*s.* 4*d.*	7*s.* 0*d.*	4*s.* 11*d.*	19*s.* 9*d.*	
Tirllannerch	27	17	4	2	—	1*s.* 2*d.*	12*s.* 4*d.*	4*s.* 8*d.*	£6. 6*s.* 10*d.*	
Trewyn	24	15	2	—	—	1*s.* 1*d.*	8*s.* 4*d.*	3*s.* 9*d.*	£4. 10*s.* 4*d.*	
Ucheldref	5	1	1	—	—	1*s.* 10*d.*	7*s.* 1*d.*	3*s.* 3*d.*	16*s.* 6*d.*	
Gwyddelwern Parish:	67	31	9	4	1	1*s.* 0*d.*	13*s.* 4*d.*	4*s.* 2*d.*	£14. 1*s.* 3*d.*	£2. 3*s.* 3*d.*
Bodgynfel	8	3	1	—	—	1*s.* 4*d.*	9*s.* 5*d.*	3*s.* 11*d.*	£1. 11*s.* 8*d.*	
Gwyddelwern	53	26	8	4	1	1*s.* 0*d.*	13*s.* 4*d.*	4*s.* 5*d.*	£11. 13*s.* 5*d.*	
Llanaelhaearn	6	2	—	—	—	1*s.* 5*d.*	4*s.* 6*d.*	2*s.* 8*d.*	16*s.* 2*d.*	
Llandrillo Parish:	127	61	24	13	6	1*s.* 1*d.*	18*s.* 2*d.*	4*s.* 6*d.*	£28. 13*s.* 6*d.*	£1. 16*s.* 0*d.*
Branas	25	12	2	1	—	1*s.* 6*d.*	12*s.* 6*d.*	3*s.* 11*d.*	£4. 18*s.* 0*d.*	
Cilan	9	6	1	—	—	1*s.* 10*d.*	8*s.* 6*d.*	4*s.* 3*d.*	£1. 18*s.* 2*d.*	
Garthiaen	16	8	3	2	—	1*s.* 8*d.*	12*s.* 3*d.*	4*s.* 7*d.*	£3. 13*s.* 9*d.*	
Hendwr	5	4	3	3	3	1*s.* 8*d.*	18*s.* 2*d.*	11*s.* 7*d.*	£2. 18*s.* 0*d.*	
Llandrillo	8	2	—	—	—	1*s.* 1*d.*	5*s.* 0*d.*	2*s.* 8*d.*	£1. 1*s.* 1*d.*	
Maerdref Isaf	19	7	1	—	—	1*s.* 5*d.*	7*s.* 8*d.*	3*s.* 4*d.*	£3. 3*s.* 1*d.*	
Maerdref Uchaf	14	4	1	1	1	1*s.* 2*d.*	14*s.* 10*d.*	3*s.* 4*d.*	£2. 6*s.* 5*d.*	
Moelysgediw	4	2	1	—	—	1*s.* 4*d.*	8*s.* 11*d.*	4*s.* 2*d.*	16*s.* 8*d.*	
Pennant	23	14	11	6	2	1*s.* 4*d.*	14*s.* 4*d.*	6*s.* 2*d.*	£7. 2*s.* 5*d.*	
Tyfos	4	2	1	—	—	2*s.* 0*d.*	7*s.* 0*d.*	3*s.* 11*d.*	15*s.* 11*d.*	
Llanfihangel Glyn Myfyr Parish:	11	6	1	—	—	1*s.* 2*d.*	9*s.* 4*d.*	3*s.* 10*d.*	£2. 2*s.* 4*d.*	
Llanfihangel	11	6	1	—	—	1*s.* 2*d.*	9*s.* 4*d.*	3*s.* 10*d.*	£2. 2*s.* 4*d.*	
Llangar Parish:	79	31	9	5	4	1*s.* 1*d.*	23*s.* 11*d.*	3*s.* 11*d.*	£15. 13*s.* 0*d.*	£2. 4*s.* 8*d.*
Cynwyd	45	19	5	3	2	1*s.* 1*d.*	23*s.* 11*d.*	3*s.* 4*d.*	£9. 2*s.* 0*d.*	
Gwnnodl	16	5	2	1	1	1*s.* 1*d.*	14*s.* 0*d.*	3*s.* 6*d.*	£2. 16*s.* 10*d.*	
Llangar & Cymer	18	7	2	1	1	1*s.* 5*d.*	15*s.* 7*d.*	4*s.* 1*d.*	£3. 14*s.* 2*d.*	
Llansanffraid Glyndyfrdwy Parish:	12	5	—	—	—	1*s.* 2*d.*	5*s.* 9*d.*	2*s.* 10*d.*	£1. 14*s.* 5*d.*	£2. 11*s.* 0*d.*
Llansanffraid	12	5	—	—	—	1*s.* 2*d.*	5*s.* 9*d.*	2*s.* 10*d.*	£1. 14*s.* 5*d.*	
Llanyblodwel Parish (part):										
Abertanat (*now* co. Salop)	26	4	—	—	—	1*s.* 0*d.*	4*s.* 6*d.*	2*s.* 1*d.*	£2. 14*s.* 11*d.*	
Unidentified – Brithdir	9	6	3	1	—	1*s.* 0*d.*	11*s.* 0*d.*	5*s.* 2*d.*	£2. 6*s.* 10*d.*	
Unnamed	1	1	1	1	1	21*s.* 1*d.*	21*s.* 1*d.*	21*s.* 1*d.*	£1. 1*s.* 1*d.*	
Assessors	6	6	6	3	3	7*s.* 5*d.*	19*s.* 2*d.*	11*s.* 10*d.*	£3. 10*s.* 11*d.*	

TABLE C Commote of Edeirnion. Local analysis of subsidy roll of 1292–3.

TABLE D	No. of taxpayers	Nos. paying more than 3*s*. 4*d*.	6*s*. 8*d*.	10*s*. 0*d*.	13*s*. 4*d*.	Min.	Max.	Average	Total	Tax. capacity per 1,000 acres
Commote of PENLLYN	493	203	54	22	14	1*s*. 0*d*.	30*s*. 0*d*.	3*s*. 11*d*.	£98. 8*s*. 6*d*.	19*s*. 11*d*.
Llandderfel Parish:	84	24	5	1	—	1*s*. 0*d*.	10*s*. 7*d*.	2*s*. 10*d*.	£11. 13*s*. 10*d*.	£1. 8*s*. 0*d*.
Crogen	5	2	—	—	—	1*s*. 2*d*.	5*s*. 0*d*.	2*s*. 10*d*.	14*s*. 5*d*.	
Cymysgadwy	9	8	3	1	—	2*s*. 11*d*.	10*s*. 7*d*.	5*s*. 9*d*.	£2. 12*s*. 0*d*.	
Doldrewyn	10	1	—	—	—	1*s*. 3*d*.	3*s*. 6*d*.	2*s*. 2*d*.	£1. 1*s*. 9*d*.	
Hengaer	10	1	—	—	—	1*s*. 4*d*.	3*s*. 6*d*.	2*s*. 5*d*.	£1. 4*s*. 10*d*.	
Llandderfel	18	5	—	—	—	1*s*. 0*d*.	4*s*. 7*d*.	2*s*. 4*d*.	£2. 1*s*. 9*d*.	
Nanffreuar	16	4	1	—	—	1*s*. 0*d*.	6*s*. 8*d*.	2*s*. 4*d*.	£1. 19*s*. 2*d*.	
Selwrn	16	3	1	—	—	1*s*. 3*d*.	8*s*. 2*d*.	2*s*. 5*d*.	£1. 19*s*. 9*d*.	
Llanfor Parish:	179	79	20	5	1	1*s*. 0*d*.	15*s*. 5*d*.	3*s*. 9*d*.	£33. 6*s*. 2*d*.	£1. 0*s*. 2*d*.
Ciltalgarth	19	11	3	1	—	1*s*. 0*d*.	11*s*. 10*d*.	3*s*. 11*d*.	£3. 14*s*. 8*d*.	
Cynlas	9	5	1	—	—	1*s*. 1*d*.	8*s*. 3*d*.	3*s*. 7*d*.	£1. 12*s*. 6*d*.	
Garn	2	2	—	—	—	4*s*. 10*d*.	5*s*. 3*d*.	5*s*. 0*d*.	10*s*. 1*d*.	
Llaethgwm	7	3	1	—	—	1*s*. 1*d*.	8*s*. 4*d*.	3*s*. 11*d*.	£1. 7*s*. 9*d*.	
Llanfor	34	9	1	—	—	1*s*. 0*d*.	10*s*. 8*d*.	2*s*. 10*d*.	£4. 17*s*. 3*d*.	
Nantlleidiog	17	9	2	—	—	1*s*. 3*d*.	8*s*. 9*d*.	3*s*. 6*d*.	£3. 2*s*. 7*d*.	
Penmaen	17	8	3	—	—	1*s*. 1*d*.	8*s*. 4*d*.	3*s*. 5*d*.	£2. 18*s*. 3*d*.	
[Rhywedog?]	64	28	8	4	1	1*s*. 0*d*.	15*s*. 5*d*.	4*s*. 2*d*.	£13. 7*s*. 8*d*.	
Ucheldref	10	4	1	—	—	1*s*. 4*d*.	6*s*. 9*d*.	3*s*. 6*d*.	£1. 15*s*. 5*d*.	
Llangywer Parish:	27	11	3	1	—	1*s*. 0*d*.	11*s*. 4*d*.	3*s*. 8*d*.	£5. 2*s*. 8*d*.	14*s*. 7*d*.
Dwygraig	16	6	2	1	—	1*s*. 0*d*.	11*s*. 4*d*.	4*s*. 1*d*.	£3. 6*s*. 3*d*.	
Llangywer	11	5	1	—	—	1*s*. 0*d*.	8*s*. 3*d*.	3*s*. 3*d*.	£1. 16*s*. 5*d*.	
Llanuwchllyn Parish:	104	44	10	6	6	1*s*. 1*d*.	30*s*. 0*d*.	4*s*. 5*d*.	£22. 7*s*. 6*d*.	15*s*. 11*d*.
Cynllwyd *or* Caergeiliog	3	2	1	—	—	2*s*. 6*d*.	7*s*. 9*d*.	4*s*. 7*d*.	13*s*. 9*d*.	
Penaran	74	29	5	3	3	1*s*. 1*d*.	24*s*. 8*d*.	3*s*. 8*d*.	£14. 2*s*. 0*d*.	
Pennant-lliw	27	13	4	3	3	1*s*. 1*d*.	30*s*. 0*d*.	5*s*. 7*d*.	£7. 11*s*. 9*d*.	
Llanycil Parish:	93	39	12	6	5	1*s*. 0*d*.	28*s*. 2*d*.	3*s*. 10*d*.	£18. 7*s*. 5*d*.	17*s*. 0*d*.
Cyffty	19	7	2	1	1	1*s*. 0*d*.	14*s*. 8*d*.	3*s*. 5*d*.	£3. 5*s*. 3*d*.	
Gwernefail	40	17	4	3	3	1*s*. 1*d*.	28*s*. 2*d*.	4*s*. 3*d*.	£8. 10*s*. 11*d*.	
Llanycil	7	3	2	—	—	1*s*. 10*d*.	8*s*. 7*d*.	3*s*. 11*d*.	£1. 7*s*. 9*d*.	
Maestran	18	8	3	1	1	1*s*. 1*d*.	13*s*. 4*d*.	3*s*. 10*d*.	£3. 9*s*. 9*d*.	
Streflyn	9	4	1	1	—	1*s*. 4*d*.	11*s*. 7*d*.	3*s*. 9*d*.	£1. 13*s*. 9*d*.	
Assessors	6	6	4	3	2	5*s*. 1*d*.	23*s*. 7*d*.	12*s*. 5*d*.	£3. 14*s*. 9*d*.	

TABLE D Commote of Penllyn. Local analysis of subsidy roll of 1292–3.

TABLE E	No. of taxpayers	Nos. paying more than 3*s.* 4*d.*	6*s.* 8*d.*	10*s.* 0*d.*	13*s.* 4*d.*	Min.	Max.	Average	Total	Tax. capacity per 1,000 acres
Commote of TAL-Y-BONT	523	269	100	38	13	1*s.* 0*d.*	36*s.* 0*d.*	4*s.* 8*d.*	£122. 2*s.* 2*d.*	£1. 18*s.* 4*d.*
Brithdir & Dolgellau Parishes:	154	76	27	6	3	1*s.* 2*d.*	19*s.* 4*d.*	4*s.* 2*d.*	£32. 7*s.* 11*d.*	£1. 5*s.* 6*d.*
Brithdir	41	20	11	1	—	1*s.* 2*d.*	10*s.* 3*d.*	4*s.* 2*d.*	£8. 17*s.* 5*d.*	
Cefnyrowen	10	7	2	1	1	1*s.* 11*d.*	14*s.* 8*d.*	5*s.* 0*d.*	£2. 10*s.* 5*d.*	
Dolgellau	3	—	—	—	—	1*s.* 8*d.*	2*s.* 4*d.*	1*s.* 11*d.*	5*s.* 9*d.*	
Dolgledr	21	13	4	—	—	1*s.* 2*d.*	9*s.* 7*d.*	4*s.* 3*d.*	£4. 8*s.* 9*d.*	
[Dyffrydan?]	20	14	3	1	1	1*s.* 4*d.*	19*s.* 4*d.*	5*s.* 3*d.*	£5. 5*s.* 4*d.*	
Garthgynfor	34	12	6	3	1	1*s.* 3*d.*	17*s.* 3*d.*	4*s.* 1*d.*	£6. 19*s.* 6*d.*	
Garthmaelan	22	7	1	—	—	1*s.* 3*d.*	7*s.* 4*d.*	2*s.* 11*d.*	£3. 4*s.* 8*d.*	
Gwanas	3	3	—	—	—	3*s.* 8*d.*	6*s.* 6*d.*	5*s.* 4*d.*	16*s.* 1*d.*	
Llanegryn Parish:	108	51	14	6	2	1*s.* 0*d.*	18*s.* 3*d.*	3*s.* 11*d.*	£21. 8*s.* 2*d.*	£3. 5*s.* 10*d.*
Peniarth	62	31	10	5	2	1*s.* 0*d.*	18*s.* 3*d.*	4*s.* 3*d.*	£13. 4*s.* 8*d.*	
Rhyd-cryw	46	20	4	1	—	1*s.* 2*d.*	12*s.* 0*d.*	3*s.* 6*d.*	£8. 3*s.* 6*d.*	
Llanfachreth Parish:	112	59	23	11	1	1*s.* 0*d.*	21*s.* 4*d.*	4*s.* 9*d.*	£26. 14*s.* 6*d.*	£1. 10*s.* 1*d.*
Nannau	112	59	23	11	1	1*s.* 0*d.*	21*s.* 4*d.*	4*s.* 9*d.*	£26. 14*s.* 6*d.*	
Llanfihangel-y-Pennant Parish:	41	22	8	3	1	1*s.* 0*d.*	16*s.* 6*d.*	4*s.* 3*d.*	£8. 15*s.* 0*d.*	17*s.* 1*d.*
Bere	16	8	3	1	—	1*s.* 0*d.*	10*s.* 0*d.*	3*s.* 5*d.*	£2. 16*s.* 10*d.*	
Llanfihangel	13	6	2	1	1	1*s.* 4*d.*	16*s.* 6*d.*	4*s.* 4*d.*	£2. 16*s.* 6*d.*	
Nantcaw	12	8	3	1	—	1*s.* 7*d.*	11*s.* 3*d.*	5*s.* 1*d.*	£3. 1*s.* 8*d.*	
Llangelynnin Parish:	100	55	23	9	3	1*s.* 0*d.*	24*s.* 0*d.*	4*s.* 8*d.*	£23. 8*s.* 7*d.*	£2. 12*s.* 0*d.*
Bodgadfan	21	10	6	3	1	1*s.* 0*d.*	24*s.* 0*d.*	5*s.* 1*d.*	£5. 7*s.* 8*d.*	
Cregennan	16	8	3	2	1	1*s.* 7*d.*	14*s.* 4*d.*	4*s.* 7*d.*	£3. 13*s.* 8*d.*	
Llanfendigaid	23	13	7	2	—	1*s.* 2*d.*	10*s.* 8*d.*	4*s.* 8*d.*	£5. 8*s.* 2*d.*	
Llwyngwril	28	17	5	1	1	1*s.* 3*d.*	18*s.* 11*d.*	4*s.* 9*d.*	£6. 13*s.* 0*d.*	
Morfa Maenog	12	7	2	1	—	1*s.* 9*d.*	11*s.* 8*d.*	4*s.* 8*d.*	£2. 16*s.* 1*d.*	
Unidentified (*unnamed*)	1	1	1	1	1	36*s.* 0*d.*	36*s.* 0*d.*	36*s.* 0*d.*	£1. 16*s.* 0*d.*	
Assessors	6	5	4	2	2	2*s.* 0*d.*	29*s.* 8*d.*	12*s.* 0*d.*	£3. 12*s.* 11*d.*	

TABLE E Commote of Tal-y-bont. Local analysis of subsidy roll of 1292–3.

TABLE F	No. of taxpayers	Nos. paying more than 3s. 4d.	6s. 8d.	10s. 0d.	13s. 4d.	Min.	Max.	Average	Total	Tax. capacity per 1,000 acres
Commote of YSTUMANNER	397	164	51	25	16	1s. 3d.	35s. 4d.	4s. 5d.	£83. 1s. 6d.	£1. 11s. 5d.
Llanfihangel-y-Pennant Parish:	26	13	1	1	1	1s. 7d.	18s. 7d.	4s. 5d.	£5. 5s. 3d.	17s. 1d.
Llanllwydau	12	5	—	—	—	1s. 9d.	5s. 8d.	3s. 5d.	£2. 1s. 2d.	
Maestrefnant	9	5	—	—	—	2s. 4d.	4s. 5d.	3s. 7d.	£1. 12s. 8d.	
Rhiwerfa	5	3	1	1	1	1s. 7d.	18s. 7d.	6s. 3d.	£1. 11s. 5d.	
Pennal Parish:	38	14	5	1	1	1s. 4d.	14s. 4d.	3s. 6d.	£6. 13s. 10d.	14s. 10d.
Pennal	38	14	5	1	1	1s. 4d.	14s. 4d.	3s. 6d.	£6. 13s. 10d.	
Tal-y-llyn Parish:	78	35	11	7	4	1s. 4d.	18s. 4d.	4s. 8d.	£17. 0s. 0d.	£1. 1s. 3d.
Ceiswyn	18	8	2	1	1	1s. 10d.	16s. 8d.	4s. 3d.	£3. 16s. 1d.	
Corris	16	8	2	1	1	1s. 4d.	18s. 4d.	4s. 6d.	£3. 12s. 8d.	
Llangedris	9	4	3	3	2	1s. 6d.	13s. 10d.	6s. 0d.	£2. 14s. 3d.	
Ystradgwyn	35	15	4	2	—	1s. 5d.	12s. 4d.	3s. 11d.	£6. 17s. 0d.	
Tywyn Parish:	209	83	25	11	7	1s. 3d.	35s. 4d.	3s. 10d.	£40. 0s. 9d.	£1. 14s. 10d.
Botalog	3	2	—	—	—	2s. 4d.	5s. 8d.	3s. 11d.	11s. 9d.	
Bron-prys	9	2	1	—	—	1s. 9d.	7s. 3d.	2s. 11d.	£1. 6s. 2d.	
Caethle	17	5	—	—	—	1s. 6d.	4s. 9d.	2s. 7d.	£2. 4s. 1d.	
Cefnrhos	41	19	6	4	3	1s. 6d.	16s. 8d.	4s. 3d.	£8. 16s. 1d.	
Cynfal	27	11	4	1	—	1s. 5d.	11s. 1d.	3s. 9d.	£5. 2s. 2d.	
Gwrych	23	9	4	1	1	1s. 6d.	16s. 7d.	3s. 11d.	£4. 10s. 1d.	
Gwyddelfynydd	17	1	—	—	—	1s. 4d.	5s. 1d.	2s. 2d.	£1. 17s. 6d.	
Llannerchgoediog	13	5	—	—	—	1s. 5d.	4s. 11d.	2s. 11d.	£1. 18s. 3d.	
Maesmor	10	7	3	1	1	2s. 0d.	16s. 7d.	5s. 3d.	£2. 13s. 0d.	
Pencoed	4	2	1	1	1	2s. 1d.	14s. 5d.	5s. 10d.	£1. 3s. 5d.	
Penllyn	1	—	—	—	—	2s. 2d.	2s. 2d.	2s. 2d.	2s. 2d.	
Penmaen	10	6	1	—	—	1s. 3d.	9s. 8d.	3s. 11d.	£1. 19s. 4d.	
Trefeddian	12	7	3	1	—	1s. 8d.	12s. 5d.	4s. 7d.	£2. 15s. 9d.	
Trefrydd	12	5	2	2	1	1s. 7d.	35s. 4d.	6s. 3d.	£3. 15s. 7d.	
[?Trefrion] Uwch Buga	1	1	—	—	—	4s. 3d.	4s. 3d.	4s. 3d.	4s. 3d.	
Tywyn	9	1	—	—	—	1s. 5d.	4s. 11d.	2s. 4d.	£1. 1s. 2d.	
Unidentified:										
Arnarou	1	1	1	1	—	11s. 10d.	11s. 10d.	11s. 10d.	11s. 10d.	
Bylan	14	5	2	1	1	1s. 6d.	13s. 9d.	3s. 8d.	£2. 11s. 9d.	
Treffeden	17	5	1	—	—	1s. 6d.	9s. 1d.	3s. 4d.	£2. 16s. 7d.	
Winas	1	1	—	—	—	5s. 4d.	5s. 4d.	5s. 4d.	5s. 4d.	
---- (*unnamed*)	7	1	—	—	—	1s. 6d.	5s. 1d.	2s. 4d.	16s. 6d.	
Assessors:	6	6	5	3	2	3s. 6d.	14s. 0d.	10s. 0d.	£3. 0s. 2d.	

TABLE F Commote of Ystumanner. Local analysis of subsidy roll of 1292–3.

TEXT

THE MERIONETH LAY SUBSIDY ROLL
[1292–3]

(Public Record Office, Exchequer, King's Remembrancer, Subsidy Roll E.179/242/53)

THE MERIONETH LAY SUBSIDY ROLL
[1292–3]

P.R.O. E.179/242/53

[m.1, left h. col.]

Comotus de Penthlyn [i.e. Penllyn][1]

(1) [?Rhywedog in the parish of Llanfor]

Gurgenu Vachan[2]	11*s.* 1¼*d.*
Gron*ou* Vachan[3]	9*s.* 8¾*d.*
Griffid Duy	22¾*d.*
Ithel Duy	5*s.* 8*d.*
Madoco Hen	3*s.* 4*d.*
Ririd Duy	15*s.* 5½*d.*

---

1 Lists of taxpayers and the amounts at which they were assessed were usually arranged under townships or hamlets, but the first 64 names here appear directly under the commote of Penllyn. The assumption must be that the name of the township has, in this instance, been omitted in error. It is suggested that the township may have been Rhywedog – for three reasons: firstly, the next township referred to is neighbouring Llanfor; secondly, that part of the parish of Llanfor to the south of the river Dee would otherwise be unaccounted for; and thirdly, in Henry V's reign, Rhywedog (Uwch and Is Llafar) was, with its 12 gavells of land (Henry Ellis (ed.), *The Record of Caernarvon* (1838), pp. 264–5), a fairly populous area, as it may well have been in 1292–3, for part of the township consists of good agricultural land. Both Tytanygraig and Tycerrig were in the township of Rhywedog-is-afon in the eighteenth century (K. Williams-Jones (ed.), *A Calendar of the Merioneth Quarter Sessions Rolls*, I (1965), 277), so that it is likely that the northern boundary of the township was the river Dee.

2 If the reasoning in the previous note is correct, that we are here dealing with a list of names for the township of Rhywedog, then it is possible that the person who heads the list – Gurgenu Vachan – was the great-grandson of Rhirid Flaidd and an ancestor of the Lloyds of Plas Rhywedog. His grandson, Einion ab Ithel, was acting as sheriff of Merioneth when he died in 1400. Co-operation with the crown may long have been a tradition in the family – Gwrgenau Fychan himself was appointed rhaglaw of Penllyn in 1306 and was acting as woodward and farming the amobr of the commote at the same time (P.R.O. S.C.6/1170/5 m. 5). He was active, too, as one of the taxors of Penllyn for the fifteenth granted in 1318 (P.R.O. E.159/95 m. 62). But it is rather curious that he is not mentioned amongst those who did homage and fealty to the prince in 1301. He appears to have been important enough to have done so, especially if he is to be identified with the 'Gweramen Vaghan de Pentll', who petitioned the prince for a licence to have a mill on his own land (*Rec. of Caern.*, p. 217). His attitude to the events of 1294–5 is not known.

3 A Gronou Vaghan of Penllyn made homage and fealty to Edward of Caernarvon in 1301 (Edward Owen, *A List of those who did homage and fealty to the First English Prince of Wales in A.D. 1301* (1901), p. 12).

Rerid ap Madoc[1]	8*s*. 7½*d*.
Kenur*ic* Duy	12¾*d*.
Gron*ou* Bach	2*s*. 11¼*d*.
Eynon ap Adaf	4*s*. 11*d*.
Eynon Pyn	2*s*. 0½*d*.
Dauid ap Eynon	2*s*. 0¾*d*.
Yer*word* Velyn	14½*d*.
Ханghar*ad* uxore Tud*er*	5*s*. 4¾*d*.
Ithel ap Cad*ugan*	3*s*. 9½*d*.
Griffid ap Eynon	11*s*. 3¾*d*.
Corniykil	2*s*. 5½*d*.
Iorword ap Griffri	2*s*. 9*d*.
Ririd Loweydwy	5*s*. 8½*d*.
Tournour	3*s*.
Ieuan ap Griffid	5*s*. 3½*d*.
Blingyn	14*d*.
D*aui*d Duy	2*s*. 1¼*d*.
Gurgenu ap D*aui*d	3*s*. 10¼*d*.
map Seis	14*d*.
Meurik*o* Poith	3*s*. 3*d*.
Gron*ou* Voyl	22¼*d*.
Eynon ap Velin	2*s*. 7*d*.
Eynon Loglev	3*s*.
Bongam	17*d*.
Yer*word* Duy	4*s*. 5½*d*.
Eynon ap Kyb	7*s*. 6½*d*.
Madoc ap Gwerith	3*s*. 2¾*d*.
Eynon Saer	3*s*. 6¼*d*.
Gron*ou* Duy	3*s*. 11½*d*.
Kenur*ic* ap D*aui*d	4*s*. 10½*d*.
Griffid Voyl	4*s*. 11¼*d*.
Madyn Loyt	13*d*.
D*aui*d ap Cad*ugan*	5*s*.
Adaf Win	15½*d*.
Madin Crak.	17½*d*.
Neste	13½*d*.
Eynon ap Eden*euet*	18½*d*.
Eden*euet* ap Kenur*ic*	12*s*. 1½*d*.
Win ap Gron*ou*	3*s*. 2*d*.
Eynon Loyt	6*s*. 11*d*.
Ph*elip*o Loyt	19½*d*.

1 He may have been the rhaglaw of Penllyn in 1282 (Martin (ed.), *Registrum . . . Peckham*, II, 455).

Yer*word* ap Yagov	4*s*. 8*d*.
Ririd ap Griffid	22½*d*.
Ieuan ap Gron*ou* Goch	2*s*. 8*d*.
Tud*er* ap Gurgeneu	14½*d*.
Atreayliu	3*s*. 11*d*.
Wyn ap D*aui*d	15½*d*.
Gron*ou* ap Meurik.	12½*d*.
Win ap Ieuan	2*s*. 1½*d*.
Eden*euet* ap Madoc	15½*d*.
Eynon Goch.	2*s*. 6*d*.
Wasmel	2*s*. 10*d*.
D*aui*d ap Keb	20½*d*.
Ieuan ap Gron*ou*	7*s*. 6*d*.
Win ap D*aui*d	6*s*. 1½*d*.
Rerid ap Win(1)	3*s*. 4½*d*.
Ieuan Loyt	13¼*d*.
Whith Vunuis	4*s*. 5½*d*.

Summa 12*li*. 7*s*. 8¼*d*.(2) probatur.

(2) Lanuaur [i.e. Llanfor]

Eden*euet* Grach.	6*s*. 0½*d*.
Botoun	12¾*d*.
Lewelino Loyt	2*s*. 0¼*d*.
Gurgenov ap Ioreword	2*s*. 4½*d*.
Edenowen	21*d*.
Eynon ap Gron*ou*	12½*d*.
Wladusa Duy	20½*d*.
Gron*ou* filio eius	21½*d*.
Weruill*a* filia Kenewr*ic*	2*s*. 1½*d*.
Eynon ap Kenur*ic*	6*s*. 3*d*.
Howello Wild	5*s*. 8½*d*.
Will*elm*o clerico	10*s*. 8*d*.
Eynon Fakeb	2*s*. 7*d*.
Madoco Duy(3)	5*s*. 5½*d*.
Tud*er* Goch filio Wasdewy	2*s*. 0¾*d*.
Gron*ou* Voyl	21½*d*.
Nest	22¾*d*.
Tyngrin	2*s*. 1*d*.

1 A Ririt filius Guyn complained that he was ill-used by the constable of Oswestry in 1282 (ibid., p. 456); a Ririt ap Wyn was acting as coroner of Penllyn in 1304–05 (*B.B.C.S.*, I (1921–3), 263).

2 An error for £13. 7*s*. 8¼*d*.

3 He may have been dead by 1318 for in that year a widow of a certain Madoc Du was assessed at 10*d*. (*infra*, p. 102).

Eden*euet* Toyl		23$\frac{3}{4}$*d.*
Ieuan Pen[. . .]thkur[1]	3*s.*	7$\frac{1}{2}$*d.*
Yer*word* Voyl[2]	2*s.*	0$\frac{3}{4}$*d.*
Eynon ap Adaf	3*s.*	11$\frac{3}{4}$*d.*
Glaffoc		18$\frac{1}{4}$*d.*
Leuk*e* Goch.		18$\frac{3}{4}$*d.*
Alano de Ruthin		12$\frac{3}{4}$*d.*
Kenur*ic* Kam		17$\frac{3}{4}$*d.*
Yer*word* Poith	5*s.*	5$\frac{1}{4}$*d.*
Weruel*a* uxore Ener	2*s.*	10*d.*
Gron*ou* Duy		19$\frac{1}{2}$*d.*
Gron*ou* ap Ririd[3]	4*s.*	1$\frac{3}{4}$*d.*
Griffid ap Howel		13$\frac{1}{2}$*d.*
D*aui*d Voyl		23$\frac{1}{2}$*d.*
Kenur*ic* ap D*aui*d	2*s.*	
Madin ap Howel	2*s.*	5$\frac{1}{2}$*d.*

Summa 4*li.* 17*s.* 10$\frac{1}{4}$*d.*[4] probatur.

(3) Penmayn [i.e. Penmaen in the parish of Llanfor][5]

Cad*ugan* ap Ospers	4*s.*	0$\frac{1}{4}$*d.*
Dauid ap Adaf	3*s.*	9$\frac{1}{4}$*d.*
Adaf ap Eynon	5*s.*	7$\frac{1}{2}$*d.*
Madoco ap Wasdewy	2*s.*	5$\frac{1}{2}$*d.*
filia fabri	3*s.*	6$\frac{3}{4}$*d.*
Madoco Whith		13$\frac{1}{2}$*d.*
Yer*word* ap Adaf	2*s.*	6*d.*
Eua filia Ade		13$\frac{1}{2}$*d.*

1 Gash in MS. Possible reading: 'Pennathkur' = Pennaethgwr.

2 Cf. *infra*, p. 99–100, for a widow of a Iorword Voel and Ririd ap Iorword Voel being assessed respectively at 4*s.* 10$\frac{1}{2}$*d.* and 2*s.* 7$\frac{1}{4}$*d.*

3 Cf. *infra*, pp. 98 and 101, for a person of the same name being assessed in 1318 *sub* Penaran and Cyffty.

4 An error for £4. 17*s.* 3$\frac{1}{4}$*d.*

5 At the time of the making of the extent of *c.* 1284 it was said that the men of Penmaen were dead and their lands laid waste (*Arch. Camb.*, (1867), p. 188) which is not altogether surprising since the vill had been in the hands of Llywelyn ap Gruffydd, prince of Wales, and Dafydd his brother. With 17 taxpayers to its credit in 1292–3, and a possible total population of about 80, the vill of Penmaen had made a good recovery in the ten years or so after the conquest.
Llanfor may, at various times, have been included in the township of Penmaen for some administrative purposes. Edward Lhuyd made no specific mention of the township of Llanfor as such; and in the seventeenth and eighteenth centuries places like Rhiwlas, Pantyffynnon, and Tomen Castell, as well as Penmaen (to the north-west) and Llwyniolyn (to the north-east) were within the township of Penmaen (Owen Parry, 'The Hearth Tax of 1662 in Merioneth', *Journal of the Merioneth Historical and Record Society*, II (1953–6), 18; K. Williams-Jones, op. cit., pp. 25, 277).

Gron*ou* ap Madoc		15½*d*.
Win ap Adaf	7*s*.	8*d*.
Gron*ou* ap Wion		13½*d*.
Dauid ap Yer*word*		20½*d*.
D*aui*d ap Madoc	3*s*.	10*d*.
Ieuan ap Ph*elip*		15*d*.
Gron*ou* ap Adaf	8*s*.	4½*d*.
Map Heylin		13*d*.
Eynon ap Thom*as*	7*s*.	9*d*.

Summa 58*s*. 3¼*d*. probatur.

De abbate de Bassingwerk.[1]	63*s*.	0½*d*.

Summa 63*s*. 0½*d*. probatur.

De abbate de Stradmarchel[2]	13*s*.	1½*d*.

Summa 13*s*. 1½*d*. probatur.

Taxatores:

Kenur*ic* ap Edeneuet	18*s*.	9*d*.
Adaf ap Eynon	23*s*.	6¾*d*.
Yer*word* ap Res[3]	12*s*.	2½*d*.
Rerid ap Eynon	9*s*.	1¼*d*.
Kenuric Vachan	6*s*.	1*d*.
Griffid ap Madoc Selour[4]	5*s*.	1*d*.

Summa 74*s*. 9½*d*. probatur.

(4) Penachlw [i.e. Pennant-lliw in the parish of Llanuwchllyn][5]

Madoc ap Yer*word*[6]	30s.	
Eynon Loyt		13¼*d*.

---

1 i.e., Basingwerk, in the old county of Flint.

2 i.e., Ystrad Marchell (Strata Marcella), in the former county of Montgomery.

3 A Yereworth ap Rees appears as one of the hostages taken by Edward I from Caernarvonshire and Merioneth after Madog's rebellion of 1294–5 (J. Griffiths, 'The Revolt of Madog ap Llywelyn 1294–5', *Transactions of the Caernarvonshire Historical Society*, 16 (1955), 24); a person of the same name from Merioneth made homage and fealty to prince Edward in 1301 (Edward Owen, op. cit., p. 25). A Iorword ap Rys was assessed at only 2*s*. 10¾*d*. *sub* Castell in 1318 (see *infra*, p. 100).

4 i.e., of Selwrn.

5 According to the extent of Merioneth of *c*. 1284, the 'land' called Pennanthlu was extended at 45*s*. a year but over two-thirds of it was devastated – clearly a result of the war of conquest of 1282–3 (*Arch. Camb.*, (1867), p. 188). As this subsidy roll shows, it had, like Penmaen, recovered remarkably well by 1292–3. Its southern boundary, at least in the seventeenth century, does not appear to have been the river Dee as one would expect: it lay about quarter of a mile to the north, for both Llwyngwern and Prys were in neighbouring Penaran (Owen Parry, art. cit., p. 21).

6 Another great-grandson (see *supra*, p. 3, n. 2) of Rhirid Flaidd and clearly a person of some consequence in Penllyn in Edward I's reign. He must be numbered amongst the many locally influential Welshmen of his day who saw great advantages in serving the crown. Nothing seems to be known about him before the conquest but it is very

Madoc ap Eynon	2*s.*	4*d.*
Griffid Duy	5*s.*	$2\frac{3}{4}$*d.*
Iorword ap Eynon	2*s.*	$2\frac{1}{2}$*d.*
Yer*word* ap Gwahalet	3*s.*	$8\frac{1}{2}$*d.*
Eynon ap Whahalet		$16\frac{3}{4}$*d.*

[m.2, left h. col.]

Adhuc Penachlow

Dauid ap Clustfold	3*s.*	$7\frac{1}{2}$*d.*
Griffid ap Gron*ou*	2*s.*	$6\frac{1}{2}$*d.*
Ieuan ap Thom*as*		14*d.*
Win ap Griffid	3*s.*	
Leuke Goch.	6*s.*	2*d.*

---

likely that he was already committed to the royal cause before 1282. From as early as 1287 he is known to have held various offices in Merioneth: in 1287 he was acting as keeper of the vaccary of Merioneth and from 1288 to 1294 he was accounting for the issues of the havottries and other offices in Merioneth (*B.B.C.S.*, XIV (1950–52), 241, 303, 309, 312). His attitude to Madog's revolt is unknown: the heavy sum at which he was assessed in 1292–3 may have strained his loyalty, but there is no hard evidence that it pushed him over the brink (unless we are to make much of the fact that he sought to reinstate himself in office in 1305 (*Rec. of Caern.*, p. 216)). If it did, he was quickly back in favour again with the crown, for on 1 April 1300 his interest in certain lands in Pennant-lliw, extended at 40*s*. a year, which he had enjoyed up till then 'during pleasure', was converted to a grant for life by Edward I (*Cal. Pat. Rolls 1292–1301*, p. 507; *Arch. Camb.*, (1867), p. 191) and he was still farming the amobr of the commote of Penllyn in 1304–05 (*B.B.C.S.*, I (1921–3), 265) despite the less favourable breezes which had sprung up since 1301. He was, it seems, not valued as highly as others in Merioneth by Edward of Caernarvon, though he had dutifully made homage and fealty to him in 1301 (Edward Owen, op. cit., p. 12). When he petitioned the prince in 1305 to restore to him the mysterious-sounding office of bailiff 'unius cantr.' in Penllyn and Ardudwy which Edward I had granted to him, he was told that the office had been given by the prince himself to Griffith ap David for life, possibly in 1303 (*Rec. of Caern.*, p. 216; W. H. Waters, *The Edwardian Settlement*, p. 33 n). The prince dismissed, too, his plea for turning a life interest in Pennant-lliw into a grant in perpetuity and in October 1315, by which time Madog ab Iorwerth had almost certainly died, the land was granted to Madog ab Athaf at the request, interestingly enough, of the king of France (*Rec. of Caern.*, p. 219; *Cal. of Fine Rolls 1307–19*, p. 234; *Cal. of Chanc. Warrants 1244–1326*, p. 410, *Cal. Pat. Rolls 1313–17*, p. 355). However, Pennant-lliw was in the hands of the Glan-llyn family, which could claim descent from Madog ab Iorwerth, in the late sixteenth and seventeenth centuries (T. I. Jeffreys-Jones (ed.), *Exchequer Proceedings Concerning Wales* (1955), p. 235). Madog ab Iorwerth himself clearly remained a formidable figure in the area in Edward I's day and Dr. C. A. Gresham accepts the suggestion that he probably held Castell Carndochan (see his *Medieval Stone Carving in North Wales* (1968), p. 178, and No. 169 for a line-drawing of his effigy in the parish church of Pennant Melangell; see also *Arch. Camb.*, (1919), p. 573, for the original assertion that Madog ab Iorwerth was connected with Castell Carndochan, and *Roy. Comm. Anc. Mon.: Inv. Merioneth*, p. 139 n, for a refutation of the idea). His grandson, if not his son – a Gruffydd ap Madog ap Iorwerth was acting as one of the taxors of Penllyn for the fifteenth granted in 1318 (P.R.O. E.159/95 m. 62) – continued to serve the crown (S. R. Meyrick (ed.), *Lewys Dwnn's Heraldic Visitations of Wales*, (1846), p. 232, n. 4). Madog ab Iorwerth seems to have had interests also in the neighbouring township of Cyffty (see *infra*, p. 12).

Ioreword Troyn	3*s*.	4*d*.
Eynon ap Cad*ugan*	2*s*.	
Yer*word* ap Thom*as*	2*s*.	0¼*d*.
Kenuric ap Ithel		13*d*.
Tud*er* Bongam	4*s*.	5*d*.
Cad*ugan* Goch.	7*s*.	4½*d*.
Gron*ou* ap Ener	17*s*.	
D*aui*d ap Ririd[1]	29*s*.	0½*d*.
Wyon		16*d*.
Ririd Loyt	2*s*.	4*d*.
Yer*word* ap Gron*ou*	2*s*.	1¾*d*.
Yer*word* ap Ithel		15*d*.
D*aui*d ap Lowarch	5*s*.	4¼*d*.
Eden*euet* Voyl	4*s*.	2¾*d*.
Ieuan ap Lowarch.	6*s*.	4½*d*.

Summa 7*li*. 11*s*. 9¼*d*. probatur.

(5) Penaran [in the parish of Llanuwchllyn][2]

Win Mautho[3]	4*s*.	10¾*d*.
Gurgeneu Goch.[4]	6*s*.	3¼*d*.
Griffid Wilour	4*s*.	4*d*.
Win Voyl	3*s*.	4¾*d*.
Win ap D*aui*d Duy	9*s*.	6¾*d*.
Dauid Crak.		18*d*.
Dauid Loyt		13½*d*.
Ithel ap Candalo	5*s*.	3½*d*.
Cantor	5*s*.	0¾*d*.
Nest filia Adaf	4*s*.	7½*d*.
Adekin	2*s*.	4½*d*.
Tegware*t*	2*s*.	8½*d*.

1 A certain David ap Ririt was fined 10*d*. for non-attendance at the county court in 1288 (P.R.O. E.101/614/3); David ap Ririth made homage and fealty to the prince of Wales in 1301 (Edward Owen, op. cit., p. 25). A person of the same name was assessed at 6*s*. 6½*d*. in the adjacent township of Penaran; and at 6*s*. 8*d*. in 1318 (*infra*, p. 97).

2 Penaran straddled the river Dee (see *supra*, p. 7, n. 5) and included an outlier in the area north-east of the village of Llanuwchllyn – Plas Madoc, e.g., was in the township of Penaran in 1461 (*Cat. of Anc. Deeds*, VI, No. C.6403) – as well as most of the area to the south of the Dee. With its 74 taxpayers, it was the most populous township in Penllyn in 1292–3. However, in 1318, only 27 persons were assessed and the total assessment of the township was a mere £4. 6*s*. 8¾*d*. as against £14. 1*s*. 11¾*d*. in 1292–3 (*infra*, p. 99).

3 Presumably from neighbouring Mawddwy, which lay outside the county until 1536.

4 A Dauid ap Gurgenu of Penaran was assessed at exactly the same sum in 1318 (*infra*, p. 98).

Madoco Voyl[1]	2*s*. 9½*d*.
Gurgeneu Duy	2*s*. 2½*d*.
Yer*word* ap Wion	2*s*. 8½*d*.
Kena	3*s*. 5¼*d*.
Adaf ap Madoc	2*s*. 10*d*.
Ithel sutore	21*d*.
Gurg*eneu* Loyt	17¼*d*.
Owein ap Lewelin[2]	24*s*. 8*d*.
Dauid ap Ririd[3]	6*s*. 6½*d*.
Madoco ap Eden*euet*	4*s*. 2*d*.
Ph*elip*o Duy[4]	14¾*d*.
Wentlian Duy	2*s*. 11½*d*.
Win ap Eynon	2*s*. 8½*d*.
Eua filia Win	2*s*. 7½*d*.
Gron*ou* Alchlwy	5*s*. 8*d*.
Eynon Osporn	2*s*. 2*d*.
Eynon ap Gron*ou*	9*s*. 8¾*d*.
D*aui*d Duy[5]	13*s*. 8½*d*.
Yer*word* Duy	4*s*. 4¼*d*.
Eden*euet* ap Ririd	19½*d*.
Win ap Dauid Pengreck.[6]	19½*d*.
Wentlian filia Dauid	3*s*. 2*d*.
Win ap Eynon	2*s*. 3¼*d*.
Yer*word* Vachan	4*s*. 6¼*d*.
Dauid Velinith	23½*d*.
Wladusa uxore map Bretwen	6*s*. 0¾*d*.
Eden*euet* ap Dauid	3*s*. 8*d*.
Loydin	17*d*.
Eynon ap Ririd	3*s*. 10½*d*.
Yer*word* ap Howel	2*s*. 1¼*d*.
Tyncrin Talennyour	4*s*. 3¼*d*.
Dauid Duy	2*s*. 5¼*d*.
Eynon ap Ieuan	18*d*.
Ririd Duy	2*s*. 9¼*d*.
D*aui*d ap Ithel	5*s*.
Eynon Kilfin	14*d*.

---

1 A Madoc Voel was assessed at 12*d*. *sub* Castell in 1318 (*infra*, p. 100).

2 An Owayn ap Thlewelyn made homage and fealty to the prince of Wales in 1301 (Edward Owen, op. cit., p. 25).

3 Cf. *supra*, p. 9, n. 1.

4 Phelip Du of Penaran was assessed at 7*d*. in 1318 (*infra*, p. 98).

5 A David Du was assessed at 12½*d*. *sub* Castell in 1318 (*infra*, p. 99).

6 It is not known which Pencraig is referred to here.

Ieuan Loyt		14*d.*
Trahern Voyl	2*s.*	8¼*d.*
Wentlian Duy		3¼*d.*(1)
Adaf Loyt(2)	5*s.*	4*d.*
Win ap Madin	3*s.*	2½*d.*
Heylin Duy		19½*d.*
Adaf ap Heilin	3*s.*	1½*d.*
Ieuan Sutore	2*s.*	4*d.*
Kenuric Voyl	2*s.*	5*d.*
Eynon ap Ithel(3)	2*s.*	10½*d.*
Eynon Duy	3*s.*	3¾*d.*
Wladusa		15½*d.*
Deshardelach	4*s.*	9*d.*
Yer*word* ap Eden*euet*		17¼*d.*
D*aui*d ap Atha		18*d.*
Rerid ap Heilin	2*s.*	10*d.*
Ririd Loyt		20½*d.*
Wentlian uxore Gwin		18¼*d.*
Meilor ap Ada	5*s.*	10¼*d.*
Iagou Voyl	4*s.*	5½*d.*
Ieuan ap Iagou	2*s.*	8¾*d.*
Madoc ap Yagou(4)		22*d.*
Eynon Offeriot(5)		14½*d.*
Ithel ap Griffid		13¼*d.*
Eynon decano	13*s.*	6½*d.*
Ieuan filio Cad*ugan*	9*s.*	7*d.*

Summa 6*li.* 7*s.* 6¾*d.*(6) probatur.

(6) Deugrek. [i.e. Dwygraig in the parish of Llangywer](7)

Madoco ap Lewelin	7*s.*	4*d.*
Griffid ap Gron*ou*	3*s.*	5*d.*
Madoco ap Kenuric	2*s.*	

1 Almost certainly an error for 13¼*d.*: no one was assessed at less than 12*d.*

2 An Adaf Loyd of Penaran was assessed at 20¼*d.* in 1318 (*infra*, p. 99).

3 He was assessed at exactly the same sum in 1318 (*infra*, p. 98).

4 A Madoc ap Yago Voel of Penaran was assessed at 2½*d.* in 1318 (*infra*, p. 99).

5 We may have here another candidate for the authorship of the earliest metrical grammar in Welsh (*Dictionary of Welsh Biography* (1959), p. 203), but in the light of recent conjectures it seems an outside possibility only (J. Beverley Smith, 'Einion Offeiriad', *B.B.C.S.*, XX (1962–4), 339–47).

6 An error for £14. 1*s.* 11¾*d.*

7 Known otherwise as the township of Isafon. The small stream, the Afon Glyn, divided Isafon from the township of Uwchafon, Glyn Bach being in Isafon (K. Williams-Jones, op. cit., p. 24) and Glyn Mawr in Uwchafon,

Dauid Saer	6*s*.	3*d*.
Madoco Goch.	2*s*.	8¼*d*.
Gwion	2*s*.	8¼*d*.
Madoco Duy[1]	8*s*.	6½*d*.
Eynon Goch	2*s*.	4½*d*.
Gen*er*ys filia Howel	2*s*.	4¾*d*.
Gronou Voyl	5*s*.	1¾*d*.
Eden*euet* ap Gron*ou*		16*d*.
Madoco ap D*aui*d ap Eden*euet*		22½*d*.
Madoco ap D*aui*d	2*s*.	8*d*.
Yer*word* ap Adaf		12½*d*.
Yer*word* Goch[2]	11*s*.	4*d*.
Eden*euet* Duy	5*s*.	2*d*.

Summa 66*s*. 3*d*. probatur.

(7) Kiftu [i.e. Cyffty in the parish of Llanycil][3]

Gurgenu ap Tud*er*		12½*d*.
Win Seis[4]	4*s*.	10*d*.
Madoco ap Yer*word*[5]	5*s*.	
Strilin	2*s*.	
Gron*ou* Berthoc[6]	14*s*.	8*d*.
D*aui*d ap Yer*word*		18*d*.
Madoc Ruth	6*s*.	11½*d*.
Adaf Loyt[7]	4*s*.	0¼*d*.
Cad*ugan* ap Kenuric	4*s*.	8*d*.
Meiler ap Gurg*enu*		16¾*d*.
Yer*word* ap Tud*er*[8]	3*s*.	4*d*.
D*aui*d Sant		17½*d*.
Tangwistel filia Ph*elip*		18½*d*.

---

1 A widow of Madoc Du was assessed at 10*d*. in 1318 (*infra*, p. 102).

2 A Iorwerth Goch was fined for not making suit at the hundred court in 1288 (P.R.O. E.101/614/3); Yerward Gouch made homage and fealty to the prince in 1301 (Edward Owen, op. cit., p. 25).

3 In the eighteenth century, Gwernhefin was considered to be in the township of Cyffty (K. Williams-Jones, op.cit., pp. 24, 258) but in the thirteenth century Gwernhefin was apparently a township in its own right (*Cal. Charter Rolls*, II, 291). By 1318, the number of those assessed in Cyffty had been reduced to 13 and the total sum at which the township was then assessed was £1. 11*s*. 8¾*d*. (*infra*, p. 101).

4 Guyn Seis was assessed at 5*s*. *sub* Cyffty in 1318 (*infra*, p. 101).

5 See *supra*, p. 7 n. 6. A widow of a certain Madoc ap Iorword was assessed at 3*s*. 1¾*d*. in 1318 (*infra*, p. 101).

6 If this refers to a place no trace of it has been found. Cf. Goronw Verthauc, assessed at 8*s*. 5¾*d*. *sub* Streflyn in 1318 (*infra*, p. 102).

7 An Adam Loyd of Cyffty was assessed at 5*d*. in 1318 (*infra*. p. 101).

8 His widow was assessed at 17¾*d*. in 1318 (ibid.).

map Yerword		22*d.*
Dugoch		20*d.*
Madoco Cam	2*s.*	10½.*d*
Scormyl	3*s.*	2*d.*
E gargam		12*d.*
Gurg*enu* ap Ririd	2*s.*	3½*d.*

Summa 65*s.* 3*d.* probatur.

(8) Maystran [i.e. Maestran in the parishes of Llanycil and Llanuwchllyn][1]

Idiaual[2]	13*s.*	4¼*d.*
Gron*ou* ap Yer*word*		20½*d.*
Isbidur	7*s.*	2*d.*
Ieuan ap Budur	5*s.*	
Yer*word* ap Griffri		17½*d.*
Howel ap D*au*id[3]	4*s.*	10½*d.*
Adam Penthlin[4]		13½*d.*
Ithel ap Eynon	6*s.*	0¾*d.*

[m.1, right h. col.]

Adhuc Maystran

Ieuan Loyt[5]	2*s.*	1½*d.*
Win Cossin	7*s.*	0½*d.*
Ririd ap Yer*word*	3*s.*	8*d.*
Meurico		16½*d.*
Eynon Loyt	2*s.*	2*d.*
Anghar*ad* filia Ririd	2*s.*	2¼*d.*
Win ap Madoc[6]		15½*d.*
Eynon Seis	3*s.*	8¼*d.*
Adaf Maystran	2*s.*	3*d.*
Madoco ap D*au*id	3*s.*	2½*d.*

Summa 69*s.* 9*d.* probatur.

---

1 Meinihirion in the parish of Llanycil was, it is known, within the township of Maestran in the sixteenth century (E. G. Jones (ed.), *Exchequer Proceedings* (*Equity*) *concerning Wales* (1939), p. 228), but so too were Caergai, Fron Gastell, and Cystyllen, which are in the parish of Llanuwchllyn (P.R.O. L.R.2/236, fos. 79–80). Hence the supposition that the township of Maestran straddled the two parishes of Llanycil and Llanuwchllyn. Its exact bounds have not, however, as yet, been discovered.

2 A Guyon ap y Dioual was assessed at only 19½*d.* in the neighbouring vill of Castell in 1318 (*infra*, p. 100).

3 A person of the same name was trading with Oswestry in 1282 (Martin (ed.), *Registrum . . . Peckham*, II, 456–7).

4 i.e., of Penllyn.

5 A Ieuan Loyd was assessed at 19¼*d.* in nearby Cyffty in 1318 (*infra*, p. 101).

6 Cf. Guyn ap Madoc, assessed at 8*s.* 11½*d.* in the neighbouring township of Streflyn in 1318 (*infra*, p. 102).

(9) Langouer [i.e. Llangywer][1]

Dauid ap Ieuan	5*s*. 0½*d*.
Hunith	13½*d*.
Tangwistel filia Eynon	3*s*. 2¼*d*.
Tud*er* ap Eynon	4*s*. 0¾*d*.
Eurerdich	18*d*.
Generys	12½*d*.
Heylin ap Glackoun	4*s*. 3½*d*.
Lewelin ap Eden*euet*	3*s*.
Wentliana filia Kenuric	8*s*. 3*d*.
Eynon ap Kenuric	17½*d*.
D*au*id Vachan	3*s*. 5½*d*.

Summa 36*s*. 5*d*. probatur.

(10) Selour [i.e. Selwrn in the parish of Llandderfel]

Yer*word* ap Madoc	4*s*. 4½*d*.
Cad*ugan* Vachan	15½*d*.
Madoco ap Rerid	2*s*. 0¼*d*.
Win ap Madoc	20½*d*.
Yer*word* ap Candalo	2*s*. 2½*d*.
map Botoun	16*d*.
D*au*id ap Cad*ugan*	2*s*. 8½*d*.
Kenuric Duy	22½*d*.
Eden*euet* ap Griffid[2]	2*s*. 3*d*.
D*au*id ap Ithel	16*d*.
Ieuan ap Heylin	3*s*. 7¾*d*.
Madoco ap Eynon	2*s*.
Wladusa uxore Wion	16½*d*.
Ieuan Iankin	8*s*. 2½*d*.
Gurg*enu* sutore	23*d*.
Adaf Turnor	18½*d*.

Summa 39*s*. 8½*d*.[3] probatur.

(11) Nanfruer [i.e. Nanffreuer in the parish of Llandderfel][4]

Leget Penglok.	16*d*.
Gron*ou* Ver	22*d*.

---

1 Sometimes referred to as the township of (Llangywer) Uwchafon. Cf. *supra*, p. 11, n. 7.

2 A person of the same name was accused of selling a horse outside the town of Oswestry in 1282 (Martin (ed.), *Registrum . . . Peckham*, II, 456).

3 An error for 39*s*. 9½*d*.

4 Edward Lhuyd numbered it one of the townships of Llanfor but modified his statement by saying that 'the Tyth of it belongs to Llan Vor' (*Arch. Camb.: Parochialia* Part ii (1910), pp. 54, 62). He noted too 'Lleidiog rh. pont Lleidiog a thre Nant Freiar' (p. 64): the stream of Nant Lleidiog now forms part of the boundary between the parishes of Llanfor and Llandderfel.

Madoco ap Heylin		21¾*d.*
Gron*ou* ap Heylin		16¾*d.*
Howel ap Eynon		16¾*d.*
Lowarch		12¾*d.*
Ierword ap Cad*ugan*	4*s.*	4¼*d.*
Ada Seysir		14¾*d.*
Madoco Bloyth	6*s.*	8*d.*
Dauid ap Yer*word*		22½*d.*
Dauid ap Meyler		22*d.*
Ieuan Medico		16*d.*
Dauid Voyl	5*s.*	8½*d.*
Ririd ap Cad*ugan*	3*s.*	8*d.*
Iorword ap Meiler[1]	2*s.*	0½*d.*
Gurgeneu ap Meiler		19½*d.*

Summa 39*s.* 2*d.* probatur.

(12) Nantleydyoc [i.e. Nantlleidiog in the parish of Llanfor]

Dauid ap Madoc	4*s.*	6*d.*
Adaf ap Eynon	8*s.*	8¾*d.*
Wladusa filia Tud*er*	2*s.*	5½*d.*
Mad*oco* ap Cad*ugan*	3*s.*	3½*d.*
Ririd ap Madoc	3*s.*	3½*d.*
Ph*elip*o Goch	2*s.*	0¼*d.*
Madoco ap Ph*elip*	4*s.*	10*d.*
Meurico ap Iorword	6*s.*	8*d.*
Yor*word* Vachan	4*s.*	1¼*d.*
Eden*euet* ap Meurik.		19*d.*
Generys uxore Wasdewy	2*s.*	3½*d.*
Ieuan ap Wasdewy	3*s.*	8*d.*
D*aui*d ap Ieuan	4*s.*	
Eden*euet* Crouthour	3*s.*	11½*d.*
Gron*ou* Loyt		18½*d.*
Gron*ou* ap Wasdewy	4*s.*	4¼*d.*
map Yer*word* ap Ada*f*		15½*d.*

Summa 72*s.* 7*d.*[2] probatur.

(13) Llaytcoum [i.e. Llaethgwm in the parish of Llanfor][3]

Candalov		13½*d.*
Eynon Edich	2*s.*	

---

1 A person of the same name was trading in Oswestry in 1282 (Martin (ed.), *Registrum . . . Peckham*, II, 456).

2 An error for 62*s.* 7*d.*

3 Llaethgwm was at one time a detached portion of the parish of Llandderfel (see, e.g., Lhuyd, op. cit., p. 59).

Eynon ap Tuder	5*s.* 7*d.*
Meurico Dathloyt	2*s.* 1½*d.*
Yer*word* ap Gron*ou*	3*s.* 2*d.*
Howel ap Tud*er*	8*s.* 3¾*d.*
Gron*ou* Cutta	5*s.* 5¼*d.*

Summa 27*s.* 9*d.* probatur.

(14) Hengayr [i.e. Hengaer in the parish of Llandderfel][1]

Eynon ap Ieuan	3*s.* 6¾*d.*
Gron*ou* ap Ieuan	2*s.* 6¾*d.*
Pengour	2*s.* 8*d.*
Houa ap Pengour	18¾*d.*
Cadug*an* ap Ieuan	16*d.*
Ieuan fabro	3*s.* 3¼*d.*
D*aui*d fabro	2*s.* 6¾*d.*
D*aui*d ap Ieuan	2*s.* 5*d.*
Lewelin Duy	2*s.* 0¾*d.*
Cala Heth	2*s.* 10½*d.*

Summa 24*s.* 10½*d.* probatur.

(15) Cregan [i.e. Crogen in the parish of Llandderfel][2]

Meiler Goch	4*s.* 6*d.*
Ithel Dapifero	5*s.* 0½*d.*
D*aui*d Duy	17¼*d.*
Dauid ap Ph*elip*	2*s.* 1*d.*
Adaf Goch	16¼*d.*

Summa 14*s.* 10½*d.*[3] probatur.

---

1 Otherwise known as Llawrybetws or Betws-y-Coed. Tythin yr Hengayr was said to be in the lordship of Bettuse y Koyd in the late sixteenth century (E. G. Jones, op. cit., p. 226). Betws was accounted one of the townships of the parish of Llanfor in the seventeenth and eighteenth centuries (Lhuyd, op. cit., pp. 54, 62).

2 Crogen was sometimes associated with Edeirnion rather than Penllyn. No mention is made of it under Penllyn in the extent of Merioneth in *c.* 1420; in all the taxation returns of the sixteenth and seventeenth centuries it appears invariably as part of Edeirnion (Univ. Coll. of N. Wales, Bangor MS. 13494, pp. 10, 112, 133); in the eighteenth century, too, the township was regarded as being in Edeirnion (K. Williams-Jones, op. cit., pp. 21, 34). What accounts for this? The confusion presumably sprang from the fact that Crogen was granted to Dafydd ap Gruffydd of Hendwr, one of the barons of Edeirnion, after the native prince of Wales had been defeated in 1277; and, as Mr. A. D. Carr has pointed out (*Journ. Mer. Hist. and Rec. Soc.*, IV (1961–4), 190), it remained thereafter in the hands of the Hendwr family. (It is significant that Crogen boasted a steward in 1292–3.) For purposes other than taxation, however, Crogen was considered to be a part of the commote of Penllyn, at least in the fourteenth century (see, e.g., *Cal. Pat. Rolls 1381–85*, p. 179; *Cal. Pat. Rolls 1385–89*, p. 533), and, as this roll shows, was still taxed under Penllyn in the late thirteenth century.

3 An error for 14*s.* 5*d.*

(16) Kywluot [i.e. ?Cynllwyd in the parish of Llanuwchllyn – or possibly [Caer]geiliog in the parish of Llanfor]

Ieuan ap Eynon	7*s*. 9½*d*.
Adaf ap D*aui*d	2*s*. 6½*d*.
Adaf Loyt	3*s*. 5½*d*.

Summa 13*s*. 9½*d*. probatur.

(17) Kenlas [i.e. Cynlas in the parish of Llanfor][1]

Adaf ap Madoc	8*s*. 3¼*d*.
Eynon ap Gron*ou*	3*s*. 5½*d*.
D*aui*d Voyl	13½*d*.
Gron*ou* Voyl	5*s*. 10*d*.
Ithel ap Cuhelin	3*s*. 10¾*d*.
Iorword ap Ithel	21¼*d*.
Ieuan Duy	3*s*. 5*d*.
Win ap Idonn	17½*d*.
Griffid ap Gron*ou*	3*s*. 3*d*.

Summa 32*s*. 5¾*d*. probatur.

(18) Doldrewen [i.e. Doldrewyn in the parish of Llandderfel][2]

Ioreword	16*d*.
Kenuric Voyl	3*s*. 1*d*.
Gurg*enu*	3*s*. 1*d*.
Ithel ap Eynon	3*s*. 6*d*.
Cad*ugan* Duy[3]	15½*d*.
Gurg*enu* Duy	14¾*d*.
Ieuan Voil	2*s*. 10½*d*.
Wentliana filia Ieuan	18½*d*.
Madoco Saer	20¾*d*.
Cad*ugan* ap D*aui*d	2*s*. 1*d*.

Summa 21*s*. 9*d*. probatur.

[m.2, right h. col.]

(19) Hucheldref [i.e. Ucheldref in the parish of Llanfor]

Wentliana uxore Ph*elipi*	2*s*. 5½*d*.
Adaf ap Madoc	6*s*. 8¾*d*.
Ieuan Kethin	2*s*. 2*d*.
Tud*er*	2*s*. 3*d*.
D*aui*d Crach	4*s*. 8¾*d*.

1 The township of Cynlas was at one time in the parish of Llandderfel (Lhuyd, op. cit., p. 59).

2 The township included not only Garthllwyd, Henblas, Hendre-ddu, Cae-pant, Caecoryn, and Bodelith, but also apparently distant Brynderw by the eighteenth century (Owen Parry, art. cit., p. 20; K. Williams-Jones, op. cit., pp. 25, 277).

3 A 'Caduganus Niger' was described as 'famulus constabularii de Penllyn' in 1282 (Martin (ed.), *Registrum . . . Peckham*, II, 456).

Ieuan Voil	4*s*. 7¾*d*.
Leget Mark.	3*s*. 3½*d*.
Madoco Whith	5*s*. 1*d*.
Griffid ap Tevet	2*s*. 8¾*d*.
Madoco ap Gurg*enu*	16¼*d*.

Summa 35*s*. 5¼*d*. probatur.

(20) Carn [i.e. Garn in the parish of Llanfor]

Bongam[1]	5*s*. 2¾*d*.
Eynon ap Ithel	4*s*. 10*d*.

Summa 10*s*. 0¾*d*. probatur

(21) Kyltalgart [i.e. Ciltalgarth in the parish of Llanfor]

Gron*ou* ap Kenuric	3*s*. 6½*d*.
Eden*euet* ap Griffid	9*s*.
map Keuenard Duy	13¼*d*.
Griffid ap D*aui*d[2]	7*s*. 9½d.
Madoco ap Cad*ugan*	3*s*. 10*d*.
Erdiduwol	14*d*.
Eden*euet* Goch	4*s*.
Candalo	4*s*. 4*d*.
Madoco Voil	2*s*. 0½*d*.
Adaf ap Gurg*enu*	13½*d*.
Ieuan With	5*s*. 0¼*d*.
Eynon ap Cad*ugan*	12½*d*.
Eynon ap Keuen*ard*	3*s*. 4*d*.
Howel ap Cad*ugan*	3*s*.
Cad*ugan* ap Ieuan	2*s*. 3½*d*.
Ph*elip*o ap Ieuan	3*s*. 8¼*d*.
Kenuric Voyl[3]	11*s*. 10*d*.
Cad*ugan* ap Yagov	2*s*. 4½*d*.
Adaf Penbras	4*s*. 1½*d*.

Summa 74*s*. 7¾*d*. probatur.

(22) Wernovel [i.e. Gwernefail in the parish of Llanycil][4]

---

1 Two servants ('famuli') of a person called 'Y bongam' were trading in Oswestry in 1282 (ibid., p. 457).

2 Probably the lord of Hendwr. See *infra*, p. 82, n. 3.

3 Cf. Carnewyk Goel who did homage and fealty to Edward of Caernarvon in 1301 (Edward Owen, op. cit., p. 25).

4 Its extent at the end of the thirteenth century is very problematical. Two hundred years later Rhydydefaid ('Maysrreyd Devayd') was included in Gwernefail (*Cat. of Anc. Deeds*, III, No. C.3676) and so too was Yr Orsedd ('Hacheb'rryd i'r Orseth' in ibid., No. C.3675). This suggests that the whole area known as Ismynydd and Uwchmynydd by the eighteenth century was simply Gwernefail at the end of the thirteenth century. The great survey of 1592 confirms this supposition: included in Gwernevell were places like Weirglodd Ddu and Maesytail in Uwchmynydd and Pencelli and Tyn-y-pant in Ismynydd (P.R.O. L.R.2/236 fos. 83–6).

Dauid	2*s*.	5½*d*.
Gron*ou* Voyl	2*s*.	
Dauid Saer	16*s*.	3½*d*.
Kenuric Vachan	2*s*.	2*d*.
Edenewein ap Kenuric	28*s*.	2½*d*.
Gron*ou* ap Meiler	19*s*.	8¼*d*.
Howello Vachan	3*s*.	8¾*d*.
Howello ap Wyn	6*s*.	8*d*.
Eden*euet* ap Howel	4*s*.	5½*d*.
Madoco ap Howel	2*s*.	8*d*.
Meiler ap Howel		13½*d*.
Eua filia Howel		12¾*d*.
Kediuor	4*s*.	7¾*d*.
Win ap Lewelin	2*s*.	6¾*d*.
Meiler ap Lewelin	4*s*.	
Wladusa filia Yor*word*		19½*d*.
Madoco ap Gurg*enu*	4*s*.	4*d*.
Madoco ap D*aui*d[1]	4*s*.	0¼*d*.
Kenuric Goch		14½*d*.
Dabyn	2*s*.	8*d*.
Madoco Duy[2]	3*s*.	0½*d*.
Ad*af* ap Madoc	3*s*.	5½*d*.
Wentliana uxore Win		13¾*d*.
Wledir	2*s*.	2*d*.
Weyruel		18*d*.
Win Gam		20¾*d*.
Ioreword Loyt	2*s*.	
D*aui*d ap Gron*ou*	6*s*.	5½*d*.
Wyn ap Ph*elip*		21½*d*.
Eynon Loyt[3]	4*s*.	1¾*d*.
Eden*euet* ap Gurg*enu*	4*s*.	5½*d*.
D*aui*d ap Eden*euet*[4]	4*s*.	9*d*.
Eynon Loyt		15¾*d*.
Cad*ugan*		14*d*.
Eden*euet* Duy		20*d*.
Adaf ap Eden*euet*		18¼*d*.
Wentliana Loyt	5*s*.	9½*d*.

1 A Maddok ap David (of Penllyn) made homage and fealty to the prince in 1301 (Edward Owen, op. cit., p. 12). A person of the same name was assessed in Dwygraig and Maestran.

2 A widow of Madoc Du was assessed at 10*d*. *sub* Bedwarian in 1318 (*infra*, p. 102).

3 An Eynon Loyd was assessed at 5*s*. 1½*d*. in Bedwarian in 1318 (*infra*, p. 102).

4 A David ap Edneuet was assessed at 3*s*. 6*d*. *sub* Bedwarian in 1318 (*infra*, p. 102).

Ithel ap Ririd		16*d.*
Madoco ap Win[1]	4*s.*	3¾*d.*
Kenuric ap Ithel		18¾*d.*

Summa 8*li.* 9*s.* 10¾*d.*[2] probatur.

(23) Llanyckyl [i.e. Llanycil]

Adaf ap Cad*ugan*	2*s.*	2½*d.*
Ririd Vachan	8*s.*	7*d.*
fabro	7*s.*	3½*d.*
Win Penbras	3*s.*	4*d.*
D*aui*d Crouthur	2*s.*	4*d.*
Griffri ap Gron*ou*	2*s.*	1½*d.*
Meurico sacrista		22½*d.*

Summa 27*s.* 9*d.* probatur.

(24) Lestreuelyn [i.e. Llystreflyn (now Streflyn) in the parish of Llanycil][3]

Madoco ap Keuen*ard*	11*s.*	7½*d.*
Wyn ap Ioreworth		20*d.*
Ririd ap Yer*word*	3*s.*	6½*d.*
Win ap Tud*er*[4]	3*s.*	4½*d.*
Yer*wor*d ap Gron*ou*	2*s.*	6½*d.*
Madoco Sutore	5*s.*	9*d.*
Eynon Voyl		16*d.*
Kedich Duy		19*d.*
D*aui*d ap Gron*ou*	2*s.*	4*d.*

Summa 33*s.* 9*d.* probatur.

(25) Kemiscadeu [i.e. Cymysgadwy in the parish of Llanfor][5]

Madoco ap Howel	6*s.*	2½*d.*
ap Tegwar*et*	10*s.*	7½*d.*
Ph*elip*o sacrista	3*s.*	11½*d.*
Madoco ap Eynon	2*s.*	11½*d.*
Kenuric ap Ithel	4*s.*	8½*d.*

---

1 Cf. Madoc ap Guyn, assessed at 4*s.* *sub* Bedwarian in 1318 (*infra*, p. 102).

2 An error for £8. 10*s.* 10¾*d.*

3 The form 'Llystreflyn' is found at least as late as 1592 (P.R.O. L.R.2/236 f. 82.).

4 A Wyn ap Tudyr was fined 6*d.* for not making suit of court at the county and hundred courts in 1288 (P.R.O. E.101/614/3); he was assessed at 3*s.* 4*d.* in 1318 (*infra*, p. 102).

5 Lhuyd noted that Kymmyskadwy was one of the mountains in the parish of Llanfor (op. cit., p. 55). The exact location and extent of the township in the thirteenth century are unknown, but in 1592 tenements included in the vill of Kymyskadoye were Tyddyn Alis, Tyddyn y ffrith, Tyddyn hen, Yr Havotty, and Tyddyn y Pant Duy (P.R.O. L.R.2/236 f. 100). This places Cymysgadwy in the north-east corner of the parish of Llanfor, in an area which was once a detached portion of the parish of Llandderfel.

Anghar*ad* uxore [*sic*]	3*s*. 11½*d*.
Ioreword Duy	7*s*. 11¾*d*.
Ithel Voyl	3*s*. 11½*d*.
Roberto forestario	7*s*. 7½*d*.

Summa 58*s*. 11¾*d*.(1) probatur.

(26) Landeruayl [i.e. Llandderfel](2)

Win capellano	4*s*. 7½*d*.
Lewk*e* Loyt	12½*d*.
Ier*word* ap Gurg*enu*	3*s*. 3½*d*.
Eynon Duy	3*s*. 10*d*.
Eynon ap Tud*er*	17½*d*.
Cad*ugan* ap Ririd	16½*d*.
Merck Heilin	18½*d*.
Madoco Pendwy	2*s*. 1½*d*.
Madoco ap Ad*af*(3)	20*d*.
Eynon	16½*d*.
Gron*ou* sutore	2*s*.
Adaf sutore	4*s*.
Gurg*enu* Ebogrh(4)	19½*d*.
Eynon ap Rerid	16*d*.
Madoco Goch	3*s*. 7*d*.
Blethint	3*s*. 5½*d*.
Ieuan ap Cathel	20¾*d*.
Ririd Loyt(5)	20¾*d*.

Summa 40*s*. 9½*d*.(6)

Summa totalis huius comoti: 97*li*. 14*s*.(7) 10¼*d*., unde de incremento ex summis particularibus 12*d*. probatur.

[m.1d., left h. col.]

Comotus de Estymaner [i.e. Ystumanner](8)

---

1 An error for £2. 11*s*. 11¾*d*.

2 The township seems to have been assessed at £2. 10*s*. 6*d*. in 1318 (*infra*, p. 97).

3 His widow was assessed at 18*d*. in 1318 (ibid.).

4 Ebogrh = ? Hebogydd (i.e., falconer). A David ap Gurgen was assessed at 14*d*. in 1318 *infra*, p. 96.

5 A David Loyd ap Ririt was assessed at 7*s*. 5*d*. in 1318 *infra*, p. 97.

6 The whole amount has been underlined for deletion. Interlineated above it is the following: '41*s*. 9½*d*., incrementum 12*d*. probatur'.

7 '14*s*.' underlined for deletion; interlineated above it: '15*s*.' The total sum is an error for £98. 8*s*. 6¼*d*.

8 The first seven entries appear directly under the name of the commote with no clear indication of which township is referred to here. It may be Cwmcadian in the parish of Pennal, to judge from the second entry; but no corroboration of the existence of a vill of Cwmcadian at this time has been found.

abbate de Kynner.[1]	18*s.* 8*d.*
Cumcadyen[2]	15*s.* 6*d.*
Anghar*ad* filia Win	18*d.*
uxore Wasdinot et Deykin	2*s.* 4½*d.*
Dauid ap Riliard	22¼*d.*
Lowarch	2*s.* 6¾*d.*
Gwin ap Eynon	3*s.* 1¼*d.*

Summa 45*s.* 6¾*d.* probatur.

Tud*er* ap Gron*ou*[3]	5*s.* 1¾*d.*

Summa 10*s.* 1*d.* [*sic*] probatur.

(1) Winas [*or possibly* Wiuas][4]

Eynon ap Cad*ugan*	5*s.* 4*d.*

Summa 5*s.* 4*d.* probatur.

(2) Pencoyd [i.e. Pencoed in the parish of ?Tywyn][5]

Ithel Duy	2*s.* 1*d.*
Madoco ap Reys	3*s.* 8¾*d.*
Madoco Cam	14*s.* 4¾*d.*
Madoco Voil	3*s.* 2¾*d.*

Summa 23*s.* 5¼*d.* probatur.

(3) Catheleu [i.e. Caethle in the parish of Tywyn]

Madin With	4*s.* 9*d.*
Dauid ap Griffid	3*s.* 4*d.*
Ada ap Ithel	2*s.* 4*d.*

---

1 i.e., Cymer.

2 i.e., Cwmcadian, land which belonged to Cymer Abbey (see *Journ. Mer. Hist. and Rec. Soc.*, III (1957–60), 69).

3 The name stands on its own: since the sum he was assessed at does not tally with the total under his name, it is more than likely that other entries have been omitted in error; nor has the name of the township been entered.

4 No trace of the name has been found and consequently the location of the township is completely unknown.

5 One cannot accept that the Pencoed mentioned here is the place of that name in the township of Uwchygarreg (K. Williams-Jones, op. cit., p. 239) in the northern half of the parish of Llanfihangel-y-Pennant, since that part of the parish was in the commote of Tal-y-bont even in the 1290s, as the reference to, e.g., Llanfihangel township under that commote makes clear. The only Pencoed in the commote of Ystumanner which has hitherto been discovered is that on the earliest 1″ O.S. map where, as Pen y coed, it appears between Rhiwerfa and Llannerchgoediog, about one third of a mile to the north-east of Tanycoedisaf and about three quarters of a mile to the south-east of Tanycoeduchaf. It is suggested, therefore, that the township of Pencoed, to which no other reference has been found, was in the parish of Tywyn.

Ithel Cam		18*d.*
Meiler ap Adaf		21$\frac{1}{2}$*d.*
Gron*ou* Grek.	2*s.*	1*d.*
Griffid Voyl		22$\frac{1}{4}$*d.*
Howel ap Griffid		21$\frac{1}{4}$*d.*
Ioreword ap Ieuan	2*s.*	4$\frac{1}{2}$*d.*
Morud		18*d.*
Gron*ou* ap Ieuan	4*s.*	2*d.*
Ririd Gorista	4*s.*	8$\frac{1}{4}$*d.*
Iorword ap Griffid	4*s.*	5*d.*
Morwid Wechef [*sic*](1)		22*d.*
Ier*word* Penath	2*s.*	
Madoco ap Lewelin		20*d.*
Ieuaf Duy	2*s.*	

Summa 44*s.* 0$\frac{3}{4}$*d.* probatur.

(4) Botaloc [i.e. Botalog in the parish of Tywyn]

Cad*ugan* Kethin	2*s.*	4$\frac{1}{2}$*d.*
Ph*elip*o ap Kediuor	5*s.*	8$\frac{1}{2}$*d.*
Adaf Goch	3*s.*	8$\frac{1}{4}$*d.*

Summa 11*s.* 9$\frac{1}{4}$*d.* probatur.

(5) Keuenros [i.e. Cefnrhos in the parish of Tywyn]

Ithel ap Crom	16*s.*	8$\frac{1}{4}$*d.*
Ithel Wan	2*s.*	10*d.*
Ithel Duy		19*d.*
D*aui*d Duy orhalt(2)	3*s.*	9$\frac{1}{4}$*d.*
Adaf Cutta	2*s.*	1$\frac{1}{4}$*d.*
Deykin	7*s.*	9$\frac{1}{2}$*d.*
D*aui*d Duy ap Deykin		21$\frac{1}{4}$*d.*
Kenuelin	3*s.*	2$\frac{1}{4}$*d.*
Gron*ou* ap Yer*word*	5*s.*	7$\frac{1}{2}$*d.*
Win ap Cad*ugan*	4*s.*	1$\frac{1}{4}$*d.*
Lewek*e* filia Madoc	2*s.*	8$\frac{1}{4}$*d.*
map Wechethes	3*s.*	8$\frac{1}{2}$*d.*
Adaf ap Yer*word*	2*s.*	4$\frac{1}{2}$*d.*
Howel ap Cad*ugan*	3*s.*	2$\frac{3}{4}$*d.*

---

1 Professor Melville Richards suggested that what was probably intended here was Wech[eth]es (for 'gwehyddes'). Cf. *infra*, the twelfth entry under Cefnrhos; and cf. further *B.B.C.S.*, V (1929–31), 147.

2 Possibly Allt Goch, north-east of Aberdyfi and directly north of Pen-helyg. Cf. also Allt-lwyd, about four miles north-east of Aberdyfi. A Tyddyn Duy Tan yr Allt is noted in 1592 (P.R.O. L.R.2/236 f. 54v). There was a Tythyn yr allt goch near Trefrydd in 1633 (*Journ. Mer. Hist. and Rec. Soc.*, II (1953–6), 314), and lands called Yr Allt Llwyd ycha in the same township of Cefnrhos (ibid., p. 316).

Ieuan ap Robert	21$\frac{1}{4}$*d.*
Moridic ap Gwin	15*s.* 3*d.*
Ier*word* ap Adaf	2*s.* 0$\frac{1}{2}$*d.*
Gwilim	22$\frac{3}{4}$*d.*
Griffri	21*d.*
Griffid ap Ieuan	3*s.* 9*d.*
Yer*word* ap Wasdewy	3*s.* 8$\frac{3}{4}$*d.*
Ieuaf	19$\frac{1}{2}$*d.*
Ithel ap Adaf	4*s.* 1*d.*
Ieuan ap Reys	5*s.* 3$\frac{1}{4}$*d.*
Tud*er* ap Griffid	3*s.* 4*d.*
Eynon Voil	2*s.* 4$\frac{1}{2}$*d.*
Ionkin	2*s.* 5*d.*
Ithel ap Lowarch	18$\frac{1}{2}$*d.*
Dauid Grek.	2*s.* 2$\frac{1}{2}$*d.*
Madoco ap Meiler	7*s.* 2*d.*
Madoco kesseloc(1)	4*s.* 3*d.*
Bromwin	3*s.* 3$\frac{3}{4}$*d.*
Gronu ap Cad*ugan*	5*s.* 7*d.*
Yago ap Dehewint	13*s.* 7$\frac{1}{2}$*d.*
Iorword ap Iokin	2*s.* 4$\frac{1}{2}$*d.*
Dechewint ap Iago	21*d.*
Ieuan hen	2*s.* 9$\frac{1}{2}$*d.*
Ieuan ap Lowarch	2*s.* 5$\frac{1}{4}$*d.*
Tangwistel filia Ithel	10*s.* 10$\frac{1}{2}$*d.*
Ieuan ap Kethin	5*s.* 4$\frac{1}{4}$*d.*
Adaf ap Lowarch	2*s.* 1*d.*

Summa 8*li.* 16*s.* 1$\frac{1}{4}$*d.* probatur.

(6) Penthlin [i.e. Penllyn in the parish of Tywyn]

Win ap Madoc	2*s.* 2*d.*

Summa 2*s.* 2*d.* probatur.

(7) Reuarua [i.e. Rhiwerfa in the parish of Llanfihangel-y-Pennant]

Win ap Madoc	20*d.*
Madoco ap Sulien	4*s.* 1*d.*
Yer*word* Goch	5*s.* 5$\frac{1}{2}$*d.*
Eden*euet* Duy	19$\frac{1}{2}$*d.*
Meiler ap Madoc	18*s.* 6$\frac{3}{4}$*d.*

Summa 31*s.* 4$\frac{3}{4}$*d.* probatur.

---

1 If this refers to a place, no trace of it has been found.

(8) Lanercoydoc [i.e. Llannerchgoediog in the parish of Tywyn]

Madoco ap Meiler	4*s*. 9*d*.
Adaf Skynnith	3*s*. 5½*d*.
Griffid ap Mereduth	4*s*. 11¼*d*.
Dauid ap Griffid	2*s*. 4¾*d*.
Wentlyana filia Griffid	2*s*. 6*d*.
Dauid ap Kediuor	3*s*. 4½*d*.
D*aui*d Grach	2*s*. 11½*d*.
Tegwar*et* Grak.	2*s*. 5*d*.
Wasmyhangel	3*s*. 5½*d*.
Adaf ap Win	3*s*.
Goch Gaur	16¾*d*.
Eynon Penath	2*s*. 1¾*d*.
Kenuric Duy	17½*d*.

Summa 38*s*. 3*d*. probatur.

(9) Maystreuenant [i.e. Maestrefnant in the parishes of Llanfihangel-y-Pennant and Tywyn]

Eynon ap Adaf	3*s*. 5*d*.
Yer*word* ap Griffid	2*s*. 4*d*.
Yer*word* Duy	4*s*. 4½*d*.
Heylin ap Dehewint	3*s*. 2½*d*.
Tudgoch uxore Dehewint	2*s*. 10*d*.
Eynon Voyl	4*s*. 5¼*d*.
Madoco ap Ieuaf	4*s*. 4*d*.
Yer*word* ap Ieuan	3*s*. 8*d*.
Madoco ap Yer*word* ap Gron*ou* With	4*s*. 1½*d*.

Summa 32*s*. 7¾*d*.(1) probatur.

(10) Langederos [i.e. Llangedris in the parish of Tal-y-llyn]

Win Voyl	10*s*. 8*d*.
Win ap Moridic	2*s*. 4*d*.
Ithel ap Colligwith	2*s*. 11*d*.
Collyguth	4*s*. 4*d*.
Tangwistel Goch	18*d*.
Gwathauc	13*s*. 6*d*.
Ph*elip*o Cam	2*s*. 4½*d*.
Cad*ugan* ap Tangwistel	2*s*. 9½*d*.
D*aui*d Voyl(2)	13*s*. 10*d*.

Summa 54*s*. 3*d*. probatur.

1 An error for 32*s*. 8¾*d*.

2 He is probably to be identified with the David Voyl who had, according to the extent of *c*. 1284, half a mill in the area, for the next entry immediately following touches 'piscaria que vocatur Tabyth Lyn' which must refer to Tal-y-llyn. (*Arch. Camb.*, (1867), p. 187).

(11) Huchbega [possibly [Trefrion] Uwch Buga in the parish of Tywyn][1]

Gwathloc ap Cad*ugan*	3*s*. 10¼*d*.
Summa 44*s*. 3*d*.[*sic*][2]	

[m. 2d., left h. col.]

(12) Arnarou[3]

Madoco Chitharista[4]	11*s*. 10*d*.
Summa 11*s*. 10*d*. *probatur*	

(13) Bylan[5]

Madoco Goch	5*s*. 2*d*.
Daykin Skinith	4*s*. 11*d*.
Wilim ap Cad*ugan*	18½*d*.
Meiler ap Gurg*enu* et Lewelin ap Dauid	2*s*. 7*d*.
Was Patrik	7*s*. 5½*d*.
Madoco ap Cad*ugan*	5*s*. 0½*d*.
Ieuan ap Dauid	13*s*. 9¼*d*.
Deykin Goch	2*s*. 0¾*d*.
Dauid filio Eden*euet* Duy	2*s*. 1*d*.
Madoco ap Riscaellus	2*s*. 11*d*.
Generis Duy	2*s*. 2*d*.
Adaf ap D*aui*d et matre eius	2*s*. 0½*d*.
Summa 51*s*. 8½*d*.[6] probatur.	

(14) Treffethian [i.e. Trefeddian in the parish of Tywyn]

Madoco ap Meiler	2*s*. 11¼*d*.
Yer*word* ap Moridic	4*s*. 4¼*d*.
Ithel ap Ieuan	3*s*. 6*d*.
Cad*ugan* ap Eboldir	2*s*. 8*d*.
Meuanou	20½*d*.

1 See Melville Richards, *Welsh Administrative and Territorial Units* (1969), p. 209.

2 Clearly some matter has been omitted here, for the total bears no relation to what has preceded it.
In the left hand margin at the bottom of the membrane the word 'loquendum' has been entered.

3 Location unknown. It is difficult to know what to make of this name: it could be Arnarou (which would give an ending 'arw', as in Garreg Arw); or it could be Aruaron (which could possibly give us something like Yr Horon, which is near Trefeddian, the next township but one).

4 He and his brothers owed 5*s*. 'de consuetudinibus', according to the extent of *c*. 1284 (*Arch. Camb*., (1867), p. 186).

5 No trace of the name has been found in the commote of Ystumanner. There is a farm called Bylan in the parish of Brithdir and Islaw'r-dref, but that is in the commote of Tal-y-bont and therefore cannot refer to the same place as is mentioned in the text.

6 An error for 51*s*. 9*d*.

Wasdewy	3*s*.	7*d*.
Kenuric ap D*auid*[1]	8*s*.	6¼*d*.
Tystywin	4*s*.	1½*d*.
Adaf ap Eynon	12*s*.	5*d*.
Ph*elip*o ap Eynon	2*s*.	9*d*.
Adaf Vachan	2*s*.	6*d*.
Gurgenu ap Adaf	6*s*.	8½*d*.
Summa 53*s*. 8¼*d*.[2]		

(15) Maesmaur [i.e. Maesmor in the parish of Tywyn][3]

Gilberto Vachan	6*s*.	10*d*.
Eynon Duy	2*s*.	5*d*.
Meiler ap Eynon	5*s*.	1*d*.
Eynon ap Griffid	3*s*.	11*d*.
Adaf ap Griffid	2*s*.	0¼*d*.
Generys uxore Win	2*s*.	
Tangwistel uxore Adaf Duy	4*s*.	1¼*d*.
Madoco ap Eynon	16*s*.	7¼*d*.
Eynon Voil	6*s*.	8¼*d*.
Ieuan Pant	3*s*.	4*d*.
Summa 53*s*. probatur.		

(16) Gwadelmenith [i.e. Gwyddelfynydd in the parish of Tywyn]

Cad*ugan* Goch		17*d*.
Tangwistel filia Lewelini	2*s*.	1½*d*.
Adaf Couppa	2*s*.	8*d*.
Win Wlossec	2*s*.	3½*d*.
Itak. Coch[4]	5*s*.	1¼*d*.

---

1 A Kenurik ap David from Ystumanner made homage and fealty to the prince of Wales in 1301 (Edward Owen, op.cit., p. 20).

2 Underlined for deletion. Interlineated above the total is the following: '55*s*. 9¼*d*. incrementum 2*s*. 1*d*., probatur'.

3 This of course cannot be the township of Maesmawr in the parish of Llangelynnin (K. Williams-Jones, op. cit., p. 171) since the latter is in the commote of Tal-y-bont. The exact location and limits of Maesmor in the commote of Ystumanner are uncertain. Professor Melville Richards, using the great Elizabethan survey of Merioneth in 1592 as a source, identified (Kae) Maesmor with part of the township of Trefri (=Trefrydd); however, a rental of crown lands in 1633 published by Mr. E. D. Jones (see *Journ. Mer. Hist. and Rec. Soc.*, II (1953–6), 318) shows that Kae Maesmor was in the township of Treverion (=Trefeirion). The late sixteenth and early seventeenth centuries appear to have been a period of great instability in the boundaries of townships, especially in the Tywyn area, but if it can be accepted that the Maesmor mentioned here was in the township of Trefeirion rather than in Trefrydd, then two things follow: firstly, that the fifth person assessed – Adaf ap Griffid – may have been an ancestor of the Dolaugwyn family; and secondly, that the Pant in the last entry may refer to either Pant y Maes or Pant y Bawe (ibid., p. 317).

4 An Isak Goth owed 1*s*. 'de consuetudinibus', according to the extent of *c*. 1284 (*Arch. Camb.*, (1867), p. 186).

Marured	16*d.*
Ad*af* Goch	19*d.*
Win Voyl	16¼*d.*
D*aui*d Cam	2*s.* 4*d.*
Eua filia Wir	2*s.* 0½*d.*
Madoc ap Eua	22*d.*
Meiler ap Madoc	2*s.* 3*d.*
Ieuan ap Win(1)	23*d.*
Kediuor ap Ieuan	2*s.* 5*d.*
Madoco ap Howel	2*s.* 2½*d.*
Eynon Goch	2*s.* 10*d.*
Adaf ap Ieuan	22*d.*

Summa 37*s.* 6½*d.* probatur.

(17) Lanloydey [i.e. Llanllwydau in the parish of Llanfihangel-y-Pennant]

Madoco ap Meiler	2*s.* 7½*d.*
Map Goch	2*s.* 5½*d.*
Kediuor ap D*aui*d	4*s.* 6¾*d.*
Gwdaws	2*s.* 2¾*d.*
Madoco ap Seysild	5*s.* 7¾*d.*
Ieuan ap Landeu	5*s.* 1*d.*
Cad*ugan* ap Griffid	5*s.* 7*d.*
Gurgenu ap Lowarch	3*s.* 5½*d.*
Madoco ap Lowarch	2*s.* 2*d.*
Madoco Ebarwith	2*s.* 9*d.*
Hirlender	2*s.* 10*d.*
Generis uxore Eden*euet*	21*d.*

Summa 41*s.* 6¾*d.*(2) probatur.

(18) Penhale [i.e. Pennal]

Generis filia Kinogam	17*d.*
Gurg*enu* Coyt maur(3)	4*s.* 10*d.*
Adaf ap Ph*elip*	5*s.* 7*d.*
Eynon Predith	4*s.* 8*d.*
Mereduth Bongam	2*s.* 9½*d.*
Adaf ap Wingam	3*s.* 4*d.*
Ieuan ap Cad*ugan*	2*s.* 8*d.*

1 A Yeuan ab Guen made homage and fealty to the prince of Wales in 1301 (Edward Owen, op. cit., p. 20); and a Ieuan ap Wyn (Gwyn) was farming the amobr of the commote of Ystumanner in 1304–05 (*B.B.C.S.*, I (1921–3), 265; P.R.O. S.C.6/1170/5 m. 5); but it is difficult to identify them with the Ieuan ap Win of the subsidy.

2 An error for 41*s.* 1¾*d.*

3 The name does not seem to have survived. Cf. Tythin y Coed in 1633 (*Journ. Mer. Hist. and Rec. Soc.*, II (1953–6), 322).

Perweur	20¼*d.*
Win ap Adaf	21*d.*
Ithel ap Heylin	19*d.*
Eua filia Hunith	2*s.* 2¼*d.*
D*aui*d ap Griffid[1]	14*s.* 4¼*d.*
Ieuan Duy	2*s.* 9¼*d.*
Yer*word* Duy	16*d.*
Meiler ap Adaf	20*d.*
Generys filia Rufut	2*s.* 0¾*d.*
Laurencio de Monte Gomery	2*s.* 5*d.*
Griffid ap Meiler	17¾*d.*
Yer*word* ap Mereduth	20½*d.*
Gurg*enu* Melinnith	4*s.* 6*d.*
Meiler ap Kenuric	8*s.* 4*d.*
Roberto	3*s.* 2¼*d.*
Map Ygwely	20*d.*
Ey*non* ap Yer*word*	5*s.* 7¼*d.*
Win Duy	20¾*d.*
Wladusa filia Ener	19*d.*
Tud*er* ap Lewelin	6*s.* 9*d.*
Eyner ap Wilim	8*s.* 4¾*d.*
Moridic ap Keuenard	2*s.* 1*d.*
Yer*word* ap Was moel	23¼*d.*
Madoco ap Adaf	5*s.* 4*d.*
Yer*word* Vachan[2]	4*s.* 4½*d.*
Llaugut	2*s.* 3¼*d.*
Ieuan ap Howel	3*s.* 8¾*d.*
Anghar*ad* filia Kenewric	16¾*d.*
Tud*er* Goch filio D*aui*d	19½*d.*
Eynon ap Madoc	2*s.* 1¾*d.*
Tegwar*et*	6*s.* 11¼*d.*

Summa 6*li.* 13*s.* 10¾*d.*[3] probatur.

(19) Wrek [i.e. Gwrych in the parish of Tywyn]

Wentliana filia Griffid	8*s.* 9*d.*

---

1 A David ap Griffith heads the list of those from Ystumanner who made homage and fealty to the prince in 1301 (Edward Owen, op. cit., p. 20), but this is the bond vill of Pennal. Was David ap Griffith an 'uchelwr' with interests in the vill?

2 Yerword Vaghan was paying an annual rent of 3*s.* 4*d.* on land in the vill of Pennal at the time of the making of the extent of Merioneth *c.* 1284 (*Arch. Camb.*, (1867), p. 186). In 1308–09 the sheriff of Merioneth was accounting for 4*d.* for rent concealed at the time of the making of the extent for six acres of Welsh land which used to belong to Iorwerth Fychan in the vill of Pennal (E. A. Lewis, 'The Decay of Tribalism in North Wales', *Trans. Hon. Soc. Cymmrodorion* (1902–03), p. 54).

3 An error for £6. 13*s.* 10½*d.*

Wr ap Cad*ugan*	8*s.* 10*d.*
Tud*er* ap Eynon	3*s.* 3½*d.*
D*aui*d ap Cad*ugan*	18*d.*
Madin	5*s.* 7*d.*
Gurg*enu* ap D*aui*d	5*s.* 8½*d.*
Dauid ap Deykin et Iago	2*s.* 8*d.*
Gurg*enu* Voil	3*s.* 1*d.*
Bichan	20½*d.*
Aurifabro et Ad*af* filio Mathei	2*s.* 6*d.*
Eynon ap D*aui*d	4*s.* 4*d.*
Wilim	2*s.* 10*d.*
Adaf ap Gurg*enu*	2*s.* 0½*d.*
Adaf ap Eyn*on* et D*aui*d	7*s.* 10*d.*
Wachly et map	3*s.* 5*d.*
D*aui*d Duy ap D*aui*d	2*s.* 4*d.*
Roberto ap Edenewint	4*s.* 3½*d.*
Lewelin ap Cad*ugan*(1)	16*s.* 7*d.*
Griffid ap Lewelin	2*s.* 10*d.*

Summa 4*li.* 10*s.* 1½*d.* probatur.

[m.1d., right h. col.]

(20) Villa Tewyn [i.e. Tywyn]

Madin Cam	21*d.*
Heylin ap Rog*er*(2)	4*s.* 11*d.*
Ph*elip*o ap Adaf	2*s.* 1½*d.*
Gron*ou*	2*s.* 9*d.*
Heylin Voyl	21½*d.*
Cad*ugan* sutore	17*d.*
Nest uxore D*aui*d	2*s.* 6*d.*
Kenet Cam	19*d.*
map Cossyn	2*s.* 4*d.*

Summa 21*s.* 2½*d.*(3) probatur.

(21) Bronpres [i.e. Bron-prys in the parish of Tywyn]

Griffid ap Cad*ugan*	3*s.* 8*d.*
Eyn*on* Goch	2*s.* 5*d.*
Kediuor ap Dehewint	2*s.* 5*d.*

---

1 In 1306 and 1309 the sheriff of Merioneth was accounting for 10*s.* annually for four acres of Welsh land which once belonged to Llywelyn ap Cadwgan who died in Madog's rebellion fighting against the crown. (P.R.O. S.C.6/1170/5; E. A. Lewis, op. cit., p. 55). Did the heavy sum at which he was assessed in 1292–3 affect his political judgement in 1294–5?

2 As a villein from Tal-y-bont, Heylin ap Roger was paying 3*s.* 4*d.* in 1284 so that he could remain freely at Tywyn (*Arch. Camb.*, (1867), p. 184).

3 An error for 21*s.* 2*d.*

Dauid ap Yago		21*d.*
Ithel Goch	2*s.*	0½*d.*
Eyno*n* ap Ph*elip*	7*s.*	3*d.*
Madoco Pengrek	2*s.*	2¾*d.*
Wladosa uxore Ph*elip*i	2*s.*	7*d.*
Wilim Skynith		22*d.*

Summa 26*s.* 1¾*d.*(1) probatur.

(22) Kenvayl [i.e. Cynfal in the parish of Tywyn]

Adaf Vachan	7*s.*	1*d.*
Ieuan ap Adaf	4*s.*	3*d.*
Kendalo Croum	7*s.*	6*d.*
Madoco ap Kenur*ic*	11*s.*	1*d.*
Gron*ou* ap Ithel	7*s.*	9*d.*
Eyn*on* Voil	2*s.*	
Gron*ou* Voil(2)	2*s.*	2*d.*
Gron*ou* ap Wilim	2*s.*	10*d.*
Griffid ap Eynon	3*s.*	1*d.*
Ad*af* ap Ey*non*	6*s.*	7½*d.*
Tud*er* ap Adaf	3*s.*	7*d.*
Lewelino ap Gron*ou*	3*s.*	1½*d.*
Wladusa filia Cad*ugan*	2*s.*	2*d.*
Ad*af* ap Madoc(3)	2*s.*	1¾*d.*
map Talennyatur	2*s.*	
Lewk*e* filia Lewelini		20*d.*
Griffid ap Ph*elip*	2*s.*	4¼*d.*
Madoco ap Mad*oc* Kethin	2*s.*	3½*d.*
Ioreword Duy	4*s.*	2*d.*
Cad*ugan* ap Yer*word*	3*s.*	6*d.*
D*aui*d ap Yago	5*s.*	9½*d.*
Win ap Yer*word*	2*s.*	9½*d.*
Griffid Whith	2*s.*	
Gron*ou* ap Hodelov	4*s.*	
D*aui*d Cam	2*s.*	2½*d.*
Ad*af* ap Cad*ugan*	2*s.*	7½*d.*
Gwerith		17*d.*

Summa 103*s.* 2½*d.*(4) probatur.

---

1 '1¾*d.*' underlined for deletion; interlineated above it: '2¼*d.* incrementum ½*d.* probatur'.

2 Cf. the entry in the extent of *c.* 1284: 'De Gronoco Voyl de exitu vaccarum suarum 4*s.* 2*d.*' (*Arch. Camb.*, (1867), p. 187) and the fact that a Gronou Voyl was a ringild of Ystumanner in 1306–07 (P.R.O. S.C.6/1170/5 m. 5). Only one other Gronou Voil was assessed in Ystumanner (see *infra* under Ystradgwyn).

3 An Adaf ab Maddok owed 40*d.* 'de consuetudinibus' in Ystumanner *c.* 1284 (*Arch. Camb.*, (1867), p. 186).

4 An error for 102*s.* 2½*d.*

(23) Villa Penmaen [i.e. Penmaen in the parish of Tywyn]

Dauid Duy	3*s*.
Madoco ap Griffid	3*s*. 10*d*.
Moridic ap Ioreword	3*s*. 1*d*.
Gron*ou* ap Kenocam	3*s*. 6*d*.
Madoco ap Kediuor	3*s*. 5½*d*.
Morur*an* ap Meiller	3*s*. 4½*d*.
Ph*elip*o ap Adaf	5*s*. 5½*d*.
Wentliana filia Lewelini	2*s*. 8*d*.
Ieuan ap Ph*elip*	9*s*. 8½*d*.
D*aui*d ap Crek.	15½*d*.

Summa 39*s*. 4½*d*. probatur.

(24) Treffeden[1]

Iockin Tuglyn	2*s*.
Wentlian*a* uxore D*aui*d	4*s*. 1*d*.
Cad*ugan* ap Adaf	3*s*. 1½*d*.
Urien Voyl	2*s*. 4*d*.
Eynon ap D*aui*d	5*s*. 9*d*.
filia Deweyd	2*s*.
Ithel Voyl	23*d*.
Eynon ap Gron*ou*	4*s*. 11*d*.
Win ap Madin	6*s*. 4*d*.
Ithel ap Win	2*s*. 5*d*.
Ivanou ap Madoc	9*s*. 1½*d*.
D*aui*d ap Madoc	3*s*.
Enith	2*s*. 6*d*.
Eynon Goch	18*d*.
D*aui*d ap Tuder	2*s*. 0½*d*.
Anghar*ad* uxore Tud*er*	18*d*.
Madoco Goch	2*s*. 0½*d*.

Summa 56*s*. 7*d*. probatur.

---

1 Probably somewhere in the parish of Tywyn. The name suggests that a Tref Ednyfed once existed – quite distinct from Trefeddian – but even the Ty-glyn in the first entry is elusive and does not help us in locating the township. Prof. G. R. J. Jones identified Treffeden with Trefeddian – it was inhabited in the late thirteenth century, he says, 'by at least seventeen family households' (see his 'Some Medieval Rural Settlements in North Wales' in *Transactions and Papers of the Institute of British Geographers* (1953), p. 55) – but it would have suited his arguments better to have referred to Treffethian with its twelve taxpayers in 1292–3 (*supra*, p. 26–7), exactly the same number of holdings as existed apparently in 1592. If Treffeden = Trefeddian, what are we to make of Treffethian, which has more obvious claims to being Trefeddian? Are we here dealing with two distinct townships? Or is one an outlier of the other? If Ty-glyn in the first entry could be identified and located, it might help to solve the mystery.

(25) Villa Treueryth [i.e. Trefrydd in the parish of Tywyn][1]

Kallwit	6*s*. 4*d*.
Gron*ou* ap Win	35*s*. 4*d*.
Madoco ap Eynon	2*s*. 5*d*.
Edenowen Cul	4*s*.
Gron*ou* Duy	4*s*. 8*d*.
Ieuan ap Ithel	3*s*. 2*d*.
Weruel uxore Gof.	20*d*.
D*aui*d ap Adaf	19*d*.
Win ap Idenerth	2*s*. 8*d*.
Madoco ap Win	10*s*. 5*d*.
uxore Griffid Gock.	20*d*.
Kediuor Of	20*d*.

Summa 75*s*. 7*d*. probatur.

(26) Corrous [i.e. Corris in the parish of Tal-y-llyn]

Kediuor ap Eynon	3*s*. 7*d*.
D*aui*d Hene	2*s*. 1¼*d*.
Griffid Porthour	5*s*. 3*d*.
Ty Map Morud	3*s*.
Yer*word* ap D*aui*d	21*d*.
D*aui*d Corrous[2]	2*s*. 3½*d*.
Griffid ap Heylin	5*s*. 5¾*d*.
Ph*elip*o ap Ithel	3*s*. 11*d*.
Ithel Goch.	4*s*. 5½*d*.
Ieuan Corrous	18*d*.
Madoco ap Lewelin	18*s*. 4½*d*.
Iuor ap Meiler	8*s*. 11½*d*.
Ier*word* ap Iuor	5*s*. 0½*d*.
Griffri ap Kediuor	2*s*. 11*d*.
Eynon ap Adaf	2*s*. 8*d*.
Eua filia Kediuor	16½*d*.

Summa 72*s*. 8*d*. probatur.

(27) Keyswyn [i.e. Ceiswyn in the parish of Tal-y-llyn]

Eynon ap Madoc	16*s*. 8*d*.
map maur	3*s*. 4*d*.
D*aui*d ap Win	6*s*. 5*d*.
Ad*af* ap Gurg*enu*	9*s*. 5*d*.

---

1 It appears as 'Trefri' on O.S. maps.

2 i.e., of Corris.

Ieuan ap Llagau	2*s*. 8½*d*.
filiis Ieuan ap D*aui*d	2*s*. 5½*d*.
Moridic Pours	2*s*. 4*d*.
Ithel Gwethel	22*d*.
Ieuan Hir	2*s*. 5½*d*.
Itha gargam	2*s*. 9*d*.
Griffid Crouthur	4*s*. 5*d*.
fil. Ad*af* ap Griffid	4*s*. 10*d*.
Tegwar*et* Velin	3*s*. 7*d*.
Ithel Warth	3*s*. 6*d*.
Wir ap Was Patrik	2*s*. 5*d*.
Reys Keyswin	2*s*. 11½*d*.
Eden*euet* Crak.	2*s*.
fil. Ad*af* Wachan	2*s*.

Summa 76*s*. 1*d*. probatur.

(28) Stradquin [i.e. Ystradgwyn in the parish of Tal-y-llyn]

D*aui*d ap Tud*er*	5*s*. 9*d*.
Ken. ap Kadogan	3*s*. 3½*d*.
Moruran ap Tud*er*	3*s*. 4¼*d*.
Tegwar*et* Voyl	2*s*. 5*d*.
Ieuan ap Iuor	2*s*. 6*d*.
Eua uxore Ithel	4*s*. 8*d*.
Yer*word* ap Ad*af*	3*s*.
Anghar*ad* uxore Eynon	2*s*. 3*d*.

[m.2d., right h. col.]

Adhuc Stradquin

Ph*elip*o Duy	2*s*. 1½*d*.
Ph*elip*o fratre eius	2*s*. 7*d*.
Madoco ap Tud*er*	2*s*. 8*d*.
Cad*ugan* Saer	12*s*. 4*d*.
Cad*ugan* ap Adkin	6*s*. 4*d*.
Eua filia Tud*er*	2*s*. 2*d*.
Tud*er* Voyl	6*s*. 0¾*d*.
Madoco ap Yer*word*	2*s*. 6*d*.
Ithel Voyl	4*s*. 10*d*.
Ithel ap Wyn	3*s*. 8½*d*.
Win ap Gron*ou*	17*d*.
Ieuan Crak.	2*s*. 3*d*.
Weruel Duy	18*d*.
Ada ap Eynon	10*s*. 9*d*.
Madoco ap Eynon	3*s*. 6*d*.
Dauid ap Win	2*s*. 11*d*.

Dauid ap Win[1]	8s. 2*d.*
Gron*ou* Voil[2]	2*s.* 8¼*d.*
Gron*ou* ap Reys et Ririd ap Gron*ou*	2*s.* 10*d.*
Wladusa filia Ithel	19½*d.*
Clerkin	2*s.* 1*d.*
Cad*ugan* ap Meiler	4*s.* 3½*d.*
D*aui*d ap Moridic	8*s.* 9*d.*
Ithel ap Was Patrik	3*s.* 11*d.*
Kediuor ap Wion	6*s.* 2*d.*
Eynon ap Ithel	19½*d.*

Summa 6*li.* 6*s.* 11¼*d.*[3] probatur.

Taxatores:

Eynon ap D*aui*d Seys	12*s.* 8*d.*
Madoco Duy	14*s.*
D*aui*d ap Win[4]	13*s.* 4*d.*
Eynon ap D*aui*d	9*s.* 10*d.*
Griffid ap Adaf	6*s.* 10*d.*
Lewelino ap Wylim	3*s.* 6*d.*

Summa 60*s.* 2*d.* probatur.

Summa istius commoti 79*li.* 16*s.* 4½*d.*[5] probatur, unde de incremento 56*s.* 4½*d.*, unde de summis particularibus 2*s.* 1½*d.* et de summa totali 54*s.* 3*d.* probatur.

[m.3, left h. col.]

Commotus de Talbunt [i.e. Tal-y-bont]

(1) Lamendyget [i.e. Llanfendigaid in the parish of Llangelynnin]

Madoco ap Ph*elip*	8*s.* 10¼*d.*
Madoco ap Yer*word*	3*s.* 9*d.*
Win ?Simmul	2*s.* 5*d.*
Anghar*ad* filia Eynon	14*d.*

1 A David ap Guen of Meirionnydd made homage and fealty to the prince of Wales in 1301 (Edward Owen, op. cit., p. 17) and a David ap Gwin was acting as woodward of Ystumanner in 1306–07 (P.R.O. S.C.6/1170/5 m. 5). Cf. *infra*, n. 4, and pp. 36, n. 2 and 51 n. 3.

2 Cf. *supra*, p. 31, n. 2.

3 An error for £6 17*s.* 0¼*d.*

4 Cf. *supra*, n. 1.

5 The whole amount has been underlined for deletion. Interlineated above the line: '£82. 12*s.* 9*d.*', an error for £83. 1*s.* 5¾*d.*

Ithel Gock.		17½d.
Nest filia Adaf		16¼d.
Treydin	2s.	5½d.
Gron*ou* Voyl	5s.	1½d.
Madoco ap Ithel	5s.	2½d.
Yer*word* sutore		16½d.
Meiler Voyl	5s.	8¾d.
Tegwaret Vaur	7s.	7¼d.
Ieuan ap Madoc	2s.	1¼d.
Eynon Vachan(1)	7s.	8½d.
Dauid ap Win(2)	9s.	
Eynon ap Kenuric	10s.	8d.
Penrin	3s.	4½d.
D*aui*d ap Madin		22¾d.
Win capellano	8s.	5¼d.
Eynon ap Madoc	2s.	2¾d.
Ph*elip*o ap Tegwar*et*	3s.	6¾d.
Eynon capellano	2s.	6½d.
Ieuan Aron	10s.	1½d.

Summa 108*s.* 1¾*d.* probatur.

(2) Bodgadevan [i.e. Bodgadfan in the parish of Llangelynnin]

Madoco ap Eynon	4s.	11¾d.
Madoco ap Moridic	2s.	5¾d.
Ithel ap Griffid		22¼d.
Angar*ad* filia Win	10s.	4½d.
Howel ap Gron*ou*	3s.	7¾d.
Madoco ap Kenuig		18½d.
fabro		14½d.
uxore D*aui*d Trefas(3)		16d.
Eynon Hir	8s.	4¼d.
Yer*word* ap Howel	3s.	11d.
Lewelin ap Madoc	8s.	8½d.
map Gron*ou* ap Ieuan	2s.	8¼d.
Adaf ap Madin	13s.	3¼d.

1 An Eynoun Vaghan held land in Tonfannau (which was within the township of Llanfendigaid – see Owen Parry, art. cit., p. 30) in *c.* 1284 (*Arch. Camb.*, (1867), p. 185), and an Eynon Vaghan was serving the office of woodward of the commote of Tal-y-bont in 1306–07 (P.R.O. S.C.6/1170/5 m. 5). A person of the same name was assessed also in the nearby township of Rhyd-cryw; and it may be noted, too, that an Eynon Vaghan ab Maddok of Meirionnydd made homage and fealty to the prince of Wales in 1301 (Edward Owen, op. cit., p. 17).

2 Cf. *supra*, p. 35, n. 1.

3 i.e., of Trefaes (see Owen Parry, art. cit., p. 30).

Wir ap Madin	7*s*.	9¾*d*.
Madin ap Adaf Hen	24*s*.	
uxore Tegwar*et* Vachan		12¼*d*.
Wion Troyn		15*d*.
Kefnauc		15¼*d*.
was Wagyl		16¼*d*.
Meiler ap Wion	2*s*.	11½*d*.
Eyn*on* Leget	3*s*.	8*d*.

Summa 107*s*. 8½*d*.[1] probatur.

(3) Redcru [i.e. Rhyd-cryw in the parish of Llanegryn]

Ph*elip*o ap D*aui*d	12*s*.	
D*aui*d ap Ph*elip*	7*s*.	5½*d*.
Eyn*on* ap Yer*word*		16¾*d*.
Madoco ap Yer*word*		18½*d*.
Eyn*on* ap Ph*elip*[2]	7*s*.	8¼*d*.
Seysild grek.	2*s*.	3½*d*.
uxore D*aui*d ap Phelip		19¼*d*.
Madoco Voyl		17*d*.
Tudgech filia Adaf	2*s*.	4¾*d*.
Gron*ou* ap Ph*elip*[3]	2*s*.	10*d*.
Dugech filia Gron*ou*		16*d*.
Eua filia D*aui*d	4*s*.	1*d*.
Cad*ugan* ap Madoc	6*s*.	2¾*d*.
D*aui*d ap Houa	2*s*.	6*d*.
Cad*ugan* ap Ieuan	2*s*.	5*d*.
Ad*af* ap Cad*ugan*	3*s*.	8*d*.
D*aui*d Duy	2*s*.	1*d*.
D*aui*d Tanbont[4]	4*s*.	11¼*d*.
Ithel ap Kenuric	3*s*.	3¼*d*.
D*aui*d ap Gron*ou*	4*s*.	7¼*d*.
Meurik*o* ap Win	9*s*.	3*d*.
Tangwistel filia Bondic	3*s*.	6*d*.
Eyn*on* Ruth	3*s*.	6¾*d*.
Iuor		21½*d*.
Rudry		14*d*.
Win ap Eyn*on*	4*s*.	8¾*d*.

---

1 An error for 107*s*. 8¼*d*.

2 According to the extent of *c*. 1284, Eynoun ap Philip and Gronoc his brother owed 5*s*. for the assize rent in the commote (*Arch. Camb.*, (1867), p. 185). For an echo of the same in the *c*. 1420 extent, see *Rec. of Caern.* p. 272.

3 See *supra*, n. 2.

4 No trace of Tanbont has been found.

Eynon ap Win	16½*d.*
Eynon ap Meirion	14¾*d.*
Mad*oco* ap Gron*ou*	21*d.*
Griffid ap Ener	3*s.* 1¾*d.*
Wladusa filia Eynon	19*d.*
Yer*word* ap Gron*ou*	16*d.*
D*aui*d Goch	4*s.* 9¼*d.*
Ithel ap D*aui*d	3*s.* 0¾*d.*
Eyn*on* Penteg	18*d.*
Heylin Voyl	6*s.* 5½*d.*
Anghar*ad* filia Gron*ou*	3*s.* 9¾*d.*
Kolmync	5*s.* 4¼*d.*
Cad*ugan* Voyl	2*s.* 5¼*d.*
Eynon Crouthur	18¾*d.*
Ier*word* ap Ithel	23¾*d.*
Angahar*ad* [*sic*] filia Moridic	4s. 6*d.*
Eyn*on* Vachan(1)	5*s.* 9*d.*
Moridic Voyl	3*s.* 5¾*d.*
Leget Cornerat	5*s.* 11¼*d.*
Eynon ap Heylin	20½*d.*

Summa 8*li.* 3*s.* 5¾*d.*(2) probatur.

(4) Pennarth [i.e. Peniarth in the parish of Llanegryn]

Tangwistel filia Ieuan	6*s.* 4*d.*
Cad*ugan* ap Eynon	3*s.* 10*d.*
Madoco ap Ithel	10*s.* 0¼*d.*
Madoco ap D*aui*d	4*s.* 8¾*d.*
D*aui*d ap Gron*ou*(3)	5*s.* 7¼*d.*
Meiler ap Lewelin	9*s.* 1¾*d.*
Adaf ap Meiler	13*s.* 1¼*d.*
Heylin ap Iuor	7*s.* 6¾*d.*
Wladusa filia Gron*ou*	3*s.* 2½*d.*
map Was Doun	2*s.* 1*d.*
Dauid(4) Galgich	10*s.* 8*d.*
Meurico ap Howel	4s.
Ieuan Vachan	3*s.* 11*d.*
Dudgech filia Wasmihangel	3*s.* 2½*d.*

---

1 See *supra*, p. 36, n. 1.

2 An error for £8. 2*s.* 5¾*d.*

3 A David ap Gronou was made clustor of Kevynteylloyn, a neighbouring township, in 1326 (*B.B.C.S.*, VI (1931–3), 357), but it is unlikely that he is to be identified with the David ap Gronou of the subsidy.

4 'Goch' added but subsequently struck through.

Kenuric ap Gock.	3*s*.	9*d*.
Ithel ap Ieuan		16¾*d*.
Cad*ugan* ap Ada	2*s*.	
map Bedar	4*s*.	2¾*d*.
Madoco ap Eyn*on*	2*s*.	9½*d*.
Adaf Wirion	3*s*.	5½*d*.
Dauid ap Eynon	3*s*.	10¼*d*.
Dauid Duy		19¾*d*.
Madoco Duy	2*s*.	2*d*.
Meiler ap Ithel		19½*d*.
Madoco ap Meiler		16¾*d*.
Wen Unwin	2*s*.	4*d*.
Anghar*ad* filia Madoci(1)		16¼*d*.
Anghar*ad* Duy		12½*d*.
[m.4, left h. col.]		
Dauid Goch		16½*d*.
Reys Duy	2*s*.	10*d*.
Genithles filia Griffri	6*s*.	5¼*d*.
Lewelin ap Madoc	10*s*.	8*d*.
Morur*an* ap Madoc		17¼*d*.
Meiler ap Lewelin	3*s*.	2¾*d*.
sorore fratris Heylin	18*s*.	3¼*d*.
Ioreword Crak.	2*s*.	8¾*d*.
Madoco ap Ithel	3*s*.	0¾*d*.
Ioreword ap Madoc	3*s*.	4*d*.
Tangwistel filia Edenowein	3*s*.	4½*d*.
Eynon Duy	3*s*.	6¾*d*.
Madin ap Ph*elip*	2*s*.	8*d*.
Madoco Skynith	2*s*.	5¼*d*.
Moridic ap Ieuan	3*s*.	0½*d*.
Ithel ap Ada		19¼*d*.
Thomas		17¼*d*.
Adaf ap Madoc		17¼*d*.
Morur*an* ap Ithel	3*s*.	8¼*d*.
Wilim ap Eynon	4*s*.	8*d*.
D*aui*d ap Ada	4*s*.	11¾*d*.
Gron*ou* Goch	3*s*.	9¼*d*.
Ithel Ney		23*d*.
Ithel Vachan	13*s*.	4*d*.
map Doyok.	3*s*.	4*d*.

1 It was, apparently, her daughters Dudgu and Leucu who paid a relief of 10*s*. to succeed to their mother's land at the hundred court held at Dolgellau on 21 December 1325 (W. H. Waters, *The Edwardian Settlement*, p. 155, n. 3).

Morur*an* ap Gurg*enu*[1]	4*s.* 2½*d.*
Madoco ap Morur*an*	2*s.* 2*d.*
Blethint	2*s.* 5¼*d.*
Madoco ap Eynon	6*s.* 8*d.*
uxore Eynon fabro	8*s.*
Hunith	20½*d.*
Lowarch Crak.	16*d.*
Elena	3*s.* 1¼*d.*
Win Voyl	6*s.* 0¼*d.*

Summa 13*li.* 18¾*d.*[2] probatur.

(5) Cragennan [i.e. Cregennan in the parish of Llangelynnin]

D*aui*d ap Ph*elip*	3*s.* 8*d.*
Houa saer	4*s.* 9¼*d.*
Ithel Crak	3*s.* 8*d.*
Dauid ap Wechethes	4*s.* 9½*d.*
Adaf ap Madoc	2*s.* 10*d.*
Adaf ap Griffid	14*s.* 4½*d.*
Ithel ap Edenowen	19½*d.*
Eynon Voil	8*s.* 2*d.*
Dauid ap Eynon	11*s.* 0¾*d.*
Ad*af* ap Tegwar*et*	2*s.* 8*d.*
Tegwar*et* ap Reis	3*s.* 1*d.*
Madoco Goch	3*s.* 5*d.*
Acherui Cam	2*s.* 4½*d.*
map Ioreword ap Reis	2*s.* 10*d.*
Anghar*ad* or pant[3]	2*s.* 5¼*d.*
Gron*ou* Whith	22¾*d.*

Summa 73*s.* 8*d.* probatur.

(6) Morvan Maynoc [i.e. Morfa Maenog in the parish of Llangelynnin]

Eynon ap Adaf	8*s.* 8*d.*
Win ap Moridic	4*s.* 1*d.*
Madoco ap D*aui*d	2*s.* 1½*d.*
Eynon ap Tegwar*et*	5*s.* 9*d.*

---

1 His land was in the hands of the crown and Roger Lestrange had taken possession of them after the conquest (*Arch. Camb.*, (1867), p. 185); and in Easter 1309 the sheriff was accounting for two acres of Welsh land which had belonged to Moruram ap Gurg. in the vill of Peniarth, so that he was dead by then (E. A. Lewis, 'The Decay of Tribalism in North Wales', *Trans. Hon. Soc. Cymmrodorion* (1902–03), p. 52).

2 An error for £13. 4*s.* 8¾*d.*

3 Possibly either Pantyllan (see K. Williams-Jones, op. cit , p. 171) or Pantphilip (see Owen Parry, art. cit., p. 30).

Wladusa filia D*au*id	5*s*. 8½*d*.
Ad*af* ap D*au*id	4*s*. 2½*d*.
D*au*id ap Moridic	3*s*. 7*d*.
Adaf ap Cad*ugan*	2*s*. 4½*d*.
Madoco ap Eyn*on*	3*s*. 0¾*d*.
D*au*id ap Tegwar*et*	3*s*. 1*d*.
Adaf ap Gron*ou*	21*d*.
D*au*id ap Kenithlin(1)	11*s*. 8*d*.
Summa 56*s*. 0¾*d*.	

(7) Longoril [i.e. Llwyngwril in the parish of Llangelynnin]

Peredur(2)	8*s*. 2*d*.
Madin Goch	7*s*. 5*d*.
Ithel ap Moridic	5*s*. 7*d*.
Wladusa filia Griffid	3*s*. 10½*d*.
Madoco ap Meiler	21*d*.
Madoco Whith	5*s*. 11½*d*.
Madoco fabro	4*s*. 3*d*.
Eynon ap Griffid	5*s*. 6*d*.
Madoco ap Lewelin	6*s*. 9*d*.
Moridic ap Keuenard	6*s*. 2¼*d*.
Gron*ou* Carpan	2*s*. 0½*d*.
Eua filia Eynon	21¼*d*.
Ieuan ap D*au*id	2*s*. 4¼*d*.
Madoco Vachan	5*s*. 6*d*.
Madoco ap Eynon	3*s*. 6*d*.
Adaf ap Gurg*enu*	8*s*. 5½*d*.
Eynon ap Aron	3*s*. 3½*d*.
Madoco ap Ithel	18*s*. 11¼*d*.
uxore Ithel ap Robert	3*s*. 3*d*.
Wion Pilis	2*s*.
Wigar.	17½*d*.
Gron*ou* vaur	5*s*. 2½*d*.
Ioreword ap Madoc	4*s*.
Madoc ap Eynon	21*d*.
Eynon Goch	18½*d*.

1 A David ap Kenythlin of Merioneth and Caernarvonshire was held hostage by the crown after the revolt of 1294–5. (*Trans. Caerns. Hist. Soc.*, 16 (1955), 24.)

2 Possibly the same person as the Peredur ap Llywelyn who died in Madog's war fighting against the crown and whose lands – 16 acres of Welsh land in Garthgynfor – the sheriff was accounting for in 1309 (P.R.O. S.C.6/1170/5). His son may have been the Gruffud ap Peredur who petitioned the crown in vain about the payment of the 'extended rent' on his land (E. A. Lewis, art. cit., pp. 32–3, 64–5). Note, however, that a Griffith ap Peredur made homage and fealty to the prince of Wales in 1301 (Edward Owen, op cit., p. 25).

Ier*word* Goch	15*d.*
Madoco ap Moridic	4*s.* 11½*d.*
uxore Ier*word* ap Yagou	6*s.* 3½*d.*
Summa 6*li.* 13*s.* probatur.	

(8) Nantcau [i.e. Nantcaw in the parish of Llanfihangel-y-Pennant][1]

Ieuan Duy	4*s.* 11*d.*
Madoco ap Gurg*enu*	19*d.*
D*aui*d ap Adaf	5*s.* 5½*d.*
Ph*elip*o Whith	8*s.* 2¾*d.*
Weruill*a* filia Ieuan	2*s.* 3½*d.*
Ithel ap Ieuan	2*s.* 2¾*d.*
Madoco Palmere	21¼*d.*
Ithel ap Tegwar*et*	3*s.* 8*d.*
Ph*elip*o Voil	11*s.* 3½*d.*
Ithel ap Adaf	8*s.* 6½*d.*
Eynon Medico	5*s.* 9*d.*
Ririd ap Madoc	5*s.* 11*d.*
Summa 61*s.* 7¾*d.*	

(9) Llamyhangel [i.e. Llanfihangel]

D*aui*d ap Grono*u*	2*s.* 1*d.*
Morur*a*n ap Grono*u*	20*d.*
Ieuan ap D*aui*d	19½*d.*
Eua filia Dauid	16*d.*
Ph*elip*o Voyl	5*s.* 2½*d.*
Lewke filia Ph*elip*i	3*s.* 5*d.*
Meiler ap Leweke	4*s.* 10*d.*
Generys filia Ioreword	21*d.*
Ph*elip*o Duy	2*s.* 7½*d.*
Adaf ap D*aui*d	5*s.* 9¼*d.*
Adaf ap Morud	21*d.*
Adaf ap Howel	16*s.* 6*d.*
Ioreword Goch[2]	7*s.* 11¼*d.*
Summa 56*s.* 5*d.*[3] probatur.	

---

1 Cf. the farm of the same name in the township of Pennant in the seventeenth century (Owen Parry, art. cit., p. 32) and in the township of Uwchygarreg by the eighteenth century (K. Williams-Jones, op. cit., p. 172.)

2 A Yereward Gouch made homage and fealty to the prince of Wales in 1301 (Edward Owen, op. cit., p. 25).

3 An error for 46*s.* 6*d.*

(10) Wonas [i.e. Gwanas in the parish of Brithdir][1]

Ithel Voyl	5*s.*	11*d.*
Tuder Glyne	6*s.*	6*d.*
Dauid Loyt	3*s.*	8*d.*
Summa 16*s.* 1*d.* probatur.		

[m.5, left h. col.]

De abbate de Kynner[2] apud Iskyvon[3]	7*s.*	6*d.*
De eodem de grangia de Abydon[4]	8*s.*	2*d.*
De eodem de eadem grangia	5*s.*	11½*d.*
De eodem apud Eskeridon[5]	3*s.*	4½*d.*
De eodem de grangia sua apud Brinbedewin[6]	3*s.*	8½*d.*
De eodem apud Redgarnet[7]	9*s.*	10*d.*
De eodem de grangia sua apud Go[v]othlyauc[8]	5*s.*	2*d.*
De eodem de grangia ap[ud] Gethlwassarrauc[9]	2*s.*	1½*d.*
De eodem de grangia in abbacia		16*d.*
Summa 47*s.* 2*d.* probatur.		

De episcopo de sancto Assapho apud grangiam de Hauot Newith[10]	10*s.*	3½*d.*
De eodem apud Eskesgaur[11]	12*s.*	6½*d.*
Summa 22*s.* 10*d.* probatur.		

Ithel ap Gurg*enu*[12]	36*s.*	
Summa 36*s.* probatur.		

1 See *infra*, p. 45, n. 2, and 47, n. 3.

2 i.e., Cymer.

3 Possibly Esgairwen, in the parish of Llanfachreth.

4 i.e. Abereiddon in the parish of Llanfachreth (see K. Williams-Jones, 'Llywelyn's Charter to Cymer Abbey in 1209', *Journ. Mer. Hist. and Rec. Soc.*, III (1957–60), 62–3).

5 i.e., Esgaireiddon, in the parish of Llanfachreth (ibid., p. 63).

6 i.e., Brynbedwyn, in the parish of Brithdir (ibid., p. 66).

7 i.e., Rhydygarnedd, in the parish of Llanegryn (ibid., p. 69).

8 i.e., Cyfeiliog, or that part of it between the Dyfi and Dulas rivers (ibid., p. 65).

9 i.e., Gellisarog, in the parish of Llanegryn (ibid., p. 71).

10 It is not known which Hafod Newydd this might refer to.

11 i.e., Esgairgawr, in the parish of Brithdir. Cymer Abbey also had an interest in it (ibid., p. 66).

12 The name of the township in which he had movables has not been entered.

(11) Garthmaylan [i.e. Garthmaelan in the parish of Brithdir][1]

Ieuan Duy	2*s*.	9*d*.
Madoco ap Win	2*s*.	0¼*d*.
Eua filia Lewelini		15¼*d*.
Leweke filia Howel[2]	7*s*.	4½*d*.
Ithel Bach	2*s*.	7½*d*.
Gurg*enu* aurifabro		17¼*d*.
Kenuric fabro	5*s*.	6½*d*.
Tangwistel filia D*aui*d		22*d*.
Generys filia Leweke		17¼*d*.
Dudgech filia D*aui*d Duy		16¼*d*.
Tantliu	5*s*.	7¼*d*.
Weruel filia Lewelini	4*s*.	
Madoc Crak.	2*s*.	3*d*.
Ener		21¼*d*.
Kenuric ap Louard		23½*d*.
Eynon Duy		19*d*.
Madoco or Dol[3]	4*s*.	7½*d*.
Cad*ugan* Goch		18*d*.
Danges	2*s*.	
Madin Duy	6*s*.	5½*d*.
Yerword ap Loward		18*d*.
Kenuric ap Blethin	3*s*.	9½*d*.

Summa 64*s*. 8¼*d*. probatur.

(12) Nannev [i.e. Nannau in the parish of Llanfachreth]

Weruel	2*s*.	6*d*.
Aniano ap Loward	4s.	5¼*d*.
Wentliana filia Kerwiot	3*s*.	4*d*.
Eua filia Howel		19*d*.
uxore Eynon ap Thomas	3*s*.	
Iorword sutore	7*s*.	8*d*.
Madin ?Cutta	2*s*.	2¾*d*.
uxore Ph*elipi*	2*s*.	8*d*.
Madin ap Ph*elip*		15*d*.
Win With	4*s*.	5½*d*.

1 The boundary between Garthmaelan and the township of Nannau, and hence the parish of Llanfachreth, was not the river Wnion as one might suppose, but a line drawn half-a-mile or so to the north of the river. See further *infra* p. 47, n. 3.

2 From this point the rest of the membrane is badly worn and the entries are consequently difficult to read.

3 Possibly Dolrhyd or Dolgun.

Madoco ap Adaf	6*s.*
Morwil	3*s.* 4*d.*
Candalo Goch	3*s.* 4*d.*
Ener Vachan[1]	8*s.* 6½*d.*
filia Madoci filii Tud*er*	2*s.*
Eynon ap Eynon kethin	2*s.* 10½*d.*
Iorword Wonas[2]	17¼*d.*
Crak coun	4*s.* 9*d.*
Ieuan Voil	3*s.* 0½*d.*
Ieuan Voil or Glastir[3]	7*s.* 6*d.*
Eynon Grek	4*s.* 1¼*d.*
Win ap Cathel	4*s.* 8*d.*
Madoco ap Eynon	2*s.* 1¾*d.*
Eua filia Kenuric	16*d.*
Madoco ap Ririd	3*s.* 9½*d.*
Thomas	2*s.* 6¼*d.*
Gron*ou* Goch	22½*d.*
Morwith filia Ithel	2*s.* 0½*d.*
Gron*ou* ap Ithel Crak.	2*s.* 11*d.*
Hunith Vachan	2*s.* 8*d.*
Lewelin ap Meiler	13*s.*
map Sely	21¼*d.*
Howel Goch	6*s.* 2½*d.*
D*aui*d ap Yagou	4*s.* 5*d.*
Guroc Gwydraus	2*s.* 3*d.*
Win ap Kenuric	2*s.* 1*d.*
uxore Eynon Duy	2*s.* 5½*d.*
Ieuaf ap Ieuan	9*s.* 3*d.*
Win Loyt	21*s.* 4*d.*
Ithel ap y mank.	3*s.* 2½*d.*

---

1 An ancestor of the Nanneys and Vaughans of Nannau. All the evidence suggests that he was a firm supporter of the crown. Nothing is known of his attitude to the events of 1282–3 or of his allegiance at the beginning of the war of 1294–5. He boasted, however, that it was he who captured Madog, the leader of the great revolt of 1294–5, and claimed, on the strength of it, the rhaglawry of Tal-y-bont quit of farm. The claim was not accepted by the authorities. Nevertheless, he remained loyal to the crown, making homage and fealty to the prince of Wales in 1301 and serving the office of rhaglaw of Tal-y-bont from, at the latest, 1303 until his son succeeded him in office on his death *c.* 1330. He was certainly acting as one of the taxors of Tal-y-bont for the fifteenth granted in 1318 (P.R.O. E.159/95 m. 62). He was implicated, too, along with a number of prominent Merioneth men in the obscure but doubtless royalist-motivated raid on Dyffryn Clwyd in 1322. For a full summary of his career, see Bryn R. Parry, 'Hugh Nanney Hên (*c.* 1546–1623) Squire of Nannau', *Journ. Mer. Hist. and Rec. Soc.*, V (1965–8), 188.

2 i.e., of Gwanas, the township on the other side of the valley.

3 i.e., Glasdir in the parish of Llanfachreth.

Ieuan Keri	4*s*. 6½*d*.
Edenowen ap Cathel	3*s*. 1½*d*.
Edenowen Ledan	18½*d*.
Eynon Goch	2*s*. 6½*d*.
Madoco Kynith	2*s*. 2½*d*.
Ph*elip*o ap Meuric	2*s*. 5*d*.
Tegwar*et* Kenith	15½*d*.
Griffid ap Meurik	22*d*.
Tegwar*et* Keri	16½*d*.
Wladusa	19*d*.
Eynon ap Ad*af*	4*s*. 3½*d*.
Eynon ap Weruel	10*s*. 8*d*.
Ad*af* ap Win	4*s*. 3½*d*.
Kenuric Vachan	5*s*. 4*d*.
Yer*word* ap Win	7*s*. 11½*d*.
Moyl Dainoc	12*s*. 5*d*.
Cad*ugan* ap Win	9*s*. 4*d*.
uxore Kenuric ap Iorword	2*s*. 4*d*.
Iorword ap Ph*elip*	4*s*. 9*d*.
Ieuan ap Cathel	8*s*. 3½*d*.
Iorword ap Madoc	12*s*. 6½*d*.
Generes filia Ruathlon	23¼*d*.
Eua Duy	6*s*. 0¼*d*.
Meuanou	3*s*. 0¼*d*.
Ithel ap Win	3*s*. 7½*d*.
Lewke filia Griffri	10*s*. 2*d*.
Iockin With	5*s*. 4*d*.
uxore Iorword With	3*s*. 3¼*d*.
Wion ap Dalwen	12*s*. 6*d*.
Cadugan ap Eynon	10*s*. 10½*d*.
Meiler	6*s*. 2½*d*.
Madoco Vachan(1)	16*s*. 3*d*.
Win ap Madoc	11*s*. 4*d*.
Tegwar*et* ap Eynon	5*s*. 10*d*.
Dauid ap Tegwar*et*	4*s*.
Anghar*ad* filia Win(2)	2*s*. 4*d*.
Tangwistel filia Eynon	5*s*. 8*d*.
Win ap Madoc	2*s*. 9½*d*.
Eynon Goch	7*s*.
Adaf ap Nannou	8*s*. 6¾*d*.

1 A Maddok Vaughan made homage and fealty to the prince of Wales in 1301 (Edward Owen, op. cit., p. 26).

2 A person of the same name paid exactly the same amount in the neighbouring township of Brithdir.

Adaf Saer	5*s*.	5½*d*.
Map Luges	3*s*.	6½*d*.
Howel ap Adaf	4*s*.	4*d*.
Madoco ap Cad*ugan*	4*s*.	
Gron*ou* ap Eden*euet*		20*d*.
Tuder ap Griffid		20½*d*.
Madoco Kennach	6*s*.	7½*d*.
Ithel Voyl	3*s*.	0½*d*.
map Oyn	5*s*.	8*d*.
Anghar*ad* filia Gron*ou*	2*s*.	0½*d*.
Eynon Duy	7*s*.	9*d*.
Win ap Wilim	4*s*.	3*d*.
Madoco ap Griffry(1)	12*s*.	
Tangwistel filia Griffri	11*s*.	1¼*d*.
Eynon ap Adaf	4*s*.	1½*d*.
Tudgech filia Tud*er*	2*s*.	3*d*.
Candalou ap Madoc		21¼*d*.
Ririd ap Eynon	2*s*.	6½*d*.
Cad*ugan* ap Win		19*d*.
Madoco filio Kenwr*ic*	4*s*.	9*d*.
Ithaelin	2*s*.	6½*d*.
Map Maur	8*s*.	5½*d*.
Kenuric ap Gurg*enu*	3*s*.	6½*d*.
Ieuan ap Gurg*enu*	4*s*.	1½*d*.
D*aui*d Salov	2*s*.	10½*d*.
Wladusa filia Arthur	2*s*.	3*d*.
Ieuan ap Edenowen	2*s*.	1½*d*.
Eynon ap Eloder	4*s*.	3*d*.
Griffid ap Iuor	9*s*.	4*d*.
Cantor		15*d*.
D*aui*d ap Lewelin		12½*d*.
Courgis		13¼*d*.

Summa 26*li*. 10*s*. 0½*d*.(2) probatur.

[m.3, right h. col.]

(13) Garthkenuaur [i.e. Garthgynfor in the parish of Brithdir](3)

Barth	2*s*.	4*d*.

---

1 A Maddok ap Griffith made homage and fealty to Edward of Caernarvon in 1301 (ibid., p. 25).

2 An error for £26. 14*s*. 5¾*d*.

3 Garthgynfor seems to have absorbed the townships of Gwanas and Garthmaelan in the course of time; certainly by the eighteenth century this was so (K. Williams-Jones (ed.), *Cal. of Mer. Quart. Sess. Rec.*, I (1965), 26). Hence the reason for the fact that the small area to the north of Dolgellau and the river Wnion is referred to on O.S. maps as Garthgynfor North (Cf. *supra*, p. 44, n. 1).

Cad*ugan* ap Kenwain	7*s*.	$4\frac{1}{2}$*d*.
Eua Vachan		18*d*.
Wladusa filia Hanalt	3*s*.	3*d*.
Dauid Saer		$20\frac{1}{4}$*d*.
Wentliana filia Hanalt		$15\frac{1}{2}$*d*.
D*aui*d ap Madoc		19*d*.
Ieuan ap Eynon	2*s*.	$4\frac{1}{2}$*d*.
D*aui*d Voyl	2*s*.	$8\frac{1}{2}$*d*.
Yer*word* ap Lewelin[1]	2*s*.	7*d*.
Ithel Penbras	3*s*.	6*d*.
Yer*word* ap Ithel	2*s*.	$4\frac{1}{4}$*d*.
Wentliana Vachan	3*s*.	$8\frac{1}{4}$*d*.
Nest Duy	2*s*.	$3\frac{1}{4}$*d*.
D*aui*d ap Ieuan	9*s*.	1*d*.
Madoco ap Win	10*s*.	
Goch Carri		21*d*.
Eynon ap Griffri	7*s*.	3*d*.
Adaf Bach	4*s*.	$2\frac{1}{2}$*d*.
Win ap Ioreword		16*d*.
Leweke filia Adaf	2*s*.	$5\frac{1}{2}$*d*.
Ithel Geurch	3*s*.	$4\frac{1}{4}$*d*.
Turgech filia Ithel	2*s*.	$10\frac{3}{4}$*d*.
Madoco ap Kenuric		18*d*.
Ithel ap Ieuan	12*s*.	$10\frac{3}{4}$*d*.
Kenuric ap Cad*ugan*	17*s*.	$2\frac{3}{4}$*d*.
Gron*ou* Goch	2*s*.	6*d*.
Adeyl	2*s*.	6*d*.
Madoco ap Ada	2*s*.	7*d*.
Meiler Loyt	4*s*.	$10\frac{3}{4}$*d*.
Win ap Ithel	2*s*.	4*d*.
Ithel ap Tegwar*et*	7*s*.	5*d*.
Ioreword ap Howel	3*s*.	$4\frac{3}{4}$*d*.
Gron*ou* ap Howel		$17\frac{1}{4}$*d*.

Summa 6*li*. 19*s*. $6\frac{1}{4}$*d*. probatur.

(14) Brithir [i.e. Brithdir]

Eynon Loyt	6*s*.	$10\frac{1}{2}$*d*.
Ieuan Loyt		$21\frac{3}{4}$*d*.
Gron*ou* ap Ieuan	7*s*.	$7\frac{1}{2}$*d*.
Ieuan Voil	5*s*.	7*d*.
Madoco ap Wion	8*s*.	7*d*.

1 A Iorwerth ap Lewelin was acting as ringild of Tal-y-bont in 1306–07 (P.R.O. S.C.6/1170/5).

Ieuan ap Ririd	2*s*. 9½*d*.
Anghar*ad* Goch	9*s*. 5*d*.
Margareta filia Ririd	16*d*.
D*aui*d ap Kenuric	4*s*. 5*d*.
Yer*word* ap Eynon	2*s*. 9*d*.
Win Crak.	7*s*. 4*d*.
Fallobr	5*s*. 1*d*.
Madoco filio Ioreword	2*s*. 6*d*.
Strasigil	8*s*. 1½*d*.
Ieuan ap Ada	2*s*. 3*d*.
Ithel ap Ithel Crek.	3*s*. 3½*d*.
Dudgech filia Tegwar*et*	20*d*.
Ithel ap Ithel	2*s*. 11*d*.
Kenuric ap Win	4*s*. 8*d*.
Lowarch ap Win	4*s*. 10½*d*.
Lowarch ap Win	20½*d*.
Anghar*ad* Loyt	18¾*d*.
D*aui*d Leget	20½*d*.
Meiler Voil	7*s*. 5*d*.
map Gurkin	15*d*.
Eua sorore eius	20*d*.
Cad*ugan* filio Cad*ugan* ap Win	5*s*.
Adaf ap Madoc	20*d*.
Madoco sutore	9*s*. 8*d*.
Anghar*ad* filia Win[1]	2*s*. 4*d*.
Ieuan sutore	2*s*. 6¼*d*.
Adaf sutore	4*s*. 3*d*.
Idernet	23*d*.
Generis filia Cele	16½*d*.
Madoco filio Ithel	2*s*. 11*d*.
Ithel ap Ioreword	6*s*. 11½*d*.
D*aui*d Goch	4*s*. 8*d*.
Ada Pen	7*s*. 3*d*.
Cad*ugan* Vachan	10*s*. 2¾*d*.
Cad*ugan* ap Howel	6*s*. 3½*d*.
Ioreword ap Seleu	14¼*d*.

Summa 8*li*. 17*s*. 5¾*d*.[2] probatur.

(15) Dolgethly [i.e. Dolgellau]

Meiler ap Tuder	21¼*d*.

---

1 Cf. *supra*, p. 46, n. 2.

2 An error for £8. 17*s*. 5¼*d*.

Ieuan ap Tuder	20*d.*
Tuder Boly	2*s.* 4*d.*

Summa 5*s.* 9¼*d.* probatur.

(16) [*Blank in MS.*][1]

Gron*ou* ap Win	5*s.* 6*d.*
Eynon Goch.	5*s.* 2*d.*
Ph*elip*o Loyt	5*s.* 8*d.*
Edenowen Voil	19*s.* 4*d.*
Dudgech filia Win	6*s.* 4*d.*
Madoco ap D*aui*d	2*s.* 8*d.*
Ririd ap Gron*ou*	9*s.* 8*d.*
Wladusa filia Griffid	19*d.*
uxore Ithel ap Griffri	3*s.* 0½*d.*
Edenowen	22*d.*
Madin ap Candalov	6*s.* 6¾*d.*
Win ap D*aui*d	3*s.* 8*d.*
Dauid ap Madin	5*s.* 9*d.*
D*aui*d ap Edenowen	16½*d.*
Eynon ap Win	5*s.* 0½*d.*
Anghar*ad* Duy	7*s.*
Eduduwel	23*d.*
Adaf ap Madoc	4*s.* 10½*d.*
uxore D*aui*d ap Yagou	4*s.* 10*d.*
Ithel ap Cad*ugan*	3*s.* 6½*d.*

Summa 105*s.* 4½*d.* [2] probatur.

(17) Dolgleder [i.e. Dolgledr in the parish of Brithdir][3]

Ririd ap Iuor	8*s.* 6*d.*
Madoc ap Gron*ou*	22¾*d.*
Gron*ou* ab [*sic*] Madoc	5*s.*
Tegwar*et* Crak.	3*s.* 4½*d.*
D*aui*d ap Ioreword	3*s.* 10¼*d.*
Ad*af* ap Gron*ou*	17½*d.*

---

1 The name of the township has not been entered here. It could possibly be Dyffrydan (immediately to the south of Dolgellau) which is not mentioned in this subsidy roll. It seems most unlikely that the list is a continuation of that of Dolgellau's, though there is a gap of about three inches after the three names appearing under that township. The Dolgellau list may be incomplete, however – though cf. *Arch. Camb.*, (1867), p. 184.

2 An error for 105*s.* 4¼*d.*

3 The township extended as far west as Erw-goed, at least in the seventeenth century (Jeffreys-Jones (ed.), *Exchequer Proceedings*, p. 236, where it appears as 'Erow Grydd').

Eynon ap Madoc	20*d.*
Tegwar*et* Goch	7*s.* 8½*d.*
Lewk*e* filia Tuder	4*s.* 9*d.*
Tuder ap Gron*ou*	2*s.* 0½*d.*
Madin ap D*aui*d	2*s.* 3½*d.*
Ieuan ap P*helip*	4*s.* 6¾*d.*
Edenowen Duy	5*s.*
Howel ap Lewelin	4*s.* 4½*d.*
Tuder*o* ap Eden*euet*	21*d.*
Eyn*on* ap Rich[?ard]	2*s.* 11½*d.*
Ieuan ap Gron*ou*	4*s.* 1½*d.*

[m.4, right h. col.]

Adhuc Dolgleder

Gurg*enu* capellano	5*s.* 8*d.*
Ithel ap Madoc	7*s.*
Eynon ap Howel[1]	9*s.* 6¾*d.*
Madin ap Gron*ou*	14½*d.*

Summa 4*li.* 8*s.* 9½*d.*[2] probatur.

(18) Kenvenrowen [i.e. Cefnyrowen in the parish of Brithdir]

Seisild ap Yer*word*	4*s.* 2½*d.*
D*aui*d ap Madoc	3*s.* 4*d.*
D*aui*d ap Madin	4*s.* 0½*d.*
Madoc Dyvoun	8*s.* 9½*d.*
Dauid ap Eynon	2*s.* 0½*d.*
Madoco ap Gurg*enu*	23*d.*
Meuedus	4*s.* 4¼*d.*
Ithel Duy	2*s* 1*d.*
Madoco Duy	14*s.* 8*d.*
Dauid ap Win[3]	5*s.*

Summa 50*s.* 5¼*d.* probatur.

(19) Bere [in the parish of Llanfihangel-y-Pennant][4]

Wilim Duy	8*s.*
Thom*as* fabro	2*s.*
Willelmo prest	3*s.* 4*d.*

---

1 In *c.* 1284 he held six bovates of land, extended when taken into the crown's hands at 6*s.* 8*d.*, and paid 20*s.* to Roger Lestrange for access to it (*Arch. Camb.*, (1867), p. 185).

2 An error for £4. 8*s.* 9*d.*

3 Cf. *supra*, p. 35, n. 1.

4 For a facsimile of this section of the roll relating to Bere see Maurice Beresford, *New Towns of the Middle Ages* (1967), Plate 12, opp. p. 300.

Ankoc	3*s*.	4*d*.
Pigis	2*s*.	4*d*.
Madoco ap Weches	6*s*.	8*d*.
Tudero	4*s*.	
Adaf Bach		16*d*.
Willelmo Pevir	2*s*.	
Alicia		16*d*.
Ad*af* sutore		12*d*.
Ph*elip*o Skinith	10*s*.	
Iockin Tylour	3*s*.	5*d*.
Henrico		12*d*.
Simone ap Wilim	5*s*.	2½*d*.
Willelmo Doun		22¾*d*.

Summa 76*s*. 11¾*d*. (1) probatur.

Taxatores:

Howello Routh	20*s*.	1½*d*.
Dauid ap Howel	29*s*.	8¼*d*.
Dauid ap Meiler	2*s*.	
Aron ap Lewelin	5*s*.	
Eynon ap D*aui*d	8*s*.	0¼*d*.
Madoco ap Wilim	8*s*.	1*d*.

Summa 72*s*. 11*d*. probatur.

Summa istius comoti 122*li*. 15*s*. 9½*d*.(2) probatur.

Comotus de Ardudou [i.e. Ardudwy](3)

(1) Trausuenith [i.e. Trawsfynydd]

Ph*elip*o Espis	19*s*.	2*d*.
?Cunnian	2*s*.	11*d*.
Madoco Imper.	16*s*.	5½*d*.
Cad*ugan* Kest	7*s*.	1¼*d*.
Eynon ap Ph*elip*	6*s*.	

1 An error for 56*s*. 10¼*d*.

2 An error for £122. 2*s*. 2½*d*.

3 For some unknown reason Ardudwy was, at a later date, unique amongst the commotes of Merioneth in not being divided into townships (K. Williams-Jones, op. cit., 18). If it can be assumed that the administrative units mentioned in this subsidy roll are, for the most part, vills, and if it can be assumed further that they represent the pre-parochial situation in Merioneth, it is clear that even at this early date the townships of Ardudwy were, generally, considerably bigger than those in other commotes, so much so indeed that at least five 'townships' – Trawsfynydd, Llanaber, Llanenddwyn, Llanbedr, and Llandecwyn – had to be divided into two for administrative purposes. It may not be simply coincidental that some parishes in Ardudwy were later divided into two, e.g., Llanaberismynydd and Llanaberuwch-mynydd, and Llanddwyweisygraig and Llanddwyweuwchygraig.

Madoco Duy	2*s*. 8*d*.
Milisandia	3*s*. 4¼*d*.
uxore Madir Len	3*s*. 8*d*.
Madoco Crek.	3*s*. 5½*d*.
Kenuric Duy[1]	4*s*.
Wentliana filia Eynon	5*s*. 6½*d*.
Eynon capellano	6*s*.
Kenuric ap Ada	10*s*.
Kenuric Skynith	2*s*. 8*d*.
Lewk*e* filia Lowarch	6*s*. 1*d*.
Anghar[ad] uxore Ade	4*s*. 0½*d*.
Nest filia Eynon	8*s*. 10¾*d*.
Wilmyn	20*d*.
Meyron Eynon Voil	17*d*.
D*aui*d Lowin	5*s*. 1½*d*.
Win carpentario	6*s*. 1*d*.
Ithel ap Lewk*e*	6*s*. 8½*d*.
Ithel Wan	6*s*. 8½*d*.
Troydir	8*s*.
uxore Gregorii	2*s*. 11*d*.
Yer*word* filio Gron*ou*	19*d*.
D*aui*d ap Wion	2*s*. 8¼*d*.
Yer*word* ap Was With	2*s*. 4*d*.
Eynon Goch	4*s*. 6*d*.
Was With	3*s*. 6*d*.
Ieuan ap Yer*word*	20¼*d*.
Iorword Duy	2*s*. 4¾*d*.
Tangwistel filia Madoc	4*s*. 7*d*.
Lowarch ap Gron*ou*[2]	8*s*. 11*d*.
Eden*euet* ap Iorword	9*s*.
Eynon ap Eden*euet*	3*s*.
Anghar*ad* Goch	20*d*.
Iorword ap Ieuan	8*s*. 9¼*d*.
Blethint Hagor	18¾*d*.
Moel Crek.	17*d*.
Kenuric map Brek.	2*s*. 1*d*.
Kenuric ap Ieuan	3*s*. 1½*d*.
Madoco Whih[*sic*]	2*s*. 7¼*d*.
Trahaern ap Eyn*on*	6*s*.

1 A Kenewrec Du fought on the English side in 1294–5 (E. B. Fryde (ed.), *Book of Prests of the King's Wardrobe for 1294–5* (1962), p. 156).

2 A Llawarth ap Gronou from Merioneth or Caernarvonshire was held as a hostage (amongst others) by the crown after the revolt of 1294–5 (*Trans. Caerns. Hist. Soc.*, 16 (1955), 24).

Ad*af* ap D*aui*d	5*s.* 8*d.*
Iorword ap Meiler	3*s.* 11½*d.*
Wentlian filia Madoc	4*s.* 4*d.*
uxore ?Anians	8*s.* 4*d.*
Gron*ou* Goch[1]	10*s.*
Candalov ap Reys	23¼*d.*
Candalo ap D*aui*d	7*s.* 1¼*d.*
Ieuan ap Heilin	5*s.* 10*d.*
Ieuan Cors	21*d.*
Dugech filia Yer*word*	2*s.*
Thom*as* Vachan	9*s.* 5*d.*

Summa 14*li.* 10¾*d.*[2] probatur.

(2) Lanaber [i.e. Llanaber]

Gron*ou* ap Madoc	3*s.* 1¼*d.*
Cogan	3*s.* 6¼*d.*
Cad*ugan* ap D*aui*d	7*s.* 5*d.*
Win ap Was Crek.	2*s.* 8*d.*
decano[3]	23*s.* 3*d.*
Benedicite [*sic*]	2*s.* 2¾*d.*
Wion ap D*aui*d	2*s.* 3*d.*
Eynon Pengrek.	2*s.* 8*d.*
D*aui*d ap Yer*word*	20*d.*

[m.5, right h. col.][4]

Adhuc Lanaber

Ioreword Vrsen	16*d.*
Adaf ap Ada	18*d.*
Madoco ap Ithel	20*d.*
Ioreword Vachan	7*s.* 4*d.*
Tangwistel	2*s.* 8*d.*
Adaf ap Tegwar*et*	21*d.*
Gron*ou* ap Adaf Eyn*on*	2*s.* 8*d.*
Adaf Whith	2*s.* 3*d.*
Osborn[5]	17*s.* 5½*d.*

---

1 A Gronne Gough made homage and fealty to the prince of Wales in 1301 (Edward Owen, op. cit., p. 25).

2 An error for £14. 2*s.* 4¾*d.*

3 Possibly Adam the dean of Ardudwy whose death is referred to in the chamberlain's account of 1304–05 (*B.B.C.S.*, I (1921–3), p. 267).

4 The membrane is badly worn in parts: the readings are consequently tentative at times, especially the amounts at which persons were assessed.

5 Possibly Osborn 'Wyddel', the founder of the tribe of the same name, who is said to have married the heiress of Corsygedol (*The Dictionary of Welsh Biography*, p. 689, but cf. *B.B.C.S.*, XIII (1948–50), p. 213). If that is so, it is possible that the portion of Llanaber dealt with here is Llanaberismynydd, as compared with, *infra*, Llanaberuwchmynydd.

Tale Moel	2*s.* 9¼*d.*
Ioreword Welour	6*s.* 11*d.*
Wion Pengam	18*d.*
Eden*euet* ap Heylin	2*s.*
Madoco ap Dynodir	18¾*d.*
Dauid ap Ioreword	16¼*d.*
Dudgech filia Lewelin	10*s.* 1¾*d.*
Yer*word* capellano	3*s.* 11*d.*
Kenuric ap Tegwar*et*	22*d.*
Eynon Duy	2*s.* 2½*d.*
Wion Voil	3*s.*
Adaf ap Ydon	5*s.* 0½*d.*
Yer*word* ap Adaf	3*s.* 1½*d.*
Wion	3*s.* 11¾*d.*
Adaf Voyl	4*s.* 6½*d.*
Eyn*on* ap Adaf	11*s.* 8¾*d.*
Kenuric ap Adaf	2*s.* 8*d.*
Tuder ap Gogan	6*s.* 6¼*d.*
Adaf ap D*aui*d ap Tegwaret	3*s.* 10¾*d.*
Madoco ap Ada ap ?Aloc	3*s.* 3½*d.*
Ada ap Ithel	2*s.* 5*d.*
Madoco Vrnant(1)	2*s.* 8*d.*
Tudgech ?Connian	6*s.*
Gron*ou* ap Gogan	3*s.*
Adaf ap Ioreword	2*s.* 8*d.*
Ph*elip*o ap Dehewint	2*s.* 8*d.*
Griffri Goch	14*s.* 8*d.*
Tangwistel filia Meiler	3*s.* 6½*d.*
D*aui*d Duy	2*s.*
Eynon Cok.	20*d.*
Gron*ou* ap Ioreword	12*d.*

Summa 10*li.* 11*s.* 4¼*d.*(2) probatur.

(3) Landewey [i.e. Llanddwywe]

Madoco Goch	3*s.* 8*d.*
Adaf ap Ruathon	7*s.* 8*d.*
Wion ap Meiler	4*s.* 2*d.*
Kenuric ap Win	7*s.*
Win ap Kenuric	2*s.* 8*d.*

1 i.e., possibly 'o'r Nant', but if so, the place has not been identified.

2 An error for £10. 11*s.* 8¼*d.*

Gron*ou* ap Heylin[1]	10*s*.	4*d*.
Madon ap Win	5*s*.	
Map Doun	3*s*.	
Vrien[2]	10*s*.	4½*d*.
Cad*ugan* ap Mad*oc*	2*s*.	8*d*.
Win Duy	6*s*.	4*d*.
D*aui*d ap Candalo		20¼*d*.
D*aui*d ap Ieuan	7*s*.	4*d*.
D*aui*d ap D*aui*d	8*s*.	4*d*.
Yer*word* ap Lewelin	3*s*.	
Dauid capellano de Lanendou[3]	3*s*.	11¼*d*.
Yer*word* ap Cad*ugan*	2*s*.	8*d*.
Candalo Cachepol[4]	4*s*.	5*d*.
Wion	3*s*.	10½*d*.
Ririd Duy	7*s*.	2½*d*.
Tuder ap D*aui*d	2*s*.	4*d*.
Wentliana filia Madoc	6*s*.	7*d*.
Tegware*t* ap Wion		17*d*.
Adaf ap Eynon[5]	2*s*.	4*d*.
Gron*ou* Duy	4*s*.	8¾*d*.

Summa 7*li*. 5*s*. 8¼*d*.[6] probatur.

(4) Landeuendon [i.e. Llanenddwyn]

Win sutore	5*s*.	5¼*d*.
Heylin Vachan		18¾*d*.
Madoco ap Eynon	8*s*.	1½*d*.
Madoco filio Win	2*s*.	5*d*.
Wion Loyt	3*s*.	1¼*d*.

---

1 In Easter 1309 the sheriff accounted for 4*s*. 4¼*d*. for six bovates of Welsh land in the vill of Llanddwywe which belonged to one Gron*ou* ap Heylyn who died in Madog's war against the crown. (*Trans. Hon. Soc. Cymmrodorion* (1902–03), p. 58.)

2 An Urien ap Tegwaret of Ardudwy made homage and fealty to prince Edward in 1301 (Edward Owen, op. cit., p. 13). The same person presumably was acting as ringild of Ardudwy late in Edward I's reign (P.R.O. S.C.6/1170/5 m. 5); and a person of the same name (and Griffith his son), along with a number of prominent Merioneth men, was accused by lord Grey of Ruthin of having attacked Dyffryn Clwyd in 1322 (Brynle R. Parry, 'A Note on Sir Gruffydd Llwyd', *B.B.C.S.*, XIX (1960–2), 316 n. 2). Everything suggests, therefore, that Urien ap Tegwaret was a firm supporter of the crown.

3 i.e., of Llanenddwyn.

4 The sheriff accounted, in Easter 1309, for 3*s*. 6*d*. for rent concealed at the time of the making of the extent (of *c*. 1284) for half an acre of Welsh land which used to belong to Kendalo Chachepol in the vill of Llanenddwyn (*Trans. Hon. Soc. Cymmrodorion* (1902–03), p. 57).

5 He held three acres of Welsh land in the vill of Llanenddwyn at 3*s*. 11*d*. annual rent in 1309 (ibid., p. 58).

6 Possibly an error for £6. 2*s*. 8¾*d*., though one cannot be certain since this membrane is badly worn.

Eynon Voyl	19*d*.
Wion ap Madoc	12*s*. 4*d*.
Yer*word* Escop	2*s*. 8*d*.
Griffri ap D*aui*d	2*s*. 6¼*d*.
Tudgech filia Eynon	18¾*d*.
D*aui*d Voil	5*s*. 10½*d*.
Kalumwy	4*s*. 4*d*.
Tegwar*et* Hen	12*s*.
Leweke uxore Lewelin	2*s*.
Adaf ap Gwion	21*d*.
Bergam	16*d*.
Gron*ou* ap Eyn*on*	18*d*.

Summa 70*s*. 1¼*d*. probatur.

(5) Landanoc [i.e. Llandanwg]

Ph*elip*o ap Madoc	6*s*. 8*d*.
Gron*ou* Vaur	4*s*. 8*d*.
D*aui*d ap Meiler	20*d*.
Yer*word* ap Adaf	6*s*. 4*d*.
Wenunwin	3*s*. 5½*d*.
Moil Wen	3*s*. 10*d*.
Eynon ap Ieuan	3*s*. 8*d*.
Win Voil	2*s*. 4*d*.
Ieuan Duy	18*d*.
D*aui*d ap Lowarch	2*s*.
Eynon ap Kenuric	2*s*. 1¼*d*.
Wentliana uxore Lowarch	3*s*. 3*d*.
Kenuric	3*s*. 6*d*.
Ririd Vaur	2*s*.
Yer*word* ap Cad*ugan*	3*s*. 9¼*d*.
Eynon Duy	2*s*.
Ririd aurifabro	7*s*.
Eynon ap Madoc	3*s*. 4*d*.
Wentliana filia Madoc	2*s*. 1½*d*.
Griffri ap Tegwar*et*	2*s*. 1½*d*.
Adaf filio Denowalt	2*s*. 5½*d*.
Gurg*enu* ap Madoc	8*s*. 2*d*.
Kenuric ap Tegwar*et*	4*s*.
Gron*ou* ap Yer*word*	17*d*.
Tegwar*et* sutore	16*d*.
Howel Kedor	2*s*. 4*d*.
Eblessenon	3*s*. 5½*d*.
Wion ap Tegwar*et*	20*d*.
Eynon ap Kenuric	2*s*. 10*d*.

Gron*ou* ap Wilim	8*s*. 8*d*.
Gron*ou* ap Adaf	2*s*. 10*d*.
Pridil	4*s*. 8*d*.
Generys Goch	16*d*.
Ioreword filio Tegwar*et*	3*s*. 8*d*.
Scotin	8*s*. 6*d*.
Doyladon	3*s*. 2½*d*.

Summa 6*li*. 6*s*. 3½*d*.[1] probatur.

(6) Taltreuethin [i.e. Taltreuddyn][2]

Pellipario	5*s*. 6*d*.
Win ap Mereduth	2*s*. 6*d*.
Win ap Kenuric	4*s*. 4*d*.
Anghar*ad* filia Reis	5*s*. 6*d*.
Dauid ap Ithel	12*d*.
Heylin ap Ithel	4*s*. 4*d*.
Madoco ?Corista	2*s*. 2*d*.
Candalo ap Tegwar*et*	16*d*.
Ithel ap Tegwar*et*	9*s*. 8*d*.
Geruasio presbitero	8*s*. 9*d*.
Eynon ap Tegwar*et*	16*d*.
Madoco sipac	18*d*.
Yer*word* ap Tegwar*et*	3*s*. 8*d*.

Summa 51*s*. 8*d*.[3] probatur.

(7) Lanpeder [i.e. Llanbedr]

Ed[eneuet] Cla[. . .]	13*s*. 8½*d*.
Ieuan ap ?Glasdwr	?
Wladusa Goch	2*s*. 2*d*.
Eynon ap Yer*word*	3*s*.
Eyn*on* ap Wilim	2*s*. 2*d*.
Yer*word* ap Gur*genu*	4*s*. 2*d*.
Karweth ap ?Rylkin With	4*s*. ?*d*.
Tegwaret sutore	16*d*.
Wladusa uxore Howel	13*s*. 4*d*.
Wladusa uxore . . .	3*s*. 8½*d*.
Kynlau	?*s*. 8*d*.
Tangwistel . . .	4*s*.
Weruel filia . . .	2*s*.

1 An error possibly for £6. 7*s*. 10½*d*.

2 It did not develop into a parish of its own. It is in the parish of Llanenddwyn.

3 Possibly an error for 51*s*. 7*d*., but some readings are uncertain.

[m.3d., left h. col.]

Adhuc Lanpeder

Cappan Eulan	5*s.*	1½*d.*
Yer*word* ap Asser		23½*d.*
Wentlian uxore Mad*oci*		17½*d.*
Moyl Dilwy		17*d.*
Win ap Kenuric	4*s.*	2*d.*
Eyn*on* ap Candalo	5*s.*	
Madoco filio Backenin	5*s.*	6¾*d.*
Ierword map Penaro		23*d.*
Ieuan fronniait	9*s.*	8*d.*
Win ap Howel	4*s.*	10½*d.*

Summa 104*s.* 7*d.*[1] probatur.

(8) Lanueyr [i.e. Llanfair]

D*aui*d ap Ph*elip*	2*s.*	8*d.*
Ioreword ap Meurik.		16*d.*
Vir ap Yer*word*		22*d.*
Ieuan Gron*ou*	2*s.*	2½*d.*
Win ap Ada	2*s.*	0¼*d.*
Gurg*enu* Voyl		21½*d.*
Yer*word* ap Wion	6*s.*	
Leweke Bran	3*s.*	6½*d.*
Yer*word* ap Gron*ou*	2*s.*	8*d.*
Win Goch	9*s.*	6*d.*
Candalo Dargois	5*s.*	6*d.*
Cad*ugan* With		14*d.*
Keuenard ap Ad*af*	2*s.*	6½*d.*
Eynon Ruth	4*s.*	2¾*d.*
Ada ap Kenuric	4*s.*	4¼*d.*
Yer*word* ap Eynon	9*s.*	4*d.*
Wilim Voil	4*s.*	
Yer*word* ap Edenoweyn	3*s.*	9*d.*
Meiler ap Cad*ugan*	2*s.*	8*d.*
Ewerich filia Ad*af*		16*d.*
Win ap Gron*ou*	3*s.*	11*d.*
Gron*ou* ap Meiler	2*s.*	8*d.*
Dudgech filia Wion		19¼*d.*
Yer*word* ap Ithel	5*s.*	1*d.*
Madoco ap Eynon	2*s.*	1½*d.*
Tegwar*et* Ruffo	2*s.*	0½*d.*

1 The final total must be taken on trust because the last portion of m. 3d is illegible in parts.

Eden*euet* ap Gogan	14*s*.	4½*d*.
Yer*word* ap D*aui*d	3*s*.	8¾*d*.
D*aui*d ap Iorword[1]	7*s*.	7*d*.
Eynon ap Lewelin		17½*d*.
Ririd ap Eynon	10*s*.	4¾*d*.
Wladusa filia Win	4*s*.	8½*d*.
Kenuric ap Madoc	3*s*.	4*d*.
Wentlian*a* filia Madoc	2*s*.	4¼*d*.
Keuen*ard* ap Madoc	3*s*.	9¼*d*.
Iohanne filio Wladusa	4*s*.	7¾*d*.
Pereuer uxore Win	2*s*.	
Ithel carpentario		22*d*.
Yer*word* ap Eyn*on*	4*s*.	10*d*.
Wentlian*a* filia Win		20½*d*.
Eynon ap Kenuric	6*s*.	5¼*d*.
Adaf ap Ca*dugan*	6*s*.	9*d*.
Adaf ap Atha	2*s*.	5½*d*.
Lowarch Goch	6*s*.	5½*d*.
Tudgech filia Iorword	4*s*.	1½*d*.
Yer*word* ap Gron*ou*	5*s*.	3*d*.
Generys uxore Ackennin	5*s*.	1½*d*.
Yer*word* ap Saleu	11*s*.	4½*d*.
D*aui*d ap Yer*word*	5*s*.	8¼*d*.
Ada ap Vdrich	3*s*.	
Candalo ap Reis	4*s*.	5*d*.
Yssec		18*d*.
Dauid ap Kenuric[2]	9*s*.	
Weruel uxore Mereduth	4*s*.	8*d*.
Ieuan ap Mereduth	7*s*.	4*d*.

Summa 12*li*. 0¼*d*.[3] probatur.

(9) Landecwin [i.e. Llandecwyn]

Gron*ou* ap Ithel	2*s*.	
Madoco ap Heylin	6*s*.	
Yer*word* ap Wasteyuol	4*s*.	
Gron*ou* Corista	2*s*.	7*d*.
Yer*word* aurifabro	4*s*.	0½*d*.
Ithel filio scriptoris	2*s*.	1½*d*.

1 A David ap Yereword made homage and fealty to the prince of Wales in 1301 (Edward Owen, op. cit., p. 26).

2 A David ap Kenewric from Merioneth or Caernarvonshire was held hostage by the crown after Madog's revolt of 1294–5. (*Trans. Caerns. Hist. Soc.*, 16 (1955), 24.)

3 An error for £12. 0*s*. 2¼*d*.

Yer*word* filio Candalo	4*s*.	4¼*d*.
Yer*word* ap Eyn*on* ap Ithel		18½*d*.
Meurico filio Reis		22*d*.
Gron*ou* ap Yer*word*	3*s*.	5¼*d*.
Eua filia Wilim		16*d*.
Iohanne filio Ph*elipi*		14*d*.
Eynon filio Edenowen	3*s*.	2*d*.

Summa 37*s*. 7*d*. probatur.

(10) Penrindeudrait [i.e. Penrhyndeudraeth][1]

Dauid ap Wion	5*s*.	6*d*.
Dauid ap Wion Scolheyk.		18*d*.
Kenuric ap Dauid	2*s*.	1¼*d*.
Adaf ap Candalo	5*s*.	
Tangwestel filia Meirion	2*s*.	10*d*.
Dauid Duy	2*s*.	
Yer*word* ap Dauid	2*s*.	2*d*.
Iohanne filio Eden*euet*		13*d*.
Madoco Duy		20*d*.
Yer*word* Bleso	5*s*.	4*d*.
Madoco ap Gron*ou*	4*s*.	
Anghar*ad* Goch		13*d*.
Anghar*ad* filia Ad*af*	3*s*.	1*d*.
Ithel ap Ph*elip*	3*s*.	4*d*.
Ieuan Voil		21*d*.
Wion Kesu [*sic*]	2*s*.	4*d*.
Cad*ugan* Pen	3*s*.	9¼*d*.
Adaf Duy	12*s*.	10¾*d*.
Adaf ap Dauid	5*s*.	8*d*.
Lewelin Goch		22½*d*.
Heylin Voil	5*s*.	4*d*.
Ada filio Ade	3*s*.	1*d*.
Eden*euet* ap Dauid	2*s*.	6½*d*.
Madin Mees	2*s*.	4*d*.
map Carrec	4*s*.	
Kenuric Cantore		17*d*.
Win ap Ad*af*		21¼*d*.
Ada ap Cradoc	4*s*.	6¼*d*.
Kenuric ap Keuenard	3*s*.	4*d*.
Ieuan Troyn	3*s*.	3*d*.
Generys filia Eyn*on*		16*d*.

1 It did not develop into a parish of its own until 1897. Until then it formed part of the parish of Llanfihangel-y-traethau.

Madoco ap Kenthlu	8*s.* 9*d.*
Adaf Ruth	18*d.*
Gron*ou* Goch	6*s.* 8*d.*
Lewelin Vachan	2*s.* 1¼*d.*
Ieuan capellano de Lamyhangel[1]	22*d.*
Eynon With	4*s.* 10½*d.*
Tegwar*et* Was	4*s.* 9¼*d.*
Eynon ap Ithel	2*s.* 8*d.*
Lewke uxore Iohannis	21¼*d.*
Ieuan Voil	2*s.* 11*d.*
Ieuan Duy	15½*d.*
Ad*af* Hudol	2*s.* 3½*d.*
Wentlian*a* uxore Ph*elipi*	19¼*d.*
Yer*word* ap Eynon	23*d.*
Ieuan Vachan	5*s.* 6*d.*
Wladusa filia Eden*euet*	2*s.* 9½*d.*
Madoco ap Eynon	3*s.* 9½*d.*
Iockin hen	2*s.* 8*d.*
Win Voil Vachan	2*s.* 7*d.*
Madoco ap Gron*ou*	3*s.* 8¾*d.*
Gron*ou* ap Eyn*on*	6*s.* 0¾*d.*
Rerid ap Ad*af*	6*s.* 2½*d.*
Adaf ap Eyn*on*	14¼*d.*
Ithel Voyl	4*s.* 10½*d.*
Edenowen ap Tegwar*et*	2*s.* 6*d.*
Madoco ap Ad*af*	2*s.* 2½*d.*

Summa 9*li.* 11*s.* 11½*d.*[2] probatur.

(11) Landecwin [i.e. Llandecwyn]

Ieuan ap Win	16*d.*
Eyn*on* ap Gron*ou*[3]	20*d.*
Eynon ap Kenuric	2*s.* 5*d.*
Yer*word* Duy	4*s.* 8*d.*
Yer*word* ap Madoc	3*s.* 10½*d.*

[m.4d., left h. col.]

Adhuc Landecwin

Eyn*on* ap Ad*af*	3*s.* 2½*d.*
Adaf ap Heylin	6*s.* 10½*d.*
Ithel ap D*aui*d	2*s.* 4*d.*

1 i.e., Llanfihangel.

2 An error for £9. 10*s.* 11½*d.*

3 In 1313, one Eynoun ap Gronagh was granted the bailiwick of the bedelry of Ardudwy during pleasure (*Cal. of Fine Rolls 1307–19*, p. 178).

Iorword ap Lewelin		18*d.*
D*aui*d ap Eynon	2*s.*	4*d.*
Anghar*ad* uxore Eynon		22*d.*
Adaf Sibero	16*s.*	4*d.*
Trahaern ap Ad*af*		22*d.*
Win ap Gogan		16*d.*
Iorword ap Tegwar*et*[1]	12*s.*	10¾*d.*
Gron*ou* ap Win		20*d.*
Tudgech uxore Eyn*on*	3*s.*	4*d.*
Adaf ap Eynon	4*s.*	2*d.*
Wion Goch	3*s.*	6*d.*
Ririd ap Thom*as*		17¼*d.*
Adekin	4*s.*	
D*aui*d fabro	4*s.*	2*d.*

Summa 4*li.* 6*s.* 8½*d.* probatur.

(12) Lanfrothin [i.e. Llanfrothen]

Griffri With	7*s.*	5*d.*
Adaf ap Lowarch	13*s.*	4*d.*
Moel West	3*s.*	
Wentliana filia Kenuric	2*s.*	
Blethin filio Gron*ou*	5*s.*	6*d.*
Dauid Goch	2*s.*	6½*d.*
Yer*word* ap Gron*ou*	2*s.*	10½*d.*
Ieuan sutore		18*d.*
Cady	7*s.*	10*d.*
Adaf filio Cadi	2*s.*	6½*d.*
Yerword ap Kenuric	5*s.*	5½*d.*
Win ap Kenuric	6*s.*	4½*d.*
Eden*euet* ap Candalo	3*s.*	5*d.*
Howel Goch	5*s.*	5½*d.*
Adaf ap Seysild	2*s.*	4*d.*
Moridic	7*s.*	0½*d.*
Weruel uxore Meiler	2*s.*	1*d.*
Ph*elip*o ap Wilim	2*s.*	9*d.*
Adaf Goch	2*s.*	
Yer*word* ap Ithel		17½*d.*
Tegw*aret* Duy	2*s.*	2*d.*
Win ap Kenuric	2*s.*	
Yer*word* ap Tegwar*et*	4*s.*	3*d.*
Gron*ou* ap Ithel	2*s.*	4*d.*

1 A Yereword ap Theguaret made homage and fealty to the prince of Wales in 1301 (Edward Owen, op. cit., p.26).

Kenuric ap Wion	6*s*. 5½*d*.
Matussalem Vachan [1]	2*s*. 8*d*.
Madoco Brothen	5*s*. 9¼*d*.
Ieuan ap Dauid	3*s*. 2*d*.
Iorword ap Kenuric ap Griffri	5*s*. 6½*d*.
Madoco ap Ieuan	2*s*. 10¾*d*.
Madoc ap Eden*euet*	3*s*. 4*d*.
Ieuan ap Iorword	3*s*. 1½*d*.
Wladusa religiosa	16*d*.
Gwynen	6*s*. 8*d*.
Meurik*o* ap Ad*af*	2*s*. 7*d*.
Morvel filia Lewelini	20*d*.
Eynon Voil	2*s*. 8*d*.
Iohanne filio Ad*af*	2*s*. 6*d*.
Ithel ap Torpen	4*s*. 1½*d*.
Ioreword ap Ph*elip*	4*s*. 8*d*.
Madin With	4*s*. 10*d*.
Win Vachan capellano	20½*d*.
Dauid filio Wechlu	4*s*. 2*d*.
Tygech	18*d*.
Ieuan Goch	2*s*. 4¼*d*.
Adaf filio Cormuly	22*d*.
Yer*word* ap Candalo	3*s*. 1*d*.
Adaf ap Lewelin	3*s*. 6*d*.
Madoco ap D*aui*d	20*d*.
Meylkin	19*d*.
Yer*word* ap Edenowen	17*d*.
map Carrac	20½*d*.
Lewelin Corn	16*d*.
Eynon ap Ieuan	3*s*. 6½*d*.
Eynon ap Ieuan	4*s*.
Dauid Vachan	2*s*. 10½*d*.
Tegwar*et* ap Ad*af*	2*s*. 8*d*.
Madoco ap Heilin	16*d*.
Ieuan ap Ad*af*	20½*d*.
Ieuan ap Kenuric	22*d*.
Ieuan ap Ithel	2*s*. 5*d*.
Madoco filio D*aui*d	16¾*d*.
Madoco ap Gogan	2*s*. 3½*d*.
Yer*word* ap Lewelin	3*s*. 4*d*.

1 It is of possible interest that one Yereworth ap Matussalem from Merioneth and Caernarvonshire was held hostage by the crown after Madog's revolt (*Trans. Caerns. Hist. Soc.*, 16 (1955), 24).

Ieuan ap Thom*as*	3*s*.	6*d*.
Pengam	3*s*.	10*d*.
Gron*ou* Bergam	5*s*.	8*d*.
Braud Waer	5*s*.	
Win ap Lewelin		21¼*d*.
Iohanne Senach	2*s*.	3*d*.
Tegwar*et* Voyl	2*s*.	4*d*.
Ada ap Madoc Duy	3*s*.	2*d*.
D*aui*d ap Ph*elip*	2*s*.	8*d*.
Gron*ou* ap Win		16*d*.
Cadogin	3*s*.	10½*d*.
Wion With	4*s*.	6*d*.
Win Voyl de Botlosked[1]	3*s*.	4*d*.
Ieuan ap Wasdewy		16*d*.
Eden*euet* ap Morur*an*	2*s*.	7*d*.
Moruel uxore Keuen*ard*		18*d*.
Madoco ap Idon		16*d*.
Ad*af* ap Ad*af* sutore	2*s*.	1*d*.
Yer*word* ap Dauid	2*s*.	8*d*.
Keuen*ard* ap Ad*af*	7*s*.	8*d*.
Gron*ou* ap Yer*word*	2*s*.	
Gwyon ap Adaf		16*d*.
Cad*ugan* Loyt	3*s*.	1½*d*.
Madoco With	4*s*.	4*d*.
Eynon filio Caur		19¾*d*.
Iohanne Tissen	3*s*.	4*d*.
Kenuric Efferioitt	2*s*.	2*d*.
Goch Yrgon		20*d*.

Summa 14*li*. 15*s*. 6½*d*.[2] probatur.

[m.5d., left h. col.]

(13) [Ha]rdelach [i.e. Harlech]

Ricardo de Oswaldstre[3]	2*s*.	7*d*.
Iohanne Carbonario[4]	11*s*.	6*d*.
Stephano Ianitore[5]	6*s*.	3½*d*.

1 i.e., Bodlosged, in the parish of Ffestiniog.

2 An error for £14. 16*s*. 11*d*.

3 He is listed among the residents of Harlech in April 1295 (J. Griffiths, 'Documents relating to the Rebellion of Madoc, 1294–5', *B.B.C.S.*, VIII (1935–7), 150).

4 A resident of Harlech in April 1295 (ibid.). John le Colier was bailiff of Harlech in 1300–01 (P.R.O. E.372/146) and ringild of Ardudwy in 1307 (P.R.O. S.C.6/1170/5). See *supra*, p. cvi–cvii, for further details about him.

5 He was active as bailiff of Harlech in 1287–8, 1290–1, and also possibly in 1293 (*B.B.C.S.*, XIV (1950–52), 241, 303, 311). He had carted materials for the building of Harlech castle in the 1280s (Brown, Colvin and Taylor (edd.), *History of the King's Works*, II, 1030–1).

Eynon Goch		16*d*.
Ada Bennard[1]	10*s*.	
Madoco Crach.[2]	8*s*.	6*d*.
Iohanne Deuenith		14¼*d*.
Roberto Scot[3]	3*s*.	5½*d*.
Cad*ugan* fabro	2*s*.	3¼*d*.
Ricardo Carnifice		22½*d*.
Wion Vachan		14*d*.
Iohanne garcione Madoc Crak.	2*s*.	5*d*.

Summa 52*s*. 7*d*. probatur.

Taxatores:[4]

Adaf ap Wion[5]	10*s*.	2½*d*.
Madoco filio Keuenard	10*s*.	1½*d*.
Madoco ap Dauid	6*s*.	
Kenuric ap Gron*ou*	4*s*.	7*d*.
Heylin Goch	3*s*.	3*d*.

Summa 34*s*. 2*d*. probatur.

[m.3d., right h. col.]
Adhuc comotus de Ardudou
(14) Kethugalc[6]

Meden	9*s*.	4*d*.

---

1 He accounted for the issues of Harlech in 1291–2, was a resident there in 1295, and served as the bailiff of the borough in 1296–7 (*B.B.C.S.*, VIII (1935–7), 150; XIV (1950–52), 309; XV (1952–4), 129) and again in 1300–01 (P.R.O. E.372/146). He was, as Dr. A. J. Taylor has shown, a Savoyard, otherwise known as 'Beynard King' and 'Adam King', who not only carted materials for the building of Harlech castle, but also probably held one of the 'key positions under Master James [of St. George] in the earlier stages of the Harlech works' (Brown, Colvin, and Taylor (edd.), *History of the King's Works*, II, 1030–3, 1038–9). See also *supra*, p. cvi.

2 Madoc Crach, or Madoc the Welshman as he was sometimes called, also carted materials for the building of Harlech castle (Brown, Colvin, and Taylor (edd.), *History of the King's Works*, II, 1030–5). He seems to have assisted in accounting for the issues of Harlech in 1287–8 and was certainly resident there in 1295 (*B.B.C.S.*, XIV (1950–52), 241; VIII (1935–7), 150).

3 Both John Deuenith and Robert Scot were residents of Harlech in 1295 (ibid.); the latter had helped in carting materials for the castle in the 1280s. (*The King's Works*, II, 1030–2).

4 Only five assessors are listed here; the usual number was six.

5 An Adaf ap Wyon from Merioneth and Caernarvonshire was one of the hostages held by Edward I after the revolt of 1294–5 (*Trans. Caerns. Hist. Soc.*, 16 (1955), 24).

6 Location uncertain. No Gelli-galch (if that would be the modern form) has been found. It is suggested very tentatively that it may be located to the north of Llandecwyn and – to account for the 'piscator' in the list – on the southern bank of the Dwyryd. On the earliest one inch O.S. map there is a place called Gallt y calch in that particular area (as well as a reference to the quay nearby) and the district abounds in place-names with Gelli as the first element in them, e.g., Gelli-grin, Gelli-lydan, Gelli-dywyll, etc. (see also Lhuyd, op. cit., p. 103).

Corthur	2*s*.	
Madin ap Ad*af*	6*s*.	
Meurico	2*s*.	2*d*.
Lewelin ap Lewelin	4*s*.	
Eynon Duy piscatore	2*s*.	2*d*.
Yer*word* ap Cad*ugan*	3*s*.	4*d*.
Howel ap Win	2*s*.	8*d*.
Ieuan fol		18½*d*.
Heylin Pannor		16*d*.
Tegwar*et* Crak.	2*s*.	
map Duy		17*d*.
Kenuric fol		16¼*d*.
Tangwistel filia Madoc	2*s*.	2*d*.

Summa 41*s*. 5¾*d*. probatur.

De abbate de Kymmer[1]

De havotto eiusdem de Dynasdeliri[2]	16*s*.	

Summa 16*s*. probatur.

(15) Tyinmeyron[3]

Eynon ap Eneas	5*s*.	8¼*d*.
Gron*ou* ap Madoc		16½*d*.
Adaf Goch	2*s*.	2*d*.
Yer*word* ap Ph*elip*	3*s*.	10½*d*.
Adaf ap Iuor		21¼*d*.
Ithel Vachan		19¾*d*.

Summa 16*s*. 6¼*d*. probatur.

(16) Adhuc Lanpeder [Llanbedr]

Win Voyl	7*s*.	3*d*.
Mereduth ap Dauid		19½*d*.
Magistro Gregorio	4*s*.	10¾*d*.
Lewke filia Eynon	2*s*.	1¼*d*.
Kenuric ap Cunach		15*d*.
Madoco ap Madin	3*s*.	3*d*.
Yer*word* ap Gwahaloc		17*d*.
Gurg*enu* carpentario	2*s*.	

Summa 25*s*. 9½*d*.[4] probatur.

---

1 i.e., Cymer.

2 i.e., Craig y Dinas, in the parish of Trawsfynydd (*Journ. Mer. Hist. and Rec. Soc.*, III (1957–60), 76).

3 Location unknown. No trace of the name has been found.

4 An error for 23*s*. 9½*d*.

(17) Adhuc Trausuenith [i.e. Trawsfynydd]

Lewelin Goch	2*s.*	8*d.*
Moil With	4*s.*	5¼*d.*
Ithel ap Ph*elip*	5*s.*	8*d.*
Ad*af* ap Ph*elip*	4*s.*	4*d.*
Iockin Dolgen[1]	4*s.*	
Eynon Druth	6*s.*	6*d.*
Yorword ap Gron*ou*	3*s.*	4*d.*
Gron*ou* Vachan	2*s.*	3*d.*
D*aui*d sutore	2*s.*	
Lippa	8*s.*	2½*d.*
Ieuan Duy	2*s.*	5*d.*
Yorword ap Eynon	7*s.*	
Win ap Madoc		17½*d.*
Madoc Duy	16*s.*	8*d.*
Yer*word* ap Madoc	13*s.*	4*d.*
Adaf Gurnaur	10*s.*	
Kenuric Loyt	4*s.*	
Yer*word* ap Iuor	4*s.*	8*d.*
Gron*ou* ap Tegwar*et*		18½*d.*
Gwion Pellipario	4*s.*	
Adaf Voil	3*s.*	4*d.*
Eynon ap Lowarch	6*s.*	8*d.*
D*aui*d Goch		22½*d.*
Iockin ap Ithel	4*s.*	5*d.*
Ieuan ap Ospern	10*s.*	1¼*d.*
Ieuan Goch	3*s.*	4*d.*
Ithel Pen	3*s.*	5½*d.*
Dauid Voyl	4*s.*	8*d.*
Ithel Duy	2*s.*	6¾*d.*
Eyn*on* ap Cad*ugan*	2*s.*	8*d.*
Yer*word* ap Kenuric	9*s.*	4*d.*
Cad*ugan* ap Talbant	2*s.*	8*d.*
Aurifabro	3*s.*	3*d.*
Ieuan ap D*aui*d	6*s.*	1¾*d.*
Iorword Duy	3*s.*	8*d.*
filia ?granmayl		18*d.*
Iorword ap Meiler	2*s.*	10*d.*
Griffri sutore		17*d.*
Candalo ap Ad*af*	4*s.*	6*d.*
Ieuan ap Candalo	2*s.*	2*d.*
Adaf ap Wilim	2*s.*	5*d.*

1 i.e., of Dolgain, in the parish of Trawsfynydd.

Ad*af* ap Ieuan	4*s*. 4*d*.
Ieuan ap Ithel	3*s*. 5*d*.
Ithel Duy	4*s*. 5*d*.
Ithel Vachan	2*s*. 11*d*.
Madoc ap Adam	3*s*. 1*d*.
Weruel uxore Iorword	4*s*. 8*d*.
Ieuan filio Morueran	3*s*. 4*d*.
Ithel ap Dauid	3*s*. 8*d*.
Kenuric ap Meiler	2*s*.

Summa 10*li*. 15*s*. 3½*d*.[1]

(18) Adhuc Lanaber [i.e. Llanaber]

Moyl Gron*ou*	3*s*. 9*d*.
Adaf Duy	8*s*. 8*d*.
D*aui*d ap Gron*ou*	3*s*. 4*d*.
Gron*ou* voil	2*s*.
Madoco filio Yer*word*	20*d*.
Dehewint	3*s*. 2½*d*.
Win ap Heylin	7*s*. 4*d*.
Win Loyt	3*s*. 5¾*d*.
Madoco Cantore	20*d*.
Iockin ap Tegwar*et*	2*s*. 0½*d*.
Adaf ap Eyn*on*	7*s*. 8*d*.
Gron*ou* ap Win	8*s*.
Cad*ugan* Duy	18¾*d*.
Wladusa	4*s*. 10*d*.
D*aui*d ap Madoc	8*s*. 11¾*d*.
Ieuan ap Rerid	3*s*. 4*d*.
Eynon Ledan	13½*d*.
Wion ap Wion	4*s*.
Madoc ap Iorword	18½*d*.
Iorword ap Madoc	4*s*. 4*d*.
Issec Goch	16¾*d*.
Anghar*ad* Goch	3*s*. 3½*d*.
Madoc Saer	2*s*. 4*d*.
Gron*ou* ap Wladus	44*s*.
D*aui*d Voyl	3*s*. 4*d*.
D*aui*d ap Was Coum	2*s*. 8*d*.
D*aui*d ap Tegwar*et*	2*s*. 10*d*.
Ithel Voyl	5*s*. 8*d*.
Moruran	10*s*. 4*d*.
Dauid Bongam	18½*d*.

1 Interlineated: '11*li*. 3*s*., incrementum 8*s*. probatur' making a total of £11. 3*s*. 3½*d*., which is correct.

Ieuan ap Was Coum		20*d.*
Griffri ap Meiler		22*d.*
Madin Meronnith[1]	6*s.*	
Meiler ap Ph*elip*	3*s.*	8½*d.*
Madoco ap Eyn*on*	2*s.*	
Wentlian*a* filia Ad*af*		16*d.*
Eden*euet* ap Meiler	5*s.*	
Generys filia Eynon	2*s.*	2½*d.*
Gronu[2] With	5*s.*	
Ieuan ap Dauid	6*s.*	10*d.*
Eynon Leget		18½*d.*
Yer*word* ap Gron*ou*		21½*d.*
Ieuan ap D*aui*d	4*s.*	6*d.*
Eden*euet* Duy	3*s.*	6*d.*
Dauid Tunbol	2*s.*	
Eden*euet* ap Eden*euet*	3*s.*	4*d.*
Madoco ap Wen		20*d.*
Iockin Keri	2*s.*	2*d.*
Adaf ap Meroc	2*s.*	5½*d.*
Generys filia Win	5*s.*	
Win ap Dauid		17¾*d.*
Iorword ap Ieuan	2*s.*	8*d.*

Summa 11*li.* 9*s.* 0¼*d.*[3] probatur.

(19) Lanendewyn [i.e. Llanenddwyn]

Dauid ap Wasmyhangel	2*s.*	9¼*d.*
Madoco medico[4]	3*s.*	10*d.*
Tuder*o* ap Madoc		18*d.*
Ririd ap D*aui*d		18*d.*
Deykin	2*s.*	1¼*d.*

[m.4d., right h. col.]

Ier*word* filio Leget	6*s.*	4*d.*
Madoc Boulton		16*d.*
Heylin Ayank		14¼*d.*
D*aui*d ap Moridic		14¾*d.*
Adaf ap Eynon		20*d.*
Madoco de Vowr[5]	3*s.*	4*d.*

1 Possibly from the cantref of Meirionnydd between the rivers Mawddach and Dyfi.

2 Written above 'Eynon' which has been struck through.

3 An error for £11. 7*s.* 7¼*d.*

4 In Easter 1309 the sheriff accounted for 2*s.* 6*d.* for three parts of one acre of Welsh land belonging to Madoc ap Ior*werth* Medyk in the vill of Llanenddwyn (*Trans. Hon. Soc. Cymmrodorion* (1902–03), p. 58).

5 Unidentified.

Adaf ap Tegwar*et*	3*s*. 4*d*.
Candalo ?An*er*in	5*s*. 4*d*.
Eynon ap Edenewen	3*s*. 4*d*.
Maderun	2*s*. 4½*d*.
Henuric [*sic*] cantore	8*s*. 2*d*.
Birgif	17*d*.
uxore Seysild	3*s*. 10½*d*.
Wion Voyl	2*s*. 1½*d*.
Generys filia Gurg*enu*	20½*d*.

Summa 58*s*. 5½*d*. probatur.

(20) Lamyhangel apud Traythe [i.e. Llanfihangel-y-traethau]

Yer*word* ap Tegwar*et*	3*s*. 4*d*.
Tegwar*et* sutore	4*s*. 0½*d*.
Adaf Hen	2*s*. 9½*d*.
Wentlian*a* uxore Win	2*s*.
Ithel ap Adaf	3*s*. 7*d*.
Candalo ap Ririd	2*s*. 10¾*d*.
Eyn*on* ap Iockin	4*s*.
Madoc ap Iockin	4*s*.
Ph*elip*o ap Cad*ugan*	5*s*. 4*d*.
Eynon ap Crossot	23*d*.
Loward ap Tegwar*et*	3*s*. 2¾*d*.
Win ap Ririd	3*s*. 2¾*d*.
Ririd ?Cannian	14½*d*.
Madoco ap Iorword	2*s*. 4*d*.
Ieuan ap Yer*word*	23¾*d*.
Adaf ap Trahairn	13¾*d*.
Gron*ou* ap D*aui*d	5*s*. 8*d*.
Ieuan ap Adaf	4*s*. 8*d*.
Dauid ap Ieuan	2*s*. 4*d*.
map Kimero	2*s*. 4*d*.
Kenuric ap Adaf	4*s*. 1*d*.
Kenuric ap Kenuric	3*s*. 2*d*.
Adaf ap Ieuan	5*s*. 4*d*.
Adaf ap D*aui*d	2*s*. 11*d*.
Eynon ap D*aui*d	2*s*. 10½*d*.
Ithel ap Eynon	2*s*. 4*d*.
Yer*word* ap Eynon	2*s*. 3*d*.
Adaf ap D*aui*d(1)	2*s*. 2½*d*.

Summa 4*li*. 7*s*. 2¼*d*. probatur.

1 Written above 'Eynon' which has been expunged.

(21) Nanmaurdeudrayth [i.e. Nanmor Deudraeth][1]

Ririd ap Adaf	13*s*. 4*d*.
Iohanne Ruffo	6*s*. 4*d*.
Kuelin Goch	9*s*. 2½*d*.
Ieuan ap D*aui*d	22¾*d*.
Ieuan ap Ieuan ap D*aui*d	4*s*. 7*d*.
Gron*ou* ap Meiler	3*s*. 11¼*d*.
Tegwar*et* ap Ada	5*s*. 10½*d*.
Adaf ap Yer*word*	6*s*. 10*d*.
Madoco ap Candalo	2*s*. 10½*d*.

Summa 61*s*. 1*d*.[2] probatur.

(22) Festinioc [i.e. Ffestiniog]

Ithel capellano	5*s*. 8*d*.
magistro Cad*ugan*[3]	2*s*. 9*d*.
Ithel ap Madoc	4*s*. 7*d*.
Gurg*enu* ap Iorword	7*s*. 1*d*.
Ithel Orellyn[4]	20*d*.
Gurg*enu* ap Trahaern	4*s*. 10*d*.
Kenuric ap Lewelin	8*s*. 9¾*d*.
Heylin ap Dauid	7*s*. 7¾*d*.
Gron*ou* cantore	21*d*.
D*aui*d cantore	2*s*. 9*d*.
Win ap Morud	7*s*. 2*d*.
Ithel Wir	5*s*. 2*d*.
Gurg*enu* ap Ithel	4*s*. 5*d*.
Madoco ap Ad*af*	9*s*. 8*d*.
Adaf Voil	2*s*. 5¼*d*.
Meiler ap Gron*ou*	4*s*. 6¾*d*.
D*aui*d ap Kenithlin[5]	4*s*. 2*d*.
Kenuric ap Madoc	3*s*. 1*d*.
Win ap Ad*af*	3*s*. 5*d*.

1 Though at one time in Merioneth, Nanmor has always been considered a part of the parish of Beddgelert. In the eighteenth century it was invariably referred to as the 'hamlet' of Nanmor. (K. Williams-Jones, op. cit., p. 18). It was transferred to the former county of Caernarvon in 1895.

2 An error for 54*s*. 10½*d*.

3 In 1309 the sheriff was accounting for three acres of land in the vill of Ffestiniog which master Cadugan, who had died without heirs, had held. (*Trans. Hon. Soc. Cymmrodorion* (1902–03), p. 59).

4 'O'r Llyn' is suggestive of legends and fables! The Ffestiniog district abounds with lakes.

5 A David ap Kenythlin from Merioneth or Caernarvonshire was held as a hostage after Madog's war in 1294–5 (*Trans. Caerns. Hist. Soc.*, 16 (1955), 24).

Gron*ou* Voil	5*s*. 1½*d*.
Morwid uxore Candalo	3*s*. 4*d*.

Summa 100*s*. 1*d*. probatur.

(23) Maynturroc [i.e. Maentwrog]

Ph*elipo* Duy	4*s*. 8*d*.
Meurico Saer	22¾*d*.
Yer*word* capellano	20*d*.
Wladusa Mursen	20*d*.
Madoco filio Wilim[1]	3*s*. 4*d*.
Tegwar*et* Corista	8*s*. 8*d*.
Eyn*on*	17*d*.
Ririd ap Eyn*on*	2*s*. 4*d*.
Yer*word* ap Kediuor	5*s*. 4*d*.
Tegwar*et* ap Candalo	5*s*. 4*d*.
Wion Voil	5*s*. 10*d*.
Iuor	4*s*. 8*d*.
Madoco ap Cad*ugan*	2*s*. 4½*d*.
Eyn*on* ap Lowarch	4*s*. 6*d*.
Eyn*on* ap Ad*af*	2*s*. 2*d*.
Win Gam	5*s*. 8*d*.
Adaf ap Kenuric	20*d*.
Madoco ap D*aui*d	5*s*. 10*d*.
Gron*ou* ap Tegwar*et*	2*s*. 6½*d*.
Heylin Predith	3*s*. 3*d*.
Trahaern ap Eden*euet*	20*d*.
Mabilia	3*s*. 4*d*.
Ithel ap Win	16*d*.
Ada ap Kyrak.	16*d*.
Mereduth	2*s*. 2*d*.
Eyn*on* ap Ieuan	2*s*. 4*d*.
Saerno	3*s*. 4*d*.
Madoco ap Heylin	2*s*. 4*d*.
Wilim Spedor	8*s*. 6*d*.
map Siboc	2*s*. 8*d*.
Lewk*e* filia Ph*elipi*	17¼*d*.
Iorword	3*s*. 2*d*.
Madoco Goch	9*s*. 9½*d*.
Ieuan With	2*s*. 4*d*.
Gron*ou* ap Ithel	3*s*. 8*d*.
Heylin Hengest[2]	3*s*. 10*d*.

1 A Maddock ap Guilin from Ardudwy made homage and fealty to the prince of Wales in 1301 (Edward Owen, op. cit., p. 17).

2 Unidentified.

Adaf ap Meiler	4*s*. 6*d*.
Madoc Corista	5*s*. 5*d*.
Ririd ap Win	16*d*.
Moil Hogi	2*s*. 1¼*d*.
D*aui*d ap Ichor	3*s*.
Enuerich uxore Ad*af*	16*d*.
Madoc sutore	4*s*. 4*d*.
Ithel ap Eyn*on*	4*s*. 11*d*.
Gwen Vaur Goch	18*d*.
Wladur	4*s*. 8*d*.
Dauid ap Tegwar*et*	4*s*. 2½*d*.

[m.5d., right h. col.]

Adhuc Maynnatur

Yer*word* ap Madoc	16*d*.
Tangwistel uxore Eyn*on*	17¼*d*.
Madoco ap Tud*er*	2*s*. 8*d*.
Madoc ap Yer*word*	20*d*.
Moil Coit	3*s*. 8*d*.
Ithel Duy	3*s*. 4*d*.
Pendauat	18*d*.
Anghar*ad* Vaur	2*s*. 10½*d*.

Summa 9*li*. 3*s*. 10*d*. probatur.

Abbate de Kimer[1]

De eodem abbate apud Winvenith[2]	5*s*. 2*d*.
De eodem in eadem	3*s*. 6*d*.
De eodem de Coumgwynnin[3]	5*s*. 6*d*.
De eodem apud Mocbrin[4]	7*s*. 2*d*.
De eodem apud Kessoylgoum[5]	8*s*. 9½*d*.
De eodem pro bonis fratris Madoci	22*d*.

Summa 31*s*. 11½*d*. probatur.

Summa totalis huius commoti 148*li*. 16*s*. 9¼*d*.; 149*li*. 4*s*. 9¼*d*.[6] probatur, unde de incremento 8*s*. . . . quintodecimo harumseptem peciarum

---

1 i.e., Cymer.

2 i.e., Gwynfynydd, in the parish of Trawsfynydd (*Journ. Mer. Hist. and Rec. Soc.*, III, (1957–60), 72).

3 i.e., Cwm-gwnin, in the parish of Llanelltud (ibid.).

4 i.e., Moel Ispri, in the parish of Llanelltud (ibid.).

5 i.e., Cesailgwm, in the parish of Llanelltud (ibid.).

6 An error for £148 15*s*. 1¾*d*.

567*li*. 13*s*. 5¼*d*.[1] probatur, unde de incremento
67*s*. 11½*d*. probatur.

[m.6, left h. col.]

Commotus de Edyrnon [i.e. Edeirnion][2]

(1) Villa de Coruan [i.e. Corwen]

Ad*af* ab D*aui*d	2*s*. 4½*d*.
Ieuan ab Dehwynt	19½*d*.
Iarward Goch	4*s*. 2*d*.
Eyno*n* ab Iarward	18*d*.
Gregorio capellano[3]	2*s*. 1*d*.
D*aui*d Wyth	3*s*. 4½*d*.
Wyon ab Eyno*n*	3*s*. 5¼*d*.
Iarward fabro	6*s*. 6½*d*.
Ad*af* ab Purrewyn	21½*d*.
Ad*af* ab Purrewyn	6*s*. 4*d*.
Ad*af* Voyl	6*s*. 8¼*d*.
Groneu Grach	4*s*. 3*d*.
Kenewrek capellano[4]	22*d*.
D*aui*d ab Cadugan	16*d*.
filio Pannour	17¼*d*.
Iarward goch	21½*d*.
Ad*af* Loyt	4*s*. 11½*d*.
Madoco Kydo	14*d*.
Gryffyth ab Ph*elip*	2*s*. 9*d*.
Ithel ab Seysyld	10*s*. 2½*d*.
Ieuan ab Seysild	7*s*. 10*d*.
Eyno*n* ab Seysild	5*s*. 9*d*.
Gryffyth ab Seysild	2*s*. 1¼*d*.
Gryffyd Goch	4*s*. 4*d*.

Summa 4*li*. 9*s*. 8*d*. probatur.

(2) Villa de Lansanfreyt [i.e. Llansanffraid in the parish of Llansanffraid Glyndyfrdwy]

Ieuan ab Eyno*n*	3*s*. 8*d*.

1 The total for the county as a whole is incorrect. The final sum should read: £566. 11*s*. 10½*d*.

2 The list for Edeirnion differs from those of the other commotes of Merioneth in three respects: it has, first of all, been drawn up by a different hand; secondly, 'ab' is used, almost without exception, instead of 'ap'; and lastly, many common personal names have been spelt differently. All this reflects the semi-autonomous position of Edeirnion, being 'in the county of Merioneth, yet not of it' (see A. D. Carr, 'The Barons of Edeyrnion, 1282–1485', *Journ. Mer. Hist. and Rec. Soc.*, IV (1961–64), 189).

3 Corwen was a portionary church divided between five priests, amongst them Gregory the priest and one Kenewyrc David (*Taxatio Ecclesiastica . . . auctoritate P. Nicholai IV* (1802), p. 286).

4 See *supra*, n. 3.

Leuk*e* filia Madocy	5*s*.	9½*d*.
Ithel Deuergy	3*s*.	4¾*d*.
Iarward ab Adam	5*s*.	8*d*.
Groneu ab Ad*a*m		22*d*.
Ithel ab Gron*ou*		17½*d*.
Cadug*an* ab Eyno*n*		14*d*.
Madoco filio Yarward		21½*d*.
Wyon ab Madok	2*s*.	1¼*d*.
Eyno*n* Duy	2*s*.	1*d*.
Ad*af* ab Eynon	4*s*.	1*d*.
Ad*af* Wyn		16½*d*.

Summa 34*s*. 5*d*. probatur.

(3) Villa de Bodoryles [i.e. Bodorlas in the parish of Corwen]

Ieuaf Duy	2*s*.	1*d*.
Loward ab Ryryd	6*s*.	
D*aui*d ab Ryryd	3*s*.	6¾*d*.
Groneu ab Cadug*an*		20¼*d*.
Eyno*n* ab D*aui*d	2*s*.	7½*d*.
D*aui*d ab Yarward	5*s*.	6*d*.
Madoco ab Meyler	3*s*.	8*d*.
Cadug*an* ab Ryryd	3*s*.	10*d*.
Ieuan ab Iarward	4*s*.	10¾*d*.
uxore Ryryd Duy	12*s*.	1½*d*.
Madyn Vachan		18½*d*.

Summa 47*s*. 6¼*d*. probatur.

(4) Villa de Hyrlannerk [i.e. Tirllannerch in the parish of Corwen]

D*aui*d ap Loward	4*s*.	3½*d*.
Iarward Duy	12*s*.	4*d*.
D*aui*d Duy	2*s*.	3*d*.
Eyno*n* ab Ad*af*	5*s*.	7¼*d*.
Ithel ab Cadug*an*	2*s*.	5¼*d*.
Madoco ab Cadug*an*		22*d*.
D*aui*d ab Meuryk	5*s*.	8¼*d*.
Heylin ab Rob*er*t	7*s*.	10*d*.
Ad*af* ab Kenewrek.		14½*d*.
Iockyn ab Rob*er*t		14¾*d*.
Cadug*an* Vachan	5*s*.	5½*d*.
Wyon ab D*aui*d	6*s*.	4½*d*.
uxore Madocy ab Ieuan	12*s*.	0½*d*.
Iarward Vachan	3*s*.	5*d*.
Madoco ab D*aui*d	5*s*.	8¼*d*.

Eyno*n* sutore	2*s.* 0¼*d.*
Dyaual	8*s.* 9*d.*
D*aui*d ab Ithel	2*s.* 10¾*d.*
D*aui*d Wyth	5*s.* 8½*d.*
Iarward Goch	6*s.* 2¾*d.*
Ieuan ab D*aui*d	2*s.* 10¾*d.*
Madoco ab Ad*af*	3*s.* 5½*d.*
Howel ab Iarward	3*s.* 4¼*d.*
Ad*af* medico	4*s.* 4¾*d.*
uxore medici	23½*d.*
Eden*euet* ab Carueth	4*s.* 9¼*d.*
Iockyn Tynven	2*s.* 9*d.*

Summa 6*li.* 6*s.* 3½*d.*[1] Incrementum 7*d.* probatur.

(5) Villa Carrok [i.e. Carrog in the parish of Corwen]

Madoco ab Gryffyd Mal[2]	4*s.* 7½*d.*
Legeth gour[3]	2*s.* 8½*d.*
D*aui*d ab Kener*ic*	5*s.* 6¾*d.*
Tudero ab Carueth	2*s.* 2¾*d.*
Howel ab Iarward	5*s.* 2*d.*
Goylour	2*s.* 0½*d.*
Ithel Gam	21½*d.*
Ken*eric* ab Ieua	3*s.* 0¼*d.*
Groneu Hyr	6*s.* 4*d.*
Groneu ab D*aui*d	21*d.*
Iarward ab Kenner*ic*	2*s.*
Groneu ab Cadug*an*	4*s.* 5*d.*
Ieuan ab Ieuaf	3*s.* 2*d.*

1 '3½*d.*' underlined for deletion; interlineated above it: '10½*d.*', which is correct.

2 Despite the obvious similarity between 'M' and 'Y' at this period, the word is almost certainly 'Mal' rather than 'Yal'. The person, therefore, cannot be identified with the great-grandfather of Owain Glyn Dŵr – Madog ap Gruffydd whose father was lord of Yale (*Cal. of Welsh Rolls*, p. 171). Glyn Dŵr's great-great-great-grandfather was indeed known as Gruffydd Maelor (Henry Lewis *et al.* (ed.), *Cywyddau Iolo Goch ac Eraill* (1937), p. 31), but Professor Melville Richards dismissed the idea that 'Mal' was an abbreviated form of Maelor. It seems unlikely, too, that 'mal' could be an abbreviation of 'malus', though it is tempting to connect Madog ap Gruffydd Mal with Madog Grupl, a name by which Glyn Dŵr's great-grandfather was sometimes known.

3 It could very well be the fine poet Llygad Gŵr who sang 'the most "nationalist" poetry in Welsh before the days of Glyn Dŵr'. If so, he clearly survived the shattering blow of the conquest and his *floruit* can be extended to 1292–3. It is interesting to speculate how far his patriotic fervour influenced the Glyndyfrdwy family in supporting Prince Llywelyn II in 1282 (see previous note). Mr. D. M. Lloyd, however, associates the poet Llygad Gŵr with Hendwr and not Carrog (see *Dictionary of Welsh Biography* (1959), p. 596).

D*au*id Succannor	2*s*.	6½*d*.
Groneu Goch	4*s*.	

Summa 51*s*. 4¾*d*.[1] probatur.

(6) Tref Wyn [i.e. Trewyn in the parish of Corwen]

Beyduch		18¾*d*.
Ieuaf filio Gryffyd		16*d*.
Ieuan goch	4*s*.	10*d*.
Madoco ab Iarward	4*s*.	2½*d*.
Eyno*n* ab Edeneuet	3*s*.	8½*d*.

[m.7, left h. col.]

D*au*id ab Hudolou	2*s*.	
D*au*id filio Kenner*ic*	4*s*.	9½*d*.
Gryffry ab Eyno*n*	2*s*.	8*d*.
Madoco ab Iarward mal	8*s*.	4½*d*.
Wentlyan filia Madok	2*s*.	3*d*.
Meiler Duy	3*s*.	9¼*d*.
Ieuaf ab Ithel	6*s*.	6½*d*.
Ithel Vachan	3*s*.	7*d*.
Eyno*n* Duy	7*s*.	8*d*.
Gurg*enu* Goch	4*s*.	8½*d*.
Madoco Wyth	5*s*.	1¼*d*.
Madoco Vachan	3*s*.	5¼*d*.
Wyon	3*s*.	4*d*.
Ad*af* ab Idenerth	3*s*.	1¼*d*.
Madoco filio Ithel	3*s*.	6*d*.
Madoco ab Adam	2*s*.	6½*d*.
uxore Madoci ab Ithel	4*s*.	8¼*d*.
D*au*id fronniart		18½*d*.
Wladus*a* filia Ryryd		13¼*d*.

Summa 4*li*. 10*s*. 4¼*d*. probatur.

(7) Villa de Mesdour [i.e. Mwstwr in the parish of Corwen]

Groneu ab Ieuaf		21½*d*.
Iarward Vachan	11*s*.	6½*d*.
uxore Houa Goch	8*s*.	2½*d*.
Kenner*ic* ab Ph*elip*		20¼*d*.
Wladus filia Madoci	5*s*.	4*d*.
Ryryd ab Iarward	3*s*.	6¾*d*.
Kenner*ic* Seys[2]	2*s*.	9¼*d*.

1 An error for 51*s*. 4¼*d*.

2 A Kenewrek Seys served with the royal armies in 1294–5 (Fryde (ed.), *Book of Prests*, p. 79).

Gryffid ab Teluwas	4*s*. 1¼*d*.
Anghar*ad* filia Eudas	2*s*. 8½*d*.
Cadugan ab Iar*ward*	2*s*. 4*d*.
Madoco ab Eynon	2*s*.
Ryryd Duy	2*s*.
Madoco Goch	4*s*. 6*d*.
Iarward ab Adam	4*s*.
Gron*eu* filio Mereduth	4*s*. 2*d*.
Madoco Kest	7*s*. 10½*d*.
Kenner*ic* ab Groneu	4*s*. 10½*d*.
Madoco ab Ph*elip*	20*d*.
Iarward ab Ieuan	5*s*. 6*d*.
Ithel ab Groneu	3*s*. 2*d*.

Summa 4*li*. 3*s*. 8½*d*.[1] Incrementum 1*d*. probatur.

Bona abbatis de Lanegwystel[2] in eodem commoto.	
De eodem abbate de grangia sua apud le Mesdour[3]	9*s*. 4½*d*.
De eodem abbate de grangia sua de Grynochoc[4]	6*s*. 10*d*.

Summa 16*s*. 2½*d*. probatur.

(8) Penant [i.e. Pennant in the parish of Llandrillo]

Eynon ab D*aui*d	6*s*. 7*d*.
Madoco Goch	7*s*. 2½*d*.
Ieuan ab Gurg*enu*[5]	11*s*. 8*d*.
Iarward ab Meiler	3*s*. 5½*d*.
Ieuan ab Ithel	10*s*. 5½*d*.
Meurico Meghen[6]	14*s*. 4½*d*.
Ieuan ab Wyon	2*s*. 9¼*d*.
D*aui*d ab Eynon	6*s*. 10½*d*.
Madoco aurifabro	2*s*. 8½*d*.
D*aui*d ab Eynon	11*s*. 4*d*.
Eynon Duy	3*s*. 5½*d*.
Madoco Goch	7*s*. 8½*d*.

1 '8½*d*.' underlined for deletion; interlineated above it: '9*d*.', which is correct.

2 i.e., Llanegwestl, otherwise known as Glynegwestl or Glyn-y-groes (=Valle Crucis), in the former county of Denbigh.

3 i.e., Mwstwr, in the parish of Corwen.

4 In *Taxatio Ecclesiastica . . . Nicholai IV*, p. 289, it is Grenwyrchant. D. R. Thomas suggested that it was Creigiog (*The History of the Diocese of St. Asaph*, I (1906), 55).

5 A Ievan ap Gourgenu from Merioneth or Caernarvonshire was held hostage by the crown after the war of 1294–5 (*Trans. Caerns. Hist. Soc.*, 16 (1955), 24).

6 i.e., of Mechain, in the former county of Montgomery.

Groneu ab Adam		18¾*d.*
Ryryd ab Gurg*enu*	2*s.*	1*d.*
Ryryd Gyn		16*d.*
Tudgech filia Ryryd	7*s.*	
Ryryd ab Tud*er*	13*s.*	4*d.*
Anghar*ad* filia Madok	2*s.*	3¼*d.*
Madoco Grach	8*s*	10*d.*
D*aui*d ab Tegwaret	13*s.*	
Ryryd ab Iarward		21¼*d.*
Madoco ab Eynon		16¼*d.*
Weruilla filia D*aui*d		16*d.*

Summa 7*li.* 2*s.* 4¾*d.*(1) probatur.

(9) Villa de Branes [i.e. Branas in the parish of Llandrillo]

Iarword ab Cuhelyn	12*s.*	6*d.*
Iarword ab Cadug*an*	2*s.*	3*d.*
Eden*euet* ab Iarword	6*s.*	2¾*d.*
Ryryd ab Ph*elip*	2*s.*	1½*d.*
Groneu Loyt	4*s.*	2½*d.*
D*aui*d Goch	4*s.*	2¾*d.*
Heylyn ab Blethyn		21½*d.*
Corryn		19*d.*
Madoco Moylgoch	3*s.*	8*d.*
Ieuan ab Blethiot [*sic*]	2*s.*	10½*d.*
Generys uxore Ieuan	2*s.*	8*d.*
Heylyn ab Eynon		21*d.*
Ieuan ab Eynon	2*s.*	1¼*d.*
Tudgech filia Meyler	9*s.*	8*d.*
Madoco Gwyde	2*s.*	3*d.*
Madoco Duy		18¼*d.*
Gurg*enu* ab D*aui*d Palmere	5*s.*	4¼*d.*
Ithel ab Ph*elip*	5*s.*	11*d.*
Ad*af* ab Candolou	4*s.*	5¼*d.*
Kyrreank.(2)	2*s.*	4*d.*
Ieuan ab Candolou		18*d.*
Groneu Ebogith	5*s.*	11*d.*
Eynon ab Candolo [*sic*]	4*s.*	9*d.*
Eynon Vachan	2*s.*	4*d.*
Ieuan ab Tuder	4*s.*	0¼*d.*

Summa 4*li.* 16*s.* 11¼*d.*(3) probatur.

1 An error for £7 2*s.* 5¼*d.*

2 A variant, presumably, of 'Gwreang'.

3 '16*s.* 11¼*d.*' underlined for deletion; interlineated: '17*s.* 11¾*d.* [which is correct], incrementum 12*d.*' [*sic*].

(10) Villa de Carthaen [i.e. Garthiaen in the parish of Llandrillo]

Ithel ab D*aui*d	12*s*. 3*d*.
Madoco ab Tuder	2*s*. 7*d*.
D*aui*d Loyt	3*s*. 6*d*.
D*aui*d carpentario	11*s*. 2*d*.
Madoco ab D*aui*d	5*s*. 10$\frac{1}{2}$*d*.
Kenner*ic* goch	6*s*. 1$\frac{1}{2}$*d*.
Ithel ab Iarword	4*s*. 9$\frac{1}{4}$*d*.
Gurgeneu ab Tud*er*	3*s*. 2*d*.
Gurgeneu ab Tuder	2*s*. 7$\frac{1}{2}$*d*.
D*aui*d ab Madok	2*s*. 4$\frac{1}{2}$*d*.
Ad*af* ab Madok	7*s*.
D*aui*d ab Wyon	20*d*.
Anghar*ad* filia Howel	2*s*. 9*d*.
Madoco Duy	23*d*.
Madoco ab Howel	3*s*. 11*d*.
Cadugan ab Howel	2*s*. 1$\frac{1}{4}$*d*.

Summa 73*s*. 8*d*.(1) probatur.

[m.6, right h. col.]

(11) Villa de Melysgederew [i.e. Moelysgediw in the parish of Llandrillo]

Dauid Loyt	4*s*. 7*d*.
Wyon Mal	8*s*. 11*d*.
D*aui*d ab Wyon	22*d*.
Gurgen*u* ab Madok	16$\frac{1}{4}$*d*.

Summa 16*s*. 8$\frac{1}{4}$*d*. probatur.

(12) Tewas [i.e. Tyfos in the parish of Llandrillo]

Eynon Goch	7*s*.
Groneu ab Tegwaret	4*s*. 9$\frac{1}{2}$*d*.
D*aui*d ab Groneu	2*s*.
Ieuan ab D*aui*d	2*s*. 1$\frac{1}{4}$*d*.

Summa 15*s*. 10$\frac{3}{4}$*d*. probatur.

(13) Gwynodyl [i.e. Gwnnodl in the parish of Llangar]

Cadugan ab Ithel	4*s*. 0$\frac{1}{2}$*d*.
Tegwar*et* ab Eynon	3*s*. 5$\frac{1}{4}$*d*.
Ad*a*m goch	14$\frac{1}{4}$*d*.
Anghar*ad* filia fabri	13*d*.
Arthour Duy	2*s*. 6*d*.

1 An error for £3. 13*s*. 9$\frac{1}{2}$*d*.

Wyn ab Adam	14*s.*
Ad*a*m ab Tuder	3*s.* 10*d.*
Houa Vel	13*d.*
Waskeyn	2*s.* 6¼*d.*
Moylgrum	13*d.*
Eynon Keyloc	22½*d.*
Iarword goch	2*s.* 10*d.*
Ad*af* goch	2*s.* 5¼*d.*
Iarword	22*d.*
Tegwar*et* ab Griffyd	4*s.* 7¼*d.*
Edeneuet Grach	8*s.* 6*d.*

Summa 56*s.* 10¼*d.* probatur.

(14) Hendor [i.e. Hendwr in the parish of Llandrillo]

Madoco ab D*aui*d[1]	6*s.*
Lewelyn Vachan[2]	14*s.* 4½*d.*
Howel ab D*aui*d	18*s.* 2*d.*
Gryffid ab D*aui*d[3]	17*s.* 10*d.*
Ieuan ab Tuder	20*d.*

Summa 58*s.* 0½*d.* probatur.

(15) Kylan [i.e. Cilan in the parish of Llandrillo]

Madoco ab Idenerth	3*s.* 0½*d.*

1 Mr. A. D. Carr, who has made a thorough study of the barons of Edeirnion, says that Madog ap Dafydd was assessed also in Tirllannerch, Garthiaen, Cilan, and Gwyddelwern – and that may well be so (*Journ. Mer. Hist. and Rec. Soc.*, IV (1961–4), 190–1). His total assessment, therefore, came to 22*s.* 7¾*d.* He served with the royal armies during Madog's war (Fryde (ed.), *Book of Prests*, pp. 58, 59, 135).

2 One of the barons of Edeirnion (see *Cal. of Welsh Rolls*, p. 286), he made homage and fealty to the prince of Wales in 1301 (Edward Owen, op. cit., p. 25).

3 The interesting suggestion has been made that he was probably the Gruffydd ap Dafydd who was 'the first Welshman to hold the office of sheriff in the principality', acting in that capacity in Merioneth in 1300–01 (A.D. Carr, art. cit., p. 289). This fits in well not only with what can reasonably be assumed to have been royal needs in Merioneth but also with what is known of the career of Gruffydd ap Dafydd, lord of Hendwr, one of the barons of Edeirnion. A squire of the king's household, he fought, like his brother Madog (see *supra*, p. 82, n. 1), on the English side in 1294–5 (*Book of Prests*, pp. 163, 169, 186) and was rewarded for his services: in 1295 Edward I committed to his care, as 'the king's yeoman', the royal forests in Penllyn, Ardudwy and Meirionnydd (*Cal. of Chanc. Warrants*, I, 63–4). It may well be that he had interests in Penllyn, for a Griffid ap David was assessed at 7*s.* 9½*d.* in Ciltalgarth (*supra*, p. 18). He made homage and fealty to the prince of Wales in 1301 (Edward Owen, op. cit., p. 24) and clearly won his confidence and favour. He must surely be identified with the person on whom the prince, in a rare fit of independence, possibly in 1302 or 1303, conferred the rhaglawry of Ardudwy and Penllyn (W. H. Waters, *The Edwardian Settlement*, p. 33 n.), and that in the teeth of claims that the office had been given to another by Edward I himself. Gruffydd ap Dafydd remained rhaglaw of Ardudwy and Penllyn until his death in 1306 (P.R.O. S.C.6/1170/5 m. 5). His son Madog held the same offices and Edward II continued to favour his family (A. D. Carr, art. cit., p. 290).

Ieuan Byr	6*s*.	4¼*d*.
D*aui*d ab Gurgen*u*	3*s*.	4¼*d*.
Gurgen*u* ab Idenerth	5*s*.	0¼*d*.
Iarward Vylein		22*d*.
D*aui*d ab Madok	8*s*.	6½*d*.
Madoco ab D*aui*d	3*s*.	5½*d*.
Madoco ab Candolo	3*s*.	4*d*.
Madoco ab Ithel	3*s*.	3*d*.

Summa 38*s*. 2¼*d*. probatur.

(16) Llanderychlou [i.e. Llandrillo]

Ad*af* ab Referyot	5*s*.	
D*aui*d ab Ad*a*m		13½*d*.
Iarword Vachan	3*s*.	8½*d*.
D*aui*d ap Ph*elip*		20*d*.
Iohanne pictore	2*s*.	2½*d*.
Madoco Gam		22½*d*.
Ieuan Vachan	3*s*.	8½*d*.
D*aui*d capellano		22*d*.

Summa 21*s*. 1½*d*. probatur.

(17) Villa de Maerdref Vchaph [i.e. Faerdref Uchaf in the parish of Llandrillo]

Ieuan ab Gryffry	4*s*.	6¾*d*.
uxore fabri		16*d*.
D*aui*d ab Eardur	4*s*.	
Adekyn	2*s*.	1½*d*.
Ad*a*m ab Gurgen*u*		19¼*d*.
Ieuan ab D*aui*d	3*s*.	0½*d*.
Iarward ab Loward		22½*d*.
Madoco ab Eynon	2*s*.	3½*d*.
Eynon ab Iarword		14*d*.
D*aui*d ab Iarword		16*d*.
Ieuan ab Gwadenerth	5*s*.	6½*d*.
D*aui*d ab Iarword		15*d*.
Iarword ab Ph*elip*		17¼*d*.
Groneu Coutta	14*s*.	10*d*.

Summa 46*s*. 4¾*d*. probatur.

(18) Villa de Dol [i.e. Dôl in the parish of Corwen]

Groneu ab Wyon	12*s*.	5*d*.
Ieua ab Iarword	6*s*.	6¼*d*.
Ad*af* ab Ithel	3*s*.	5*d*.

Ieuan ab Kenewr*ic*	7*s*.	$1\frac{1}{2}$*d*.
Adaf ab Ryryd	4*s*.	$9\frac{1}{2}$*d*.

Summa 34*s*. $2\frac{1}{4}$*d*.(1) probatur.

(19) Villa de Llygadoc [i.e. Llygadog in the parish of Corwen]

Anghar*ad* filia Lewelini	7*s*.	5*d*.
Madoco ab Iarword	6*s*.	$1\frac{1}{4}$*d*.
Meurico Vachan	10*s*.	$9\frac{1}{2}$*d*.
Madoco ab Ryryd	6*s*.	$5\frac{1}{4}$*d*.
Ryryd Voyl	6*s*.	
D*aui*d ab Eynon		23*d*.

Summa 38*s*. 8*d*. probatur.

(20) Villa de Gothelwern [i.e. Gwyddelwern]

Iarword ab Eynon	8*s*.	3*d*.
Madoco ab D*aui*d		$19\frac{1}{2}$*d*.
Adaf Duy	2*s*.	
Ad*a*m Voyl	12*s*.	$10\frac{1}{2}$*d*.
Groneu ab Lewelyn		$20\frac{1}{2}$*d*.
Kennewr*ic* ab Ithel	6*s*.	$5\frac{1}{2}$*d*.
uxore Kenner*ic* ab Madoc	3*s*.	$0\frac{1}{4}$*d*.
Esgobyn	2*s*.	$0\frac{1}{4}$*d*.
Houa ab Ad*a*m	4*s*.	8*d*.
Madoco medico	10*s*.	3*d*.
Iarword medico		$17\frac{1}{4}$*d*.

[m.7, right h. col.]

Maderoun goch	2*s*.	1*d*.
Iarword ab Gron*eu*	5*s*.	9*d*.
Madoco ab Edeneweyn	7*s*.	$4\frac{1}{2}$*d*.

Summa 70*s*. $6\frac{1}{4}$*d*.(2) probatur.

(21) Villa de Aberalwen [in the parish of Corwen]

Iarword ab Eyno*n*	7*s*.	11*d*.
Eynon ab Groneu	5*s*.	$2\frac{1}{2}$*d*.
Ithel ab Groneu	7*s*.	5*d*.
Ph*elip*o ab Meyler	3*s*.	$2\frac{1}{2}$*d*.
Howel ab Blethin	8*s*.	8*d*.
Tudgech filia Ithel		$19\frac{1}{4}$*d*.
Blethint ab Tud*er*		17*d*.
D*aui*d ab Gron*eu*	10*s*.	$8\frac{1}{4}$*d*.

Summa 46*s*. $1\frac{1}{2}$*d*. probatur.

---

1 An error for 34*s*. $3\frac{1}{4}$*d*. See *infra*, p. 85 for another section on Dôl.

2 An error for 69*s*. $6\frac{1}{4}$*d*. Another part of Gwyddelwern is dealt with *infra*, p. 87–8.

(22) Villa de Hucheldref [i.e. Ucheldref in the parish of Corwen]

Eden*euet* Duy[1]	7*s*. 1*d*.
Iarword ab Howeyn	2*s*. 10½*d*.
Eyno*n* ab Morlin	2*s*. 2*d*.
Iarword ab Adam	22*d*.
Eynon ab Mereduth	2*s*. 6½*d*.
Summa 16*s*. 6*d*. probatur.	

(23) Villa de Dol [i.e. Dôl in the parish of Corwen][2]

Iarword Voil	4*s*. 1*d*.
uxore Meuric goch	2*s*. 2*d*.
Gron*eu* ab Meuryk.	6*s*. 3½*d*.
Ieuan goch	6*s*. 3*d*.
Ad*af* ab Ieuaf	5*s*. 7½*d*.
Wyon ab Madoc	5*s*. 6*d*.
Madoco ab Wyon	6*s*. 4½*d*.
Eynon ab Wyon	6*s*. 0¼*d*.
Gron*eu* Vachan	3*s*. 11½*d*.
D*aui*d ab Gron*eu* Goch	21*d*.
Ph*elip*o ab Gryffry	2*s*. 0½*d*.
Ithel ab Ryryd	3*s*. 2½*d*.
D*aui*d ab Iarword	5*s*. 6*d*.
Kenner*ic* Goch	17½*d*.
Iarword ab Tegwar*et*	5*s*. 4*d*.
Summa 64*s*. 11¾*d*.[3]	

(24) Villa de Maerdref Elisse et Gryffid [i.e. Faerdref Isaf][4]

D*aui*d aurifabro	18*d*.
Iarword ab Wyon	5*s*. 7½*d*.
Gurgen*u* ab Wyon	2*s*. 10¾*d*.
Ieuan Mendour	7*s*. 8¼*d*.
Mad[o]co ab Ieuan	2*s*. 10½*d*.
Madoco Bleyth	6*s*. 0¼*d*.
D*aui*d ab Ithel	4*s*. 5¼*d*.

1 An Edenaved Theu made homage and fealty to the prince in 1301 (Edward Owen, op. cit., p. 25).

2 Cf. *supra*, p. 83–4. Dôl may have been divided into two for some administrative purposes.

3 Underlined for deletion; interlineated: '65*s*. 6¾*d*., incrementum 7*d*. probatur', which is correct.

4 Elisse and Gryffid were the sons of Iorwerth ab Owain Brogyntyn (A. D. Carr, art. cit., p. 300). Cf. *supra*, p. 83, for Faerdref Uchaf, which devolved on the descendants of Gruffydd ab Owain Brogyntyn.

Madoco ab Ithel		21*d.*
Meurico ab Ithel		17*d.*
Eynon Alauour	2*s.*	3*d.*
Cadug*an* ab Gryffri	3*s.*	
Eynon ab Ad*af*	2*s.*	1¼*d.*
Meurico ab Tud*er*		19½*d.*
Gron*eu* ab Iarword	2*s.*	0¾*d.*
Eynon ab Ithel		18¾*d.*
filia map Coun		18¾*d.*
D*aui*d ab Blethint	4*s.*	1½*d.*
Groneu ab Madoc	6*s.*	2½*d.*
map Blayn	4*s.*	4¼*d.*

Summa 79*s.* 7¾*d.*[1] probatur.

(25) Villa de Conryt [i.e. Cynwyd in the parish of Llangar][2]

D*aui*d ab Eden*euet*	6*s.*	4¼*d.*
Madoco ab Yarword	3*s.*	8*d.*
Eynon Wyth		17*d.*
Iohanne sutore		17*d.*
uxore sutoris		18*d.*
Cad*ugan* sutore		19¼*d.*
Madoco ab Griffry[3]	3*s.*	4½*d.*
Eynon Wyr		18½*d.*
Weruilla filia Iarword		19¼*d.*
Madoco Kethyn		21*d.*
Madoco Goch	10*s.*	
Edeneuet Voyl		13*d.*
Ieuan ab Ph*elip*		14½*d.*
Groneu ab Gurg*enu*	5*s.*	3½*d.*
Groneu mercatore		14½*d.*
Iarword fabro		16½*d.*
Ph*elip*o Voil	7*s.*	1½*d.*
Cadvaur	9*s.*	3½*d.*
Ph*elip*o ab Adam		20½*d.*
Madoco ab Iarword		19¼*d.*
Kenner*ic* ?Veeyth	5*s.*	8½*d.*
Eynon ab Griffry		20¼*d.*

1 An error for 63*s.* 0¾*d.*

2 This can be none other than Cynwyd – the references to the merchant, the doctor, the cobblers, etc., indicate an embryonic 'borough' – though the spelling might not lead one to suppose that it is. Cynwyd was in the parish of Gwyddelwern until the late nineteenth century.

3 One hesitates to identify him with Glyn Dŵr's great-grandfather, though no other person with exactly the same name appears *sub* Edeirnion.

Gron*eu* ab Meyler		17*d.*
D*aui*d ab Iarword	2*s.*	3*d.*
Madoco ab Edeneuet	2*s.*	4½*d.*
Madoco ab Ryryd	6*s.*	2¼*d.*
D*aui*d Goch	4*s.*	6½*d.*
Eynon medico	4*s.*	4*d.*
Madoco Vachan		21*d.*
Iarword goch	4*s.*	10¾*d.*
Eynon ab Yarword	4*s.*	2*d.*
Madoco ab Ithel	4*s.*	2*d.*
D*aui*d ab Yarword	2*s.*	10½*d.*
Crouthores		22½*d.*
Yarword ab Meuryk	6*s.*	3¼*d.*
Yarword Duy	6*s.*	
Blethin ab Wyon		18*d.*
Groneu ab Kennewr*ic*		17½*d.*
uxore Ade Goch	2*s.*	2*d.*
Leuk*e* filia D*aui*d		16*d.*
Ryryd Seys		16*d.*
Elisse ab Yarword[1]	19*s.*	3*d.*
Gryffid ab Yarword	23*s.*	11*d.*
Iarword ab Gryffid	3*s.*	1*d.*
Iarword Coutta	3*s.*	4½*d.*

Summa 9*li.* 2*s.* 0½*d.* probatur.

[m.6d., left h. col.]

(26) Villa de Gwydelwern [i.e. Gwyddelwern][2]

Kennewr*ic* ab Glochet	3*s.*	1*d.*
Kennewr*ic* ab Edenewen	3*s.*	1¼*d.*
Ieuan ap Madoc	4*s.*	11*d.*
Candolou		22*d.*
Ieuan ap Gron*eu*		22¾*d.*
Iarward ab Adam	2*s.*	8½*d.*
Eynon ab Adam		19¾*d.*
Groneu ab Kenuug	2*s.*	10*d.*
Ph*elip*o ab menach	3*s.*	6½*d.*
Yarword ab Madoc	3*s.*	6*d.*
Cadugan ab Idon	3*s.*	9*d.*
D*aui*d ab Blethint	6*s.*	4*d.*

1 Both he and his brother Gruffydd – the next person assessed – were barons of Edeirnion (*Cal. of Welsh Rolls*, p. 286). Elisse was lord of Llangar and his two sons made homage and fealty to the prince in 1301; so too did one son of Gruffydd's. For a full summary see A. D. Carr, art. cit., pp. 294–5.

2 Cf. *supra*, p. 84. The parish of Gwyddelwern was composed of three detached portions until the nineteenth century.

Kenner*ic* ab Ithel gam	3*s*.	11½*d*.
Groneu ab Eynon	13*s*.	4¼*d*.
Madoco ab Ph*elip*	5*s*.	10*d*.
Ieuan Duy		14½*d*.
Madoco ab Meyryk.		19½*d*.
Madoco		14½*d*.
D*aui*d ab Keuenard	3*s*.	2½*d*.
Wledyr Wyth	3*s*.	10*d*.
Tegwar*et* medico	2*s*.	11¼*d*.
Kenner*ic* sutore	3*s*.	3½*d*.
Wentlian filia Ithel Goch	2*s*.	10½*d*.
Iarword ab Edeneweyn	2*s*.	8½*d*.
Eynon grach		15½*d*.
Howel ab Eynon	4*s*.	8¼*d*.
Ithel ab D*aui*d	5*s*.	5*d*.
Ieuan Voil	5*s*.	7¼*d*.
D*aui*d ab Wynku	2*s*.	10¼*d*.
Yarword ab Ph*elip*	9*s*.	4¼*d*.
Groneu goch		12½*d*.
Madoco Duy	3*s*.	2¼*d*.
Seysild ab Yarword	12*s*.	1¼*d*.
Ithel ab Ryrid	6*s*.	4*d*.
Madoco ab Adam	5*s*.	4*d*.
Madoco sutore	4*s*.	6½*d*.
Iarword ab Ieuan	9*s*.	
Ad*af* ab Madoc	2*s*.	10*d*.
Ryrid ab Adam	5*s*.	1½*d*.

Summa 8*li*. 4*s*. 9¾*d*.[1] probatur.

(27) Villa de Bodekenvayl [i.e. Bodgynfel in the parish of Gwyddelwern]

Wentlyan filia Yarword	3*s*.	8¼*d*.
Ryrid ab Madoc	3*s*.	2½*d*.
Eynon ab Moridic	3*s*.	8*d*.
Howel ab Madoc	2*s*.	7*d*.
Yarword ab Howel		16½*d*.
Ieuan ab Morydic	9*s*.	5¼*d*.
Madoco Loyt	6*s*.	5*d*.
D*aui*d Wyth		16*d*.

Summa 31*s*. 8½*d*. probatur.

(28) Villa de Llangar et Kymmer [i.e. Llangar and Cymer]

Eynon ab D*aui*d	5*s*.	4½*d*.

1 An error for £8. 3*s*. 10¾*d*.

Ad*af* ab Eynon	2*s*.	4½*d*.
Wyon goch	15*s*.	7*d*.
Edeneuet capellano	3*s*.	2½*d*.
Yarword ab Elisse	5*s*.	2½*d*.
Wentliana filia Gryffini		21½*d*.
Eua filia Lewelini	2*s*.	5*d*.
uxore persone	4*s*.	8½*d*.
Groneu Kennit	5*s*.	
Ph*elip*o ab Madok	5*s*.	4¼*d*.
uxore Ph*elip*i filii Madocy		18*d*.
Madoco ab Reys	2*s*.	7*d*.
Meuanov filia Ithel	2*s*.	1¼*d*.
D*aui*d Bone		23*d*.
Cadug*an* ab Adam		17*d*.
D*aui*d ab Yarword	2*s*.	2½*d*.
Yarward ab Adam	9*s*.	10½*d*.
uxore Adam Llewych		18½*d*.

Summa 74*s*. 0½*d*.(1) probatur.

(29) Villa Brythyr(2)

Groneu ab Cadugon	3*s*.	9*d*.
Madoco filio Meuryk	3*s*.	7¾*d*.
D*aui*d ab Ithel	7*s*.	4*d*.
Howel ab Eynon		12½*d*.
Ad*a*m ab Ithel	5*s*.	
Ieuan ab Meuryk	3*s*.	
Cadugan Crimwas	9*s*.	
Cadugon ab Ithel	3*s*.	1*d*.
Adaf ab Gronou	11*s*.	0¼*d*.

Summa 46*s*. 9¼*d*.(3)

(30) Villa de Gruc in terra Gryffid ab Howeyn [i.e. Rug in the parish of Corwen](4)

Ieuan ab Yarword	7*s*.

---

1 An error for 74*s*. 2*d*.

2 The location of this hitherto unknown township is uncertain. It may have been in the region of Bryn-brith, a farm about 1½ mile to the north-west of Corwen or Ty-brith about 1½ mile to the east of Glyndyfrdwy; or it may have been the Brithdir four miles to the west of Corwen and on the west bank of the river Alwen – and therefore outside the present county boundaries. The latter seems the more likely.

3 '9¼*d*.' underlined for deletion; interlineated: '10½*d*., incrementum 1¼*d*.', which is correct.

4 There was later a close connection between Rug and Llanaelhaearn (Lhuyd, op. cit., p. 49 noted, e.g., that 'Ryg is always tax'd with Ayl Hayarn tho' it be in Korwen parish') and it may be because a person like Gryffid ab Howeyn had at one time interests in both townships.

Madoco ab Ithel	3*s.* 4*d.*
Iarword ab Heylin	5*s.* 4*d.*
Eynon ab Blaynwyn	4*s.* 1*d.*

Summa 19*s.* 9*d.* probatur.

(31) Villa de Pengreyk [i.e. Pencraig in the parish of Betws Gwerful Goch]

Eynon ab Lewelyn	7*s.* 4*d.*
Madoco ab Yarword	7*s.* 6*d.*
Meiler ab Madok	13*s.* 4*d.*
Ryrid ab Yarword	7*s.* 8*d.*
Groneu ab Melogyn	7*s.* 8*d.*
Tudero ab Melogin	6*s.* 8*d.*
Howel ab Melogyn	9*s.* 4*d.*

[m.7d., left h. col.]

Madoco ab Lewelin[1]	15*s.*
Wentlyan*a* filia Kenner*ic*	7*s.*
D*aui*d ab Lewelin	20*d.*
Ieuan ab Ryryd	9*s.* 8*d.*
Tegwar*et* Duy	3*s.* 4*d.*
Kenner*ic* ab Yarword	6*s.* $2\frac{1}{2}$*d.*
D*aui*d Mon	2*s.* 8*d.*
Ph*elip*o ab Thomas	6*s.* 4*d.*
Groneu Grach	2*s.* 8*d.*
Eynon ab Yarword	5*s.* 4*d.*

Summa 119*s.* $4\frac{1}{2}$*d.* probatur.

(32) Villa de Lamyangel [i.e. Llanfihangel (Glyn Myfyr)]

Eynon grach	18*d.*
Edeneuet ab Edenewen	3*s.* 7*d.*
Madoco Voyl	2*s.* $10\frac{1}{2}$*d.*
uxore Earthur	2*s.* 6*d.*
Ryrid Duy	9*s.* 4*d.*
Eynon Voil	3*s.* $6\frac{1}{2}$*d.*
Eynon ab Dehewint	6*s.* 4*d.*
Tud*er*o Goch	3*s.* 3*d.*
Eden*euet* ab Edeneweyn	4*s.*
Eden*euet* ab Madok	4*s.* 3*d.*
Yarword ab Eden*euet*	14*d.*

Summa 42*s.* 4*d.* probatur.

---

1 One of the barons of Edeirnion (*Cal. of Welsh Rolls*, p. 286).

(33) Villa de Llanerhaern [i.e. Llanaelhaearn in the parish of Gwyddelwern]

Yarword ab Meuryk	4*s*. 6*d*.
Yarword ab Adam	4*s*. 2*d*.
Eynon ab Groneu	20*d*.
Howel ab Meuryk	17*d*.
Houa ab Ithel	21*d*.
Ieuan aurifabro	2*s*. 8*d*.
Summa 17*s*. 10*d*.(1) probatur.	

Bona sex taxatorum in eodem commoto

D*aui*d ab Gryffid de Trewen(2)	8*s*. 3½*d*.
Madoco ab Ad*af* de Wothewern(3)	14*s*. 4¼*d*.
Ryrid Vachan de Garthyaen(4)	19*s*. 2½*d*.
Gryffid ab D*aui*d ab Howel	13*s*. 10¾*d*.
Madoco ab Meuryk.	7*s*. 9*d*.
Eyno*n* ab Ryrid de Mesdour(5)	7*s*. 5*d*.
Summa 70*s*. 8½*d*.(6)	

Villa de Abertanet que extra comitatum(7)

Yarword goch	2*s*. 4*d*.
Madoco ab Lewelin	23*d*.
Tudero Voyl	16*d*.
Madoco goch	20*d*.
Eynon gam	22*d*.
Gryffin Crouthor	2*s*. 9*d*.
Grun. carpentario	22*d*.
Wyn ab Heylin	4*s*. 6*d*.
Ieuan ab Madoc	12*d*.
Ieuan Pengul	2*s*. 11*d*.
D*aui*d ab G*ri*ffid	3*s*. 7*d*.
Gryffid ab Lewelyn	2*s*. 5*d*.
Morydic ab G*ri*ffid	2*s*. 1*d*.

1 An error for 16*s*. 2*d*.

2 i.e., Trewyn. A David ap Gruffydd made homage and fealty to the prince in 1301 (Edward Owen, op. cit., p. 26). A person of the same name had been fined 8*d*. for not attending the county court in 1288 (P.R.O. E.101/614/3).

3 i.e., Gwyddelwern.

4 i.e., Garthiaen, in the parish of Llandrillo.

5 i.e., Mwstwr, in the parish of Corwen.

6 '8½*d*.' underlined for deletion; interlineated: '11*d*., incrementum 2½*d*. probatur' which is correct.

7 i.e., Abertanat, in the parish of Llanyblodwel, co. Salop. It was transferred from Merioneth in 1536.

D*aui*d Goch		23*d*.
Gryffid cantore	2*s*.	
Iarword goch	2*s*.	3*d*.
D*aui*d ab Wyn		13*d*.
Ieuan ab Gryffin	4*s*.	4*d*.
Ieuan fratre eius	3*s*.	9*d*.
D*aui*d ab Eynon		21*d*.
Eynon Trudo		20*d*.
Ieuan Duy		12*d*.
Ieuan Scoleyk.		20*d*.
Wyn ab Mary		12*d*.
Eynon Goch		12*d*.
Mereduth ab Howel		16*d*.

Summa 54*s*. 11*d*. probatur.

Lewelyno filio Ad*af* de Iskyngaynok[1]	21*s*.	1*d*.

Summa 21*s*. 1*d*. probatur.

Summa summarum istius commoti 115*li*. 4*s*. 4*d*.[2]
unde de incremento 2*s*. 7*d*. probatur.

1 i.e., ?Esgaingaenog, in the parish of Gwyddelwern. No indication is given of the township in which Llywelyn ab Adda was assessed.

2 An error for £114. 4*s*. 6$\frac{1}{4}$*d*.

APPENDIX

Fragment of a 'local' LAY SUBSIDY ROLL for part of the commote of PENLLYN, Merioneth

[1318]

(Public Record Office, Exchequer, King's Remembrancer, Accounts, Various E.101/506/15 mm. 1 and 2)

APPENDIX

Fragment of a 'local' LAY SUBSIDY ROLL for part of the commote of PENLLYN, Merioneth

[1318]

'Local' lay subsidy rolls,(1) giving details of the movable goods of persons assessed for taxation, are extremely rare for Wales. Only five such rolls have been preserved, four of them relating to areas in the former counties of Anglesey and Caernarvon – Aberffraw, Nefyn, Creuddyn, and Cafflogion, all of them dating from 1292–3(2) – the fifth being the undated fragment for part of the commote of Penllyn printed below. The latter was found – and is still preserved – not with the other subsidy rolls, but amongst the records now classified as 'Accounts, Various' in the office of the King's Remembrancer of the Exchequer. Though it deals fully with only four townships (Penaran, Castell, Cyffty, and Bedwarian) and partially with two others (Streflyn and possibly Llandderfel) in the commote of Penllyn, it is none the less unique as far as Merioneth is concerned. Hence the decision to publish it here *in extenso*. An attempt to assess its importance has been made at various points in the introduction to this volume.

The roll, which consists of two isolated membranes, is undated. There can be no doubt that it did not serve as the basis upon which part of the 'county' roll of 1292–3 (printed above) was drawn up, for although the same names appear now and again in both, the sums at which they were assessed are, with two exceptions, entirely different. In other words, this fragment cannot be dated 1292–3. There are only two other possible dates – namely 1300 and 1318, when further subsidies were demanded of the principality(3) – for the document cannot be dated much later than the early fourteenth century. We find that the widows of persons taxed in 1292–3 were assessed in this 'local' roll so that it could have been drawn up in either 1300 or 1318. However, the subsidy demanded from the principality in 1300 was for a lump sum, whereas that of 1318, like that of 1292–3, was for a fifteenth; and since two persons were assessed at exactly the same sum in the 'county' roll of 1292–3 and

---

1 See *supra*, p. xi, for the distinction between 'local' and 'county' rolls.

2 Seebohm, *Tribal System*, App. A. f.; *B.B.C.S.*, V (1929–31), 54–71, 143–8; P.R.O. E.179/242/51.

3 Strayer and Rudisill, 'Taxation and Community in Wales and Ireland, 1272–1327', *Speculum*, XXIX (1954), 410.

in this fragment of a 'local' roll, we cannot but conclude that the latter should be dated 1318 and not 1300. The document transcribed below was then, without much doubt, drawn up for the purposes of the fifteenth (the word 'quintadecima', with the sum assessed, has been entered against every name listed) imposed in 1318. This conclusion is reinforced by the fact that the remaining documents classified under E.101/506/15, though in no way related to mm. 1 and 2, all belong to a period later than the reign of Edward I.

The procedure whereby the subsidy of 1318 was assessed and collected followed closely that adopted in 1292–3, but the number of local assessors seems to have been reduced from six to two per commote. These were Gwrgenau Fychan and Gruffydd ap Madog ab Iorwerth for Penllyn; Dafydd ap Madog and Iorwerth ap Howel for Ardudwy; Ynyr Fychan and Einion 'Legleu' for Tal-y-bont; and Gruffydd ab Adda and Einion ap Dafydd ap Madog for Ystumanner.[1] For some undisclosed reason the assessment and levy of the subsidy was halted late in 1318,[2] and in early 1319 a pardon was issued, at the request of Hugh le Despenser the younger, to the commonalties of Dryslwyn and Newton and Cantref Mawr in West Wales 'of the fifteenth of their goods lately granted as a subsidy for the war in Scotland'.[3] But the principality of North Wales did not escape. The tax brought in £928 from there, made up of £377, £325, and £226 from the former counties of Caernarvon, Anglesey, and Merioneth respectively,[4] certainly a considerable drop from the heavy assessments of 1292–3 when Merioneth alone contributed £566. The imposition of the subsidy in 1318 did not lead to disturbances in North Wales, but it remains a moot point how much the lower assessments of 1318 reflect the 'normal' situation, how much the result of the appalling famine of 1315–17, how much the consequence of learning the tricks of tax-evasion.

P.R.O. E.101/506/15 mm. 1 and 2

[m.1] [*possibly part of the vill of* Llandderfel][5]
D*aui*d ap Gurgen*u* [habet] 1 vaccam, 2 aueria duorum annorum, 6 oues, 18 grenockas auene. Quintadecima: 14*d.*

---

1 P.R.O. E.159/95 m. 62. The taxors for the commote of Edeirnion are not named.

2 *Cal. Close Rolls 1318–23*, p. 19.

3 *Cal. Pat. Rolls 1317–21*, p. 266.

4 P.R.O. E.359/14 m. 13d.

5 The reason for thinking that the vill referred to here is Llandderfel rests mainly on the fact that the widow of Madog ap Adda appears in the list. Cf. *supra*, p. 21.

D*aui*d apRirid: 8 boues, 12 vaccas, 4 aueria trium annorum, 20 crenockas auene. Quintadecima: 6*s*. 8*d*.
D*aui*d Ruth: 2 vaccas, 5 oues, 1 iumentum, 8 grenockas auene. Quintadecima: 14¾*d*.
Relicta Mad*oci* ap Ad*af*:(1) 4 vaccas, 6 grenockas auene. Quintadecima: 18*d*.
Ieu*an* Goch: 1 bouem, 7 vaccas, 2 aueria duorum annorum, 6 oues, 1 iumentum. Quintadecima: 2*s*. 8¼*d*.
Guyn ap D*aui*d: 1 bouem, 3 vaccas, 2 aueria trium annorum, 5 oues, 1 caballum, 4 aueria duorum annorum, 6½ grenockas auene. Quintadecima: 2*s*. 3¾*d*.
D*aui*d Loyd ap Ririd:(2) 8 boues, 6 vaccas, 3 aueria trium annorum, 2 aueria duorum annorum, 2 iumenta, 10 oues, 64 crenockas auene. Quintadecima: 7*s*. 5*d*.
Guyn ap Saer: 3 boues, 6 vaccas, 1 auerium trium annorum, 3 aueria duorum annorum, 6 oues, 1 iumentum, 6 crenockas auene. Quintadecima: 3*s*. 8½*d*.
Mad*oc* ap Ith*el*: 5 vaccas, 6 oues, 8 crenockas auene. Quintadecima: 19*d*.
Summa predicte ville: 2*li*. 10*s*. 6*d*. probatur.

Villa de Pennaran [i.e. Penaran in the parish of Llanuwchllyn]
Guyn ap Edneuet [habet] 5 boues, 6 vaccas, 2 aueria trium annorum, 10 oues, 1 iumentum, 40 crenockas auene. inde Quintadecima: 5*s*. 4*d*.
Goron*w* ap Mad*oc*: 2 boues, 3 vaccas, 20 crenockas auene. Quintadecima: 2*s*. 0*d*.
Eyn*on* ap Bussel: 6 vaccas, 1 auerium trium annorum et dimidiam [*sic*], 2 aueria duorum annorum, 8 oues, 4 crenockas auene. Quintadecima: 2*s*. 3*d*.
Tuder ap Houel: 7 boues, 26 vaccas, 9 aueria trium annorum, 8 aueria duorum annorum, 2 iumenta, 8 oues, 8 crenockas auene. Quintadecima: 11*s*. 10¾*d*.
Mad*oc* Loyd: 2 boues, 5 vaccas, 1 auerium trium annorum, 3 aueria duorum annorum, 1 iumentum, 7 oues, 8 crenockas auene. Quintadecima: 3*s*. 2¼*d*.
Guyon ap Guidraus: 3 boues, 18 vaccas, 6 aueria trium annorum, 6 aueria duorum annorum, 16 oues, 2 iumenta, 12 crenockas auene. Quintadecima: 8*s*. 5*d*.

---

1 Madoc ap Adaf was assessed at 20*d*. *sub* Llandderfel in 1292–3 (*supra*, p. 21).
2 Cf. Ririd Loyt assessed at 20¾*d*. *sub* Llandderfel in 1292–3 (*supra*, p. 21).

Guenll*ian* filia Guion: 2 vaccas, 1 auerium trium annorum, 1 auerium duorum annorum, 5 oues. Quintadecima: 11¼*d.*
Ph*elip* Du:[1] 2 vaccas, 5 oues. Quintadecima: 7*d.*
Eyno*n* Loyd:[2] 11 vaccas, 2 aueria trium annorum, 2 aueria duorum annorum, 20 oues, 16 crenockas auene. Quintadecima: 4*s.* 3¼*d.*
Guenll*ian* filia Eyno*n*: 2 vaccas, 1 auerium trium annorum, 1 auerium duorum annorum, 5 oues. Quintadecima: 11¼*d.*
Ior*word* ap Guion:[3] 2 boues, 6 vaccas, 5 aueria trium annorum, 1 auerium duorum annorum, 9 oues, 1 iumentum, 20 crenockas auene. Quintadecima: 4*s.* 3¼*d.*
Lewel*in* grach: 7 boues, 11 vaccas, 2 aueria duorum annorum, 2 iumenta, 40 crenockas auene. Quintadecima: 7*s.* 0¾*d.*
Mad*oc* ap Yago ap Guyn: 2 vaccas et dimidiam [*sic*], 2 aueria trium annorum, 1 iumentum, 3 oues, 16 crenockas auene. Quintadecima: 2*s.* 4½*d.*,
Goron*w* ap Ririd: 2 boues, 6 vaccas, 3 aueria duorum annorum, 1 iumentum, 15 crenockas auene. Quintadecima: 3*s.* 4*d.*
Eyno*n* ap Ith*el*:[4] 2 boues, 5 vaccas, 1 auerium duorum annorum, 1 iumentum, 12 crenockas auene. Quintadecima: 2*s.* 10½*d.*
Heil*in* ap Kediuor: 3 boues, 9 vaccas, 1 auerium trium annorum, 2 aueria duorum annorum, 1 iumentum, 4 oues, 12 crenockas auene. Quintadecima: 4*s.* 3¾*d.*
Ieu*an* Goch: 3 boues, 3 vaccas, 2 aueria trium annorum, 2 aueria duorum annorum, 12 oues, 2 iumenta, 16 crenockas auene. Quintadecima: 3*s.* 1¾*d.*
Mad*oc* ap Ieu*an*: 4 vaccas, 2 aueria duorum annorum, 6 oues, 1 iumentum, 8 crenockas auene. Quintadecima: 2*s.* 0*d.*
Ad*af* ap Meilyr: 4 vaccas, 1 auerium trium annorum, 2 aueria duorum annorum, 6 oues, 8 crenockas auene. Quintadecima: 22*d.*
Houel sutor: 1 bouem, 4 vaccas, 2 aueria duorum annorum, 13 oues, 16 crenockas auene. Quintadecima: 2*s.* 8*d.*
Meilyr ap Ith*el*: 2 vaccas, 8 oues, 4 crenockas auene. Quintadecima: 10½*d.*
D*aui*d ap Gurgen*u*: 1 bouem, 15 vaccas, 6 aueria trium annorum, 6 aueria duorum annorum, 6 oues, 1 iumentum, 8 crenockas auene. Quintadecima: 6*s.* 3¼*d.*

---

1 Phelip Du was assessed at 14¾*d.* in 1292–3 (*supra*, p. 10).

2 An Eynon Loyt was assessed at 13¼*d.* in neighbouring Pennant-lliw in 1292–3 and at 2*s.* 2*d.* in nearby Maestran (*supra*, pp. 7 and 13).

3 Cf. *supra*, p. 10, where Yerward ap Wion was assessed at 2*s.* 8½*d.* *sub* Penaran.

4 He was assessed at exactly the same sum in 1292–3 (see *supra*, p. 11).

Ad*af* Loyd:[1] 4 vaccas, 1 auerium trium annorum, 3 aueria duorum annorum, 2 oues, 4 crenockas auene.
Quintadecima: 20¼*d.*
Hag*ra*t Wastat: [3] vaccas, 6 oues, 3 crenockas auene.
Quintadecima: 11¾*d.*
[M]ad*oc* ap Yago Voel:[2] 6 crenockas auene.
Quintadecima: 2½*d.*
Edneuet: 5 vaccas, 1 iumentum, 7 oues, 16 crenockas auene.
Quintadecima: 2*s.* 2½*d.*
Ior*word* ap Yago: 3 vaccas, 3 crenockas auene.
Quintadecima: 9¾*d.*

Summa: 4*li.* 6*s.* 8¾*d.*

[m.2] Villa de Kastel [i.e. Castell in the parish of Llanuwchllyn][3]
D*aui*d Du[4] [habet] 1 vaccam, 2 aueria duorum annorum, 6 oues, 1 iumentum, 4 crenockas auene. Quintadecima: 12½*d.*
Mad*oc* ap Ad*af*:[5] 1 bouem, 4 vaccas, 1 auerium trium annorum, 3 aueria duorum annorum, 1 iumentum, 4 crenockas auene.
Quintadecima: 2*s.* 3½*d.*
Mad*oc* Loyd ap Eyno*n*: 9 vaccas, 1 iumentum, 4 crenockas auene.
Quintadecima: 2*s.* 5¾*d.*
D*aui*d ap Mad*oc* Coch: 2 boues, 8 vaccas, 3 aueria trium annorum, 4 aueria duorum annorum, 2 oues, 1 iumentum, 24 crenockas auene. Quintadecima: 4*s.* 6¾*d.*
Ieu*an* Goch: 3 boues, 2 vaccas, 2 aueria trium annorum, 1 auerium duorum annorum, 2 iumenta, 5 oues, 36 crenockas auene.
Quintadecima: [3*s.*]11½*d.*
Relicta Ior*word* Voel:[6] 3 boues, 15 vaccas, 1 iumentum, 6 crenockas auene. Quintadecima: 4*s.* 10½*d.*

---

1 Cf. Adaf Loyt assessed at 5*s.* 4*d.* *sub* Cyffty in 1292–3 (*supra*, p. 12).

2 Almost certainly the same man who was assessed at 22*d.* in 1292–3 (see *supra* p. 11).

3 The vill of Castell does not appear in the 1292–3 roll.

4 Two men called Dauid Duy were assessed in nearby Penaran in 1292–3, one at 13*s.* 8½*d.* and the other at 2*s.* 5¼*d.* (*supra*, p. 10).

5 It is difficult to see how he is to be identified with Madoc ap Athaf, king's yeoman, who was granted, at the request of the king of France, the 'land' of Pennant-lliw, extended at £6. 10*s.* 0*d.* a year, in 1315, a grant which was converted to a grant for life in 1320 and which was enjoyed by him until his death in 1328 (*Cal. Pat. Rolls 1313–17*, p. 355; *Cal. Pat. Rolls 1317–21*, p. 499; *Cal. Pat. Rolls 1327–30*, p. 244.)

6 The only Iorword Voel assessed in the commote of Penllyn in 1292–3 appears *sub* Llanfor in that list with the sum of 2*s.* 0¾*d.* against his name (*supra*, p. 6).

Mad*oc* Voel:[1] 1 vaccam, 5 oues, 1 iumentum, 8 crenockas auene.
Quintadecima: 12*d.*

Goronw Wr: 3 vaccas, 3 aueria trium annorum, 9 oues, 1 iumentum, [4] crenockas auene. Quintadecima: 23*d.*

Ieu*an* Du: 4 boues, 15 vaccas, 2 aueria trium annorum, 4 aueria duorum annorum, 5 oues, 2 mutones, 1 iumentum, 32 crenockas auene. Quintadecima: 7*s.* 2¼*d.*

Ydei: 2 vaccas, 1 auerium duorum annorum, 8 crenockas auene.
Quintadecima: 10½*d.*

Ririd ap Ior*word* Voel: 1 vaccam, 13 aueria duorum annorum, 6 oues, 1 iumentum, 4 crenockas auene.
Quintadecima: 2*s.* 7¼*d.*

Eyno*n* Vychan: 2 boues, 5 vaccas, 1 auerium trium annorum, 1 auerium [duorum] annorum. Quintadecima: 2*s.* 1*d.*

Hag*ra*t filia Eyno*n*: 4 vaccas. Quintadecima: 11*d.*

Galk. ap Goron*w*: 2 boues, 9 vaccas, 2 aueria trium annorum, 7 aueria duorum annorum, 1 iumentum, 8 oues, 32 crenockas auene. Quintadecima: 5*s.* 7¼*d.*

Ieu*an* Geth*in*: 1 bouem, 5 vaccas, 1 auerium duorum annorum, 1 iumentum, 4 oues, 8 crenockas auene.
Quintadecima: 2*s.* 4¼*d.*

Guyon ap y Dioual:[2] 2 vaccas, 1 auerium duorum [annorum], 5 oues, 1 iumentum, 16 crenockas auene.
Quintadecima: 19½*d.*

Y guas t*ru*sgul: 6 vaccas, 5 oues, 1 iumentum, 13 crenockas [?auene].
Quintadecima: 2*s.* 3¾*d.*

Ior*word* ap Rys: 2 boues, 4 vaccas, 3 aueria trium annorum, 2 aueria duorum annorum, 16 crenockas auene.
Quintadecima: 2*s.* 10¾*d.*

Summa: 50*s.* 7*d.* probatur.

Villata de Kefdu [i.e. Cyffty in the parish of Llanycil]

Ior*word* Du[3] [habet] 1 bouem, 6 vaccas, 3 aueria trium annorum, 3 aueria duorum annorum, 10 oues, 1 iumentum, 16 crenockas auene. Quintadecima: 3*s.* 4¼*d.*

---

1 Cf. Madoc Voyl assessed at 2*s.* 9½*d.* *sub* Penaran in 1292–3 (*supra*, p. 10).

2 Possibly the son of Idiaual assessed at 13*s.* 4¼*d.* *sub* neighbouring Maestran in 1292–3 (*supra*, p. 13).

3 Cf. Yerword Duy assessed at 4*s.* 4¼*d.* *sub* the nearby vill of Penaran in 1292–3 (*supra*, p. 10).

Guyn Seys:[1] 3 boues, 9 vaccas, 4 aueria trium annorum, 5 aueria duorum annorum, 1 iumentum, 10 crenockas auene.
Quintadecima: 5*s*. 0*d*.

Tuder ap Guyn Seys: 3 vaccas, 3 aueria trium annorum, 1 auerium duorum annorum, 1 iumentum, 8 oues, 4 crenockas auene.
Quintadecima: 2*s*. 4½*d*.

Ior*word* ap Grifri:[2] 3 boues, 3 vaccas, 1 auerium duorum annorum, 8 oues, 1 iumentum, 24 crenockas auene.
Quintadecima: 3*s*. 3½*d*.

Ieu*an* ap Ior*word*: 2 boues, 4 vaccas, 8 oues, 1 iumentum, 4 crenockas auene. Quintadecima: 2*s*. 4*d*.

Goronw ap Ririd: 1 bouem, 4 vaccas, 3 aueria duorum annorum, 1 iumentum, 5 oues, 8 crenockas auene.
Quintadecima: 2*s*. 5¼*d*.

Ieu*an* Loyd:[3] 3 vaccas, 5 aueria duorum annorum, 8 crenockas auene. Quintadecima: 19¼*d*.

Ad*af* Loyd:[4] 9 oues. Quintadecima: 5*d*.

Relicta Ior*word* ap Tuder:[5] 6 vaccas, 4 oues.
Quintadecima: 17¾*d*.

Relicta Mad*oci* ap Ior*word*:[6] 4 boues, 6 vaccas, 1 iumentum, 4 crenockas auene. Quintadecima: 3*s*. 1¾*d*.

Eyno*n* Loyd: 1 bouem, 7 vaccas, 10 oues, 1 iumentum, 8 crenockas auene. Quintadecima: 2*s*. 6*d*.

Goron*w* Loyd: 4 boues, 2 vaccas, 2 aueria duorum annorum, 1 iumentum, 5 oues, 11 crenockas auene.
Quintadecima: 3*s*. 1*d*.

Ior*word* ap Mad*oc* creyd: 3 vaccas. Quintadecima: 8½*d*.

Summa: 1*li*. 11*s*. 8¾*d*. probatur.

Villa de Bedouoren [i.e. Bedwarian in the parish of Llanycil][7]

---

1 Win Seis was assessed at 4*s*. 10*d*. in Cyffty in 1292–3 (*supra*, p. 12).

2 Cf. Yerwoıd ap Griffri, assessed at 17½*d*. in the neighbouring vill of Maestran in 1292–3 (*supra*, p. 13).

3 Cf. also Ieuan Loyt, assessed at 2*s*. 1½*d*. in the same township in 1292–3 (*supra*, p. 13).

4 Adaf Loyt was assessed at 4*s*. 0¼*d*. in 1292–3 (*supra*, p. 12).

5 Yerword ap Tuder was assessed at 3*s*. 4*d*. in 1292–3 (*supra*, p. 12).

6 Madoc ap Ierword was assessed at 5*s*. in Cyffty in 1292–3, but he may have had interests in Pennant-lliw as well (*supra*, p. 12, n. 5).

7 The vill of Bedwarian does not appear in the 1292–3 roll. Those having movables there seem to have been included in the lists for the vill of Gwernefail (in the same parish of Llanycil) in 1292–3. (See the four succeeding notes.)

Eyno*n* Loyd[1] [habet] 6 boues, 5 vaccas, 2 aueria trium annorum, 3 aueria duorum annorum, 8 oues, 1 iumentum, 20 crenockas auene. Quintadecima: 5*s.* 1½*d.*

D*aui*d ap Edneuet:[2] 3 boues, 6 vaccas, 3 aueria duorum annorum, 6 oues, 1 iumentum, 4 crenockas auene.
Quintadecima: 3*s.* 6*d.*

Ken*uric* Kenyd: 4 vaccas, 4 aueria duorum annorum, 4 oues.
Quintadecima: 17½*d.*

Relicta Mad*oci* Du:[3] 1 vaccam, 1 auerium duorum annorum, 1 iumentum, 3 oues, 1 crenockam auene.
Quintadecima: 10*d.*

Mad*oc* ap Guyn:[4] 2 boues, 15 vaccas. Quintadecima: 4*s.* 0*d.*

Summa: 14*s.* 11*d.*

Villa de Lestreflyn [i.e. [Lly]streflyn in the parish of Llanycil]

Guyn ap Mad*oc* [habet] 6 boues, 21 vaccas, 5 aueria duorum annorum, 16 oues, 1 iumentum, 32 crenockas auene.
Quintadecima: 8*s.* 11½*d.*

Go*ronw* Verthauc:[5] 2 boues, 24 vaccas, 4 aueria trium annorum, 5 aueria duorum annorum, 1 iumentum, 24 crenockas auene.
Quintadecima: 8*s.* 5¾*d.*

Guyn ap Tuder: 2 boues, 6 vaccas, 15 oues, 1 iumentum, 15 crenockas auene. Quintadecima: 3*s.* 4*d.*

Eua relicta Mad*oci*: 3 vaccas, 1 auerium trium annorum, 14 oues, 4 crenockas auene. Quintadecima: 17¼*d.*

Cad*ugan* Du: 4 boues, 12 vaccas, 5 aueria trium annorum, 8 aueria duorum annorum, 6 oues, 1 iumentum.
Quintadecima: 6*s.* 5*d.*

[*End of membrane* 2. *Incomplete*]

---

1 Cf. Eynon Loyt assessed at 4*s.* 1¾*d.* *sub* Gwernefail in 1292–3 (*supra*, p. 19).

2 A person of the same name was assessed at 4*s.* 9*d.* *sub* Gwernefail in 1292–3 (*supra*, p. 19).

3 Cf. Madoc Duy assessed at 3*s.* 0½*d.* *sub* Gwernefail in 1292–3 (*supra*, p. 19).

4 Cf. Madoc ap Win assessed at 4*s.* 3¾*d.* *sub* Gwernefail in 1292–3 (*supra*, p. 20).

5 He is probably to be identified with Gronou Berthoc, assessed at 14*s.* 8*d.* *sub* the neighbouring vill of Cyffty in 1292–3 (*supra*, p. 12).

INDEX

All places referred to are in co. Gwynedd, unless otherwise stated

ABER, cxiv
Aberalwen, co. Clwyd, cxxxix, cxli, 84
Aberconwy, abbey, cvii n. 4, cxiv
Aberdaron, cxi
Aberdyfi, 23 n. 2
Abereiddon (Abydon), 43 and n. 3
Aberffraw, x and n. 2, xi and n. 1, xiv, xv, xxxix n. 4, xlviii and n. 3, lxxxii, cxiii and n. 2, cxiv, cxv, cxvii, cxviii, cxix, cxx, 95
Abergavenny, co. Gwent, xlix
— , lordship of, x, xi and n. 1, xxx n. 6, xlviii, lxix, lxxxii
Aber Ia, lxxvi
Abertanat, co. Salop, xxxviii, cxl, cxli, 91 and n. 7
Aberystwyth, co. Dyfed, lx, lxiv, cxxiii, cxxix, cxxx
Abydon, *see* Abereiddon
Acherui Cam, Cregennan, 40
Adda (Ada, Adaf, Adam, Atha)
— ap Ada, Llanaber, 54
— — Adaf sutore, Llanfrothen, 65
— — Atha, Llanfair, 60
— — Cadugan, Cynfal, 31
— — — , Llanfair, 60
— — — , Llanycil, 20
— — — , Morfa Maenog, 41
— — — , Rhyd-cryw, 37
— — Candalo, Penrhyndeudraeth, 61
— — Candolou, Branas, 80
— — Cradoc, Penrhyndeudraeth, 61
— — Dauid, Bylan, 26
— — — , Corwen, 75
— — — , Cynllwyd, 17
— — — , Llanfihangel, 42
— — — , Llanfihangel-y-traethau, 71
— — — , Morfa Maenog, 41
— — — , Penrhyndeudraeth, 61
— — — , Trawsfynydd, 54
— — — ap Tegwaret, Llanaber, 55
— — Edeneuet, Gwernefail, 19
— — Eynon, Cynfal, 31
— — — , Gwrych, 30
— — — , Llanaber, 69
— — — , Llanddwywe, 56
— — — , Llandecwyn, 63
— — — , Llanenddwyn, 70
— — — , Llangar, 89
Adda ap Eynon, Llansanffraid, 76
— — — , Nantlleidiog, 15
— — — , Penmaen, 6
— — — , Penrhyndeudraeth, 62
— — — , *taxator*, 7
— — — , Trefeddian, 27
— — — , Ystradgwyn, 34
— — Griffid, Ceiswyn, son(s) or daughter(s) of, 34
— — — , Cregennan, 40
— — — , Maesmor, 27 and n. 3
— — Gronou, Brythyr, 89
— — — , Dolgledr, 50
— — — , Morfa Maenog, 41
— — Gurgenu, Ceiswyn, 33
— — — , Ciltalgarth, 18
— — — , Faerdref Uchaf, 83
— — — , Gwrych, 30
— — — , Llwyngwril, 41
— — Gwion, Llanenddwyn, 57
— — Heilin, Penaran, 11
— — Heylin, Llandecwyn, 62
— — Howel, Llanfihangel, 42
— — Idenerth, Trewyn, 78
— — Ieuaf, Dôl, 85
— — Ieuan, Gwyddelfynydd, 28
— — — , Llanfihangel-y-traethau, 71
— — — , Trawsfynydd, 69
— — Ioreword, Llanaber, 55
— — Ithel, Brythyr, 89
— — — , Caethle, 22
— — — , Dôl, 83
— — — , Llanaber, 55
— — Iuor, Tyinmeyron, 67
— — Kenewrek, Tirllannerch, 76
— — Kenuric, Maentwrog, 73
— — Kenwric, Llanfair, 59
— — Kyrak, Maentwrog, 73
— — Lewelin, Llanfrothen, 64
— — Lowarch, Cefnrhos, 24
— — — , Llanfrothen, 63
— — Maddok, 31 n. 3
— — Madin, Bodgadfan, lxxxii, 36
— — Madoc, Brithdir, 49
— — — , Cregennan, 40
— — — , Cynfal, 31
— — — , Cynlas, 17
— — — , Dyffrydan, 50
— — — , Gwernefail, 19
— — — , Gwyddelwern, 88
— — — , Penaran, 10

Adda ap Madoc, Peniarth, 39
— — — , Ucheldref, 17
— — Madoc Duy, Llanfrothen, 65
— — Madok, Garthiaen, 81
— — Meiler, Maentwrog, 74
— — — , Peniarth, 38
— — Meilyr, Penaran, 98
— — Meroc, Llanaber, 70
— — Morud, Llanfihangel, 42
— — Nannou, Nannau, 46
— — Phelip, Pennal, 28
— — — , Trawsfynydd, 68
— — Purrewyn, Corwen, xxxviii, 75
— — Referyot, Llandrillo, c, 83
— — Ruathon, Llanddwywe, 55
— — Ryryd, Dôl, 84
— — Seysild, Llanfrothen, 63
— — Tegwaret, Cregennan, 40
— — — , Llanaber, 54
— — — , Llanenddwyn, 71
— — Trahairn, Llanfihangel-y-traethau, 71
— — Tuder, Gwnnodl, 82
— — Vdrich, Llanfair, 60
— — Wilim, Trawsfynydd, 68
— — Win, Llannerchgoediog, 25
— — — , Nannau, 46
— — Wingam, Pennal, 28
— — Wion, 66
— — Wyon, 66 n. 5
— — Ydon, Llanaber, 55
— — Yerword, Cefnrhos, 23
— — — , Nanmor, 72
— Bach, Bere, 52
— — , Garthgynfor, 48
— Bennard, Harlech, cvi, 66
— Couppa, Gwyddelfynydd, 27
— Cutta, Cefnrhos, 23
— dean of Ardudwy, 54 n. 3
— Duy, Gwyddelwern, 84
— — , Llanaber, 69
— — , Penrhyndeudraeth, 61
— *filius* Ade, Penrhyndeudraeth, 61
— — Cadi, Llanfrothen, 63
— — Cormuly, Llanfrothen, 64
— — Denowalt, Llandanwg, 57
— — Mathei, Gwrych, 30
— Goch, Botalog, 23
— — , Crogen, 16
— — , Cynwyd, wife of, 87
— — , Gwnnodl, 81, 82
— — , Gwyddelfynydd, 28
— — , Llanfrothen, 63
— — , Tyinmeyron, 67
— Gurnaur, Trawsfynydd, 68
— Hen, Bodgadfan, lxxxiii
— — , Llanfihangel-y-traethau, 71
— Hudol, Penrhyndeudraeth, 62
— 'King', 66 n. 1
— Llewych, Llangar, wife of, 89
— Loyd, Cyffty, 12 n. 7
— — , Penaran, 11 n. 2, 99
— Loyt, Corwen, 75
— — , Cyffty, 12, 99 n. 1, 101 and n. 4
— — , Cynllwyd, 17
Adda Loyt, Penaran, 11
— Maystran, Maestran, 13
— *medicus*, Tirllannerch, 77
— Pen, Brithdir, 49
— Penbras, Ciltalgarth, 18
— Penthlin, Maestran, 13
— Ruth, Penrhyndeudraeth, 62
— Saer, Nannau, 47
— Seysir, Nanffreuer, 15
— Sibero, Llandecwyn, 63
— Skynnith, Llannerchgoediog, 25
— Sutor, Bere, 52
— — , Brithdir, 49
— — , Llandderfel, 21
— Turnor, Selwrn, 14
— Vachan, Cynfal, 31
— — , Trefeddian, 27
— Voil, Ffestiniog, 72
— — , Trawsfynydd, 68
— Voyl, Corwen, 75
— — , Gwyddelwern, 84
— — , Llanaber, 55
— Wachan, Ceiswyn, son(s) or daughter(s) of, 34
— Whith, Llanaber, 54
— Win, Rhywedog, 4
— Wirion, Peniarth, 39
— Wyn, Llansanffraid, 76
Adekin, Llandecwyn, 63
— , Penaran, 9
Adekyn, Faerdref Uchaf, 83
Adeyl, Garthgynfor, 48
Agyston, co. Clwyd, lxiii
Alicia, Bere, 52
Allt Goch, 23 n. 2
Allt Llwyd ycha, Yr, 23 n. 2
Allt-lwyd, 23 n. 2
Alltuelin, xxxvii n. 2, cxxxix
Alwen, river, 89 n. 2
Angharad (Angaharad, Angarad, Hangharad)
— Duy, Dyffrydan, 50
— — , Peniarth, 39
— *filia* Adaf, Penrhyndeudraeth, 61
— — Eynon, Llanfendigaid, 35
— — Eudas, Mwstwr, 79
— — *fabri*, Gwnnodl, 81
— — Gronou, Nannau, 47
— — — , Rhyd-cryw, 38
— — Howel, Garthiaen, 81
— — Kenewric, Pennal, 29
— — Lewelini, Llygadog, 84
— — Madoci, Peniarth, 39
— — Madok, Pennant, 80
— — Moridic, Rhyd-cryw, 38
— — Reis, Taltreuddyn, 58
— — Ririd, Maestran, 13
— — Win, Bodgadfan, 36
— — — , Brithdir, 49
— — — , Nannau, 46
— — — , Ystumanner, 22
— Goch, Brithdir, 49
— — , Llanaber, 69
— — , Penrhyndeudraeth, 61
— — , Trawsfynydd, 53

Angharad Loyt, Brithdir, 49
— o'r Pant, Cregennan, 40
— *uxor* . . . , Cymysgadwy, 21
— — Ade, Trawsfynydd, 53
— — Eynon, Llandecwyn, 63
— — — , Ystradgwyn, 34
— — Tuder, Rhywedog, 4
— — — , Treffeden, 32
— Vaur, Maentwrog, 74
Anglesey, ix, x, xv, xix n. 5, xxv, xxvii, xxxi, xxxv, xxxix n. 4, xlviii, liv, lix, lxii, lxix, lxxi, lxxx, lxxxii, lxxxiii, cv, cxi, cxiii, cxiv, cxvii, cxxx, cxxxi, 95, 96
Anian ap Loward, Nannau, 44
Anian, bishop of St. Asaph, xcix, cxiv, cxv
Anians, Trawsfynydd, wife of, 54
Ankoc, Bere, 52
Ap Tegwaret, Cymysgadwy, 20
Ardudwy (Ardudou), commote of, xxxiii, xxxvii n. 2, xl, xliii, xliv, xlvii, lvii, lxvi, lxvii, lxix, lxxii, lxxiii, lxxiv, lxxvi, lxxvii, lxxix, lxxxi, lxxxvii, lxxxviii, lxxxix, xc, xciv, xcvii, c, ciii, cviii, cix, cxii, cxvi, cxxxvi, cxxxix, cxl, 8 n, 52 and n. 3, 54 n. 3, 56 n. 2, 62 n. 3, 66, 73 n. 1, 82 n. 3, 96
Argaun, Crogen, xcvi
Arnarou, cviii, cxxxix, cxliv, 26 and n. 3
Aron ap Lewelin, 52
Arthour Duy, Gwnnodl, 81
Aruaron (Arvaron), cviii
Arwystli, cantref of, co. Powys, x, xxxi n., xlviii, lxx, lxxiii
Asney, co. Clwyd, li
Assessors (*taxatores*), xiii–xvi, lxxxvi, cxl, cxli, cxlii, cxliii, cxliv, 7, 8 n., 35, 52, 66 and n. 4, 91, 96
Atha, *see* Adda
Atreayliu, Rhywedog, 5
Aurifaber, Gwrych, 30
— , Trawsfynydd, 68
Ayl Hayarn, *see* Llanaelhaearn

BALA, xxxvii n. 2, xlvii, lxv, lxxxi, cviii, cxxxix
Bangor, bishop of, xliv, c, cxxiii
— , borough of, civ, cv, cx
— , church at, xx
— , co. Clwyd, xxxiii, li
Barth, Garthgynfor, cxxxvi, 47
Basingwerk, abbey, co. Clwyd, xxxvii n. 2, lxxv, c, 7 and n. 1
Baynard, Adam, cvi; *see also* Bennard, Beynard 'King', *and* Boynard.
Beaumaris, xlvi, n. 3, lx and n. 4, lxi and n. 1, lxii, lxiv and n. 6, cv, cxxx
Beddgelert, parish of, cxl, 72 n. 1
Bedwarian (Bedouoren), xi n. 2, xxxvii n. 2, cxiii, cxxxix, 19 n. 2, 3, and 4, 20 n. 1, 95, 101 and n. 7
Belvero, Robert de, xxxi
Benedict, Llanaber, 54
Bennard, Ada, Harlech, 66; *see also* Baynard
Bere, lx, lxiv, lxv, lxxiv, cxxix, cxxxix, cxliii, 51 and n. 4
Bergam, Llanenddwyn, 57
Berwyn, mountain, lxxx
Bettisfield, co. Clwyd, li, lxiii
Betws Gwerful Goch, co. Clwyd, xlv, lxxvi, lxxix, lxxx n. 2, cxli, 90
Betws-y-coed (Bettuse y Koyd), 16 n. 1
Beyduch, Trewyn, 78
Beynard 'King', 66 n. 1; *see also* Baynard
Bichan, Gwrych, 30
Birgif, Llanenddwyn, 71
Black Death, liii, liv, lv, lvi, lix
Bleddfa, lordship of, co. Powys, x, xxxi n., lxiii
Blethin ab Wyon, Cynwyd, 87
Blethin *filius* Gronou, Llanfrothen, 63
Blethint, Llandderfel, 21
— , Peniarth, 40
— ab Tuder, Aberalwen, 84
— Hagor, Trawsfynydd, 53
Blingyn, Rhywedog, 4
Bodekenvayl, *see* Bodgynfel
Bodelith, 17 n. 2
Bodfel, cxiv
Bodgadfan (Bodgadevan), xxxviii, lxxxii, cxxxix, cxliii, 36
Bodgynfel (Bodekenvayl), co. Clwyd, cxxxix, cxli, 88
Bodidris, co. Clwyd, li
Bodington, Adam de, viii n. 2, xii
Bodlosged (Botlosked), 65
Bodorlas (Bodoryles), co. Clwyd, xxxviii, cxxxix, cxli, 76
Bohun, lordships, cxvi
Bongam, Garn, 18 and n. 1
— , Rhywedog, 4
Bonwm, co. Clwyd, xxxvii n. 2, cxxxix
Botalog (Botaloc), cxxxix, cxliv, 23
Botlosked, *see* Bodlosged
Botoun, Llanfor, 5
Boynard, Gilbert, cvi; *see also* Baynard
Branas (Branes), co. Clwyd, cxxxix, cxli, 80
Braud Waer, Llanfrothen, 65
Brecon, co. Powys, xlix, lvii, lxxxiv
— , castle, cxxiii
— , county of, x, lxiii, lxix
Brinbedewin, *see* Brynbedwyn
Bristol, co. Avon, lxv, cxxx
Brithdir (Brithir), parish of, lxxvi, lxxix, cxliii, 26 n. 5, 43 and n. 6 and 11, 44, 47, 50, 51; *see also under* Dolgellau
— , vill of, xlvi, lxxxi, cxxxix, cxliii, 46 n. 2, 48
— , — , co. Clwyd, cxli, 89 n. 2
Bromfield and Yale, lordship of, co. Clwyd, xxxii, lxiii, lxxxvii
Bromwin, Cefnrhos, 24
Bronington, co. Clwyd, li
Bronllys, lordship of, co. Powys, x, xiii, xxx and n. 6, lxix, lxxxiv
Bron-prys (Bronpres), lxxxiii
— , vill of, cxxxix, cxliv, 30

Brynbanon, xxxvii n. 2, cxxxix
Brynbedwyn (Brinbedewin), 43 and n. 6
Bryn-brith, co. Clwyd, 89 n. 2
Brynderw, 17 n. 2
Brythyr, co. Clwyd, cxxxix, 89
Buckley, co. Clwyd, civ
Builth, castle, co. Powys, lxxxv, n. 5, cxxiii n. 3
— , lordship of, viii
Burleigh, lord, lxxxv
Bylan, 26 and n. 5
— , vill of, cxxxix, cxliv

C-, Cf. also K-
Cadvaur, Cynwyd, 86
Cadwgan (Cadogin, Cadugan, Cadugn, Cadugon)
— , Gwernefail, 19
— , Llanfrothen, 65
— ap Ada, Peniarth, 39
— — Adaf, Treffeden, 32
— — Adam, Llangar, 89
— — Adkin, Ystradgwyn, 34
— — Dauid, Doldrewyn, 17
— — — , Llanaber, 54
— — Eboldir, Trefeddian, 26
— — Eynon, Llansanffraid, 76
— — — , Nannau, 46
— — — , Peniarth, 38
— — Griffid, Llanllwydau, 28
— — Gryffri, Faerdref Isa, 86
— — Howel, Brithdir, 49
— — — , Garthiaen, 81
— — Ieuan, Ciltalgarth, 18
— — — , Hengaer, 16
— — — , Rhyd-cryw, 37
— — Iarward, Mwstwr, 79
— — Idon, Gwyddelwern, 87
— — Ithel, Brythyr, 89
— — — , Gwnnodl, 81
— — Kenuric, Cyffty, 12
— — Kenwain, Garthgynfor, 48
— — Madoc, Llanddwywe, 56
— — — , Rhyd-cryw, 37
— — Meiler, Ystradgwyn, 35
— — Ospers, Penmaen, 6
— — Ririd, Llandderfel, 21
— — Ryryd, Bodorlas, 76
— — Talbant, Trawsfynydd, 68
— — Tangwistel, Llangedris, 25
— — Win, Nannau, 46, 47
— — Yagov, Ciltalgarth, 18
— — Yerword, Cynfal, 31
— Crimwas, Brythyr, 89
— Du, Llystreflyn, 102
— Duy, Doldrewyn, 17
— — , Llanaber, 69
— *faber*, Harlech, 66
— *filius* Cadugan ap Win, Brithdir, 49
— Goch, Garthmaelan, 44
— — , Gwyddelfynydd, 27
— — , Pennant-lliw, 9
— Kest, Trawsfynydd, 52
— Kethin, Botalog, 23
Cadwgan Loyt, Llanfrothen, 65
— *magister*, Ffestiniog, c, 72 and n. 3
— Niger, Penllyn, 17 n. 3
— Pen, Penrhyndeudraeth, 61
— Saer, Ystradgwyn, 34
— Sutor, Cynwyd, 86
— — , Tywyn, 30
— Vachan, Brithdir, 49
— — , Selwrn, 14
— — , Tirllannerch, 76
— Voyl, Rhyd-cryw, 38
— With, Llanfair, 59
Cady, Llanfrothen, 63
Caecoryn, 17 n. 2
Cae-pant, 17 n. 2
Caereinion, commote of, co. Powys, x, xlviii, lxx, lxxiii
Caerffili, castle, co. Mid Glamorgan, xviii, cxxii, cxxiii
Caergai, lxxxi, 13 n. 1
Caergeiliog (Kywluot), cxxxix, cxlii, 17
Caernarvon, xxxv, xxxvii, xlvi n. 3, xlix, lx n. 3, lxiv, cv, cviii, cxiv
— , castle, xxxv, cxxix, cxxx
— , county of, x and n. 1, xi n. 1, xxv and n. 2, xxvii, xxxi, xxxii, xxxiv, xxxix, xl, xlviii, lvii, lx, lxviii n. 4, lxix, lxxi, xcvi, xcix, ciii, civ, cv, cviii, cxiii, cxiv, cxvi, cxvii, cxix n. 1, cxxx, cxxxiii n. 7, cxxxvii, 7 n. 3, 53 n. 2, 60 n. 2, 64 n. 1, 66 n. 5, 72 n. 1, 79 n. 5, 95, 96
Caerwys, co. Clwyd, liii and n. 4, lv
— , 'merchant town' of, lx, lxiv
— , vill, xxvi n. 1, lii and n. 2
Caethle (Catheleu), cxxxix, cxliv, 22
Cafflogion, commote of, x and nn. 1 and 2, xi and n. 1, xiv, xxxi n., xxxix, xl, xlviii, lxix, lxxiii, cxiii and n. 2, cxiv, cxviii, cxix, 95
Cala Heth, Hengaer, 16
Calcot, co. Clwyd, liv
Candalo, Candalou, Candalov, Candolou, *see* Cynddelw
Cantor, Nannau, 47
— , Penaran, 9
Cantref Mawr, co. Dyfed, viii n. 4, cxxxiv, 96
Cappan Eulan, Llanbedr, 59
Carbonarius, *see* Colier
Cardiff, co. South Glamorgan, lvi
Cardigan, co. Dyfed, l, lxiv
— , castle, cxxiii, cxxx
— , county of, xxxii, l, lxviii, lxix, ciii, cxxviii
Carmarthen, co. Dyfed, xlix, liii n. 2, lxiv
— , county of, x, xxii, xxxii, l, lxix, cxxxiv
Carn, *see* Garn
Carndochan, *see* Castell Carndochan
Carnewyk Goel, 18 n. 3

Carreghofa, co. Powys, x, xlviii and n. 3
Carrog (Carrok), co. Clwyd, cxxxvi, cxxxix, cxli, 77 and n. 3
Carthaen, *see* Garthiaen
Castell (Kastel), xi n. 2, xxxvii n. 2, cxiii, cxxxix, 7 n. 3, 10 n. 1 and 5, 13 n. 2, 95, 99 and n. 3
Castell Carndochan, lxxxi, 8 n.
Castell Deudraeth, lxxvi
Catheleu, *see* Caethle
Cedifor (Kediuor)
— , Gwernefail, 19
— ap Dauid, Llanllwydau, 28
— — Dehewint, Bron-prys, 30
— — Eynon, Corris, 33
— — Ieuan, Gwyddelfynydd, 28
— — Wion, Ystradgwyn, 35
— Of, Trefrydd, 33
Cefnrhos, (Keuenros), lxxxi, cxxxix, cxliv, 23 and n. 1 and 2
Cefnyclawdd, cxxxix
Cefnyrowen (Kenvenrowen), lxxxiii
— , vill of, xlvi, cxxxix, cxliii, 51
Ceiswyn (Keiswyn), xxxviii, cxxxix, cxliv, 33
Cesailgwm (Kessoylgoum), 74 and n. 5
Cheddington, co. Salop, xv, xxix
Chester, co. Ches., civ, cv, cxxi, cxxx
— , co. of, lxxv, cxxi, cxxxi
— , earl of, cxxxi
— , earldom of, xviii, xxxi
— , justiciar of, xiii
Chirk, lordship of, co. Clwyd, ix, xxx, xxxi n., lvii, lxiii, lxvi, lxvii, lxxxiv
Cilan (Kylan), co. Clwyd, cxxxix, cxli, 82 and n. 1
Cilgerran, hundred of, co. Dyfed, xl n. 1, xlviii, lxx
— , lordship of, x, xi and n. 1, xii n. 6, xxxi n., li, lxiii, lxx
Ciltalgarth (Kyltalgart), cxxxix, cxlii, 18, 82 n. 3
Clare, estate, xviii n. 2, cxxxi
— , Gilbert de, xviii, cxxxi n. 2; *see also* Gloucester, earl of
Clerkin, Ystradgwyn, 35
Clifford and Middlewood, lordship of, co. Hereford, xiii
Clun, lordship of, co. Salop, xciv n. 5
Clwyd, county of, lv, lxvi, cxxxv; *see also* Denbigh, county of, *and* Flint, co. of
— , vale of, cix, cxxxi, 45 n. 1, 56 n. 2
Cnwclas, castle, co. Powys, cxxiii n. 3
Cogan, Llanaber, 54
Coleshill, commote of, co. Clwyd, lii, lxiii, lxvi, lxix, lxxiii, lxxxvii
Colier, family, cvi, cvii
— , John le (John Carbonarius), cvi, cvii, 65 n. 4
Collyguth, Llangedris, 25
Conryt, *see* Cynwyd
Conwy, xxii, xlvi n. 3, lx and n. 3, lxi, lxiv, cv, cx, cxiv
— , castle, cxxix, cxxx
Corniykil, Rhywedog, 4
Cornwall, co. of, xxvi and n. 2, cxvi
Corris (Corrous), cxxxix, cxliv, 33 and n. 2
Corryn, Branas, 80
Corsygedol, lxxxiii, 54 n. 5
Corthur, Kethugalc, 67
Corwen (Coruan, Korwen), cvii, 75 n. 3
— , parish of, xlv, lxxvi, lxxvii, lxxix, lxxx n. 2, cxli, 76 77, 78, 79 n. 3, 83, 84, 85, 89 and n. 2, 91 n. 5
— , vill of, xxxviii, cxxxix, cxli, 75
Coumgwynnin, *see* Cwm-gwnin
Courgis, Nannau, 47
Coyt maur, 28
Craig y Dinas (Dynasdeliri), 67 and n. 2
Crak coun, Nannau, 45
Cregan, *see* Crogen
Cregennan, cxxxix, cxliii, 40
Creigiog, co. Clwyd, 79 n. 4
Creuddyn, commote of, x and n. 2, xi and n. 1, xxxix, xl, xlviii, lxix, lxxiii, cxiii, cxiv, cxvi, cxvii, cxviii, cxix, 95
Cricieth, xli n. 1, lxii, lxv, cv
— , castle, cxxix, cxxx
Crogen (Cregan), xxxvi, xciv, xcvi, cxxxix, cxlii, 16 and n. 2
Crouthores, Cynwyd, 87
Cuelin (Kuelin) Goch, Nanmor, 72
Cumberland, co. of, cxv
Cunnian, Trawsfynydd, 52
Cuxham, co. Oxon., xv, xxix, cv
Cwmcadian, 21 n. 8, 22 and n. 2
Cwm-gwnin (Coumgwynnin), 74 and n. 3
Cwmhir, abbey, co. Powys, cxv
Cyfeiliog (Gofothlyauc), commote of, co. Powys, x, xxxi n., xlviii, lxx, lxxiii, 43 and n. 8
Cyffty (Kefdu, Kiftu), lxxxiii, 6 n. 3
— , vill of, xi n. 2, xxviii, cxiii, cxxix, cxxxix, cxlii, 8 n., 12 and n. 3, 4, and 7, 13 n. 5, 95, 99 n. 1, 100 and n. 1, 101 n. 6, 102 n. 5
Cyfnerth (Keuenard)
— ap Adaf, Llanfair, 59
— — — , Llanfrothen, 65
— — Madoc, Llanfair, 60
— Duy, Ciltalgarth, *see* Map Keuenard Duy
Cymer (Kimer, Kymmer, Kynner), abbey, c, cxv, 22 and n. 1 and 2, 43 and n. 2 and 11, 67 and n. 1, 74 and n. 1
— , co. Clwyd, *see* Llangar
— , lake, cxiv
Cymydmaen, commote of, x and n. 1, xi n. 1, xlviii, lxix, lxxii, lxxiii, cxxxvii
Cymysgadwy (Kemiscadeu, Kymmyskadwy, Kymyskadoye), cxxxix, cxlii, 20 and n. 5
Cynddelw (Candalo, Candalou, Candalov, Candolo, Candolou, Kendalo)
— , Ciltalgarth, 18
— , Gwyddelwern, 87

Cynddelw, Llaethgwm, 15
— Anerin, Llanenddwyn, 71
— ap Adaf, Trawsfynydd, 68
— — Dauid, Trawsfynydd, 54
— — Madoc, Nannau, 47
— — Reis, Llanfair, 60
— — Reys, Trawsfynydd, 54
— — Ririd, Llanfihangel-y-traethau, 71
— — Tegwaret, Taltreuddyn, 58
— Cachepol, Llanddwywe, 56 and n. 4
— Croum, Cynfal, 31
— Dargois, Llanfair, 59
— Goch, Nannau, 45
Cynfal (Kenvayl), cxxxix, cxliv
Cynfelin (Kenuelin), Cefnrhos, 23
Cynlas (Kenlas), lxxxiii
— , vill of, cxxxix, cxlii, 17 and n. 1, 31
Cynllaith, commote of, co. Clwyd, x, xlviii, lxix, lxxiii
Cynllwyd (Kywluot), cxxxix, cxlii, 17
Cynwrig (Keneric, Kenewrec, Kenewrek, Kenewric, Kenneric, Kennewric, Kenuric, Kenurik, Kenwric)
— , Llandanwg, 57
— ap Ada, Trawsfynydd, 53
— — Adaf, Llanaber, 55
— — — , Llanfihangel-y-traethau, 71
— — Blethin, Garthmaelan, 44
— — Brek, Trawsfynydd, 53
— — Cadugan, Garthgynfor, 48
— — Cunach, Llanbedr, 67
— — Dauid, Llanfor, 6
— — — , Penrhyndeudraeth, 61
— — — , Rhywedog, 4
— — — , Trefeddian, 27
— — — , Ystumanner, 27 n. 1
— — Edeneuet, *taxator*, 7
— — Edenewen, Gwyddelwern, 87
— — Glochet, Gwyddelwern, 87
— — Gock, Peniarth, 39
— — Groneu, Mwstwr, 79
— — Gronou, *taxator*, 66
— — Gurgenu, Nannau, 47
— — Gwion, Nanconwy, xcvi
— — Ieua, Carrog, 77
— — Ieuan, Trawsfynydd, 53
— — Iorword, Nannau, wife of, 46
— — Ithel, Cymysgadwy, 20
— — — , Gwernefail, 20
— — — , Gwyddelwern, 84
— — — , Pennant-lliw, 9
— — Ithel gam, Gwyddelwern, 88
— — Kenuric, Llanfihangel-y-traethau, 71
— — Keuenard, Penrhyndeudraeth, 61
— — Lewelin, Ffestiniog, 72
— — Louard, Garthmaelan, 44
— — Madoc, Ffestiniog, 72
— — — , Gwyddelwern, wife of, 84
Cynwrig ap Madoc, Llanfair, 60
— — Meiler, Trawsfynydd, 69
— — Phelip, Mwstwr, 78
— — Tegwaret, Llanaber, 55
— — — , Llandanwg, 57
— — Win, Brithdir, 49
— — — , Llanddwywe, 55
— — Wion, Llanfrothen, 64
— — Yarword, Pencraig, 90
— Cantor, Penrhyndeudraeth, 61
— *capellanus*, Corwen, 75
— David, 75 n. 3
— Du, 53 n. 1
— Duy, Llannerchgoediog, 25
— — , Rhywedog, 4
— — , Selwrn, 14
— — , Trawsfynydd, 53
— Efferioitt, Llanfrothen, 65
— *faber*, Garthmaelan, 44
— Foel, Madryn, xxxiv
— Fol, Kethugalc, 67
— Goch, Dôl, 85
— — , Garthiaen, 81
— — , Gwernefail, 19
— Kam, Llanfor, 6
— Kenyd, Bedwarian, 102
— Loyt, Trawsfynydd, 68
— Sais, co. Flint, xxi, lxxxvii
— Seys, 78 n. 2
— — , Mwstwr, 78
— Skynith, Trawsfynydd, 53
— Sutor, Gwyddelwern, 88
— Vachan, Gwernefail, 19
— — , Nannau, 46
— — , *taxator*, 7
— Veeyth, Cynwyd, 86
— Voyl, Ciltalgarth, 18
— — , Doldrewyn, 17
— — , Penaran, 11
Cynwyd (Conryt), co. Clwyd, xiv, lxiv, lxxxi, ciii, cxxxix, cxli, 86 and n. 2
Cystyllen, 13 n. 1

DABYN, Gwernefail, 19
Dafydd (Dauid, David)
— , Gwernefail, 19
— , Gwrych, 30
— ap Ada, Peniarth, 39
— — Adaf, Nantcaw, 42
— — — , Penmaen, 6
— — — , Trefrydd, 33
— — Adam, Llandrillo, 83
— — Atha, Penaran, 11
— — Blethint, Faerdref Isaf, 86
— — — , Gwyddelwern, 87
— — Cadugan, Corwen, 75
— — — , Gwrych, 30
— — — , Rhywedog, 4, 5
— — — , Selwrn, 14
— — Candalo, Llanddwywe, 56
— — Clustfold, Pennant-lliw, 8
— — Crek, Penmaen, 32
— — Dauid, Llanddwywe, 56
— — Deykin, Gwrych, 30
— — Eardur, Faerdref Uchaf, 83

Dafydd ap Edeneuet, Cynwyd, 86
— — — , Gwernefail, 19
— — Edenowen, Dyffrydan, 50
— — Edneuet, Bedwarian, 19 n. 4, 102
— — Einion, Beaumaris, lxi, lxii; *see also* Dafydd ab Eynon, Llan-faes
— — Eynon, Abertanat, 92
— — — , Cefnyrowen, 51
— — — , Cregennan, 40
— — — , Llandecwyn, 63
— — — , Llan-faes, lxi n. 1; *see also* Dafydd ab Einion, Beaumaris
— — — , Llygadog, 84
— — — , Peniarth, 39
— — — , Pennant, 79
— — — , Rhywedog, 4
— — Griffid, Abertanat, 91
— — — , Caethle, 22
— — — , Llannerchgoediog, 25
— — — , Pennal, 29
— — Griffith, Ystumanner, 29 n. 1
— — Groneu, Aberalwen, 84
— — — , Tyfos, 81
— — Groneu Goch, Dôl, 85
— — Gronou, Gwernefail, 19
— — — , Kevynteylloyn, 38 n. 3
— — — , Llanaber, 69
— — — , Llanfihangel, 42
— — — , Peniarth, 38
— — — , Rhyd-cryw, 37
— — — , Streflyn, 20
— — Gruffydd, 91 n. 2
— — — , Hendwr, 16 n. 2
— — — , prince, 6 n. 5
— — Gruffydd Fantach, xcvi
— — Gryffid, Trewyn, *taxator*, 91
— — Guen, Meirionnydd, 35 n. 1
— — Gurgenu, 21 n. 4, 96
— — — , Cilan, 83
— — — , Penaran, 9 n. 4, 98
— — Guyon, Llanaber, cxxxiii n. 7
— — Gwin, Ystumanner, 35 n. 1
— — Houa, Rhyd-cryw, 37
— — Howel, *taxator*, 52
— — Hudolou, Trewyn, 78
— — Iarword, Cynwyd, 87
— — — , Dôl, 85
— — — , Faerdref Uchaf, 83
— — Ichor, Maentwrog, 74
— — Ieuan, Garthgynfor, 48
— — — , Hengaer, 16
— — — , Llanddwywe, 56
— — — , Llanfihangel-y-traethau, 71
— — — , Llangywer, 14
— — — , Nantlleidiog, 15
— — Ioreword, Dolgledr, 50
— — — , Llanaber, 55
— — Iorwerth Geyrgogh, xxxiii, cxxxv
— — Iorword, Llanfair, 60
— — Ithel, Brythyr, 89
Dafydd ap Ithel, Faerdref Isaf, 85
— — — , Penaran, 10
— — — , Selwrn, 14
— — — , Taltreuddyn, 58
— — — , Tirllannerch, 77
— — Keb, Rhywedog, 5
— — Kediuor, Llannerchgoediog, 25
— — Keneric, Carrog, 77
— — Kenewric, 60 n. 2
— — Kenithlin, Ffestiniog, 72 and n. 5
— — — , Morfa Maenog, 41
— — Kenuric, Brithdir, 49
— — — , Llanfair, 60
— — Kenythlin, 41 n. 1
— — Keuenard, Gwyddelwern, 88
— — Lewelin, Nannau, 47
— — — , Pencraig, 90
— — Lowarch, Llandanwg, 57
— — — , Pennant-lliw, 9
— — Loward, Tirllannerch, 76
— — Madin, Cefnyrowen, 51
— — — , Dyffrydan, 50
— — — , Llanfendigaid, 36
— — Madoc, Cefnyrowen, 51
— — — , Garthgynfor, 48
— — — , Llanaber, 69
— — — , Nantlleidiog, 15
— — — , Penmaen, 7
— — — , Treffeden, 32
— — Madoc Coch, Castell, 99
— — Madog, Ardudwy, 96
— — Madok, Cilan, 83
— — — , Garthiaen, 81
— — Meiler, Llandanwg, 57
— — — , *taxator*, 52
— — Meuryk, Tirllannerch, 76
— — Meyler, Nanffreuer, 15
— — Moridic, Llanenddwyn, 70
— — — , Morfa Maenog, 41
— — — , Ystradgwyn, 35
— — Phelip, Cregennan, 40
— — — , Crogen, 16
— — — , Llandrillo, 83
— — — , Llanfair, 59
— — — , Llanfrothen, 65
— — — , Rhyd-cryw, 37
— — — , — , wife of, 37
— — Riliard, Ystumanner, 22
— — Ririd, 97
— — — , Penaran, 10
— — — , Pennant-lliw, 9
— — Ririt, 9 n. 1
— — Ryryd, Bodorlas, 76
— — Tegwaret, Llanaber, 69
— — — , Maentwrog, 74
— — — , Morfa Maenog, 41
— — — , Nannau, 46
— — — , Pennant, 80
— — Tuder, Treffeden, 32
— — — , Ystradgwyn, 34
— — Was Coum, Llanaber, 69
— — Wasmyhangel, Llanenddwyn, 70
— — Wechethes, Cregennan, 40

Dafydd ap Win, Cefnyrowen, 51
— — —, Ceiswyn, 33
— — —, Llanfendigaid, 36
— — —, *taxator*, 35
— — —, Ystradgwyn, 34, 35
— — Wion, Penrhyndeudraeth, 61
— — —, Trawsfynydd, 53
— — Wion Scholheyk, Penrhyndeudraeth, 61
— — Wyn, Abertanat, 92
— — Wynku, Gwyddelwern, 88
— — Wyon, Garthiaen, 81
— — —, Moelysgediw, 81
— — Yago, Bron-prys, 31
— — —, Cynfal, 31
— — —, Dyffrydan, wife of, 50
— — Yagou, Nannau, 45
— — Yarward, Bodorlas, 76
— — Yarword, Cynwyd, 87
— — —, Llangar, 89
— — Yereword, 60 n. 1
— — Yerword, Cyffty, 12
— — —, Llanaber, 54
— — —, Llanfair, 60
— — —, Nanffreuer, 15
— — —, Penmaen, 7
— *aurifaber*, Faerdref Isaf, 85
— Bone, Llangar, 89
— Bongam, Llanaber, 69
— Cam, Cynfal, 31
— —, Gwyddelfynydd, 28
— *cantor*, Ffestiniog, 72
— *capellanus*, Llandrillo, 83
— —, Llanenddwyn, 56
— Carpenter, Garthiaen, ci, 81
— Corrous, Corris, 33
— Crach, Ucheldref, 17
— Crak, Penaran, 9
— Crouthur, Llanycil, 20
— Du, Castell, 10 n. 5, 99
— Duy, Crogen, 16
— —, Llanaber, 55
— —, Penaran, 10, 99 n. 4
— —, Peniarth, 39
— —, Penmaen, 32
— —, Penrhyndeudraeth, 61
— —, Rhyd-cryw, 37
— —, Rhywedog, 4
— —, Tirllannerch, 76
— Duy ap Dauid, Gwrych, 30
— Duy ap Deykin, Cefnrhos, 23
— Duy orhalt, Cefnrhos, 23
— *faber*, Hengaer, 16
— —, Llandecwyn, 63
— *filius* Edeneuet Duy, Bylan, 26
— — Kenneric, Trewyn, 78
— — Wechlu, Llanfrothen, 64
— Fronniart, Trewyn, 78
— Fychan, West Wales, lxxxv
— Galgich, Peniarth, 38
— Goch, Abertanat, 92
— —, Branas, 80
— —, Brithdir, 49
— —, Cynwyd, 87
— —, Llanfrothen, 63
— —, Peniarth, 39
Dafydd Goch, Rhyd-cryw, 38
— —, Trawsfynydd, 68
— Grach, Llannerchgoediog, 25
— Grek, Cefnrhos, 24
— Hene, Corris, 33
— Leget, Brithdir, 49
— Lowin, Trawsfynydd, 53
— Loyd ap Ririd, 21 n. 5, 97
— Loyt, Garthiaen, 81
— —, Gwanas, 43
— —, Moelysgediw, 81
— —, Penaran, 9
— Mon, Pencraig, 90
— Ruth, 97
— Saer, ci
— —, Dwygraig, 12
— —, Garthgynfor, 48
— —, Gwernefail, ci, 19
— Salov, Nannau, 47
— Sant, Cyffty, 12
— Succannor, Carrog, 78
— Sutor, Trawsfynydd, 68
— Tanbont, Rhyd-cryw, 37
— Trefas, Bodgadfan, wife of, 36
— Tunbol, Llanaber, 70
— Vachan, Llanfrothen, 64
— —, Llangywer, 14
— Velinith, Penaran, 10
— Voil, Llanenddwyn, 57
— Voyl, 25 n. 2
— —, Cynlas, 17
— —, Garthgynfor, 48
— —, Llanaber, 69
— —, Llanfor, 6
— —, Llangedris, 25
— —, Nanffreuer, 15
— —, Trawsfynydd, 68
— Wyth, Bodgynfel, 88
— —, Corwen, 75
— —, Tirllannerch, 77
Danges, Garthmaelan, 44
Dauid, David, *see* Dafydd
Daykin Skinith, Bylan, 26
Decanus, Llanaber, 54
Dechewint ap Iago, Cefnrhos, 24
Dee, river, liii, 3 n. 1, 7 n. 5, 9 n. 2
Dehewint, Llanaber, 69
Denbigh, co. Clwyd, xlvi n. 3, xlviii, xlix, lxv, cxxxiv n. 5
—, county of, x, xlviii, lx, lxiv, lxix, lxxi, c, 79 n. 2
—, lordship of, lvi, lxiii, xcv, n. 5, cxv, cxxviii, cxxxi, cxxxiii
Deshardelach, Penaran, 11
Despenser, Hugh le, the younger, viii n. 4, 96
Deuddwr, commote of, co. Powys, lxx, lxxiii
Deudraeth, *see* Castell
Deuenith, John, Harlech, 66 and n. 3
Deugrek, *see* Dwygraig
Deutrayth, Le, *see* Penrhyndeudraeth
Devon, co. of, xxvi
Deweyd, Treffeden, daughter of, 32
Deykin, Cefnrhos, 23
—, Llanenddwyn, 70

Deykin, Ystumanner, 22
— Goch, Bylan, 26
Dinas Mawddwy, lv
Dinefwr, co. Dyfed, cxxiii, cxxx
Diriyon, *see* Edeirnion
Diserth, co. Clwyd, xxvii, cxxiii
Dôl, *see* Dolgun; Dolrhyd
— , vill of, co. Clwyd, cxxxix, cxli, 83, 84 n. 1, 85 and n. 2
Dolaugwyn, 27 n. 3
Doldrewyn, cxxxix, cxlii, 17
Dolforwyn, castle, co. Powys, xx
Dolgain, 68
Dolgellau (Dolgethly), xlvi and n. 3, xlvii, lxxiv, 39 n. 1, 47 n. 3, 50 n. 1
— , parish of, xlv, xlvi, lxxvi, lxxvi n. 2; *see also under* Brithdir
— , vill of, lxiv, lxxv, cxxxix, cxliii, 49
Dolgledr, xiv, xlvi, xcviii n. 1, cxxxix, cxliii, 50, 51
Dolgun, 44 n. 3
Dolrhyd, 44 n. 3
Dolwyddelan, castle, lxxxv
Doncaster, William de, cvi
Doyladon, Llandanwg, 58
Dryslwyn, co. Dyfed, viii n. 4, xviii, cxxiii, cxxx, 96
Dublin, Ireland, archbishopric of, xxvii
Dudgech (=? Dyddgu); Cf. *also* Tudgech, Tudgoch, Turgech, *and* Tygech
— *filia* Dauid Duy, Garthmaelan, 44
— — Lewelin, Llanaber, 55
— — Tegwaret, Brithdir, 49
— — Wasmihangel, Peniarth, 38
— — Win, Dyffrydan, 50
— — Wion, Llanfair, 59
Dudgu dau. of Angharet, 39 n. 1
Dugech filia Gronou, Rhyd-cryw, 37
— — Yerword, Trawsfynydd, 54
Dugoch, Cyffty, 13
Dulas, river, 43 n. 8
Dwygraig (Deugrek), ci, cxxxix, cxlii, 11, 19 n. 1
Dwygyfylchi, manor of, xcvi
Dwyryd, river, 66 n. 6
Dyaual, Tirllannerch, 77
Dyfed, lxiii, cxxiv n. 1
— , county of, xlix, lvi, lxiv
Dyffrydan, xlvi, cxxxix, cxliii, 50 n. 1
Dyfi, river, 43 n. 8, 70 n. 1
— , valley, cxxi n. 1
Dynasdeliri, *see* Craig y Dinas
Dysynni, river, lxxxi

EARTHUR, Llanfihangel, wife of, 90
East Anglia, cxxx
Eblessenon, Llandanwg, 57
Edeirnion (Diriyon, Edyrnon). co. Clwyd
— , barons of, xxxiv, 82 n. 1, 2, 87 n. 1, 90 n. 1
Edeirnion, commote of, xl, xliv, xlvi, xlvii, lxvi, lxix, lxxii, lxxiii, lxxiv and n. 1, lxxv, lxxvii, lxxix, lxxxi, lxxxix, xciv, ci, cviii, cix, cx, cxii, cxviii, cxxvi, cxxxv, cxxxvi, cxxxvii, cxxxix, cxl, cxli, 16 n. 2, 75 and n. 2, 86 n. 3, 96 n. 1
Edenaved, Edeneuet, Edenuet, *see* Ednyfed
Edenewein, Edenowen, *see* Ednowain
Edmund, lord, xii
Edneuet, *see* Ednyfed
Ednowain (Edenewein, Edenowen)
— , Dyffrydan, 50
— , Llanfor, 5
— ap Cathel, Nannau, 46
— — Kenuric, Gwernefail, 19
— — Tegwaret, Penrhyndeudraeth, 62
— Cul, Trefrydd, 33
— Duy, Dolgledr, 51
— Ledan, Nannau, 46
— Voil, Dyffrydan, 50
Ednyfed, (Edenaved, Edeneuet, Edenuet, Edneuet)
— , Llanbedr, 58
— , Penaran, 99
— ap Candalo, Llanfrothen, 63
— — Carueth, Tirllannerch, 77
— — Dauid, Penaran, 10
— — — , Penrhyndeudraeth, 61
— — Edeneuet, Llanaber, 70
— — Edenewen, Llanfihangel, 90
— — Edeneweyn, Llanfihangel, 90
— — Gogan, Llanfair, 60
— — Griffid, Ciltalgarth, 18
— — — , Selwrn, 14
— — Gronou, Dwygraig, 12
— — Gurgenu, Gwernefail, 19
— — Heylin, Llanaber, 55
— — Howel, Gwernefail, 19
— — Iarword, Branas, 80
— — Iorword, Trawsfynydd, 53
— — Kenuric, Rhywedog, 4
— — Madoc, Rhywedog, 5
— — Madok, Llanfihangel, 90
— — Meiler, Llanaber, 70
— — Meurik, Nantlleidiog, 15
— — Moruran, Llanfrothen, 65
— — Ririd, Penaran, 10
— *capellanus*, Llangar, 89
— Crak, Ceiswyn, 34
— Crouthour, Nantlleidiog, 15
— Duy, Dwygraig, 12
— — , Gwernefail, 19
— — , Llanaber, 70
— — , Rhiwerfa, 24
— — , Ucheldref, 85
— Goch, Ciltalgarth, 18
— Grach, Gwnnodl, 82
— — , Llanfor, 5
— Theu, 85 n. 1
— Toyl, Llanfor, 6
— Voyl, Cynwyd, 86
— — , Pennant-lliw, 9

Eduduwel, Dyffrydan, 50
Edward, I, king, vii, viii, xii, xiii, xviii, xix and n. 5, xx, xxi, xxiv, xxvi, xxvii, xxviii, xxxiii, xxxiv, xxxvii n. 2, lxi, lxxii, lxxxiii, cxxi, cxxii, cxxvi, cxxix, cxxx, 7 n. 3, 8 n., 56 n. 2, 66 n. 5, 82 n. 3
— , II, king, xxiii, xxviii, xcv, 82 n. 3
— , III, king, cx
— , prince, ('of Caernarvon'), xviii, xc, cxxv, 3 n. 3, 7 n. 3, 8 n., 18 n. 3, 47 n. 1
— , — , (the Black Prince), ix, xxix, liii
Edyrnon, *see* Edeirnion
Efa (Eua)
— Duy, Nannau, 46
— *filia* Ade, Penmaen, 6
— — Dauid, Llanfihangel, 42
— — — , Rhyd-cryw, 37
— — Eynon, Llwyngwril, 41
— — Howel, Gwernefail, 19
— — — , Nannau, 44
— — Hunith, Pennal, 29
— — Kediuor, Corris, 33
— — Kenuric, Nannau, 45
— — Lewelin, Garthmaelan, 44
— — — , Llangar, 89
— — Tuder, Ystradgwyn, 34
— — Wilim, Llandecwyn, 61
— — Wir, Gwyddelfynydd, 28
— — Wyn, Penaran, 10
— *relicta* Madoc, Streflyn, 102
— *soror* map Gurkin, Brithdir, 49
— *uxor* Ithel, Ystradgwyn, 34
— Vachan, Garthgynfor, 48
E gargam, *see* Gargam, Y
Egryn, cv
Eifionydd, commote of, x n. 1, lxv, lxxxvii
Einion (Eynon, Eynoun)
— , Llandderfel, 21
— , Maentwrog, 73
— Alauour, Faerdref Isaf, 86
— ap Adaf, Corris, 33
— — — , Faerdref Isaf, 86
— — — , Llanaber, 55
— — — , Llandecwyn, 62
— — — , Llanfor, 6
— — — , Maentwrog, 73
— — — , Maestrefnant, 25
— — — , Morfa Maenog, 40
— — — , Nannau, 46, 47
— — — , Rhywedog, 4
— — — , Tirllannerch, 76
— — Adam, Gwyddelwern, 87
— — Aron, Llwyngwril, 41
— — Blaynwyn, Rug, 90
— — Bussel, Penaran, 97
— — Cadugan, Ciltalgarth, 18
— — — , Pennant-lliw, 9
— — — , Trawsfynydd, 68
— — — , Winas, 22
— — Candalo, Branas, 80
— — — , Llanbedr, 59
Einion ap Crossot, Llanfihangel-y-traethau, 71
— — Dafydd ap Madog, Ystumanner, 96
— — Dauid, Bodorlas, 76
— — — , Gwrych, 30
— — — , Llanfihangel-y-traethau, 71
— — — , Llangar, 88
— — — , Pennant, 79
— — — , *taxator*, Tal-y-bont, 52
— — — , — , Ystumanner, 35
— — — , Treffeden, 32
— — Dauid Seys, *taxator*, 35
— — Dehewint, Llanfihangel, 90
— — Edeneuet, Rhywedog, 4
— — — , Trawsfynydd, 53
— — — , Trewyn, 78
— — Edenewen, Llanenddwyn, 71
— — Eloder, Nannau, 47
— — Eneas, Tyinmeyron, 67
— — Eynon kethin, Nannau, 45
— — Griffid, Llwyngwril, 41
— — — , Maesmor, 27
— — Griffri, Garthgynfor, 48
— — Griffry, Cynwyd, 86
— — Gronagh, 62 n. 3
— — Groneu, Aberalwen, 84
— — — , Llanaelhaearn, 91
— — Gronou, Cynlas, 17
— — — , Llandecwyn, 62
— — — , Llanfor, 5
— — — , Penaran, 10
— — — , Treffeden, 32
— — Gronou Voel, xiv–xv
— — Heylin, Rhyd-cryw, 38
— — Howel, Dolgledr, 51
— — Iarward, Corwen, 75
— — — , Faerdref Uchaf, 83
— — Ieuan, Hengaer, 16
— — — , Llandanwg, 57
— — — , Llanfrothen, 64
— — — , Maentwrog, 73
— — — , Penaran, 10
— — Iockin, Llanfihangel-y-traethau, 71
— — Ithel, 3 n. 2
— — — , Faerdref Isaf, 86
— — — , Garn, 18
— — — , Penaran, 11, 98
— — — , Penrhyndeudraeth, 62
— — — , Ystradgwyn, 35
— — Kenuric, Llandanwg, 57
— — — , Llandecwyn, 62
— — — , Llanfair, 60
— — — , Llanfendigaid, 36
— — — , Llanfor, 5
— — — , Llangywer, 14
— — Keuenard, Ciltalgarth, 18
— — Kyb, Rhywedog, 4
— — Lewelin, Llanfair, 60
— — Lewelyn, Pencraig, 90
— — Lowarch, Maentwrog, 73
— — — , Trawsfynydd, 68
— — Madoc, Ceiswyn, 33

Einion ap Madoc, Dolgledr, 51
— — — , Llandanwg, 57
— — — , Llanfendigaid, 36
— — — , Pennal, 29
— — Meirion, Rhyd-cryw, 38
— — Mereduth, Ucheldref, 85
— — Moridic, Bodgynfel, 88
— — Morlin, Ucheldref, 85
— — Phelip, Bron-prys, 31
— — — , Rhyd-cryw, 37 and n. 2
— — — , Trawsfynydd, 52
— — Rerid, Llandderfel, 21
— — Richard, Dolgledr, 51
— — Ririd, Penaran, 10
— — Ryrid, Mwstwr, *taxator*, 91
— — Seysild, Corwen, 75
— — Tegwaret, Morfa Maenog, 40
— — — , Taltreuddyn, 58
— — Thomas, Nannau, wife of, 44
— — — , Penmaen, 7
— — Tuder, Llaethgwm, 16
— — — , Llandderfel, 21
— — Velin, Rhywedog, 4
— — Weruel, Nannau, 46
— — Whalalet, Pennant-lliw, 8
— — Wilim, Llanbedr, 58
— — Win, Dyffrydan, 50
— — — , Rhyd-cryw, 38
— — Wyon, Dôl, 85
— — Yarword, Cynwyd, 87
— — — , Pencraig, 90
— — Yerword, Llanbedr, 58
— — — , Pennal, 29
— — — , Rhyd-cryw, 37
— *capellanus*, Llanfendigaid, 36
— — , Trawsfynydd, 53
— Cok, Llanaber, 55
— Crouthur, Rhyd-cryw, 38
— *decanus*, Penaran, 11
— Druth, Trawsfynydd, 68
— Duy, Garthmaelan, 44
— — , Llanaber, 55
— — , Llandanwg, 57
— — , Llandderfel, 21
— — , Llansanffraid, 76
— — , Maesmor, 27
— — , Nannau, 47
— — , — , wife of, 45
— — , Penaran, 11
— — , Peniarth, 39
— — , Pennant, 79
— — , Trewyn, 78
— Duy, *piscator*, Kethugalc, 67
— Edich, Llaethgwm, 15
— *faber*, Peniarth, wife of, 40
— Fakeb, Llanfor, 5
— *filius* Caur, Llanfrothen, 65
— — Edenowen, Llandecwyn, 61
— Gam, Abertanat, 91
— Goch, Abertanat, 92
— — , Bron-prys, 30
— — , Dwygraig, 12
— — , Dyffrydan, 50
— — , Gwyddelfynydd, 28
— — , Harlech, 66
— — , Llwyngwril, 41
Einion Goch, Nannau, 46
— — , Rhywedog, 5
— — , Trawsfynydd, 53
— — , Treffeden, 32
— — , Tyfos, 81
— Grach, Gwyddelwern, 88
— — , Llanfihangel, 90
— Grek, Nannau, 45
— Hir, Bodgadfan, 36
— Keyloc, Gwnnodl, 82
— Kilfin, Penaran, 10
— Ledan, Llanaber, 69
— Leget, Bodgadfan, 37
— — , Llanaber, 70
— Logleu, Rhywedog, 4
— — , Tal-y-bont, 96
— Loyd, Bedwarian, 19 n. 3, 102 and n. 1
— — , Cyffty, 101
— — , Penaran, 98
— Loyt, Brithdir, 48
— — , Gwernefail, 19
— — , Maestran, 13
— — , Pennant-lliw, 7, 98 n. 2
— — , Rhywedog, 4
— *medicus*, Cynwyd, 87
— — , Nantcaw, 42
— Offeriot, Penaran, cxxxvi, 11
— Osporn, Penaran, 10
— Penath, Llannerchgoediog, 25
— Pengrek, Llanaber, 54
— Penteg, Rhyd-cryw, 38
— Predith, Pennal, cxxxvi, 28
— Pyn, Rhywedog, 4
— Ruth, Llanfair, 59
— — , Rhyd-cryw, 37
— Saer, Rhywedog, 4
— Seis, Maestran, 13
— Sutor, Tirllannerch, 77
— Trudo, Abertanat, 92
— Vachan, Branas, 80
— — , Llanfendigaid, 36
— — , Rhyd-cryw, 38
— Vaghan, Llanfendigaid, 36 n. 1
— Vaghen ab Maddok, Meirionnydd, 36 n. 1
— Voil, Cefnrhos, 24
— — , Cregennan, 40
— — , Cynfal, 31
— — , Llanfihangel, 90
— — , Llanfrothen, 64
— — , Maesmor, 27
— Voyl, Llanenddwyn, 57
— — , Maestrefnant, 25
— — , Streflyn, 20
— Vychan, Castell, 100
— With, Penrhyndeudraeth, 62
— Wyr, Cynwyd, 86
— Wyth, Cynwyd, 86
Elena, Peniarth, 40
Elisse ab Iorwerth ab Owain Brogyntyn, 85 n. 4, 87 n. 1
— — Yarword, 87
Ellesmere, lordship of, co. Salop, viii n. 3
Englefield, cantref, co. Clwyd, xxvi n. 1, lxxxvii, lxxxviii, cxxvi

Ener, *see* Ynyr
Enith, Treffeden, 32
Enuerich *uxor* Adaf, Maentwrog, 74
Erbistock, co. Clwyd, li
Erdiduwol, Ciltalgarth, 18
Erw-goed (Erow Grydd), 50 n. 3
Esgaingaenog (Iskyngaynok), co. Clwyd, 92 and n. 1
Esgaireiddon (Eskeridon), 43 and n. 5
Esgairgawr (Eskesgaur), 43 and n. 11
Esgairwen (Iskyvon), 43 and n. 3
Esgobyn, Gwyddelwern, 84
Eskeridon, *see* Esgaireiddon
Eskesgaur, *see* Esgairgawr
Eston, co. Clwyd, lxiii
Estymaner, *see* Ystumanner
Eua, *see* Efa
Eurerdich, Llangywer, 14
Ewerich *filia* Adaf, Llanfair, 59
Ewloe, co. Clwyd, lxiii, civ
Eyner, *see* Ynyr
Eynon, Eynoun, *see* Einion
Eynoon (=? Eifionydd), *see* Eifionydd

FABER, Bodgadfan, 36
— , Faerdref Uchaf, wife of, 83
— , Llanycil, 20
— , Penmaen, dau. of, 6
Faerdref Isaf (Maerdref Elisse and Gryffid), co. Clwyd, cxxxix, cxli, 85
Faerdref Uchaf (Maerdref Vchaph), co. Clwyd, cxxxix, cxli, 83, 85 n. 4
Fallobr, Brithdir, 49
Ffestiniog, parish of, xliii, xlv, lxxvii, lxxix, 65
— , vill of, c, cxxxix, cxl, 72 and n. 3
Flanders, Belgium, xxix, lxv
Flint, co. Clwyd, lx, lxiv
— , borough of, lii and n. 2, liii and n. 4, lxxxii n. 1
— , county of, viii, ix, x, xi, xii, xvi n. 3, xxi, xxiv and n. 2, xxv, xxvi, xxx, xxxii, xxxiii, xlviii, li, lii, liii, liv, lix, lx, lxiii, lxiv, lxvi, lxvii, lxix, lxx, lxxii, lxxxii, lxxxiv, lxxxix, c, civ, cxxviii, cxxxv, 7 n. 1
France, xxix, xxx and n. 2, 8, 99 n. 5
Fron Gastell, 13 n. 1

GALK ap Goronw, Castell, 100
Gallt y calch, 66 n. 6
Gargam, Y (E gargam), 13
Garn (Carn), cxxxix, cxlii, 18
Garreg Arw, 26 n. 3
Garthgynfor (Garthkenuaur), xlvi, cxxxvi, cxxxix, cxliii, 41 n. 2, 47 and n. 3
Garthiaen (Carthaen, Garthyaen), co. Clwyd, ci, cxxxix, cxli, 81, 82 n. 1, 91 n. 4
Garthllwyd, 17 n. 2
Garthmaelan, xlvi, cxxxix, cxliii, 44 and n. 1, 47 n. 3
Gascony, France, viii
Gellidywyll, 66 n. 6
Gelli-galch, 66 n. 6
Gelli-grin, 66 n. 6
Gellilydan, 66 n. 6
Gellisarog (Gethlwassarrauc), 43 and n. 9
Generys (Generes, Generis)
— , Llangywer, 14
— Duy, Bylan, 26
— *filia* Cele, Brithdir, 49
— — Eynon, Llanaber, 70
— — — , Penrhyndeudraeth, 61
— — Gurgenu, Llanenddwyn, 71
— — Howel, Dwygraig, 12
— — Ioreword, Llanfihangel, 42
— — Kinogam, Pennal, 28
— — Lewke, Garthmaelan, 44
— — Ruathlon, Nannau, 46
— — Rufut, Pennal, 29
— — Win, Llanaber, 70
— Goch, Llandanwg, 58
— *uxor* Ackennin, Llanfair, 60
— — Edeneuet, Llanllwydau, 28
— — Ieuan, Branas, 80
— — Wasdewy, Nantlleidiog, 15
— — Win, Maesmor, 27
Genithles *filia* Griffri, Peniarth, 39
Gerald of Wales, xlii, ciii and n. 3, cviii, cxi, cxvi, cxviii, cxxv, cxxxii
Geruasius *presbiter*, Taltreuddyn, 58
Gethlwassarrauc, *see* Gellisarog
Giffard, John, xxx n. 3
Gilbert Vachan, Maesmor, 27
Glaffoc, Llanfor, 6
Glamorgan, lord of, xviii, cxv
— , lordship of, xiv, xviii n. 2, xxviii, xcii, cxxxiv
— , shire of, xxxii, lxviii, lxix
Glan-llyn, 8 n.
Glasbury, sub-lordship of, co. Powys, x, xiii, xxxi n.
Glasdir, 45 n. 3
Gloucester, earl of, xviii, cxxii, cxxxi; *see also under* Clare
Glyn Bach, 11 n. 7
Glyn Dŵr, xxxiv, lx, xcii, xcvi, cxxxv, 77 n. 2, 86 n. 2
— — , revolt of, viii, liii, liv, lviii, lix and n. 2, lxxiv, cvii, 77 n. 3
Glyndyfrdwy, co. Clwyd, 77 n. 3, 89 n. 2
Glynegwestl, *see* Llanegwestl
Glyn Mawr, 11 n. 7
Glyn-y-groes, *see* Llanegwestl
Goch Carri, Garthgynfor, 48
Goch Caur, Llannerchgoediog, 25
Goch Yrgon, Llanfrothen, 65
Godelegh, John de, xxxi
Goronw, *see* Gronw
Gothelwern, *see* Gwyddelwern
Govothlyauc, *see* Cyfeiliog
Gower, co. West Glamorgan, xxxii

Goylour, Carrog, 77
Granmayl, dau. of, Trawsfynydd, 68
Gregorius, Trawsfynydd, wife of, 53
Gregorius *capellanus*, Corwen, 75 and n. 3
Gregorius, *magister*, Llanbedr, c, 67
Grenwyrchant, co. Clwyd, 79 n. 4
Grey, lord Reginald de, xiii, 56 n. 2
Griffid, Griffith, Griffri, *see* Gruffydd
Gronw (Goronw, Groneu, Gronne, Gronou, Gronu)
— , Tywyn, 30
— ap Adaf, Llandanwg, 58
— — — , Penmaen, 7
— — Adaf Eynon, Llanaber, 54
— — Adam, Llansanffraid, 76
— — — , Pennant, 80
— — Cadugan, Bodorlas, 76
— — — , Brythyr, 89
— — — , Carrog, 77
— — — , Cefnrhos, 24
— — Dauid, Carrog, 77
— — — , Llanfihangel-y-traethau, 71
— — Edeneuet, Nannau, 47
— — Ener, Pennant-lliw, 9
— — Eynon, Gwyddelwern, 88
— — — , Llanenddwyn, 57
— — — , Penrhyndeudraeth, 62
— — Gogan, Llanaber, 55
— — Gurgenu, Cynwyd, 86
— — Heylin, Llanddwywe, xxxiii, 56 and n. 1
— — — , Nanffreuer, 15
— — Hodelou, Cynfal, 31
— — Howel, Garthgynfor, 48
— — Iarword, Faerdref Isaf, 86
— — Ieuaf, Mwstwr, 78
— — Ieuan, Bodgadfan, *see* Map Gronou
— — — , Brithdir, 48
— — — , Caethle, 23
— — — , Hengaer, 16
— — Ioreword, Llanaber, 55
— — Ithel, Cynfal, 31
— — — , Llandecwyn, 60
— — — , Llanfrothen, 63
— — — , Maentwrog, 73
— — Ithel Crak, Nannau, 45
— — Kennewric, Cynwyd, 87
— — Kenocam, Penmaen, 32
— — Kenuric, Ciltalgarth, 18
— — Kenuug, Gwyddelwern, 87
— — Lewelyn, Gwyddelwern, 84
— — Madoc, Dolgledr, 50
— — — , Faerdref Isaf, 86
— — — , Llanaber, 54
— — — , Penaran, 97
— — — , Penmaen, 7
— — — , Tyinmeyron, 67
— — Meiler, Gwernefail, 19
— — — , Llanfair, 59
— — — , Nanmor, 72
— — Melogyn, Pencraig, 90
— — Meurik, Rhywedog, 5
— — Meyler, Cynwyd, 87
Gronw ap Meyryk, Dôl, 85
— — Phelip, Rhyd-cryw, 37 and n. 2
— — Reys, Ystradgwyn, 35
— — Ririd, Cyffty, 101
— — — , Llanfor, 6
— — — , Penaran, 98
— — Tegwaret, Maentwrog, 73
— — — , Trawsfynydd, 68
— — — , Tyfos, 81
— — Wasdewy, Nantlleidiog, 15
— — Wilim, Cynfal, 31
— — — , Llandanwg, 58
— — Win, Dyffrydan, 50
— — — , Llanaber, 69
— — — , Llandecwyn, 63
— — — , Llanfrothen, 65
— — — , Trefrydd, 33
— — Wion, Penmaen, 7
— — Wladus, Llanaber, 69
— — Wyon, Dôl, 83
— — Yerword, Cefnrhos, 23
— — — , Llandanwg, 57
— — — , Llandecwyn, 61
— — — , Llanfrothen, 65
— — — , Maestran, 13
— Alchlwy, Penaran, 10
— Bach, Rhywedog, 4
— Bergam, Llanfrothen, 65
— Berthoc, Cyffty, 12, 102 n. 5; *see also* Gronw Verthauc
— Cantor, Ffestiniog, 72
— Carpan, Llwyngwril, 41
— Corista, Llandecwyn, 60
— Coutta, Faerdref Uchaf, 83
— Cutta, Llaethgwm, 16
— Duy, Llanddwywe, 56
— — , Llanfor, 6
— — , Rhywedog, 4
— — , Trefrydd, 33
— Ebogith, Branas, 80
— *filius* Mereduth, Mwstwr, 79
— — Wladusa Duy, Llanfor, 5
— Goch, Carrog, 78
— — , Garthgynfor, 48
— — , Gwyddelwern, 88
— — , Nannau, 45
— — , Peniarth, 39
— — , Penrhyndeudraeth, 62
— — , Trawsfynydd, 54
— Gough, 54 n. 1
— Grach, Corwen, 75
— — , Pencraig, 90
— Grek, Caethle, 23
— Hyr, Carrog, 77
— Kennit, Llangar, 89
— Loit, Dolgledr, xv
— Loyd, Cyffty, 101
— Loyt, Branas, 80
— — , Nantlleidiog, 15
— *mercator*, Cynwyd, 86
— Sutor, Llandderfel, 21
— Vachan, Dôl, 85
— — , Rhywedog, 3
— — , Trawsfynydd, 68
— Vaghan, Penllyn, 3 n. 3
— Vaur, Llandanwg, 57

Gronw Vaur, Llwyngwril, 41
— Ver, Nanffreuer, 14
— Verthauc, Streflyn, 12 n. 6, 102; *see also* Gronw Berthoc
— Voil, Cynfal, 31
— — , Ffestiniog, 73
— — , Llanaber, 69
— — , Ystradgwyn, 35
— Voyl, Cynlas, 17
— — , Dwygraig, 12
— — , Gwernefail, 19
— — , Llanfendigaid, 36
— — , Llanfor, 5
— — , Rhywedog, 4
— — , Ystumanner, 31 n. 2
— With, Cregennan, 40
— — , Llanaber, 70
— Wr, Castell, 100
Grosmont, lordship of, co. Gwent, x, xii, xxx n. 6, lxix
Gruc, *see* Rug
Gruffydd (Griffid, Griffith, Griffri, Gruffud, Gryffid, Gryffin, Gryffry, Gryffyd, Gryffyth)
— , Cefnrhos, 24
— ap Adaf, *taxator*, 35
— — Adda, Ystumanner, 96
— — Cadugan, Bron-prys, 30
— — Cynan, prince, xlii
— — Dafydd, lord of Hendwr, xxxiv, lxxxvi, xcii, 82 n. 3; *see also* Gruffydd ap Dauid, Hendwr
— — Dauid, Ciltalgarth, 18
— — — , Hendwr, 8 n., 82 and n. 3; *see also* Gruffydd ap Dafydd
— — — , Llanenddwyn, 57
— — Dauid ab Howel, *taxator*, 91
— — Ener, Rhyd-cryw, 38
— — Eynon, Cynfal, 31
— — — , Rhywedog, 4
— — — , Trewyn, 78
— — Gronou, Cynlas, 17
— — — , Dwygraig, 11
— — — , Llanycil, 20
— — — , Pennant-lliw, 8
— — Heylin, Corris, 33
— — Howel, Llanfor, 6
— — Howeyn, Rug, 89 and n. 4
— — Ieuan, Cefnrhos, 24
— — Iorwerth ab Owain Brongyntyn, 87 n. 1
— — Iuor, Nannau, 47
— — Kediuor, Corris, 33
— — Lewelin, Gwrych, 30
— — Lewelyn, Abertanat, 91
— — Llywelyn, prince, xvii
— — Madoc Selour, *taxator*, 7
— — Madog ab Iorwerth, Penllyn, 8 n., 96
— — Meiler, Llanaber, 70
— — — , Pennal, 29
— — Mereduth, Llannerchgoediog, 25
Gruffydd ap Meurik, Nannau, 46
— — Owain Brogyntyn, 85 n. 4
— — Peredur, 41 n. 2
— — Phelip, Corwen, 75
— — — , Cynfal, 31
— — Seysild, Corwen, 75
— — Tegwaret, Llandanwg, 57
— — Teluwas, Mwstwr, 79
— — Tevet, Ucheldref, 18
— — Tudur, Dolwyddelan, lxxxv
— — — , Englefield, lxxxvii
— — Urien ab Tegwaret, 56 n. 2
— — Yarword, Cynwyd, 87
— Cantor, Abertanat, 92
— Crouthor, Abertanat, 91
— — , Ceiswyn, 34
— Duy, Pennant-lliw, 8
— — , Rhywedog, 3
— Fantach, xcvi
— Goch, Corwen, 75
— — , Llanaber, 55
— Gock, Trefrydd, wife of, 33
— Llwyd, poet, xcii
— — , sir, civ
— Maelor, 77 n. 2
— Porthour, Corris, 33
— Sutor, Trawsfynydd, 68
— Voyl, Caethle, 23
— — , Rhywedog, 4
— Whith, Cynfal, 31
— Wilour, Penaran, 9
— With, Llanfrothen, 63
Gruffud, *see* Gruffydd
Grun carpenter, Abertanat, 91
Gryffid, Gryffin, Gryffry, Gryffyd, Gryffyth, *see* Gruffydd
Grynochoc, co. Clwyd, 79
Guenllian, *see* Gwenllïan
Gurgeneu, Gurgenov, Gurgenu, *see* Gwrgenau
Guroc Gwydraus, Nannau, 45
Guyn, *see* Gwyn
Guyon, *see* Gwion
Gwadelmenith, *see* Gwyddelfynydd
Gwanas (Wonas), xlvi, cxxxix, cxliii, 43, 45 n. 2, 47 n. 3
Gwathauc, Llangedris, 25
Gwathloc ap Cadugan, Uwch Buga, 26
Gwdaws, Llanllwydau, 28
Gwedir, xcvi, xcvii
Gwen Vaur Goch, Maentwrog, ciii, 74
Gwenllïan (Guenllian, Wentlian, Wentliana, Wentlyan, Wentlyana)
— Duy, Penaran, 10, 11
— *filia* Adaf, Llanaber, 70
— — Dauid, Penaran, 10
— — Eynon, Penaran, 98
— — — , Trawsfynydd, 53
— — Griffid, Gwrych, 29
— — — , Llannerchgoediog, 25
— — Gryffini, Llangar, 89
— — Guion, Penaran, 98
— — Hanalt, Garthgynfor, 48
— — Ieuan, Doldrewyn, 17

Gwenllïan *filia* Ithel Goch, Gwyddelwern, 88
— — Kenneric, Pencraig, 90
— — Kenuric, Llanfrothen, 63
— — — , Llangywer, 14
— — Kerwiot, Nannau, 44
— — Lewelin, Penmaen, 32
— — Madoc, Llandanwg, 57
— — — , Llanddwywe, 56
— — — , Llanfair, 60
— — — , Trawsfynydd, 54
— — Madok, Trewyn, 78
— — Win, Llanfair, 60
— — Yarword, Bodgynfel, 88
— Loyt, Gwernefail, 19
— *uxor* Dauid, Treffeden, 32
— — Gwin, Penaran, 11
— — Lowarch, Llandanwg, 57
— — Madoc, Llanbedr, 59
— — Phelip, Penrhyndeudraeth, 62
— — — , Ucheldref, 17
— — Win, Gwernefail, 19
— — — , Llanfihangel-y-traethau, 71
— Vachan, Garthgynfor, 48
Gwent, co. of, lxiii
Gwenwynwyn (Wenunwin)
— , Llandanwg, 57
— , Peniarth, 39
Gweramen Vaghan, *see* Gwrgenau Fychan
Gwerful (Weruel, Weruela, Weruilla, Weyruel)
— , Gwernefail, 19
— , Nannau, 44
— Duy, Ystradgwyn, 34
— *filia* . . . , Llanbedr, 58
— — Dauid, Pennant, 80
— — Iarword, Cynwyd, 86
— — Ieuan, Nantcaw, 42
— — Kenewric, Llanfor, 5
— — Lewelin, Garthmaelan, 44
— *uxor* Ener, Llanfor, 6
— — Gof, Trefrydd, 33
— — Iorword, Trawsfynydd, 69
— — Meiler, Llanfrothen, 63
— — Mereduth, Llanfair, 60
Gwerith, Cynfal, 31
Gwernefail (Gwernevell, Wernovel) lxxxi, ci, cxxxix, cxlii, 18 and n. 4, 101 n. 7, 102 n. 1, 2, 3, 4
Gwernhefin, xxxvii n. 2, cxxxix, 12 n. 3
Gwilym (Gwilim, Wilim); Cf. *also* Willelmus
— , Cefnrhos, 24
— , Gwrych, 30
— ap Cadugan, Bylan, 26
— — Eynon, Peniarth, 39
— Duy, Bere, 51
— Skynith, Bron-prys, 31
— Spedor, Maentwrog, cviii, 73
— Voil, Llanfair, 59
Gwin, *see* Gwyn
Gwion (Guyon, Gwyon, Wion, Wyon)
— , Dwygraig, 12
— , Llanaber, 55
Gwion, Llanddwywe, 56
— , Pennant-lliw, 9
— , Trewyn, 78
— ap Adaf, Llanfrothen, 65
— — Dalwen, Nannau, 46
— — Dauid, Llanaber, 54
— — — , Tirllannerch, 76
— — Eynon, Corwen, 75
— — Guidraus, Penaran, 97
— — Madoc, Dôl, 85
— — — , Llanenddwyn, 57
— — Madok, Llansanffraid, 76
— — Meiler, Llanddwywe, 55
— — Tegwaret, Llandanwg, 57
— — Wion, Llanaber, 69
— — y Dioual, Castell, 13 n. 2, 100
— Goch, Llandecwyn, 63
— — , Llangar, 89
— Kesu, Penrhyndeudraeth, 61
— Loyt, Llanenddwyn, 56
— Mal, Moelysgediw, 81
— Pelliparius, Trawsfynydd, 68
— Pengam, Llanaber, 55
— Pilis, Llwyngwril, 41
— Troyn, Bodgadfan, 37
— Vachan, Harlech, 66
— Voil, Llanaber, 55
— — , Maentwrog, 73
— Voyl, Llanenddwyn, 71
— With, Llanfrothen, 65
Gwladus (Wladosa, Wladus, Wladusa)
— , Llanaber, 69
— , Nannau, 46
— , Penaran, 11
— Duy, Llanfor, 5
— *filia* Arthur, Nannau, 47
— — Cadugan, Cynfal, 31
— — Dauid, Morfa Maenog, 41
— — Edeneuet, Penrhyndeudraeth, 62
— — Ener, Pennal, 29
— — Eynon, Rhyd-cryw, 38
— — Griffid, Dyffrydan, 50
— — — , Llwyngwril, 41
— — Gronou, Peniarth, 38
— — Hanalt, Garthgynfor, 48
— — Ithel, Ystradgwyn, 35
— — Madoc, Mwstwr, 78
— — Ryryd, Trewyn, 78
— — Tuder, Nantlleidiog, 15
— — Win, Llanfair, 60
— — Yorword, Gwernefail, 19
— Goch, Llanbedr, 58
— Mursen, Maentwrog, 73
— *religiosa*, Llanfrothen, 64
— *uxor* . . . , Llanbedr, 58
— — Howel, Llanbedr, 58
— — map Bretwen, Penaran, 10
— — Phelip, Bron-prys, 31
— — Wion, Selwrn, 14
Gwnnodl (Gwynodyl), co. Clwyd, cxxxix, cxli, 81
Gwreang, 80 n. 2
Gwrgenau (Gurgeneu, Gurgenov, Gurgenu)
— , Doldrewyn, 17

Gwrgenau ap Adaf, Trefeddian, 27
— — Dauid, Gwrych, 30
— — — , Rhywedog, 4
— — Dauid Palmere, Branas, 80
— — Idenerth, 83
— — Iorword, Ffestiniog, 72
— — — , Llanfor, 5
— — Ithel, Ffestiniog, 72
— — Lowarch, Llanllwydau, 28
— — Madoc, Llandanwg, 57
— — — , Moelysgediw, 81
— — Meiler, Nanffreuer, 15
— — Ririd, Cyffty, 13
— — Trahaern, Ffestiniog, 72
— — Tuder, Cyffty, 12
— — — , Garthiaen, 81
— — Wyon, Faerdref Isaf, 85
— *aurifaber*, Garthmaelan, 44
— *capellanus*, Dolgledr, 51
— carpenter, Llanbedr, 67
— Coyt maur, Pennal, 28
— Duy, Doldrewyn, 17
— — , Penaran, 10
— Ebogrh, Llandderfel, 21
— Fychan, Penllyn, lxxxviii, 3 n. 2, 96; *see also* Gwrgenau Vachan
— Goch, Penaran, 9
— — , Trewyn, 78
— Loyt, Penaran, 10
— Melinnith, Pennal, 29
— Sutor, Selwrn, 14
— Vachan, Rhywedog, 3 and n. 2; *see also* Gwrgenau Fychan
— Voil, Gwrych, 30
— Voyl, Llanfair, 59
Gwrych (Wrek), xxxiii, cxxxix, cxliv, 29
Gwyddelfynydd (Gwadelmenith), cxxxix, cxliv, 27
Gwyddelwern (Gothelwern, Gwydelwern, Wothewern), co. Clwyd
— , parish of, xlv, lxxvii, lxxix, lxxx n. 2, lxxxi, cxli, 86 n. 2, 88, 91 and n. 3, 92 n. 1
— , vill of, cxxxix, cxli, 82 n. 1, 84 and n. 2, 87 and n. 2
Gwyn (Guyn, Gwin, Win, Wyn)
— ap Ada, Llanfair, 59
— — Adaf, Ffestiniog, 72
— — — , Penmaen, 7
— — — , Pennal, 29
— — — , Penrhyndeudraeth, 61
— — Adam, Gwnnodl, 82
— — Cadugan, Cefnrhos, 23
— — Cathel, Nannau, 45
— — Dauid, 97
— — — , Dyffrydan, 50
— — — , Llanaber, 70
— — — , Rhywedog, 5
— — Dauid Duy, Penaran, 9
— — Dauid Pengreck, Penaran, 10
— — Edneuet, Penaran, 97
Gwyn ap Eynon, Penaran, 10
— — — , Rhyd-cryw, 37
— — — , Ystumanner, 22
— — Gogan, Llandecwyn, 63
— — Griffid, Pennant-lliw, 8
— — Gronou, Llanfair, 59
— — — , Rhywedog, 4
— — — , Ystradgwyn, 34
— — Heylin, Abertanat, 91
— — — , Llanaber, 69
— — Howel, Llanbedr, 59
— — Idenerth, Trefrydd, 33
— — Idonn, Cynlas, 17
— — Ieuan, Rhywedog, 5
— — Ioreword, Garthgynfor, 48
— — Ioreworth, Streflyn, 20
— — Ithel, Garthgynfor, 48
— — Kenuric, Llanbedr, 59
— — — , Llanddwywe, 55
— — — , Llanfrothen, 63
— — — , Nannau, 45
— — — , Taltreuddyn, 58
— — Lewelin, Gwernefail, 19
— — — , Llanfrothen, 65
— — Madin, Penaran, 11
— — — , Treffeden, 32
— — Madoc, Llystreflyn, 13 n. 6, 102
— — — , Maestran, 13 and n. 6
— — — , Nannau, 46
— — — , Penllyn, 24
— — — , Rhiwerfa, 24
— — — , Selwrn, 14
— — — , Trawsfynydd, 68
— — Mary, Abertanat, 92
— — Mereduth, Taltreuddyn, 58
— — Moridic, Llangedris, 25
— — — , Morfa Maenog, 40
— — Morud, Ffestiniog, 72
— — Phelip, Gwernefail, 19
— — Ririd, Llanfihangel-y-traethau, 71
— — Saer, 97
— — Tuder, Streflyn, 20, 102
— — Was Crek, Llanaber, 54
— — Wilim, Nannau, 47
— — Yerword, Cynfal, 31
— *capellanus*, Llandderfel, 21
— — , Llanfendigaid, 36
— carpenter, Trawsfynydd, 53
— Cossin, Maestran, 13
— Crak, Brithdir, 49
— Duy, Llanddwywe, 56
— — , Pennal, 29
— Gam, Gwernefail, 19
— — , Maentwrog, 73
— Goch, Llanfair, 59
— Loyt, Llanaber, 69
— — , Nannau, 45
— Mautho, Penaran, xxxviii, 9
— Penbras, Llanycil, 20
— Seis, Cyffty, 12 and n. 4, 101 and n. 1
— Simmul, Llanfendigaid, 35
— Sutor, Llanenddwyn, 56
— Vachan *capellanus*, Llanfrothen, 64
— Voil, Llandanwg, 57

Gwyn Voil Vachan, Penrhyndeudraeth, 62
— Voyl, Gwyddelfynydd, 28
— — , Llanbedr, 67
— — , Llangedris, 25
— — , Penaran, 9
— — , Peniarth, 40
— Voyl de Botlosged, Llanfrothen, 65
— With, Nannau, 44
— Wlossec, Gwyddelfynydd, 27
Gwynedd, xv, xvi, xvii, xix, xxv, xxxix and n. 4, lxi, lxvi, lxxxiii, lxxxiv, lxxxv, cix, cxii, cxix, cxx, cxxi, cxxix, cxxxii, cxxxiii; *see also* North Wales
— , princes of, xvii, xlii, cxiv, cxxi, cxxii, cxxiv
Gwynen, Llanfrothen, 64
Gwynfynydd (Winvenith), 74 and n. 2
Gwynodyl, *see* Gwnnodl
Gwyon, *see* Gwion

HACHEB'RRYD i'r Orseth, *see* Orsedd, Yr
Hafodelwy, co. Clwyd, cxxxiv n. 5
Hafod Newydd (Havot Newith), 43 and n. 10
Hagrat *filia* Eynon, Castell, 100
Hagrat Wastat, Penaran, 99
Halghton, co. Clwyd, li
Halt-, *see* Allt-
Hangharad, *see* Angharad
Hanmer, co. Clwyd, li, liii
Harlech (Hardelach), xiv, xli and n. 1, xlvii, lx, lxiv, lxv, lxxii, lxxiv, lxxxviii, cv, cvi, cvii, cix, cxx, cxxxix, cxl, 65 and n. 4 and 5, 66 n. 1, 2
— , castle, xli n. 1, lxi, lxxvi, lxxxvi, cv, cvi, cxxix, 65 n. 5, 66 n. 2, 3
Hastings, lord John, lxxxii
Hauot Newith, *see* Hafod Newydd
Haverfordwest, co. Dyfed, ix, xlix, lxx
Havering, John de, xli n. 1
Havotty, Yr, 20 n. 5
Heilin (Heylin, Heylyn)
— , Landderfel, *see* Merck Heilin
— , Penmaen, *see* Map Heylin
— ap Blethyn, Branas, 80
— — Dauid, Ffestiniog, 72
— — Dehewint, Maestrefnant, 25
— — Eynon, Branas, 80
— — Glackoun, Llangywer, 14
— — Ithel, Taltreuddyn, 58
— — Iuor, Peniarth, 38
— — Kediuor, Penaran, 98
— — Robert, Tirllannerch, 76
— — Roger, Tywyn, xciv, 30 and n. 2
— Ayank, Llanenddwyn, 70
— Duy, Penaran, 11
— , *frater*, sister of, 39
— Goch, *taxator*, 66
— Hengest, Maentwrog, 73
Heilin Pannor, Kethugalc, cvii, 67
— Predith, Maentwrog, cxxxvi, 73
— Vachan, Llanenddwyn, 56
— Voil, Penrhyndeudraeth, 61
— Voyl, Rhyd-cryw, 38
— — , Tywyn, 30
Henblas, 17 n. 2
Hendre-ddu, 17 n. 2
Hendwr (Hendor), co. Clwyd, xxxiv, lxxxi, lxxxvi, xcii, cxxxix, cxli, 16 n. 2, 17 n. 2, 77 n. 3, 82 and n. 3
Hengaer (Hengayr), cxxxix, cxlii, 16
Hengest, 73
Henricus, Bere, 52
Henry, III, king, xvii, xviii
— , IV, king, ix
— , VII, king, xcvii
— , VIII, king, xxvii
— , of Monmouth, prince, lxxiv
Henuric Cantor, Llanenddwyn, 71
Hereford, co. Heref., xxii
Hertford, co. of, lxxxiii, lxxxix
Heylin, Heylyn, *see* Heilin
Hirlender, Llanllwydau, 28
Holt, co. Clwyd, xlix, lv and n. 1, lvi n. 4, lxiii, lxiv
Holywell, co. Clwyd, lii and n. 2, lv
Hope, co. Clwyd, xxvi n. 1, lv, lx, lxiv, lxxiii
Hopedale, lordship of, co. Clwyd, ix
Horon, Yr, 26 n. 3
Houa, *see* Hwfa
Houel, Howel, Howell, *see* Hywel
Huchbega, *see* Trefrion Uwch Buga
Hucheldref, *see* Ucheldref
Hunydd (Hunith)
— , Llangywer, 14
— , Peniarth, 40
— Vachan, Nannau, 45
Hwfa ap Adam, Gwyddelwern, 84
— — Ithel, Llanaelhaearn, 91
— — Pengour, Hengaer, 16
— Goch, Mwstwr, wife of, 78
— Saer, Cregennan, 40
— Vel, Gwnnodl, 82
Hwlcyn Bach, *nativus*, xcvii
Hyrlannerk, *see* Tirllannerch,
Hywel (Houel, Howel, Howell)
— ap Adaf, Nannau, 47
— — Blethin, Aberalwen, 84
— — Cadugan, Cefnrhos, 23
— — — , Ciltalgarth, 18
— — Dauid, Hendwr, 82
— — — , Maestran, 13
— — Eynon, Brythyr, 89
— — — , Gwyddelwern, 88
— — — , Nanffreuer, 15
— — Griffid, Caethle, 23
— — Gronou, Bodgadfan, 36
— — Iarward, Carrog, 77
— — — , Tirllannerch, 77
— — Lewelin, Dolgledr, 51
— — Madoc, Bodgynfel, 88
— — Melogyn, Pencraig, 90
— — Meuric, Builth, lxxxv n. 5
— — Meyryk, Llanaelhaearn, 91

Hywel ap Tuder, Llaethgwm, 16
— — Win, Kethugalc, 67
— — Wyn, Gwernefail, 19
— Dda, cviii
— Goch, Llanfrothen, 63
— — , Nannau, 45
— Kedor, Llandanwg, 57
— Routh, *taxator*, 52
— Sutor, Penaran, 98
— Vachan, Gwernefail, 19
— Wild, Llanfor, 5

IAGO, Gwrych, 30
Iagou Voyl, Penaran, 11
Iarward, Iarword, *see* Iorwerth
Idernet, Brithdir, 49
Idiaual, Maestran, 13, 100
Ierword, *see* Iorwerth
Ieua ab Iarword, Dôl, 83
Ieuaf, Cefnrhos, 24
— ab Ithel, 78
— Duy, Bodorlas, 76
— — , Caethle, 23
— *filius* Gryffyd, Trewyn, 78
Ieuan ap Ada, Brithdir, 49
— — Adaf, Cynfal, 31
— — — , Llanfihangel-y-traethau, 71
— — — , Llanfrothen, 64
— — Blethiot, Branas, 80
— — Budur, Maestran, 13
— — Cadugan, Pennal, 28
— — Candalo, Trawsfynydd, 68
— — Candolou, Branas, 80
— — Cathel, Llandderfel, 21
— — — , Nannau, 46
— — Dauid, Bylan, 26
— — — , Ceiswyn, *filiis*, 34
— — — , Faerdref Uchaf, 83
— — — , Llanaber, 70
— — — , Llanfihangel, 42
— — — , Llanfrothen, 64
— — — , Llwyngwril, 41
— — — , Nanmor, 72
— — — , Tirllannerch, 77
— — — , Trawsfynydd, 68
— — — , Tyfos, 81
— — David ab Eynon, Llan-faes, lxi n. 1
— — Dehwynt, Corwen, 75
— — Edenowen, Nannau, 47
— — Eynon, Branas, 80
— — — , Cynllwyd, 17
— — — , Garthgynfor, 48
— — — , Llansanffraid, 75
— — Glasdwr, Llanbedr, 58
— — Gourgenu, 79 n. 5
— — Griffid, Rhywedog, 4
— — Groneu, Gwyddelwern, 87
— — Gronou, Dolgledr, 51
— — — , Rhywedog, 5
— — Gronou Goch, Rhywedog, 5
— — Gryffin, Abertanat, 92
— — Gryffry, Faerdref Uchaf, 83
— — Guen, Ystumanner, 28 n. 1
Ieuan ap Gurgenu, Nannau, 47
— — — , Pennant, 79
— — Gwadenerth, Faerdref Uchaf, 83
— — Heilin, Selwrn, 14
— — — , Trawsfynydd, 54
— — Howel, Pennal, 29
— — Iagou, Penaran, 11
— — Ieuaf, Carrog, 77
— — Ieuan, Nannau, 45
— — Ieuan ap Dauid, Nanmor, 72
— — Iarward, Bodorlas, 76
— — Iorword, Cyffty, 101
— — — , Llanfrothen, 64
— — Ithel, Llanfrothen, 64
— — — , Pennant, 79
— — — , Trawsfynydd, 69
— — — , Trefrydd, 33
— — Iuor, Ystradgwyn, 34
— — Kenewric, Dôl, 84
— — Kenuric, Llanfrothen, 64
— — Kethin, Cefnrhos, 24
— — Landeu, Llanllwydau, 28
— — Llagau, Ceiswyn, 34
— — Lowarch, Cefnrhos, 24
— — — , Pennant-lliw, 9
— — Madoc, Abertanat, 91
— — — , Gwyddelwern, 87
— — — , Llanfendigaid, 36
— — Madog Fychan, villein, xcvi
— — Mereduth, Llanfair, 60
— — Meyryk, Brythyr, 89
— — Morydic, Bodgynfel, 88
— — Ospern, Trawsfynydd, 68
— — Phelip, Cynwyd, 86
— — — , Dolgledr, 51
— — — , Penmaen, Penllyn, 7
— — — , — , Ystumanner 32
— — Rerid, Llanaber, 69
— — Reys, Cefnrhos, 24
— — Ririd, Brithdir, 49
— — Robert, Cefnrhos, 24
— — Ryryd, Pencraig, 90
— — Seysild, Corwen, 75
— — Thomas, Llanfrothen, 65
— — — , Pennant-lliw, 8
— — Tuder, Branas, 80
— — — , Dolgellau, 50
— — — , Hendwr, 82
— — Was Coum, Llanaber, 70
— — Wasdewy, Llanfrothen, 65
— — — , Nantlleidiog, 15
— — Win, Gwyddelfynydd, 28
— — — , Llandecwyn, 62
— — Wyn, Ystumanner, 28 n. 1
— — Wyon, Pennant, 79
— — Yarword, Rug, 89
— — Yerword, Llanfihangel-y-traethau, 71
— — — , Trawsfynydd, 53
— Aron, Llanfendigaid, 36
— *aurifaber*, 91
— Byr, Cilan, 83
— *capellanus* de Lamyhangel, Penrhyndeudraeth, 62
— Corrous, Corris, 33

Ieuan Cors, Trawsfynydd, 54
— Crak, Ystradgwyn, 34
— Du, Castell, 100
— Duy, Abertanat, 92
— —, Cynlas, 17
— —, Garthmaelan, 44
— —, Gwyddelwern, 88
— —, Llandanwg, 57
— —, Nantcaw, 42
— —, Pennal, 29
— —, Penrhyndeudraeth, 62
— —, Trawsfynydd, 68
— *faber*, Hengaer, 16
— *filius* Cadugan, Penaran, 11
— — Morueran, Trawsfynydd, 69
— fol, Kethugalc, 67
— *frater* Ieuan, Abertanat, 92
— fronniait, Llanbedr, 59
— Gethin, Castell, 100
— Goch, 97
— —, Castell, 99
— —, Dôl, 85
— —, Llanfrothen, 64
— —, Penaran, 98
— —, Trawsfynydd, 68
— —, Trewyn, 78
— Gronou, Llanfair, 59
— Hen, Cefnrhos, 24
— Hir, Ceiswyn, 34
— Iankin, Selwrn, 14
— Keri, Nannau, 46
— Kethin, Ucheldref, 17
— Loyd, Cyffty, 13 n. 5, 101 and n. 3
— Loyt, Brithdir, 48
— —, Maestran, 13
— —, Penaran, 11
— —, Rhywedog, 5
— *medicus*, Nanffreuer, 15
— Mendour, Faerdref Isaf, 85
— Pant, Maesmor, 27
— Pengul, Abertanat, 91
— Pen . . . thkur, Llanfor, 6
— Scoleyk, Abertanat, 92
— Sutor, Brithdir, 49
— —, Llanfrothen, 63
— —, Penaran, 11
— Troyn, Penrhyndeudraeth, 61
— Vachan, Llandrillo, 83
— —, Peniarth, 38
— —, Penrhyndeudraeth, 62
— Voil, Brithdir, 48
— —, Doldrewyn, 17
— —, Gwyddelwern, 88
— —, Nannau, 45
— —, Penrhyndeudraeth, 61, 62
— —, Ucheldref, 18
— Voil or Glastir, Nannau, 45
— With, Ciltalgarth, 18
— —, Maentwrog, 73
Iocyn (Iockin, Iockyn)
— ap Ithel, Trawsfynydd, 68
— — Robert, Tirllannerch, 76
— — Tegwaret, Llanaber, 69
— Dolgen, Trawsfynydd, 68
— Hen, Penrhyndeudraeth, 62
— Keri, Llanaber, 70
Iocyn Tuglyn, Treffeden, 32
— Tylour, Bere, 52
— Tynven, Tirllannerch, 77
— With, Nannau, 46
Iohannes Carbonarius, Harlech, 65; *see also* Colier, John le
Iohannes Deuenith, Harlech, 66
Iohannes *filius* Adaf, Llanfrothen, 64
— — Edeneuet, Penrhyndeudraeth, 61
— — Phelip, Llandecwyn, 61
— — Wladusa, Llanfair, 60
Iohannes *garcio* Madoc Crak, Harlech, 66
Iohannes *pictor*, Llandrillo, 83
Iohannes Ruffo, Nanmor, 72
Iohannes Senach, Llanfrothen, 65
Iohannes Sutor, Cynwyd, 86
Iohannes Tissen, Llanfrothen, 65
Iolo Goch, xci, n. 1, cxviii
Ionkin, Cefnrhos, 24
Iorwerth (Iarward, Iarword, Ierword, Ioreword, Iorword, Yarward, Yarword, Yerword, Yorword)
—, Cyffty, *see* Map Yerword
—, Doldrewyn, 17
—, Gwnnodl, 82
—, Maentwrog, 73
— ap Adaf, Cefnrhos, 24
— — —, Dwygraig, 12
— — —, Llanaber, 55
— — —, Llandanwg, 57
— — —, Nantlleidiog, *see* Map Yerword ap Adaf
— — —, Penmaen, 6
— — —, Ystradgwyn, 34
— — Adam, Gwyddelwern, 87
— — —, Llanaelhaearn, 91
— — —, Llangar, 89
— — —, Llansanffraid, 76
— — —, Mwstwr, 79
— — —, Ucheldref, 85
— — Asser, Llanbedr, 59
— — Cadugan, Branas, 80
— — —, Kethugalc, 67
— — —, Llandanwg, 57
— — —, Llanddwywe, 56
— — —, Nanffreuer, 15
— — Candalo, Llanfrothen, 64
— — —, Selwrn, 14
— — Cuhelyn, Branas, 80
— — Dauid, Corris, 33
— — —, Llanfair, 60
— — —, Llanfrothen, 65
— — —, Penrhyndeudraeth, 61
— — Edeneuet, Llanfihangel, 90
— — —, Penaran, 11
— — Edeneweyn, Gwyddelwern, 88
— — Edenowen, Llanfrothen, 64
— — Edenoweyn, Llanfair, 59
— — Elisse, Llangar, 89
— — Eynon, Aberalwen, 84
— — —, Brithdir, 49
— — —, Gwyddelwern, 84
— — —, Llanfair, 59, 60

Iorwerth ap Eynon, Llanfihangel-y-traethau, 71
— — —, Pennant-lliw, 8
— — —, Penrhyndeudraeth, 62
— — —, Trawsfynydd, 68
— — Eynon ap Ithel, Llandecwyn, 61
— — Griffri, Cyffty, 101 and n. 2
— — —, Maestran, 13
— — —, Rhywedog, 4
— — Griffid, Caethle, 23
— — —, Maestrefnant, 25
— — Gronou, Gwyddelwern, 84
— — —, Llaethgwm, 16
— — —, Llanaber, 70
— — —, Llanfair, 59, 60
— — —, Llanfrothen, 63
— — —, Pennant-lliw, 9
— — —, Rhyd-cryw, 38
— — —, Streflyn, 20
— — —, Trawsfynydd, 68
— — Gryffid, Cynwyd, 87
— — Gurgenu, Llanbedr, 58
— — —, Llandderfel, 21
— — Gwahalet, Pennant-lliw, 8
— — Gwahaloc, Llanbedr, 67
— — Guion, Penaran, 98
— — Heylin, Rug, 90
— — Howel, Ardudwy, 96
— — —, Bodgadfan, 36
— — —, Bodgynfel, 88
— — —, Garthgynfor, 48
— — —, Penaran, 10
— — Howeyn, Ucheldref, 85
— — Ieuan, Caethle, 23
— — —, Gwyddelwern, 88
— — —, Llanaber, 70
— — —, Maestrefnant, 25
— — —, Mwstwr, 79
— — —, Trawsfynydd, 53
— — Iokin, Cefnrhos, 24
— — Ithel, Cynlas, 17
— — —, Garthgynfor, 48
— — —, Llanfair, 59
— — —, Llanfrothen, 63
— — —, Pennant-lliw, 9
— — —, Rhyd-cryw, 38
— — Iuor, Corris, 33
— — —, Trawsfynydd, 68
— — Kediuor, Maentwrog, 73
— — Kenuric, Carrog, 77
— — —, Llanfrothen, 63
— — —, Trawsfynydd, 68
— — Kenuric ap Griffri, Llanfrothen, 64
— — Lewelin, Garthgynfor, 48
— — —, Llanddwywe, 56
— — —, Llandecwyn, 63
— — —, Llanfrothen, 64
— — —, Tal-y-bont, 48 n. 1
— — Loward, Faerdref Uchaf, 83
— — —, Garthmaelan, 44
— — Madoc, Gwyddelwern, 87
— — —, Llanaber, 69
— — —, Llandecwyn, 62
Iorwerth ap Madoc, Llwyngwril, 41
— — —, Maentwrog, 74
— — —, Nannau, 46
— — —, Peniarth, 39
— — —, Selwrn, 14
— — —, Trawsfynydd, 68
— — Madoc creyd, Cyffty, 101
— — Matussalem, 64 n. 1
— — Meiler, Nanffreuer, 15
— — —, Pennant, 79
— — —, Trawsfynydd, 54, 68
— — Mereduth, Pennal, 29
— — Meurik, Llanfair, 59
— — Meyryk, Cynwyd, 87
— — —, Llanaelhaearn, 91
— — Moridic, Trefeddian, 26
— — Owain Brongyntyn, 85 n. 4
— — Penaro, Llanbedr, 59
— — Phelip, Faerdref Uchaf, 83
— — —, Gwyddelwern, 88
— — —, Llanfrothen, 64
— — —, Nannau, 46
— — —, Tyinmeyron, 67
— — Rees, 7 n. 3
— — Reis, Cregennan, *see* Map Ioreword
— — Res, *taxator*, 7
— — Rys, Castell, 7 n. 3, 100
— — Saleu, Llanfair, 60
— — Seleu, Brithdir, 49
— — Tegwaret, Dôl, 85
— — —, Llandecwyn, 63
— — —, Llanfihangel-y-traethau, 71
— — —, Llanfrothen, 63
— — —, Taltreuddyn, 58
— — Theguaret, 63 n. 1
— — Thomas, Pennant-lliw, 9
— — Tuder, Cyffty, 12, 101 n. 5
— — —, —, widow of, 101
— — Wasdewy, Cefnrhos, 24
— — Was Moel, Pennal, 29
— — Wasteyuol, Llandecwyn, 60
— — Was With, Trawsfynydd, 53
— — Win, Nannau, 46
— — Wion, Llanfair, 59
— — —, Penaran, 10, 98 n. 3
— — Wyon, Faerdref Isaf, 85
— — Yago, Penaran, 99
— — Yagou, Llwyngwril, wife of, 42
— — Yagov, Rhywedog, 5
— athro, xcviii n. 1
— *aurifaber*, Llandecwyn, 60
— Bleso, Penrhyndeudraeth, 61
— *capellanus*, Llanaber, 55
— —, Maentwrog, 73
— Coutta, Cynwyd, 87
— Crak, Peniarth, 39
— Du, Cyffty, 100
— Duy, Cymysgadwy, 21
— —, Cynfal, 31
— —, Cynwyd, 87
— —, Llandecwyn, 62
— —, Maestrefnant, 25
— —, Penaran, 10, 100 n. 3

Iorwerth Duy, Pennal, 29
— — , Rhywedog, 4
— — , Tirllannerch, 76
— — , Trawsfynydd, 53, 68
— Escop, Llanenddwyn, c, 57
— *faber*, Corwen, 75
— — , Cynwyd, 86
— *filius* Candalo, Llandecwyn, 61
— — Gronou, Trawsfynydd, 53
— — Leget, Llanenddwyn, 70
— — Tegwaret, Llandanwg, 58
— Foel, Aberffraw, cxiv
— Fychan, Pennal, 29 n. 2
— Goch, 12 n. 2, 91
— — , Abertanat, 92
— — , Corwen, 75
— — , Cynwyd, 87
— — , Dwygraig, 12
— — , Gwnnodl, 82
— — , Llanfihangel, 42
— — , Llwyngwril, 42
— — , Rhiwerfa, 24
— — , Tirllannerch, 77
— Gouch, 12 n. 2, 42 n. 2
— Loyt, Gwernefail, 19
— *medicus*, Gwyddelwern, 84
— Penath, Caethle, 23
— Poith, Llanfor, 6
— Sutor, Llanfendigaid, 36
— — , Nannau, 44
— Troyn, Pennant-lliw, 9
— Vachan, Llanaber, 54
— — , Llandrillo, 83
— — , Mwstwr, 78
— — , Nantlleidiog, 15
— — , Penaran, 10
— — , Pennal, 29 and n. 2
— — , Tirllannerch, 76
— Velyn, Rhywedog, 4
— Voel, Castell, widow, 99
— — , Llanfor, 6 n. 2
— Voil, Dôl, 85
— Voyl, Llanfor, 6, 99 n. 6
— Vrsen, Llanaber, 54
— Vylein, Cilan, 83
— Welour, Llanaber, 55
— With, Nannau, wife of, 46
— Wonas, Nannau, 45
Ireland, xxvii, cxxv, cxxvi, cxxx
Isaf, commote of, x n. 1
Isafon, vill of, 11 n. 7
Isak Goth, 27 n. 4
Isbidur, 13
Is Cennen, commote of, co. Dyfed, x, xxxi n., lxiii, lxviii, lxix, lxxxiv
Is-coed, co. Clwyd, li
Iscoed Is Hirwern, co. Dyfed, l
Iskyngaynok, *see* Esgaingaenog
Iskyvon, *see* Esgairwen
Ismynydd, 18 n. 4
Issec Goch, Llanaber, 69
Itak Coch, Gwyddelfynydd, 27
Italy, lxv
Itha gargam, Ceiswyn, 34
Ithaelin, Nannau, 47
Ithel ap Adaf, Cefnrhos, 24
Ithel ap Adaf, Llanfihangel-y-traethau, 71
— — — , Nantcaw, 42
— — — , Peniarth, 39
— — Cadugan, Dyffrydan, 50
— — — , Rhywedog, 4
— — — , Tirllannerch, 76
— — Candalo, Penaran, 9
— — Colligwith, Llangedris, 25
— — Crom, Cefnrhos, 23
— — Cuhelin, Cynlas, 17
— — Dauid, Garthiaen, 81
— — — , Gwyddelwern, 88
— — — , Llandecwyn, 62
— — — , Rhyd-cryw, 38
— — — , Trawsfynydd, 69
— — Edenowen, Cregennan, 40
— — Eynon, Doldrewyn, 17
— — — , Llanfihangel-y-traethau, 71
— — — , Maentwrog, 74
— — — , Maestran, 13
— — Griffid, Bodgadfan, 36
— — — , Penaran, 11
— — Griffri, Dyffrydan, wife of, 50
— — Groneu, Aberalwen, 84
— — — , Llansanffraid, 76
— — — , Mwstwr, 79
— — Gurgenu, Tal-y-bont, 43
— — Heylin, Pennal, 29
— — Iarword, Garthiaen, 81
— — Ieuan, Garthgynfor, 48
— — — , Nantcaw, 42
— — — , Peniarth, 39
— — — , Trefeddian, 26
— — Ioreword, Brithdir, 49
— — Ithel, Brithdir, 49
— — Ithel Crek, Brithdir, 49
— — Kenuric, Rhyd-cryw, 37
— — Lewke, Trawsfynydd, 53
— — Lowarch, Cefnrhos, 24
— — Madoc, Dolgledr, 51
— — — , Ffestiniog, 72
— — Moridic, Llwyngwril, 41
— — Phelip, Branas, 80
— — — , Penrhyndeudraeth, 61
— — — , Trawsfynydd, 68
— — Ririd, Gwernefail, 20
— — Robert, Llwyngwril, 41
— — Ryrid, Gwyddelwern, 88
— — Ryryd, Dôl, 85
— — Seysyld, Corwen, 75
— — Tegwaret, Garthgynfor, 48
— — — , Nantcaw, 42
— — — , Taltreuddyn, 58
— — Torpen, Llanfrothen, 64
— — Was Patrik, Ystradgwyn, 35
— — Win, Maentwrog, 73
— — — , Nannau, 46
— — — , Treffeden, 32
— — Wyn, Ystradgwyn, 34
— — Y Mank, Nannau, 45
— Bach, Garthmaelan, 44
— Cam, Caethle, 23
— *capellanus*, Ffestiniog, 72
— carpenter, Llanfair, 60
— Crak, Cregennan, 40

Ithel *dapifer*, Crogen, xxxvii, 16
— Deuergy, Llansanffraid, 76
— Duy, Cefnrhos, 23
— — , Cefnyrowen, 51
— — , Maentwrog, 74
— — , Pencoed, 22
— — , Rhywedog, 3
— — , Trawsfynydd, 68, 69
— *filius scriptoris*, Llandecwyn, 60
— Gam, Carrog, 77
— Geurch, Garthgynfor, 48
— Gwethel, Ceiswyn, 34
— Goch, Bron-prys, 31
— — , Corris, 33
— Gock, Llanfendigaid, 36
— Ney, Peniarth, 39
— Orellyn, Ffestiniog, 72
— Pen, Trawsfynydd, 68
— Penbras, Garthgynfor, 48
— Sutor, Penaran, 10
— Vachan, Peniarth, 39
— — , Trawsfynydd, 69
— — , Trewyn, 78
— — , Tyinmeyron, 67
— Voyl, Cymysgadwy, 21
— — , Gwanas, 43
— — , Llanaber, 69
— — , Nannau, 47
— — , Penrhyndeudraeth, 62
— — , Treffeden, 32
— — , Ystradgwyn, 34
— Wan, Cefnrhos, 23
— — , Trawsfynydd, 53
— Warth, Ceiswyn, 34
— Wir, Ffestiniog, 72
Iuor, Maentwrog, 73
— , Rhyd-cryw, 37
— ap Meiler, Corris, 33
Ivanou ap Madoc, Treffeden, 32

JAMES of St. George, master, 66 n. 1
Johannes, *see* Iohannes
John Carbonarius, *see* Colier, John le

K-, Cf. also C-
Kae Maesmor, *see* Maesmor
Kallwit, Trefrydd, 33
Kalumwy, Llanenddwyn, 57
Karweth ap Rylkin With, Llanbedr, 58
Kastel, *see* Castell
Kedich Duy, Streflyn, 20
Kediuor, *see* Cedifor
Kefdu, *see* Cyffty
Kefnauc, Bodgadfan, 37
Kelston, co. Clwyd, xxxiii, cxxxv
Kemiscadeu, *see* Cymysgadwy
Ken. ap Kadogan, Ystradgwyn, 34
Kena, Penaran, 10
Kendalo, *see* Cynddelw
Keneric, *see* Cynwrig
Kenet Cam, Tywyn, 30
Kenewrec, Kenewrek, Kenewric, *see* Cynwrig
Kenfig, co. Dyfed, liii n. 2
Kenlas, *see* Cynlas
Kenneric, Kennewric, *see* Cynwrig
Kenuelin, *see* Cynfelin
Kenuric, Kenurik, *see* Cynwrig
Kenvayl, *see* Cynfal
Kenvenrowen, *see* Cefnyrowen
Kenwric, *see* Cynwrig
Kesseloc, 24
Kessoylgoum, *see* Cesailgwm
Kethugalc, xiv, cvii, cxxxix, cxl, 66
Keuenard, *see* Cyfnerth
Keuenros, *see* Cefnrhos
Keventeylloyn, xxxvii n. 2, cxxxix, 38 n. 3
Keyswyn, *see* Ceiswyn
Kiftu, *see* Cyffty
Kimer, *see* Cymer
Knighton, sub-lordship of, co. Powys, xxxi n.
Knolton, co. Clwyd, li
Kolmync, Rhyd-cryw, 38
Kuelin, *see* Cuelin
Kylan, *see* Cilan
Kyltalgart, *see* Ciltalgarth
Kymmer, *see* Cymer
Kymmyskadwy, Kymyskadoe, *see* Cymysgadwy
Kynlau, Llanbedr, 58
Kynner, *see* Cymer
Kyrreank, Branas, 80
Kywluot, *see* Cynllwyd, *or* Caergeiliog

LACY, de, cxxxi; *see also* Lincoln, earl of
Lamendyget, *see* Llanfendigaid
Lampeter, co. Dyfed, lxiii n. 6, lxiv, ciii
Lamyhangel, *see* Llanfihangel Glyn Myfyr, Llanfihangel-y-Pennant, Llanfihangel-y-traethau
Lanaber, *see* Llanaber
Lancaster, county of, xxvi, cxxxi
— , earldom of, cxxxi
Land-, *see* Lland-
Lane-, *see* Llane-
Lanfrothin, *see* Llanfrothen
Lang-, *see* Llang-
Lanl-, *see* Llanll-
Lanpeder, *see* Llanbedr
Lans-, *see* Llans-
Lanu-, *see* Llanf-
Lasynys, cv
Le deutrayth, *see* Penrhyndeudraeth
Leget, Legeth, *see* Llygad
Leland, John, xlvii, xlix, lii, liii, cxi
Le Neve, c
Lestrange, Roger, lxxv, 40 n. 1, 51 n. 1
Lestreflyn, Lestreuelyn, *see* Llystreflyn, *and also* Streflyn
Leuke, Leweke, Lewke, *see* Lleucu
Lhuyd, Edward, cxviii n. 1, 6 n. 5, 14 n. 4, 15 n. 3, 16 n. 1, 20 n. 5
Lincoln, co. of, xxvi
— , earl of, cxxxi
Lippa, Trawsfynydd, 68

Llaethgwm (Llaytcoum), cxxxix, cxlii, 15 and n. 3
Llanaber (Lanaber), parish of, xlii, xlv, lxxvi, lxxix, xc
— , vill of, xliii, xc, cxxxiii n. 7, cxxxix, cxl, 52 n. 3, 54 and n. 5, 69
Llanaberismynydd, 52 n. 3, 54 n. 5
Llanaberuwchmynydd, 52 n. 3, 54 n. 5
Llanaelhaearn (Ayl Hayarn, Llanerhaern), co. Clwyd, cxxxix, cxli, 89 n. 4, 91
Llanbadarn, co. Dyfed, lv n. 5, cxxviii
Llanbedr (Lanpeder), parish of, xlv, lxxix
— , vill of, c, cxxxix, cxl, 52 n. 3, 58, 59, 67
Llandanwg (Landanoc), xlv, lxxvii, lxxix, cxxxix, cxl, 57
Llandderfel, parish of, xlv, lxxix, lxxx n. 2, cxlii, 14 and n. 4, 15 n. 3, 16, 17 and n. 1, 20 n. 5
— , vill of, xi n. 2, cxxxix, cxlii, 21, 95, 96 and n. 5, 97 n. 1 and 2
Llanddwywe (Landewey), parish of, xlv, lxxix
— , vill of, xxxiii, xciv, cxxxix, cxl, 55, 56 n. 1
Llanddwyweisygraig, 52 n. 3
Llanddwyweuwchygraig, 52 n. 3
Llandecwyn, parish of, xlv, lxxix
— , vill of, cix, cxxxix, cxl, 52 n. 3, 60, 62, 66 n. 6
Llandrillo, parish of, xlv, lxvi, lxxvi, lxxix, lxxx n. 2, xc, cxli, 79, 80, 81, 82, 83, 91 n. 4
— , vill of, cix, cxxxix, cxli, 83
Llanegryn, parish of, xlv, xlvi, lxxvi, lxxix, lxxx n. 2, lxxxi, cxliii, 37, 38 43 n. 7 and 9
Llanegwestl (Lanegwystel, Glynegwestl, Glyn-y-groes, Valle Crucis), abbey, co. Clwyd, c, cxv, 79
Llanelltud, parish of, xxxvii, xliii, xlv, lxxix, cxxxix, 74 n. 3, 4, 5
Llanenddwyn (Landeuendou, Lanendewyn, Lanendou), parish of, xlv, lxxix, cxl, 58 n. 2
— , vill of, c, cxxxix, cxl, 52 n. 3, 56 and n. 3, 4, 5, 70 and n. 4
Llanerhaern, *see* Llanaelhaearn
Llanfachreth, parish of, xlv, lxxvi, lxxix, lxxx n. 2, cxliii, 43 n. 3, 4, and 5, 44 n. 1, 45 n. 3
Llan-faes (Lanuays), lxi
Llanfair, Merioneth, xlv, lxxvii, lxxix, lxxx n. 2, cxxxix, cxl, 59
— , Uchaf commote, xcvi
Llanfendigaid (Lamendyget), xciv, c, cxxxix, cxliii, 35, 36 n. 1
Llanfihangel, commote Ardudwy, lxxx n. 2, xciii, 62 n. 1
— , commote Edeirnion, cxxxix, cxli
Llanfihangel, commote Tal-y-bont, cxxxix, cxliii, 22 n. 5, 42
Llanfihangel Glyn Myfyr, pa. of, co. Clwyd, cxli, 90
Llanfihangel-y-Pennant, parish of, xlv, lxxix, lxxx n. 2, cxliii, cxliv, 22 n. 5, 24, 25, 28, 42, 51
Llanfihangel-y-Traethau, parish of, xlv, lxxix, cxxxix, cxl, 61 n. 1, 71
Llanfor, parish of, xlv, lxxvi, lxxix, lxxx n. 2, cxlii, 3 and n. 1, 6, 15, 16 n. 1, 17, 18, 20 and n. 5
— , vill of, c, cxxxix, cxlii, 3 n. 1, 5, 6n. 5, 14 n. 4, 99 n. 6
Llanfrothen, xxxix n. 1, cxxxix, cxl
— , parish of, xlv, lxxix, lxxxi, 63
Llanfyllin, co. Powys, lxiv
Llangar, lord of, 87 n. 1
— (and Cymer), parish of, co. Clwyd, xlv, lxxvii, lxxix, lxxx n. 2, cxli, 81, 86, 88
— , vill of, cxxxix, cxli
Llangedris, cxxxix, cxliv, 25
Llangelynnin, parish of, xlv, lxvii, lxxvi, lxxix, lxxx n. 2, cxliii, 27 n. 3, 35, 36, 40, 41
Llangyfelach, hundred of, co. West Glamorgan, lxviii
Llangywer (Langouer), parish of, xlv, lxxix, cxxxix, cxlii, 11
— , vill of, cxlii, 14 and n. 1
Llanidloes, co. Powys, xlviii, lxv
Llanllwydau, vill of, cxxxix, cxliv, 28
Llannerchgoediog, vill of, cxxxix, cxliv, 22 n. 5, 25
Llansanffraid Glyn Dyfrdwy, parish of, co. Clwyd, xlv, lxxvi–lxxvii, lxxix, lxxx n. 2, cxli
— , vill of, cxxxix, cxli, 75
Llanstephan, lordship of, co. Dyfed, lv
Llantrisant, co. Mid Glamorgan, cxxx
Llanuwchllyn, parish of, xlv, lxvi, lxxvi, lxxix, xc, cviii, cxlii, 7, 9, 13 and n. 1, 17, 97, 99
— , village of, lxxxi, 9 n. 2
Llanyblodwel, parish of, co. Salop, cxli, 91 n. 7
Llanycil, parish of, xlv, lxxix, cviii, cxlii, 12, 13 and n. 1, 18, 100, 101 and n. 7
— , vill of, xciv, cxxxix, cxlii, 20
Llanymawddwy, parish of, lxxix
Llaugut, Pennal, 29
Llawarth, *see* Llywarch
Llawrybetws, 16 n. 1
Llaytcoum, *see* Llaethgwm
Lleidiog, stream, 14 n. 4
Lleucu (Leuke, Leweke, Lewke)
— Bran, Llanfair, 59
— *filia* Adaf, Garthgynfor, 48
— — Angharet, 39 n. 1
— — Dauid, Cynwyd, 87
— — Eynon, Llanbedr, 67

Lleucu *filia* Griffri, Nannau, 46
— — Howel, Garthmaelan, 44
— — Lewelin, Cynfal, 31
— — Lowarch, Trawsfynydd, 53
— — Madoc, Cefnrhos, 23
— — — , Llansanffraid, 76
— — Phelip, Llanfihangel, 42
— — — , Maentwrog, 73
— — Tuder, Dolgledr, 51
— Goch, Llanfor, 6
— — , Pennant-lliw, 8
— Loyt, Llandderfel, 21
— *uxor* Iohannis, Penrhyndeudraeth, 62
— — Lewelin, Llanenddwyn, 57
Llwyngwern, 7 n. 5
Llwyniolyn, 6 n. 5
Llwyngwril, xxxiii, cxxxix, cxliii, 41
Llygad (Leget, Llegeth)
— Cornerat, Rhyd-cryw, 38
— Gour (i.e. Llygad Gŵr), Carrog, cxxxvi, 77 and n. 3
— Mark, Ucheldref, 18
— Penglok, Nanffreuer, 14
Llygadog, vill of, co. Clwyd, cxxxix, cxli, 84
Llŷn, cantref, xxxiv, xlii, liv, lxvi, lxvii, lxxii, cxi, cxxx
Llystreflyn (Lestreflyn, Lestreuelyn), 20 and n. 3, 102; *see also* Streflyn
Llywarch (Loward, Lowarch, Llawarth)
— , Nanffreuer, 15
— , Ystumanner, 22
— ap Gronou, 53 n. 2
— — — , Trawsfynydd, 53
— — Ryryd, Bodorlas, 76
— — Tegwaret, Llanfihangel-y-traethau, 71
— — Win, Brithdir, 49
— Crak, Peniarth, 40
— Goch, Llanfair, 60
Llywelyn (Lewelin, Lewelyn)
— ap Adda, 92 n. 1
— — Cadugan, Gwrych, xxxiii, 30 and n. 1
— — Dauid, Bylan, 26
— — Edeneuet, Llangywer, 14
— — Gronou, Cynfal, 31
— — Gruffydd, prince of Wales, xvii, xviii, xix and n. 5, xx, xxvii, xxxiv, xxxvii n. 2, xlii, lxi, lxxxvi, cxxi, cxxii, cxxiii and n. 3, cxxiv and n. 1, cxxvi, cxxvii, cxxviii, cxxxii, 6 n. 5, 77 n. 3
— — Iorwerth, prince of Gwynedd, xvii
— — Lewelin, Kethugalc, 67
— — Madoc, Bodgadfan, 36
— — — , Peniarth, 39
— — Meiler, Nannau, 45
— — Wylim, *taxator*, 35
— Bren, xxviii, xcii, cxiv
— Corn, Llanfrothen, 64
— Duy, Hengaer, 16
Llywelyn *filius* Adaf, Esgaingaenog, 92
— Goch, Penrhyndeudraeth, 61
— — , Trawsfynydd, 68
— Grach, Penaran, 98
— Loyt, Llanfor, 5
— Vachan, Hendwr, 82
— — , Penrhyndeudraeth, 62
London, city of, population of, lxv
Longoril, *see* Llwyngwril
Loward, Lowarch, *see* Llywarch
Loydin, Penaran, 10

MABILIA, Maentwrog, 73
Macclesfield Park, co. Ches., cxxxi
Machynlleth, co. Powys, xlviii, lxiv
Maderoun Goch, Gwyddelwern, 84
Maderun, Llanenddwyn, 71
Madin (Madon, Madyn)
— , Gwrych, 30
— ap Adaf, Kethugalc, 67
— — Adaf Hen, Bodgadfan, lxxxii, lxxxiii, 37
— — Candalov, Dyffrydan, 50
— — Dauid, Dolgledr, 51
— — Gronou, Dolgledr, 51
— — Howel, Llanfor, 6
— — Phelip, Nannau, 44
— — — , Peniarth, 39
— — Win, Llanddwywe, 56
— Cam, Tywyn, 30
— Crak, Rhywedog, 4
— Cutta, Nannau, 44
— Duy, Garthmaelan, 44
— Goch, Llwyngwril, 41
— Loyt, Rhywedog, 4
— Mees, Penrhyndeudraeth, 61
— Meronnith, Llanaber, 70
— Vachan, Bodorlas, 76
— With, Caethle, 22
— — , Llanfrothen, 64
Madir Len, Trawsfynydd, wife of, 53
Madog (Maddok, Madoc)
— , Gwyddelwern, 88
— ap Ada, Garthgynfor, 48
— — — ap Aloc, Llanaber, 55
— — Adaf, Castell, 99
— — — , Ffestiniog, 72
— — — , Llandderfel, 21, 97 n. 1
— — — , Nannau, 45
— — — , Pennal, 29
— — — , Penrhyndeudraeth, 62
— — — , *taxator*, 91
— — — , Tirllannerch, 77
— — — , widow of, 97
— — Adam, Gwyddelwern, 88
— — — , Trawsfynydd, 69
— — — , Trewyn, 78
— — Adda, 96 n. 5
— — Athaf, 8 n., 99 n. 5
— — Cadugan, Bylan, 26
— — — , Ciltalgarth, 18
— — — , Maentwrog, 73
— — — , Nannau, 47
— — — , Nantlleidiog, 15
— — — , Tirllannerch, 76

Madog ap Candalo, Cilan, 83
— — — , Nanmor, 72
— — Dafydd, 82 n. 1
— — Dauid, Cilan, 83
— — — , Dwygraig, 12
— — — , Dyffrydan, 50
— — — , Garthiaen, 81
— — — , Gwernefail, 19
— — — , Gwyddelwern, 84
— — — , Hendwr, 82
— — — , Llanfrothen, 64
— — — , Maentwrog, 73
— — — , Maestran, 13
— — — , Morfa Maenog, 40
— — — , Peniarth, 38
— — — , *taxator*, 66
— — — , Tirllannerch, 76
— — Dauid ap Edeneuet, Dwygraig, 12
— — David, 19 n. 1
— — Dynodir, Llanaber, 55
— — Edeneuet, Cynwyd, 87
— — — , Llanfrothen, 64
— — — , Penaran, 10
— — Edeneweyn, Gwyddelwern, 84
— — Eua, Gwyddelfynydd, 28
— — Eynon, Bodgadfan, 36
— — — , Cymysgadwy, 20
— — — , Faerdref Uchaf, 83
— — — , Llanaber, 70
— — — , Llanenddwyn, 56
— — — , Llanfair, 59
— — — , Llwyngwril, 41
— — — , Maesmor, 27
— — — , Morfa Maenog, 41
— — — , Mwstwr, 79
— — — , Nannau, 45
— — — , Peniarth, 39, 40
— — — , Pennant, 80
— — — , Pennant-lliw, 8
— — — , Penrhyndeudraeth, 62
— — — , Selwrn, 14
— — — , Trefrydd, 33
— — — , Ystradgwyn, 34
— — Gogan, Llanfrothen, 64
— — Griffid, Penmaen, 32
— — Griffith, 47 n. 1
— — Griffry, Cynwyd, 86
— — — , Nannau, 47
— — Gronou, Dolgledr, 50
— — — , Penrhyndeudraeth, 61, 62
— — — , Rhyd-cryw, 38
— — Gruffydd, 77 n. 2
— — Gruffydd ap Dafydd, Hendwr, 82 n. 3
— — Gruffydd Mal, Carrog, 77 and n. 2
— — Guilin, 73 n. 1
— — Gurgenu, Cefnyrowen, 51
— — — , Gwernefail, 19
— — — , Nantcaw, 42
— — — , Ucheldref, 18
— — Guyn, Bedwarian, 20, 102
— — Gwerith, Rhywedog, 4
— — Heilin, Llanfrothen, 64
Madog ap Heylin, Llandecwyn, 60
— — — , Maentwrog, 73
— — — , Nanffreuer, 15
— — Howel, Cymysgadwy, 20
— — — , Garthiaen, 81
— — — , Gwernefail, 19
— — — , Gwyddelfynydd, 28
— — Iarward, Trewyn, 78
— — Iarward Mal, Trewyn, 78
— — Iarword, Cynwyd, 86
— — — , Llygadog, 84
— — Idenerth, Cilan, 82
— — Idon, Llanfrothen, 65
— — Ierword, Cyffty, 101 n. 6
— — Ieuaf, Maestrefnant, 25
— — Ieuan, Faerdref Isaf, 85
— — — , Llanfrothen, 64
— — — , Penaran, 98
— — — , Tirllannerch, wife of, 76
— — Iockin, Llanfihangel-y-traethau, 71
— — Iorwerth, Pennant-lliw, xxxiii, lxxxi, 7, 8 n.
— — Iorwerth Medyk, 70 n. 4
— — Iorword, Cyffty, widow of, 12 n. 5, 101
— — — , Llanaber, 69
— — — , Llanfihangel-y-traethau, 71
— — Ithel, 97
— — — , Cilan, 83
— — — , Cynwyd, 87
— — — , Faerdref Isaf, 86
— — — , Llanaber, 54
— — — , Llanfendigaid, 36
— — — , Llwyngwril, 41
— — — , Peniarth, 38, 39
— — — , Rug, 90
— — — , Trewyn, wife of, 78
— — Kediuor, Penmaen, 32
— — Kenthlu, Penrhyndeudraeth, 62
— — Kenuig, Bodgadfan, 36
— — Kenuric, Cynfal, 31
— — — , Dwygraig, 11
— — — , Garthgynfor, 48
— — Keuenard, Streflyn, 20
— — Lewelin, Abertanat, 91
— — — , Caethle, 23
— — — , Corris, 33
— — — , Dwygraig, 11
— — — , Llwyngwril, 41
— — — , Pencraig, 90
— — — , prince, revolt of, xxx, xxxiii, xxxiv, xxxv, xli n. 1, liii, lxi, lxxiv, 7 n. 3, 8 n., 30 n. 1, 41 n. 2, 45 n. 1, 56 n. 1, 60 n. 2, 64 n. 1, 72 n. 5, 82 n. 1
— — Lowarch, Llanllwydau, 28
— — Madin, Llanbedr, 67
— — Madoc Kethin, Cynfal, 31

Madog ap Meiler, Cefnrhos, 24
— — —, Llannerchgoediog, 25
— — —, Llanllwydau, 28
— — —, Llwyngwril, 41
— — —, Peniarth, 39
— — —, Trefeddian, 26
— — Meyler, Bodorlas, 76
— — Meyryk, Gwyddelwern, 88
— — —, *taxator*, 91
— — Moridic, Bodgadfan, 36
— — —, Llwyngwril, 42
— — Moruran, Peniarth, 40
— — Phelip, Gwyddelwern, 88
— — —, Llanfendigaid, 35
— — —, Mwstwr, 79
— — —, Nantlleidiog, 15
— — Rerid, Selwrn, 14
— — Reys, Llangar, 89
— — —, Pencoed, 22
— — Ririd, Nannau, 45
— — Riscaellus, Bylan, 26
— — Ryryd, Cynwyd, 87
— — —, Llygadog, 84
— — Seysild, Llanllwydau, 28
— — Sulien, Rhiwerfa, 24
— — Tuder, Garthiaen, 81
— — —, Maentwrog, 74
— — —, Ystradgwyn, 34
— — Wasdewy, Penmaen, 6
— — Weches, Bere, 52
— — Wen, Llanaber, 70
— — Wilim, *taxator*, 52
— — Win, Garthgynfor, 48
— — —, Garthmaelan, 44
— — —, Gwernefail, 20, 102 n. 4
— — —, Trefrydd, 33
— — Wion, Brithdir, 48
— — Wyon, Dôl, 85
— — Yago ap Guyn, Penaran, 98
— — Yago Voel, Penaran, 11 n. 4, 99
— — Yagou, Penaran, 11
— — Yarword, Cynwyd, 86
— — —, Pencraig, 90
— — Yerword, Cyffty, 12
— — —, Llanfendigaid, 35
— — —, Maentwrog, 74
— — —, Pennant-lliw, 7
— — —, Rhyd-cryw, 37
— — —, Ystradgwyn, 34
— — Yerword ap Gronou With, Maestrefnant, 25
— *aurifaber*, Pennant, 79
— Bleyth, Faerdref Isaf, 85
— Bloyth, Nanffreuer, 15
— Boulton, Llanenddwyn, 70
— Brothen, Llanfrothen, 64
— Cam, Cyffty, 13
— —, Pencoed, 22
— Cantor, Llanaber, 69
— Chitharista, cviii and n. 3, 26
— *clericus*, Nefyn, xcix
— Corista, Maentwrog, 74
— —, Taltreuddyn, 58
— Crach, Harlech, 66 and n. 2
— Crak, Garthmaelan, 44
Madog Crek, Trawsfynydd, 53
— de Vowr, Llanenddwyn, 70
— Du, 5 n. 3
— —, Bedwarian, 12 n. 1, 19 n. 2, 102 and n. 3
— Duy, Branas, 80
— —, Cefnyrowen, 51
— —, Dwygraig, 12
— —, Garthiaen, 81
— —, Gwernefail, 19
— —, Gwyddelwern, 88
— —, Llanfor, 5
— —, Peniarth, 39
— —, Penrhyndeudraeth, 61
— —, *taxator*, 35
— —, Trawsfynydd, 53, 68
— Dyvoun, Cefnyrowen, 51
— Ebarwith, Llanllwydau, 28
— *faber*, Llwyngwril, 41
— *filius* Backenin, Llanbedr, 59
— — Dauid, Llanfrothen, 64
— — Ioreword, Brithdir, 49
— — Ithel, Brithdir, 49
— — —, Trewyn, 78
— — Kenwric, Nannau, 47
— — Keuenard, *taxator*, 66
— — Meyryk, Brythyr, 89
— — Tuder, Nannau, dau. of, 45
— — Wilim, Maentwrog, 73
— — Win, Llanenddwyn, 56
— — Yarward, Llansanffraid, 76
— — Yerword, Llanaber, 69
— *frater*, 74
— Gam, Llandrillo, 83
— Goch, Abertanat, 91
— —, Bylan, 26
— —, Cregennan, 40
— —, Cynwyd, 86
— —, Dwygraig, 12
— —, Flintshire, xxxiii
— —, Llandderfel, 21
— —, Llanddwywe, 55
— —, Maentwrog, 73
— —, Mwstwr, 79
— —, Pennant, 79
— —, Treffeden, 32
— Grach, Pennant, 80
— Grupl, 77 n. 2
— Gwyde, Branas, 80
— Hen, Rhywedog, 3
— Imper, Trawsfynydd, 52
— Kennach, Nannau, 47
— Kesseloc, Cefnrhos, 24
— Kest, Mwstwr, 79
— Kethyn, Cynwyd, 86
— Kydo, Corwen, 75
— Kynith, Nannau, 46
— Loyd, Penaran, 97
— Loyd ap Eynon, Castell, 99
— Loyt, Bodgynfel, 88
— *medicus*, Gwyddelwern, 84
— —, Llanenddwyn, 70
— Moylgoch, Branas, 80
— o'r Dol, Garthmaelan, 44
— Palmer, Nantcaw, xcviii, 42
— Pendwy, Llandderfel, 21

Madog Pengrek, Bron-prys, 31
— Ruth, Cyffty, 12
— Saer, Doldrewyn, 17
— — , Llanaber, 69
— Sipac, Taltreuddyn, 58
— Skynith, Peniarth, 39
— Sutor, Brithdir, 49
— — , Gwyddelwern, 88
— — , Maentwrog, 74
— — , Streflyn, 20
— Vachan, Cynwyd, 87
— — , Llwyngwril, 41
— — , Nannau, 46
— — , Trewyn, 78
— Vaughan, 46 n. 1
— Voel, Castell, 10 n. 1, 100
— Voil, Ciltalgarth, 18
— — , Pencoed, 22
— Voyl, Llanfihangel, 90
— — , Penaran, 10, 100 n. 1
— — , Rhyd-cryw, 37
— Vrnant, Llanaber, 55
— Welshman, 66 n. 2
— Whih, Trawsfynydd, 53
— Whith, Llwyngwril, 41
— — , Penmaen, 6
— — , Ucheldref, 18
— With, Llanfrothen, 65
— Wyth, Trewyn, 78
Madon, *see* Madin
Madryn, xxxiv
Madyn, *see* Madin
Maelor, co. Clwyd, xlvii, li, lii, liii, lxiii, lxix, lxxiii, 77 n. 2
Maenordeilo, commote of, co. Dyfed, xxii
Maentwrog, xlv, lxxxix, lxxxi, ciii, cxxxvi, cxxxix, cxl, 73, 74
Maerdref, *see* Faerdref
Maesmawr, Tal-y-bont, lxvii, 27 n. 3
Maesmor, Ystumanner, cxxxix, cxliv, 27 and n. 3
Maestran, cviii, cxxxix, cxlii, 13 and n. 1, 19 n. 1, 98 n. 2, 100 n. 2, 101 n. 2
Maestrefnant, cxxxix, cxliv, 25
Maesytail, 18 n. 4
Malltraeth, commote of, lxix, lxxiii
Mallwyd, parish of, lxxix
Map Bedar, Peniarth, 39
Map Blayn, Faerdref Isaf, 86
Map Botoun, Selwrn, 14
Map Carrac, Llanfrothen, 64
Map Carrec, Penrhyndeudraeth, 61
Map Cossyn, Tywyn, 30
Map Coun, Faerdref Isaf, dau. of, 86
Map Doun, Llanddwywe, 56
Map Doyok, Peniarth, 39
Map Duy, Kethugalc, 67
Map Goch, Llanllwydau, 28
Map Gronou ap Ieuan, Bodgadfan, 36
Map Gurkin, Brithdir, 49
Map Heylin, Penmaen, 7
Map Ioreword ap Reis, Cregennan, 40
Map Keuenard Duy, Ciltalgarth, 18
Map Kimero, Llanfihangel-y-traethau, 71
Map Luges, Nannau, 47
Map Maur, Ceiswyn, 33
Map Maur, Nannau, 47
Map Oyn, Nannau, 47
Map Seis, Rhywedog, 4
Map Sely, Nannau, 45
Map Siboc, Maentwrog, 73
Map Talennyatur, Cynfal, 31
Map Was Doun, Peniarth, 38
Map Wechethes, Cefnrhos, 23
Map Yerword, Cyffty, 13
Map Yerword ap Adaf, Nantlleidiog, 15
Map Ygwely, Pennal, 29
Maredudd (Mereduth)
— , Maentwrog, 73
— ap Dauid, Llanbedr, 67
— — Howel, Abertanat, 92
— — Rhys, Dryslwyn, xviii
— Bongam, Pennal, 28
Margam, abbey, co. West Glamorgan, cxv
Margareta *filia* Ririd, Brithdir, 49
Marured, Gwyddelfynydd, 28
Massy, Richard de, viii n. 2, xii
Mathrafal, co. Powys, xxx n. 6
Matthew Paris, xvii
Matussalem, Vachan, Llanfrothen, 64
Mautho, *see* Mawddwy
Mawddach, river, 70 n. 1
Mawddwy, commote of, xlii n. 2, xliv, lxix, lxxiii, lxxix, cxxxix
— , lordship of, xxxviii, lxix and n., 9 n. 3
Maynnatur, Maynturroc, *see* Maentwrog
Maysrreyd Devayd, *see* Rhydydefaid
Mayst-, *see* Maest-
Mechain, commote of, co. Powys, lxx, lxxiii, 79 n. 6
Meden, Kethugalc, 66
Medicus, Tirllannerch, wife of, 77
Mefenydd, commote of, co. Dyfed, lvi, lxxxv
Meghen, *see* Mechain
Meilyr (Meiler, Meilor)
— , Nannau, 46
— ap Ada, Penaran, 11
— — Adaf, Caethle, 23
— — — , Pennal, 29
— — Cadugan, Llanfair, 59
— — Eynon, Maesmor, 27
— — Gronou, Ffestiniog, 72
— — Gurgenu, Bylan, 26
— — — , Cyffty, 12
— — Howel, Gwernefail, 19
— — Ithel, Peniarth, 39
— — — , Penaran, 98
— — Kenuric, Pennal, 29
— — Lewelin, Gwernefail, 19
— — — , Peniarth, 38, 39
— — Lewke, Llanfihangel, 42
— — Madoc, Gwyddelfynydd, 28
— — — , Rhiwerfa, 24
— — Madok, Pencraig, 90
— — Phelip, Llanaber, 70
— — Tuder, Dolgellau, 49
— — Wion, Bodgadfan, 37
— Duy, Trewyn, 78

Meilyr Goch, Crogen, 16
— Loyt, Garthgynfor, 48
— Voil, Brithdir, 49
— Voyl, Llanfendigaid, 36
Meinihirion, 13 n. 1
Meirionnydd (Meronnith), cantref of, xlii and n. 1, 35 n. 1, 36 n. 1, 70 n. 1
Melysgederew, *see* Moelysgediw
Merck Heilin, Llandderfel, 21
Mereduth, *see* Maredudd
Merioneth, xvii, xxii, xxx n. 1, xxxiv, xxxviii, xlviii, li, lii, liv, lxvii, lxxiv, lxxv, lxxvii, lxxx, lxxxi, lxxxii, lxxxiv, lxxxv, cxviii, cxxxiii, 45 n. 1, 52 n. 3, 56 n. 2, 72 n. 1, 75 n. 2, 91 n. 7
— , assessors of, xiii–xvi, lxxxvi, cxl–cxliv, 7, 8 n., 35, 52, 66 and n. 4, 91, 96
— , clergymen in, xcvii–c
— , commotes of, cxl; *and see* Ardudwy, Edeirnion, Penllyn, Tal-y-bont and Ystumanner
— , — , comparative wealth of, lxxii–lxxv
— , extent of, referred to, lxxxi, cxii, 7 n. 5, 16 n. 2, 29 n. 2
— , hostages possibly from, 7 n. 3, 53 n. 2, 60 n. 2, 64 n. 1, 66 n. 5, 72 n. 5, 79 n. 5
— , movables of persons from, cxiv, cxix, 96–102
— , occupations in, ci–cx, cxii
— , — , listed, cii
— , offices in, lxxxiv–lxxxix
— , parishes of, xlv, lxxix
— , — , comparative wealth of, lxxv–lxxvii
— , population of, xxiv, xxxvii–xlvii, lvii, lix, lx, lxiv–lxvii, cxl
— , sheriff of, xxxi, lxxxvi, xcii, 3 n. 2, 29 n. 2, 30 n. 1, 82 n. 3
— , subsidies granted by, viii n. 4, xiv, xv, xxiv, xxv and n. 2, xxvi, xxvii, xxx and n. 6, xxxii, lxviii n. 4, lxix, lxx, cxxxiv, 96
— , subsidy payable by religious houses in, c, 7, 22, 43, 67, 74, 79
— , subsidy rolls relating to, x and n. 1, xi and n. 2, xii, xiii, xxviii, xxxvi, xxxviii, lxvi, xciii, cxiii, cxxxv, cxxxvi, 95
— , towns of, lx, lxiv–lxv, civ–cv; *and see* Bere, Cynwyd, Dolgellau, Harlech, Tywyn
— , townships of, comparative wealth of, lxxx–lxxxii, cxl–cxliv
— , — , listed, cxxxix
Merioneth, townships of, population of, lxv–lxvii
— , trade in, civ, cviii
— , *uchelwyr* in, lxxxiii–lxxxiv, lxxxix–xciii
— , unfree in, xxxiv, xciii–xcvii
— , wealth of, lxix–lxxii
Meronnith, *see* Meirionnydd
Mesdour, *see* Mwstwr
Meuanou, Meuanov, *see* Myfanwy
Meuedus, Cefnyrowen, 51
Meurig (Meuric, Meurik)
— , Kethugalc, 67
— , Maestran, 13
— ap Adaf, Llanfrothen, 64
— — Howel, Peniarth, 38
— — Iorword, Nantlleidiog, 15
— — Ithel, Faerdref Isaf, 86
— — Tuder, Faerdref Isaf, 86
— — Win, Rhyd-cryw, 37
— Dathloyt, Llaethgwm, 16
— *filius* Reis, Llandecwyn, 61
— Goch, Dôl, wife of, 85
— Meghen, Pennant, 79
— Poith, Rhywedog, 4
— *sacrista*, Llanycil, 20
— Saer, Maentwrog, 73
— Vachan, Llygadog, 84
Meylkin, Llanfrothen, 64
Meyron Eynon Voil, Trawsfynydd, 53
Middlesex, county of, xxvi
Milisandia, Trawsfynydd, 53
Mocbrin, *see* Moel Ispri
Mochnant, commote of, co. Powys, x, xlviii, lxix, lxx, lxxiii
Moel, Cf. Moil, Moyl
Moel Crek, Trawsfynydd, 53
Moel Ispri, 74 and n. 4
Moel West, Llanfrothen, 63
Moel y Feidiog, cxxxiv
Moelysgediw, co. Clwyd, cxxxix, cxli, 81
Moil, Cf. Moel, Moyl
Moil Coit, Maentwrog, 74
Moil Hogi, Maentwrog, 74
Moil Wen, Llandanwg, 57
Moil With, Trawsfynydd, 68
Mold, co. Clwyd, lxix, cxxiii
Monmouth, co. Gwent, lvi
— , county of, x, xxxii, xlviii, lxix
— , lordship of, x, xii, xxx n. 6, lxix
Montegomery, Laurence de, xxxviii, civ, 29
Montfort, earl Simon de, xviii
Montgomery, co. Powys
— , county of, x, xlviii, lx, lxvi, lxvii, lxx, lxxii, lxxxiv, c, 7 n. 2, 79 n. 6
— , lordship of, viii, lxx, lxxiii
— , treaty of, xviii, xix, xx, cxxii
Morfa Maenog, cxxxix, cxliii, 40
Morfran (Moruran, Moruram)
— , Llanaber, 69
— ap Gronou, Llanfihangel, 42

Morfran ap Gurgenu, Peniarth, 40 and n. 1
— — Ithel, Peniarth, 39
— — Madoc, Peniarth, 39
— — Meiller, Penmaen, 32
— — Tuder, Ystradgwyn, 34
Morfudd (Morud, Morwid, Morwith)
— , Caethle, 23
— *filia* Ithel, Nannau, 45
— *uxor* Candalo, Ffestiniog, 73
— Wechef, Caethle, 23
Morgan, bishop William, xcvii
Moridic, Llanfrothen, 63
— ap Gwin, Cefnrhos, 24
— — Ieuan, Peniarth, 39
— — Ioreword, Penmaen, 32
— — Keuenard, Llwyngwril, 41
— — — , Pennal, 29
— Pours, Ceiswyn, 34
— Voyl, Rhyd-cryw, 38
Mortimer, lordships, cxv
— , Roger, cxxiv n. 1
Morud, *see* Morfudd
Moruel *uxor* Keuenard, Llanfrothen, 65
Moruran, Moruram, *see* Morfran
Morvan Maynoc, *see* Morfa Maenog
Morvel *filia* Lewelin, Llanfrothen, 64
Morwid, *see* Morfudd
Morwil, Nannau, 45
Morwith, *see* Morfudd
Morydic ab Griffid, Abertanat, 91
Mostyn, co. Clwyd, lxiii
Moyl, Cf. Moel, Moil
Moyl Dainoc, Nannau, 46
Moyl Dilwy, Llanbedr, 59
Moyl Gronou, Llanaber, 69
Moylgoch, co. Clwyd, 80
Moylgrum, Gwnnodl, 82
Murycastell, cviii
Mwstwr (Mesdour), co. Clwyd, cxxxix, cxli, 78, 79 and n. 3, 91 n. 5
Myfanwy (Meuanou, Meuanov)
— , Nannau, 46
— , Trefeddian, 26
— *filia* Ithel, Llangar, 89

NANCONWY, commote of, x n. 1, lxxxviii and n. 6, xcvi
Nanffreuer (Nanfruer, Nant Freiar), cxxxix, cxlii, 14 and n. 4
Nanheudwy, commote of, co. Clwyd, x, xlviii, lxix, lxxiii
Nanmor Deudraeth, cxxxix, cxl, 72 and n. 1
Nannau (Nannev), lxxxiii, lxxxv, lxxxviii, xc, 45 n. 1
— , vill of, lxv, lxvi, lxxv, lxxxi, cxxxix, cxliii, 44 and n. 1
Nant, 55
Nantcaw (Nantcau), cxxxix, cxliii, 42
Nant Freiar, *see* Nanffreuer
Nantlleidiog, cxxxix, cxlii, 14 n. 4, 15
Neath, abbey, co. West Glamorgan, cxv
— , castle, cxxx
Neath, hundred of, lxviii
Nefyn, x and n. 2, xi and n. 1, xiv, xxxix and n. 4, xl, xlviii, lv, lxix, xcix, ciii, civ, cviii, cxi, cxiii and n. 2, cxiv, cxvii, cxviii, cxix, cxx, 95
Nest, Llanfor, 5
— , Rhywedog, 4
— Duy, Garthgynfor, 48
— *filia* Adaf, Llanfendigaid, 36
— — — , Penaran, 9
— — Eynon, Trawsfynydd, 53
— *uxor* Dauid, Tywyn, 30
Newborough, lxii
Newcastle Emlyn, co. Dyfed, cxxiii
Newport, co. Dyfed, xlix
Newton, co. Dyfed, viii n. 4, 96
Nicholas IV, pope, xxvi, lxxvii
North Wales, ix n. 3, xvi, xxii, xxiii, xxiv, xxv, xxxiv, xli, lvi, lix, lx, lxii, lxiii, lxiv, lxv, lxvi, lxx, lxxi, lxxii, lxxv, lxxxvii, xcvii, civ, cv, cvii, cx, cxv, cxviii, cxix, cxxi, cxxxii; *see also* Gwynedd
— — , principality of, viii, ix, xiii, xviii, xxviii, xxx, xxxi and n. 5, xxxii, cxxxiv n. 3, 96
— — , — , officials of, xiii, xiv, xvi, xxxi, xli n. 1, lxii
Norton, sub-lordship of, co. Powys, x, xxxi n.
Norwich, 'Valuation' of, lxxvii and n. 4, lxxx, xcviii
Nynnyaw, br. of Madog Goch, xxxiii

ORELLYN, 72 and n. 4
Orhalt, *see* Allt-
Orsedd, Yr (Hacheb'rryd i'r Orseth), 18 n. 4
Osborn, Llanaber, 54
— Wyddel, 54 n. 5
Oswaldstre, Richard de, 65
Oswestry (Oswaldstre), co. Salop, civ, 5 n. 1, 13 n. 3, 14 n. 2, 15 n. 1, 18 n. 1
Overton, co. Clwyd, lii and n. 2, liii and n. 4, lx, lxiv
— , manor of, xxxiii
— , vill of, li
Overton Foreign, co. Clwyd, xxxiii, li
Owain ap Gruffydd ap Llywelyn I, xvii
Owain Glyn Dŵr, *see* Glyn Dŵr
Owayn ap Thlewelyn, 10 n. 2
Owein ap Lewelin, Penaran, 10
Oxford, Council of, xcviii
— , county of, cv, cxvii

PAINSCASTLE, co. Powys, cxxiii
Pannour, son of, Corwen, cvii, 75
Pant, 27 n. 3
Pantphilip, 40 n. 3
Pantybawe, 27 n. 3
Pantyffynnon, 6 n. 5
Pant-y-llan, 40 n. 3
Pant-y-maes, 27 n. 3
Parsona, Llangar, wife of, 89
Pecham, archbishop, lxi, xcix, c, civ
Pelliparius, Taltreuddyn, 58
Pembroke, co. Dyfed
— , county of, x, xxxii, xxxix n. 2, xl n. 1, xlviii, lxiii, lxx
— , earl of, lxxxiv
— , lordship of, lxx
Penachlw, Penachlow, *see* Pennant-lliw
Penant, *see* Pennant
Penaran, xi and n. 2, xxviii, xlviii n. 2, lxvi, lxxxi, xciii, cxiii, cxxix, cxxxvi, cxxxix, cxlii, 6 n. 3, 7 n. 5, 9 and nn. 1, 2 and 4, 10 n. 4, 11 n. 2 and 4, 95, 97 and n. 3, 99 n. 4
Pencelli, 18 n. 4
Pencoed, 22 n. 5
— , vill of, cxxxix, cxliv, 22 and n. 5
Pencraig, 10 n. 6
— , co. Clwyd, xxxviii, cxxxix, cxli, 90
Pendauat, Maentwrog, 74
Pengam, Llanfrothen, 65
Pengour, Hengaer, 16
Pengreck, Pengreyk, *see* Pencraig
Penhale, *see* Pennal
Penhelyg, 23 n. 2
Peniarth, lxxxiii
— , vill of, xxxviii, lxxxi, cxxxix, cxliii, 38, 40 n. 1
Penley, co. Clwyd, xxxiii, li
Penllyn (Penthlin, Penthlyn)
— , commote of, xi n. 2, xxx n. 1, xxxiv, xl, xliii, xlvii, xlviii n. 2, lvii, lxvi, lxix, lxxii, lxxiii, lxxiv, lxxv, lxxvii, lxxix, lxxxi, lxxxvi, lxxxviii, lxxxix, xciii, xciv, ci, cviii, cx and n. 6, cxiii, cxiv, cxvi, cxvii, cxviii, cxix, cxxi, cxxix, cxxxvi, cxxxix, cxl, cxlii, 3–21, 82 n. 3, 95, 99 n. 6
— , vill of, cxxxix, cxliv, 24
Penmaen, 6 n. 5
— , commote of Penllyn, cxxxix, cxlii, 6 and n. 5, 7 n. 5
— , commote of Ystumanner, cxxxix, cxliv, 32
Pennal, pa. of, xliii, xlv, lxxix, lxxx n. 2, cxliv, 21 n. 8
— , vill of, lxvi, cxxxvi, cxxxix, cxliv, 28, 29 n. 2
Pennant, commote of Edeirnion, co. Clwyd, lxvi, lxxx, cxxxix, cxli, 79
— , commote of Tal-y-bont, 42 n. 1
Pennant-lliw, xxxiii, cxxxix, cxlii, 7 and n. 5, 8 and n., 98 n. 2, 99 n. 5, 101 n. 6
Pennant Melangell, co. Powys, 8 n.
Pennaran, *see* Penaran
Pennarth, *see* Peniarth
Penrhyn, estate, xcvii
Penrhyndeudraeth (Le deutrayth, Penrindeudrait), cvi, cxxxix, cxl, 61
— , parish of, lxxvi, lxxvii, lxxix
Penrin, Llanfendigaid, 36
Penthlin, Penthlyn, Pentll., *see* Penllyn
Pen y coed, *see* Pencoed
Peredur, Llwyngwril, 41
— ap Llywelyn, xxxiii, 41 n. 2
Pereuer *uxor* Win, Llanfair, 60
Perweur, Pennal, 29
Phelip, Nannau, wife of, 44
— ap Adaf, Penmaen, 32
— — — , Tywyn, 30
— — Adam, Cynwyd, 86
— — Cadugan, Llanfihangel-y-traethau, 71
— — Dauid, Rhyd-cryw, 37
— — Dehewint, Llanaber, 55
— — Eynon, Trefeddian, 27
— — Gryffry, Dôl, 85
— — Ieuan, Ciltalgarth, 18
— — Ithel, Corris, 33
— — Kediuor, Botalog, 23
— — Madoc, Llandanwg, 57
— — — , Llangar, 89
— — Menach, Gwyddelwern, c, 87
— — Meuric, Nannau, 46
— — Meyler, Aberalwen, 84
— — Tegwaret, Llanfendigaid, 36
— — Thomas, Pencraig, 90
— — Wilim, Llanfrothen, 63
— Cam, Llangedris, 25
— Duy, Llanfihangel, 42
— — , Maentwrog, 73
— — , Penaran, 10 and n. 4, 98 and n. 1
— — , Ystradgwyn, 34
— Espis, Trawsfynydd, 52
— *filius* Madoc, Llangar, wife of, 89
— *frater* Phelip, Ystradgwyn, 34
— Goch, Nantlleidiog, 15
— Loyt, Dyffrydan, 50
— — , Rhywedog, 4
— Sacrista, Cymysgadwy, 20
— Skinith, Bere, 52
— Voil, Cynwyd, 86
— — , Llanfihangel, 42
— — , Nantcaw, 42
— Whith, Nantcaw, 42
Pigis, 52
Pipton, treaty of, xviii
Plas Madoc, 9 n. 2
Plas Rhywedog, 3 n. 2
Pole, Griffith de la, viii n. 3
Ponthieu, France, xviii
Powys, county of, lxiv
— , lordship of, viii and n. 3
— , principality of, xlii, cxii, cxxv

Prestatyn, commote of, co. Clwyd, lii, lxiii, lxvi, lxix, lxxiii, lxxxvii and n. 6
— , vill of, lxiii
Presteign, sub-lordship of, co. Powys, x, xxxi n.
Pridil, Llandanwg, 58
Provence, France, lvii
Prydydd y Moch, xcvi
Prys, 7 n. 5
Prysor, xxxvii n. 2, cxxxiv, cxxxix
Pulesdon, Roger de, xxxv
Pumlumon, mountain, cxviii n. 1
Pwllheli, xliii, xlviii, xlix n., lv, lvi, cxiv

RADNOR, county of, x, xiii, xlviii, lxiii, lxx, lxxi
— , lordship of, x, xxx n. 6, xxxi n., xlviii, lxiii, lxviii, lxx
Redcru, *see* Rhyd-cryw
Redgarnet, *see* Rhydygarnedd
Rerid, *see* Rhirid
Reuarua, *see* Rhiwerfa
Reys, *see* Rhys
Rhagad, co. Clwyd, xxxvii n. 2, cxxxix
Rhedynog Felen, cvii n. 4
Rhirid (Rerid, Ririd, Ririt, Ryrid, Ryryd)
— ap Adaf, Nanmor, 72
— — — , Penrhyndeudraeth, 62
— — Adam, Gwyddelwern, 88
— — Cadugan, Nanffreuer, 15
— — Dauid, Llanenddwyn, 70
— — Eynon, Llanfair, 60
— — — , Maentwrog, 73
— — — , Nannau, 47
— — — , *taxator*, 7
— — Griffid, Rhywedog, 5
— — Gronou, Dyffrydan, 50
— — — , Ystradgwyn, 35
— — Gurgenu, Pennant, 80
— — Heilin, Penaran, 11
— — Iarward, Mwstwr, 78
— — — , Pennant, 80
— — Iorword Voel, Castell, 6 n. 2, 100
— — Iuor, Dolgledr, 50
— — Madoc, Bodgynfel, 88
— — — , Nantcaw, 42
— — — , Nantlleidiog, 15
— — — , Penllyn, lxxxvi
— — — , Rhywedog, 4
— — Phelip, Branas, 80
— — Thomas, Llandecwyn, 63
— — Tuder, Pennant, 80
— — Win, Maentwrog, 74
— — — , Penllyn, 5 n. 1
— — — Rhywedog, 5
— — Yarword, Pencraig, 90
— — Yerword, Maestran, 13
— — — , Streflyn, 20
— *aurifaber*, Llandanwg, 57
— Cannian, Llanfihangel-y-traethau, 71
— Duy, Bodorlas, wife of, 76
Rhirid Duy, Llanddwywe, 56
— — , Llanfihangel, 90
— — , Mwstwr, 79
— — , Penaran, 10
— — , Rhywedog, 3
— *filius* Guyn, 5 n. 1
— Flaidd, 3 n. 2, 7 n. 6
— Gorista, Caethle, 23
— Gyn, Pennant, 80
— Loweydwy, Rhywedog, 4
— Loyt, Llandderfel, 21, 97 n. 2
— — , Penaran, 11
— — , Pennant-lliw, 9
— Seys, Cynwyd, 87
— Vachan, Llanycil, 20
— — , Garthiaen, *taxator*, 91
— Vaur, Llandanwg, 57
— Voyl, Llygadog, 84
Rhiwerfa (Reuarua), lxxxiii, 22 n. 5
— , vill of, cxxxix, cxliv, 24
Rhiwlas, lxxxiii, 6 n. 5
Rhodri (Rudry)
— , Rhyd-cryw, 37
— ap Gruffydd, prince, xix
Rhos, cantref, co. Clwyd, lxxxv
Rhuddlan, co. Clwyd, lii and n. 2, liii and n. 4, liv, lx, lxiv, cv
— , commote of, lii, lxiii, lxix, lxxiii, lxxxvii
Rhuthun, co. Clwyd, liv, lv n. 3, lvi n. 4, lvii, lx, cv, 56 n. 2; *see also* Ruthin
— Court Rolls, lvi
— , lordship of, lxiii
Rhyddallt, xxxvii n. 2, cxxxix
Rhyd-cryw (Redcru), xxxviii, lxxxi, xciii, cviii, cxxxix, cxliii, 36 n. 1, 37
Rhydydefaid, 18 n. 4
Rhydygarnedd, 43 and n. 7
Rhys (Reys)
— ap Hywel, lxxxv
— — Maredudd, Dinefwr, xxx, xxxv, xli n. 1, lxviii, cxiv
— Duy, Peniarth, 39
— Keyswin, Ceiswyn, 34
Rhywedog, lxxxiii; *see also* Plas Rhywedog
— , vill of, cxxxix, cxlii, 3 and n. 1 and 2
Rhywedog Is Afon, 3 n. 1
Rhywedog Is Llafar, 3 n. 1
Rhywedog Uwch Llafar, 3 n. 1
Richard, I, king, xviii
— , II, king, viii, ix
Richard *carnifex*, Harlech, 66
Ririd, Ririt, *see* Rhirid
Robert, Pennal, 29
— ap Edenewint, Gwrych, 30
— *forestarius*, Cymysgadwy, 21
— Scot, Harlech, 66 and n. 3
Rossendale, co. Lanc., cxxxi
Rudry, *see* Rhodri
Rug (Gruc, Ryg), co. Clwyd, cxxxix, cxli, 89 and n. 4
Ruthin, Alan de, xxxviii, civ, 6
Rutland, county of, xxvi

Ryg, *see* Rug
Ryrid, Ryryd, *see* Rhirid

SAERNO, Maentwrog, 73
St. Asaph, bishop of, xci n. 1, xcix, c, cxiv, cxv, 43
Salop, county of, xxix, cxl, cxli, 91 n. 7
Scormyl, Cyffty, 13
Scot, Robert, Harlech, 66 and n. 3
Scotin, Llandanwg, 58
Scotland, cxxvi, 96
Seisyll (Seysild)
— , Llanenddwyn, wife of, 71
— ap Yerword, Cefnyrowen, 51
— — — , Gwyddelwern, 88
— Grek, Rhyd-cryw, 37
Selwrn (Selour), cxxxix, cxlii, 7 n. 4, 14
Senena, mother of Llywelyn II, xvii
Seysild, *see* Seisyll
Shaldeford, Henry de, lxii
Shrewsbury, co. Salop, xxxiii, lxi and n. 4, civ, cxxi
— , earl of, cxxv
Sicily, Italy, king of, viii
Simon ap Wilim, Bere, 52
Sion Tudur, xcii n. 1
Skenfrith, lordship of, co. Gwent, x, xii, xxx n. 6, xlviii, lxix
South Wales, ix n. 6, xii, xviii, xxii, lxxi; *see also* West Wales
Spain, lxiv, cxxv
Stafford, county of, xxvi
Stapleton, sub-lordship of, co. Hereford, xxxi n.
Stephen *ianitor*, Harlech, 65
Stradquin, *see* Ystradgwyn
Strasigil, Brithdir, 49
Strata Florida (Ystrad Fflur), abbey, co. Dyfed, cxv
Strata Marcella (Ystrad Marchell), abbey, co. Powys, lxxv, c, cxv, 7 and n. 2
Streflyn, xi n. 2, cxiii, cxxxix, cxlii, 12 n. 6, 13 n. 6, 20 and n. 3, 95, 102; *see also* Llystreflyn
Strilin, Cyffty, 12
Sutor, Cynwyd, wife of, 86
Swansea, hundred of, co. West Glamorgan, lxviii
Sycharth, co. Powys, xci n. 1
Sychdyn, co. Clwyd, lxiii

TABYTH LYN, *see* Tal-y-llyn
Talbunt, *see* Tal-y-bont
Tale Moel, Llanaber, 55
Talgarth, co. Powys, lxix
Taltreuddyn, c, cxxxix, cxl, 58
Tal-y-bont, commote of, xvii, xxxiii, xl, xlii n. 1, xliii, xliv, xlvi, xlvii, lvii, lxvi, lxvii, lxix, lxxii, lxxiii, lxxiv, lxxv, lxxvi, lxxix, lxxxii, lxxxviii, lxxxix, xciv, c, cviii, cix, cxxxvi, cxxxix, cxl, cxliii, 22 n. 5, 26 n. 5, 27 n. 3, 30 n. 2, 35–52, 96
Tal-y-llyn, xlv, lxxix, cxliv, 25 and n. 2, 33, 34
Tanbont, 37 n. 4
Tangwistl (Tangwistel)
— , Llanaber, 54
— , Llanbedr, 58
— *filia* Bondic, 37
— — Dauid, Garthmaelan, 44
— — Edenowein, Peniarth, 39
— — Eynon, Llangywer, 14
— — — , Nannau, 46
— — Griffri, Nannau, 47
— — Ieuan, Peniarth, 38
— — Ithel, Cefnrhos, 24
— — Lewelin, Gwyddelfynydd, 27
— — Madoc, Kethugalc, 67
— — — , Trawsfynydd, 53
— — Meiler, Llanaber, 55
— — Meirion, Penrhyndeudraeth, 61
— — Phelip, Cyffty, 12
— Goch, Llangedris, 25
— *uxor* Adaf Duy, Maesmor, 27
— — Eynon, Maentwrog, 74
Tantliu, Garthmaelan, 44
Tanycoedisaf, 22 n. 5
Tanycoeduchaf, 22 n. 5
Taylour, William le, Harlech, cv
Tegwaret, Penaran, 9
— , Pennal, 29
— ap Ada, Nanmor, 72
— — Adaf, Llanfrothen, 64
— — Candalo, Maentwrog, 73
— — Eynon, Gwnnodl, 81
— — — , Nannau, 46
— — Griffyd, Gwnnodl, 82
— — Reis, Cregennan, 40
— — Wion, Llanddwywe, 56
— Corista, Maentwrog, 73
— Crak, Dolgledr, 50
— — , Kethugalc, 67
— Duy, Llanfrothen, 63
— — , Pencraig, 90
— Goch, Dolgledr, 51
— Grak, Llannerchgoediog, 25
— Hen, Llanenddwyn, 57
— Kenith, Nannau, 46
— Keri, Nannau, 46
— *medicus*, Gwyddelwern, 88
— Ruffo, Llanfair, 59
— Sutor, Llanbedr, 58
— — , Llandanwg, 57
— — , Llanfihangel-y-traethau, 71
— Vachan, Bodgadfan, wife of, 37
— Vaur, Llanfendigaid, 36
— Velin, Ceiswyn, 34
— Voyl, Llanfrothen, 65
— — , Ystradgwyn, 34
— Was, Penrhyndeudraeth, 62
Tenby, co. Dyfed, li
Tewas, *see* Tyfos
Tewyn, *see* Tywyn
Thomas, Nannau, 45
— , Peniarth, 39

Thomas *faber*, Bere, 51
— Vachan, Trawsfynydd, 54
Tintern, abbey, co. Gwent, cxv
Tirllannerch, co. Clwyd, cxxxix, cxli, 76, 82 n. 1
Tomen Castell, 6 n. 5
Tonfannau, 36 n. 1
Tournour, Rhywedog, 4
Trahaearn (Trahaern, Trahern)
— ap Adaf, Llandecwyn, 63
— — Edeneuet, Maentwrog, 73
— — Eynon, Trawsfynydd, 53
— Voyl, Penaran, 11
Trawsfynydd, parish of, xlv, lxxvi, lxxix, cxxxiv, 67 n. 2, 68 n. 1, 74 n. 2
— , 'township' of, lxv, cxxxix, cxl, 52 and n. 3, 68
Trefaes, 36 n. 3
Trefeddian (Treffethian), cxxxix, cxliv, 26 and n. 3, 32 n. 1
Tref Ednyfed (Treffeden), 32 n. 1
Treffeden, cxxxix, cxliv, 32 and n. 1
Treffethian, *see* Trefeddian
Trefrion (Huchbega, Treverion), xxxvii n. 2, cxxxix, cxliv, 26, 27 n. 3
Trefrydd (Trefri, Treueryth), cxxxix, cxliv, 23 n. 2, 27 n. 3, 33 and n. 1
Tref Wyn, *see* Trewyn
Treueryth, *see* Trefrydd
Trewyn (Tref Wyn, Trewen), co. Clwyd, cxxxix, cxli, 78, 91 n. 2
Treydin, Llanfendigaid, 36 .
Troydir, Trawsfynydd, 53
Tuder, *see* Tudur
Tudgech; Cf Dudgech, Tudgoch, Turgech, *and* Tygech
— *filia* Adaf, Rhyd-cryw, 37
— — Eynon, Llanenddwyn, 57
— — Iorword, Llanfair, 60
— — Ithel, Aberalwen, 84
— — Meyler, Branas, 80
— — Ryryd, Pennant, 80
— — Tuder, Nannau, 47
— Connian, Llanaber, 55
— *uxor* Eynon, Llandecwyn, 63
Tudgoch; Cf. Dudgech, Tudgech, Turgech, *and* Tygech
— *uxor* Dehewint, Maestrefnant, 25
Tudur, (Tuder)
— , Bere, 52
— , Ucheldref, 17
— ap Adaf, Cynfal, 31
— — Carueth, Carrog, 77
— — Dauid, Llanddwywe, 56
— — Edeneuet, Dolgledr, 51
— — Eynon, Gwrych, 30
— — — , Llangywer, 14
— — Gogan, Llanaber, 55
— — Griffid, Cefnrhos, 24
— — — , Nannau, 47
— — Gronou, Dolgledr, 51
— — — , Ystumanner, 22
— — Gurgeneu, Rhywedog, 5
— — Guyn Seys, Cyffty, 101
Tudur ap Houel, Penaran, 97
— — Lewelin, Pennal, 29
— — Madoc, Llanenddwyn, 70
— — Melogin, Pencraig, 90
— Boly, Dolgellau, 50
— Bongam, Pennant-lliw, 9
— Glyne, Gwanas, 43
— Goch, Llanfihangel, 90
— Goch *filius* Dauid, Pennal, 29
— — — Wasdewy, Llanfor, 5
— Voyl, Abertanat, 91
— — , Ystradgwyn, 34
Turgech filia Ithel, Garthgynfor, 48
— ; *Cf. also* Dudgech, Tudgech, Tudgoch, *and* Tygech
Twrcelyn, commote of, lxxxvii, cxvii
Ty-brith, co. Clwyd, 89 n. 2
Tybroughton, co. Clwyd, li
Tycerrig, 3 n. 1
Tyddyn-, *see also* Tythin, Tythyn
Tyddyn Alis, 20 n. 5
Tyddyn Duy Tan yr Allt, 23 n. 2
Tyddyn hen, 20 n. 5
Tyddyn y ffrith, 20 n. 5
Tyddyn y Pant Duy, 20 n. 5
Tyfos (Tewas), co. Clwyd, cxxxix, cxli, 81
Tygech, Llanfrothen, 64
— ; Cf. *also* Dudgech, Tudgech, Tudgoch, *and* Turgech
Ty-glyn, 32 n. 1
Tyinmeyron, cxxxix, cxl, 67
Ty Map Morud, Corris, 33
Tyncrin Talennyour, Penaran, 10
Tyngrin, Llanfor, 5
Tyn-y-pant, 18 n. 4
Tystywin, Trefeddian, 27
Tytanygraig, 3 n. 1
Tythin, Tythyn, *see also* Tyddyn
Tythin y Coed, 28 n. 3
Tythin yr Hengayr, 16 n. 1
Tythyn yr Allt Goch, 23 n. 2
Tywyn, parish of, xlv, lxxvi, lxxix, lxxx n. 2, xc, cxliv, 22 and n. 5, 23, 24, 25, 26, 27, 29 30, 31, 32 and n. 1, 33
— , vill of, lxiv, xciv, cxxxix, cxliv, 27 n. 3, 30 and n. 2

UCHAF, commote of, xcvi
Ucheldref (Hucheldref), lxxxiii, 85
— , commote of Edeirnion, cxxxix, cxli
— , commote of Penllyn, cxxxix, cxlii, 17
Urien ap Tegwaret, 56 n. 2
Urien Voyl, Treffeden, 32
Uwchafon, 11 n. 7, 14 n. 1
Uwchmynydd, 18 n. 4
Uwchygarreg, 22 n. 5, 42 n. 1

VAHGHAN, William, lxi n. 4
Valle Crucis, *see* Llanegwestl
Vir ap Ierword, Llanfair, 59
Vowr, 70
Vrien, Llanddwywe, 56

WACHLY, Gwrych, 30
Warenne, John de, xii
Wasdewy, Trefeddian, 27
Wasdinot, Ystumanner, wife of, 22
Waskeyn, Gwnnodl, 82
Wasmel, Rhywedog, 5
Wasmyhangel, Llannerchgoediog, 25
Was Patrik, Bylan, 26
Was Wagul, Bodgadfan, 37
Was With, Trawsfynydd, 53
Weirglodd Ddu, 18 n. 4
Welles, Richard de, lxxxiii
Welshpool, co. Powys, x, xxx n. 6, xlvi n. 3, l, lxiv, lxx, lxxii, lxxxiv
Wenunwin, *see* Gwenwynwyn
Wentlian, Wentliana, Wentlyan, Wentlyana, *see* Gwenllïan
Wernouel, *see* Gwernefail
Weruel, Weruela, Weruilla, Weyruel, *see* Gwerful
West Midlands, lxvii, cxxxiii
West Wales, xvii, xxxiv, lv and n. 5, lxiii, lxxxiv, lxxxv, lxxxvii, cxxvi; *see also* South Wales
— — , principality of, viii, ix, x n. 1, xxiii, xxx and n. 3, xxxii, l, 96
— — , — , officials of, lvi, lxxxiv, lxxxv
Whetenhall, Adam de, xxxi
Whitecastle, lordship of, co. Gwent, x, xii, xxx n. 6, lxix
Whith Vunuis, Rhywedog, 5
Wigar, Llwyngwril, 41
Wilim, *see* Gwilym
Willelmus, *clericus*, Llanfor, 5
— Doun, Bere, 52
— Pevir, Bere, 52
— Prest, Bere, 51
— ; Cf. *also* Gwilym
Willington, co. Clwyd, li
Wilmyn, Trawsfynydd, 53
Win, *see* Gwyn
Winas, cxxxix, cxliv, 22
Windsor, co. Berks, xxiii
Winforton, lordship of, co. Hereford, xxxi n.
Winvenith, *see* Gwynfynydd
Wion, *see* Gwion
Wir ap Madin, Bodgadfan, lxxxii, 37
Wir ap Was Patrik, Ceiswyn, 34
Wiuas, 22
Wladur, Maentwrog, 74
Wladosa, Wladus, Wladusa, *see* Gwladus
Wledir, Gwernefail, 19
Wledyr Wyth, Gwyddelwern, 88
Wnion, river, 44 n. 1, 47 n. 3
Wonas, *see* Gwanas
Worcester, county of, xxvi
Worthenbury, co. Clwyd, li
Wothewern, *see* Gwyddelwern
Wr ap Cadugan, Gwrych, 30
Wrek, *see* Gwrych
Wrexham, co. Clwyd, xlix, lv and n. 1, lxi
Wulfinton, co. Clwyd, lxiii
Wyn, *see* Gwyn
Wynn, sir John, Gwedir, xcvi, xcvii
Wyon, *see* Gwion

YAGO ap Dehewint, Cefnrhos, 24
Yale, lord of, 77 n. 2
Yarward, Yarword, *see* Iorwerth
Ydei, Castell, 100
Yerward, Yerword, Yorward, Yorword, *see* Iorwerth
Y guas trusgul, Castell, 100
Ynyr (Ener, Eyner)
— , Garthmaelan, 44
— ap Wilim, Pennal, 29
— Fychan (Vachan), Nannau, lxxxv, lxxxviii, xc, 45, 96
York, archbishopric of, xxvii
— , city of, lxv
— , county of, cxv
Ysgeifiog, co. Clwyd, liii
Yssec, Llanfair, 60
Ystradgwyn (Stradquin), cxxxix, cxliv, 31 n. 2, 34
Ystrad Marchell, *see* Strata Marcella
Ystrad Meurig, co. Dyfed, cxxiii
Ystumanner (Estymaner), commote of, xvii, xxxiii, xxxix, xlii n. 1, xliii, xliv, xlvii, lvii, lxvi, lxix, lxxii, lxxiii, lxxiv, lxxv n. 4, lxxvii, lxxix, lxxxix, xciv, xcvii, cviii, cix, cx, cxxxvi, cxxxix, cxl, cxliv, 21–35, 96